Achebe, Head, Marechera

A Three Continents Book

Achebe, Head, Marechera

On Power and Change in Africa

Annie Gagiano

LYNNE RIENNER PUBLISHERS

BOULDER
LONDON

Published in the United States of America in 2000 by
Lynne Rienner Publishers, Inc.
1800 30th Street, Boulder, Colorado 80301
www.rienner.com

and in the United Kingdom by
Lynne Rienner Publishers, Inc.
3 Henrietta Street, Covent Garden, London WC2E 8LU

Library of Congress Cataloging-in-Publication Data
Gagiano, Annie H., 1947–
Achebe, Head, Marechera : on power and change in Africa / Annie Gagiano.
p. cm.
"A three continents book."
Includes bibliographical references (p.) and index.
ISBN 0-89410-887-5 (alk. paper)
1. African literature (English)—History and criticism. 2. Politics and literature—Africa—History—20th century. 3. Power (Social sciences)—Africa—History—20th century. 4. Literature and society—Africa—History—20th century. 5. Social change—Africa—History—20th century. 6. Achebe, Chinua—Political and social views. 7. Head, Bessie, 1937—Political and social views. 8. Marechera, Dambudzo—Political and social views. 9. Power (Social sciences) in literature. 10. Social change in literature. I. Title.

PR9340.5.G34 2000
820.9'358—dc21 99-056357

British Cataloguing in Publication Data
A Cataloguing in Publication record for this book
is available from the British Library.

Printed and bound in the United States of America

The paper used in this publication meets the requirements
of the American National Standard for Permanence of
Paper for Printed Library Materials Z39.48-1984.

5 4 3 2 1

Contents

1

Introductory Considerations

Do battle for the creation of a human world—that is, a world of reciprocal recognitions.
Frantz Fanon, *Black Skin, White Masks*

Broad Strokes

Power and change in various forms affect all human lives. Possibly, though, Africans in the late twentieth century experience these ubiquitous presences with a particular intensity and urgency. The task of intellectuals—African and other—is to attempt to speak or write usefully and lucidly about such huge and usually vague, slippery notions. It is on the assumption that intellectuals need to justify their professional training and privilege by contributing—or at least attempting to contribute—to greater understanding of the crucial issues of their own time and place in the world that the present study has been undertaken.

The approach of theorists to the task of comprehension tends to be definitional; the approach of creative writers, representational: literary critics tend to oscillate uneasily between allegiance (at different times) to one or the other of these modes—neither scientists nor artists, but something of both. Yet the questions to be addressed are uncomfortable, and the task to be faced impossibly large and simultaneously ineluctable. One's choices might be said to involve and reveal moralities as much as analyses—and so, without in the least implying that anything as straightforward as an obviously "correct" strategy is available, I do adopt clearly partisan positions, while explaining such preferences in the course of this work.

In the late twentieth century no one within reach of the public media remains enclosed or isolated within his or her own locality. As our perceptions have enlarged (at least spatially) and our involvements across the globe grown more complex, our responsibilities have grown more difficult—more tricky. The colonizing thrusts of the late nineteenth and early twentieth centuries entangled the economies and cultures of most of the world's peoples—but this huge change was effected in terms of, and consequently embedded, a power imbalance of titanic proportions.[1] The basic assumption in terms of which this enquiry proceeds is that the most crucial question of our time is both a moral and a material demand: how are the perceived inequalities of the global system to be addressed?

Intellectuals tend to embark on investigations by looking at and articulating the ways in which questions of this kind have been, and are being, addressed before proceeding to their own analyses and recommendations. One prevalent way of understanding the global power imbalance is seldom openly articulated—at least by intellectuals—because the protocols of our time make it so unfashionable to do so. It is no less potent and present for all that, frequently disguised even in avowedly liberal discourse. It is the belief—felt to be a perception—that reads the global inequalities as signposting the supposed fact that there are some strong, hence superior, nations/cultures and some weak, hence inferior, nations/cultures, and that the imbalances between them are the merely natural—or at any rate unavoidable—consequences of the prevalence of one or the other economic-cultural ethos in such societies. Those who *do* better *are* better—if not morally, at least culturally. Success is taken as self-justifying.

Resting his argument on Max Weber's[2] suggestion of a close link between the Protestant ethic and the growth of capitalism, Ernest Gellner states that

> in the one great and irreversible transition or *coupure* between the traditional and the rational spirit, pragmatic considerations overwhelmingly and decisively favour one of the two contestants. At one particular crossroads, the verdict of history is categorical, unambiguous, decisive, and irreversible. (*Reason and Culture,* 165)

Gellner, in an earlier work (*Plough, Sword and Book: The Structure of Human History*—1988), in which he alludes to Karl Polyani's "typology of economic stages" (180) leading to the "great transformation" that brought about the upsurge of capitalism in and from Europe, writes of Britain:

> The combination of effective but law-bound government, the presence of an entrepreneurial class neither wholly disfranchised politically nor eager to become dominant, and endowed with some inclination to continue in its calling beyond the point of satisfying its needs; the presence of opportunity, not merely through a geographically expanding world, but also through a rising ceiling of available potential discovery—all these clearly did have their part to play, and could only play it jointly. (Gellner, *Plough, Sword and Book,* 170–171)

Noticeable in this somewhat celebratory account is the deeply veiled nature of the allusion to capitalist expansion ("endowed with some inclination to continue in its calling beyond the point of satisfying its needs") and to colonialism ("a geographically expanding world"), which have the effect of euphemizing, almost erasing, those aspects of the process.[3] In a more recent (1992) work of his it is easier to discern the outline of a "European bubble" enclosing this philosopher's perspective. In *Reason and Culture: The Historic Role of Rationality and Rationalism*, Gellner asks and answers:

> How did we build this *new world?* It was built up *by new men* imbued by the Crusoe/Descartes spirit. Robinson Crusoe was a man who carried the essential part of *his culture* in himself and could re-erect it on the island *on his own*. He needed no complementary fellow-specialists, whose zone of competence he is ritually or legally barred from entering. In other words, all the specialisms of his culture employ the same idiom, which he has mastered, and they are open to him.
>
> That which was presented as a solitary, Descartes-Crusoe enterprise, was in fact the charter of a radically new social order. (Gellner, *Reason and Culture,* 162—emphases added)[4]

Although the novelist, Defoe, and the protagonist, Crusoe, overlay the black worker's name with the servant's appellation "Friday," his presence is not *erased* by them as it is in this contemporary philosopher's oddly revealing, curtailed metaphor/book report! Revealing, too, is the last sentence in the above extract, where Crusoe's presence is expanded, not to include the (black) man without whose assistance Crusoe could not have succeeded, but to name the absent presence (in Crusoe) of the "new social order" of *Europe*. Elsewhere, however, Gellner gives a tellingly sardonic—or harsh—definition of capitalist expansion:

> But it was not greed which engendered capitalism and rational production: it was the *disciplining* of greed, its ruthless taming by order and calculation, and its conversion into a curiously disinterested compulsion, indulged for its own sake rather than for its fruits, which really did the trick. (Gellner, *Reason and Culture,* 170)[5]

The so-called culture wars of the late 1980s and 1990s in the United States furnish more instances of the triumphalist (bragging) or insouciant (shrugging) attitude toward the gap in well-being between the affluent Western countries and the poor Third World areas. The concerted attacks on Martin Bernal's thesis in his *Black Athena: The Afroasiatic Roots of Classical Civilization,* especially volume 1 (*The Fabrication of Ancient Greece: 1785–1985* [1987]), confirm the persistence of a fiercely primitive resistance, in the minds of many First World academics, against associating the notion of civilization with the lives of black Africans. When the editorial board of the influential publisher Random House in mid-1998 brought out its list of the century's one hundred best books in English, it included not a single work by an African author, whereas in the counterlist drawn up by young publishers studying at Harvard, only one work by an African (predictably, Achebe's *Things Fall Apart*) made the list, ranked at number 70.[6]

A prominent participant in the fierce debates concerning the academic necessity/unnecessary foolishness of "revising the canon" (i.e., exchanging some classical texts for those more clearly foregrounding contemporary concerns with politics, gender, race, and class) has been Harold Bloom, Sterling Professor of Humanities at Yale University and Berg Professor of English at New York University. His position rests on his belief that "the mind's dialogue with itself is not primarily a social reality" (Bloom 30). His position reflects an ancient anxiety that the classics will be replaced[7] by the new, the vulgar, the strange, the "other" (alien), the fashionable, the merely "politically correct" texts. For a sophisticated intellectual, Bloom sounds uncommonly like a proverbial American redneck when he proclaims doom in such a sentence as the following: "We are destroying all intellectual and aesthetic standards in the humanities and social sciences, in the name of social justice" (35).[8]

The "cognitive acuity, linguistic energy, and power of invention" (Bloom 46) that readers like myself find abundantly present in the African texts here discussed in detail are in Bloom's assessment preeminently manifested in the works of mainly Western provenance of his canon. He bluntly, almost smugly, asserts that "canons always do indirectly serve the social and political, and indeed the spiritual, concerns and aims of the wealthier classes of each generation, of Western society. It seems clear that capital is necessary for the cultivation of aesthetic values" (32–33).

This is the ancient, and snobbish, view of culture as a club with highly exclusive—and expensive—membership. Elsewhere, though, "primal aesthetic value" is said to be "available to whoever can be educated to read and view it"! (Bloom 65). It is a familiar coupling of attitudes: of the defiant brag of exclusivity with the liberal gesture of open access. Bloom's academic target—what he sneeringly terms "the School of Resentment"—includes "Feminists, Marxists, Lacanians, New Historicists, Deconstructionists, Semioticians" (527). He stops short of mentioning proponents of Black Studies or of African/Third World literature, although it is difficult to imagine that he does not somehow have them in mind as well. (To be fair to Bloom, his "expanded" canon does—out of hundreds of titles—list a small percentage of African and other "Other" works—548–567.)

Nevertheless these examples from the heart of the high courts of "Western civilization" do seem to illustrate aspects of what Jan P. Nederveen Pieterse, writing on "Empire and Race" in his *Empire and Emancipation: Power and Liberation on a World Scale* (1989), has called "the intestines of empire": racism. He emphasizes that "racism is not simply a by-product of empire" but in fact "is the psychology of imperialism, . . . because racism supplies the element that makes for the righteousness of empire" (Pieterse

235). If races *are* inherently unequal, occupation and domination by "the stronger," which long outlive the formal ending of colonialism, are both natural and just. Unfortunately, racism goes underground with the formal ending of political domination and the dwindling of politically visible empires, as my earlier examples are intended to illustrate. Seizure of African lands by Western powers in the previous period can be related to a deafness to African voices in the present: a similar power hierarchy is indexed in both eras.

Observing dryly that "in secret, intentions are often spelled out honestly," Noam Chomsky reports that

> in the early post–World War II period, when George Kennan, one of the most influential planners (in the U.S.A.) and considered a leading humanist, assigned each sector of the world its "function": Africa's function was to be "exploited" by Europe for its [i.e., for Europe's] reconstruction, he observed, the U.S. having little interest in it. A year earlier, a high-level planning study had urged "that co-operative development of the cheap foodstuffs and raw materials of northern Africa could help forge European unity and create an economic base for continental recovery," an interesting concept of "cooperation." (Chomsky, "Market Democracy," 29)[9]

In his work *Burundi: Ethnocide as Discourse and Practice*, René Lemarchand comments on the departure from Burundi of the U.S. ambassador

> at the height of the 1972 massacre. "On May 25, 1972," according to Roger Morris, "Melady [the ambassador] routinely left the country for a new assignment. He departed with a decoration from the Burundi government, he and his home office . . . maintaining total silence about the horror" (Morris 1977, 267). From then on, perceptions of Burundi as an "autistic and suspicious society," to quote from a 1972 State Department policy paper (ibid.), seemed entirely consistent with the kind of benign neglect displayed by U.S. policymakers in the face of irrefutable evidence of ethnocide. (Lemarchand xiii)[10]

Here I move on to a discussion of the position that broadly represents the main alternative to the viewpoint of those who seem undismayed by the gulf between the world's affluent and its indigent areas and people—it might be referred to as the School of Redress. Its ranks include many members of affluent societies—scholars like the historian Basil Davidson and the classicist Martin Bernal or the philosopher-linguist Noam Chomsky. Though undoubtedly fed by a thirst for justice and intellectual readjustment of the "color-coded" clichés of the world, this position is the very reverse of the triumphalist one. Indeed, the Malawian poet Jack Mapanje, who was long imprisoned for his resistance to political repression in his country, refers in a recent essay collection called *Writing and Africa* to "this thankless war against the injustices of the world" (quoted in Msiska and Hyland 216).

The role of cultural production in this struggle has been memorably articulated by Amilcar Cabral in one of his speeches (translated and collected under the title *Return to the Source*):

> A people who free themselves from foreign domination will be free culturally only if, without complexes and without underestimating the importance of positive accretions from the oppressor and other cultures, they return to the upward paths of their own culture, which is nourished by the living reality of its environment and which negates both harmful influences and any kind of subjection to foreign culture. Thus, it may be seen that if imperialist domination has the vital need to practise cultural oppression, national liberation is necessarily an act of culture. (Cabral 42–43)

From an African perspective, the triumph of rationalism celebrated by Gellner takes on another aspect. To represent this position, I quote from Cheikh Hamidou Kane's novel, *Ambiguous Adventure*.[11] Asked by his intellectual French host, "from what you have been able to grasp of the history of our [i.e., Western] thought, has it seemed to you radically foreign, or have you indeed recognised yourself a little, just the same?"(Kane 113), the Senegalese philosophy student Samba Diallo replies "without hesitation as if he had already pondered this question for a long time":

> "It seems to me that this history has undergone an accident which has shifted it and, finally, drawn it away from its plan. Do you understand me? Socrates' scheme of thinking does not seem to me, at bottom, different from that of Saint Augustine although there was Christ between them. The plan is the same, as far as Pascal. It is still the plan of all the thought which is not occidental. . . . I do not know. But don't you feel as if the philosophical plan were already no longer the same with Descartes as with Pascal? It is not the mystery which has changed but the questions which are asked of it and the revelations which are expected from it. Descartes is more niggardly in his quest. If, thanks to this and also to his method, he obtains a greater number of responses, what he reports also concerns us less and is of little help to us." (Kane 113–114)

It is in this novel that a divergence between "success" and desert is ironically ascribed to the West, to which Samba Diallo is sent, after much agonizing by his people, in order that he may "learn from them the art of conquering without being in the right" (Kane 37, 152). It destroys him.

Another illustration of the point that the Western style of conquest extends far beyond political possession is cited in one of Achebe's essays. He writes:

> In the area of literature, I recall that we have sometimes been informed by the West and its local zealots that the African novels we write are not novels

> at all because they do not quite fit the specifications of that literary form which came into being at a particular time in specific response to the new spirit of individual freedom set off by the decay of feudal Europe and the rise of capitalism. This form, we were told, was designed to explore individual rather than social predicaments. (Achebe, *Hopes*, 54)

What Achebe's testimony makes clear is how justifiably indignant, in his tone, the great German student of African folklore, Harold Scheub, is when he writes the following in his long essay "A Review of African Oral Traditions and Literature": "The assumption that the novel form evolved in the West and was transported to the rest of the world is as blind as it is arrogant" (Scheub 45).[12]

So brilliantly does an African novel like Kane's *Ambiguous Adventure* "answer," from another perspective, the European philosopher Gellner's recognition of the spirit of rationalism in the triumph of the West, *and* a cultural critic like Bloom in the elegance of its language and the profundity of its mediative prose, that I cite several more passages from the English translation of this work to represent the "alternative" (recuperative, "redressing") position, which I am presenting as the necessary qualification to the celebration of "Western rationality." It is to be emphasized that neither Kane nor the other writers I am discussing propose a mere antirationalist, primordialist position (African or other), but that they do have a much more complex, troubled, and even tragic recognition of what that Western triumph has cost the rest of the world—*and* the West itself, too.

"The entire black continent," Kane writes of colonialism, "had been awakened by a great clamour." His narrator remarks sarcastically that "those who had no history were encountering those who carried the world on their shoulders" (Kane 48).[13] In the end, it made no difference whether Africans cooperated with or resisted the invaders—"they all found themselves . . . checked by census, divided up, classified, labelled, conscripted, administrated."[14] On the black continent, concerning the "strange people," the Europeans, "it began to be understood that their true power lay not in the cannons of the first morning, but rather in what followed the cannons." For "the new school," it is seen, is "better than the cannon"; it "makes conquest permanent"; it is "bound up with a new order." "The cannon compels the body, the school bewitches the soul,"[15] says the narrator (49). The protagonist's father, one of the novel's wise commentators, recognizes the shameful, irresistible attraction of "this new egotism which the West is scattering abroad" (69). Yet he believes that Westerners and their adherents "are so fascinated by the returns they get from the implement that they have lost sight of the infinite immensity of the workyard" (76). I would paraphrase by suggesting that Kane's point is that the price of efficiency is a type of desacralization: "Evidence is a quality of the surface," his spokesman points out to the representative of Western learning:

"Your science is the triumph of evidence. . . . It makes you the masters of the external, but at the same time it exiles you there, more and more" (78).

The crucial point is made in what follows—and it is a position shared by all the African writers I discuss here. In their criticism of "Western rationality" they adopt no plea for the return to a supposedly pristine, precolonial situation, which would, in any case, be impossible. What the battle for redress aims for is a recognition of the human worth and value of Africans and other "by-passed" people. For, says Kane's spokesman to the Western man, "we have not had the same past, you and ourselves, but we shall have, strictly, the same future. The era of separate destinies has run its course" (Kane 79).

Again and again, African writers insist that account be taken of the ugly underbelly of the Western region's gleaming successes—that those who were materially and spiritually dislodged must be noticed—"we the underdeveloped, who feel ourselves to be clumsy in a world of perfect mechanical adjustment" (Kane 80). "Sometimes the metamorphosis is not even finished. We have turned ourselves into hybrids" . . . and are "filled with shame" (113),[16] says the main protagonist: "there is no longer any resonance from myself . . . like a musical instrument that has gone dead." His older friend adds, "The West passes you by, you are ignored, you are useless . . . when you yourself can no longer pass by the West" (150). Another speaker makes the point that "the West victoriously pursues its investiture of the actual. . . . There is no instant that is not filled with this victory" (151).

At this point in the discussion, the main point returns: the need to integrate the world anew—to achieve an acknowledgment of the non-Western world in the victorious West. "What we miss so much in the West, those of us who come from the outlying regions," says Kane's main protagonist, "is perhaps that: that original nature where our identity bursts forth *with* theirs" (emphasis added).[17] He continues: "The result is that the Most Royal Lady is right: their victory over us is also an accident. This feeling of exile which weighs upon us does not mean that we should be useless, but . . . indicates our most urgent task, which is that of clearing the ground around nature. This task is ennobling" (Kane 153).

Here, I believe, Kane's term "nature" must be understood to signify the common human nature, and the responsibility that its recognition entails, when Africans, Westerners, and others are reminded of their essential relatedness. The final, qualifying point that Kane's novel contributes as a literary expression of the argument I am pursuing is that the attempt is not to "beat the West at its own game." Indeed, says his protagonist:

> we shall never have the mastery of the object. For we shall have no more dignity than it has. We shall not dominate it. Have you noticed that? It's the same gesture as that of the West, which masters the object and colonizes us

> at the same time. *If we do not awake the West to the difference which separates us from the object, we shall be worth no more than it is.* (Kane 154, emphases added)

This imperative of change, confronting "the West" as the major power embodiment of our time, is the point fundamentally addressed in the present study.

A comment by Abiola Irele on Nigerian writing is broadly applicable to the African texts examined in the chapters to follow: "It is no exaggeration to say that every work of literature produced in this country is in some way or other a testimony to the inner realities of the social processes at work among us and to the tensions these have set up in our collective consciousness" (Irele, quoted in Ola 6).

The existential urgency with which questions of power and of change are addressed by novelists from Africa and the recognition of tragedy and loss to humanity if we fail to adjust the global imbalances make novels like those by Kane, Head, Achebe, and Marechera works of wider reach and value than texts concerned exclusively with the success stories or agonies of the "Western world" in the great power shift of the twentieth century.[18] To make these points is not, however, to overlook the status of novels such as these as artworks—indeed, it is by means of their fineness as literary artifacts that these texts convey the importance and the resonance of the insights they contain. Reductive readings of African novels as mere anthropological or sociopolitical evidence to support others' arguments is an all too prevalent distortion—not only in "Western" texts, but, unfortunately, also in some works by scholars who are themselves of African origin. The African-American academic Henry Louis Gates Jr. has tellingly made this critical point. In *Black Literature and Literary Theory* (1984), which he edited, Gates writes that

> *mimetic and expressive theories* of black literature continue to predominate over the sorts of theories concerned with discrete uses of figurative language. . . . [This is so, he suggests,] because of this curious valorization of the social and polemical *functions* of black literature, [and so] *the structure of the black text has been repressed* and treated as if it were *transparent* . . . as if it were invisible, or literal, or a one-dimensional document. (Gates 5–6, some emphases added)[19]

This, too, illustrates a traceable working of power in the literary-academic sphere. The tendency to "anthropologize" African creations—that is, to relegate the study of what Africans produce to the sphere of anthropology—is another illustration of the after-effects of the power inequality of the first major encounter between the "West" and Africa. What it illustrates is the difficulty of changing a conquest into a meeting of peoples. "But if we want humanity to advance a step further, if we want to bring it up to a different level than that which Europe has shown it, then we must invent and we must make discoveries,"[20] says Fanon.

Contexts: Actual

Arjun Appadurai, in "Globalisation and the Research Imagination," a paper he delivered at the international symposium on Globalisation and Social Sciences in Africa,[21] makes the important point that "regions are best viewed as initial contexts for themes which generate variable geographies, rather than as fixed geographies marked by pre-given themes" (8). He adds that "areas are not facts but artefacts—of our interests and our fantasies as well as of our needs to know, to remember and to forget" (10). Yet borders, however imaginary, to whatever extent imagined (that is, delusions, or choices), are often where we stake ourselves—in the sense both of a risk and an anguish.[22] They are the points at which we are required to declare our loyalties. The community to which we affiliate ourselves may be one imagined by us, a choice, but it is also something that impinges upon us, often demandingly.

Achebe expresses the idea of an African identity as a demarcation as well as a responsibility:

> I'm an Ibo writer, because this is my basic culture; Nigerian, African and a writer . . . no, black first, then a writer. Each of these identities does call for a certain kind of commitment on my part. I must see what it is to be black . . . what does Africa mean to the world? . . . There is an identity coming into existence. . . . Each of these tags has a meaning, and a penalty and a responsibility. (Quoted in Appiah, *House,* 73–74)

Africa and its people form the large, imagined context within which this study proceeds. Compared with the other continents, the very name of Africa seems to carry a peculiar potency and, however vague or various, an identity claim. Use of the inclusive, continental name "Africa" is both unavoidable and appropriate as a basket term to contain studies of the writings of Nigerian, South African–Botswanan, and Zimbabwean novelists. Yet the "penalty" involved in this identity that Achebe warns against is overwhelmingly evident when the condition of African societies is measured against that of the prosperous nations. In Nuruddin Farah's novel *Sweet and Sour Milk,* the words of a young man with an impeccable record of local commitment are reported: "Africa is humiliation. 'Africa,' Soyaan used to say, 'embarrasses me'" (124).

Movements and cries for change emanate from Africa precisely because of a deep sense of powerlessness experienced by many Africans. "Measured by the prevalence of poverty," one expert notes, "sub-Saharan Africa is the world's most marginal region" (Adedeji 3). According to the UN Development Programme (UNDP, *Human Development Report 1992*—New York, 1992), "In 1960, the richest 20 per cent [of countries] received 30 times more [of global GNP] than the bottom 20 per cent, but by 1980 they were receiving 60 times more." The position has since worsened. A more recent UNDP report (published in mid-1998) states, "The number of under-nourished Africans more than doubled between 1970 and 1990, from 103 million to 215 million."[23] The AIDS pandemic, interstate and civil wars, and the millions of refugees and displaced persons are other well-known features of social collapse in Africa. To remove responsibility for this from African shoulders is as pernicious as it is to overlook the extent to which the colonial devastation initially and neocolonialism (i.e., international capitalist domination, in which the weak "partners" are inevitably exploited) presently have disempowered African societies.

A sober description that fits neatly into the terms of the present study is the following:

> The centre, more or less visible, is the place from which power—political, military, economic, social, religious or ethical—emanates. At a second level, marginality thus becomes synonymous with the relative or absolute lack of power to influence a defined social entity while being a recipient of the exercise of power by other parts of that entity. (Adedeji 1)

"Yet, while Africa has been marginalised for centuries," he adds, "this latest wave of dispossession is threatening to lock Africa into . . . the periphery of the periphery" (Adedeji 1).

The difficulty—the obscurity and the complexity—of the accountability issue is itself at the root of the daunting task of tackling the vast human problems that have arisen here. Defining "neocolonialism" as "displaced colonialism" ("Neocolonialism" 224), Spivak mentions that "as Said and many others have argued, the British empire passes into the hands of the United States."[24] She says, "Now at that point the colonialism that you need is more economic and less territorial," pointing out that such long-distance economic domination "is neocolonialism" (221). Spivak provides an image: "Neocolonialism is like radiation . . . you feel like you're independent" (221). Accordingly, "neocolonialism happens by remote control and is immediately managed by the hyperreal. . . . And economic coercion cannot really be felt like domination can be felt" (223).[25] In fact, local, democratically elected governments are forced to execute economic measures decided upon in continents where conditions differ greatly from their own. "The notion of globalisation is structured by power," writes Stuart Hall, and it "*reconfigures* the relationship between the *global*, the *local*, the *national* and the *regional*" (Hall, "Random," 8, 9). As he recognizes, however,

> it's not simply what *they* are doing to *us*. There is an old answer to that: Get rid of them if you can! But when *they* are doing that to *us,* and some of *us* are doing that to *us* as well, the question of who is *there,* who is *here*; where is *inside* and where is *outside,* becomes much more complicated.
>
> When we say it's a complicated question, what we are talking about is politics. Politics, however complicated at a certain point, divides into *those* over there and *us* over here. In reality, some of *them* are over here, and some of *us* are over there. That is really what it is like. The colour of who is doing what to whom cannot be predicted from outside. It is necessary to know something about the local situation. (Hall, "Random," 7)

His point is confirmed by Pius Okigbo: "This third liberation is therefore more difficult, not only because this slavery is more insidious, but also because indigenous supporters and collaborators of the neo-colonial powers are drawn from the highest echelons of local society" (Okigbo 29).

Notions of exclusion and of marginalization haunt accounts of present conditions in Africa. Some "see things in terms of Africa falling off the world map" (Adebayo Williams 350, 362). "In economic terms," writes the French Africanist Chabal, "Africa is becoming marginal to world industrial development and to global commerce." He adds that "there is a sense today that the continent has become irrelevant in the world perspective" (Chabal, "Crisis," 34). Marginalization of Africans has both external (global) and local dimensions. In the international context, "marginalisation is . . . a process of devaluation which results in ever-diminishing freedom to act and space to move within the international economic environment," and "international charity has become the principal means of relieving suffering. The longer the charity is operating, the more economic and social marginalisation becomes ingrained in the culture, creating despair and apathy" (Adedeji 8).

Within many African countries there is what has been described as "a crisis of failed states" (A. Williams 349). Mary Chinery-Hesse refers to "the internal marginalisation of almost half Africa's population. . . . This is roughly the proportion that lives in poverty" (Chinery-Hesse 150). "But it is the personalisation and monopolisation of power in many African states," writes Adedeji, "that has led to the increasing privatisation of the state in the hands of the powerful. . . . The cumulative effect is a state set apart from its society, in which 80 per cent of the population are at the margin" (Adedeji 8). Such a state (Marechera is one novelist who in his later works focuses on its working) is in fact to a large extent a tool in the hands of the "transnational" corporations: Africans who occupy the state serving as local black masks to much more powerful, inaccessible white faces.

In *Race, Nation, Class—Ambiguous Identities*, Immanuel Wallerstein suggests an imbrication between racial stereotyping and international wealth disparity. "It is precisely because racism is anti-universalistic in doctrine," he says, that it helps to maintain capitalism as a system. "It allows a far lower reward to a major segment of the work force than could ever be justified on the basis of merit" (Balibar and Wallerstein 34). The working of "racial" notions, Wallerstein states, establishes "an international status group. . . . One grouping is by skin colour. . . . Another more common one is by continent." He believes that religion has been replaced by "race" in the "contemporary world [as] the only international status group category" (Balibar and Wallerstein 199). This harmonizes with Stuart Hall's observation: "As soon as power sees differences, it knows it can begin to classify them and us. . . . Difference invites the play of power" (Hall, "Random," 14).

But it seems widely accepted that there is no opting out of the international industrial system, and the need for the type of development called "modernization" in Africa, despite its numerous drawbacks and its costs, cannot be denied. It is how such development occurs, where it originates, by whom it is managed, and to whose benefit that are the crucial issues. The difficulty faced by Africa's peoples at the present juncture, as study after study insists, is that they must simultaneously globalize and localize; they have to find or rediscover their own identity and modernize, that is, internationalize. It is indeed a tall order, especially when compounded with the "crushing [international] debt burden" (Chabal, "Crisis," 34) against which so many voices have lately been raised in protest.

Basil Davidson, a well-known historian of Africa, argues that "the essential solution . . . is to renew the flow of history, of indigenous self-development, that was broken by the dispossessions" ("Restitution," 23).[26] At a time when, all over the world, educational policies stress the need to train more scientists and engineers, "scientific" studies of the African condition nevertheless emphasize again and again the foundational need for an improved social self-conception of the kind to which artists and literary works and study of the humanities contribute. One study mentions "the continent's loss of self-confidence" and calls for "reorientation of curricula and teaching methods by relating to the rehabilitation of Africa's culture, traditions and value systems" (Adedeji 217, 209). In Africa especially, "development must be a human-centred process," writes Louis Emmerij, to which "everything else—economic growth, fiscal policy, exchange rate management—is no more than the means to achieve the fundamental objective of improving human welfare" (Emmerij 108). Reporting on an international conference on the theme "Africa Within the World—Beyond Dispossession and Dependence," Adebayo Adedeji, executive director of the African Centre for Development and Strategic Studies, which sponsored the conference, mentioned the "broad agreement that sustainable development could only come from within Africa, and that the goal of all policies should be to improve the human condition and develop Africa's human resources" (Adedeji 11). Acceptance of this goal would ensure a recentering of the continent within a global context.

One way of achieving such a change is for Africans themselves to take the initiative. International economic power structures and local political élites are allowed to be too intimidating. African communities themselves need to elevate as many as possible of their lowly members—and to discipline and demote those members of their élites who selfishly appropriate scarce resources and allow themselves to be bribed by international financial institutions. "Africa's development efforts will come to nothing unless governance is improved" (Emmerij 109). Chabal, although he denounces "the vacuousness of causalities which reduce violence in Africa to 'tribal' history, political greed or incompetence," which are "attributes shared equally throughout the world," acknowledges that "it seems difficult to avoid the conclusion that postcolonial Africa has been afflicted by an extraordinarily high degree of wilful political violence" (Chabal, "Crisis," 32, 31). What is called for, as he says, is "an analysis . . . which respects rather than demeans Africans" (32).[27]

Chabal turns the tables by proposing an analysis of "Western" attitudes to African disasters: "We are disturbed by the atrocities," he suggests, "perhaps primarily, because it makes us wonder about the potential barbarity present in us all" (Chabal, "Crisis," 36). He links the phenomenon with the "increasingly strong and vocal right-wing xenophobic movement" in Europe and the attempt there to "return to our 'real' (that is, in fact, imaginary) preimperial roots"—a European postcolonialism, so to speak (38); an attempt to deny links with, and responsibility for, the former colonies. Chabal rightly insists simultaneously on the recognition of African uniqueness and contemporaneity by "Africanists [who] have been prone to seek in Africa a counterpoint to their own history" (45). "Although this is perhaps most obvious in respect of the anthropologist," writes Chabal, "it is also visible in the work of almost all other Africanists." He defines this typically "Africanist" attitude to Africa as "looking for the 'primitive' societies from which we are supposed to have evolved" (45).[28]

In a careful and subtle analysis of both the mutual and the separate responsibilities of Europe and Africa for the latter's present, problematic condition,[29] Chabal warns against the mistaken "search for an all-conquering theory of causal explanation," which he disparagingly calls "simple causality": "a tendency to look for the African (as opposed to universal) causality[30] of events in Africa" (48). Chabal, too, returns the unfashionable "identity issue" to the table by quoting Lonsdale's suggestion that "to imagine the existence of a new 'tribe' may be the best way to look outward, to embrace social progress" (quoted in Chabal, "Crisis," 49). The need to foreground "ordinary" people, of which Bessie Head is so consistently aware, is expressed by Chabal as "the injunction to take on board *'politique par le bas'*—low rather than high politics" or "what is sometimes called the politics of civil society." He mentions "the search for the appropriate African metaphor for the business of politics" (50) in order to address "the three most fundamental notions of political analysis: identity, political community and political accountability" (52). In all these respects, as the following three chapters illustrate, the texts of Achebe, Marechera, and Head abundantly illustrate their command of these rare, but crucial, skills.

In the inevitably, and unfortunately, merely rhetorical frame here proposed, two appropriate concluding questions are supplied by Adebayo Adedeji: "Can marginality unleash collective energies for change and transformation?" and "Do we not indeed have a moral obligation as intellectual, community, national and international leaders to express a vision for a qualitatively global society?" (Adedeji 13). It seems that Africa's parlous condition as the wrinkled, empty belly of the world's body signposts and indexes a great flaw in the global system. It is a flaw that Africans, especially, are obliged to address—in themselves and their own situations, in the leaders whom they allow to govern their societies, and in the global power holders and the beneficiaries from the present state of affairs.

Contexts: Theoretical

It will be evident at this juncture that the present inquiry is not proceeding strictly in terms of an identifiable theory among those theoretical frameworks particularly influential in the final decade of this century. This is a choice that will be discussed more fully under the rubric "Choices." Equally evident, however, must be the recognition that the study of Head's, Marechera's, and Achebe's depictions of power and of change has profited in innumerable obvious, as well as subtle, ways from the work of many theoreticians working in literary and surrounding areas. If, at the beginning of the latter part of the twentieth century, philosophers seemed to be taking over or invading the literary field, it is perhaps at present the case that academics who root their studies in literature have expanded their commentaries into areas like sociology, politics, and philosophy, so that literary commentaries have moved forcefully, perhaps domineeringly, into a central position among the social sciences. A leading and, to some extent, initiating figure in this field is Edward Said, who explains why there has been a shift[31] in literary studies toward a so much more inclusive vision of its subject field:

> Criticism cannot assume that its province is merely the text, not even the great literary text. It must see itself, with other discourse, inhabiting a much more contested cultural space, in which what has counted in the continuity and transmission of knowledge has been the signifier, as an event that has left lasting traces upon the human subject. Once we take that view, then literature as an isolated paddock in the broad cultural field disappears, and with it too the harmless rhetoric of self-delighting humanism. Instead we

> will be able, I think, to read and write with a sense of the greater stake in historical and political effectiveness that literary as well as other texts have had. (Said, *World,* 225)

Orientalism, Said's densely documented and powerfully rendered presentation of the argument proposing the relativity, for all its dominance, of the European perspective on other cultures to its east, has been by far the single most influential of the works that energized the change in intellectual focus referred to above. The essays in Said's *Culture and Imperialism* (1994) expanded the argument, with the demonstration of the extent to which the great works of the European literary tradition were unconsciously complicit in furthering the hierarchically ordered, European-dominated "worldview" of the time. Not strictly postcolonial studies—Said's writings mentioned here can be more correctly described as colonial discourse analysis, in which he seems ultimately more interested—they nevertheless helped bring about the move toward the study of the formerly politically dominated regions and their literatures.

Postcolonial theory or, more generally, postcolonial studies, is an achieved body of work to which a study like the present one is indebted and with which it has to contend; however, the postcolonial field is by no means monolithic. It is in fact characterized by a high degree of internal dissension,[32] occasionally deteriorating into mere point scoring. Serious criticisms of the procedures, aims, and terminology of postcolonial theory have been offered especially by scholars who, ironically, would themselves be classified by "outsiders" as "postcolonialists." But it is when debate heats up that it becomes discernible that a great deal of not only intellectual, but also emotional, capital has been invested in an undertaking. Perhaps the underlying question remains of how intellectuals can or should contribute to the eternally unfinished undertaking of beginning to right the great wrongs of the world. Playing this role outlined by intellectuals for themselves and their colleagues is seldom simple or easy—because, even though the noblesse oblige morality attendant upon the *privilege* of their education is obvious, the precise way in which intellectual undertaking can contribute in the "real world" is never clear-cut.[33]

In a thoughtful essay titled "Once More With Feeling: What Is Postcolonialism?" (1995), Deepika Bahri writes that "the academy at large has supported and encouraged, even eulogised, the field for various reasons and under circumstances that cannot be left unexplored" (53). Noting that "the compound word . . . first appeared in the *Oxford English Dictionary* in 1959" (65) and that "the term 'postcolonial', hyphenated or not, has been used largely to describe the literatures of former colonies" (63), the critic adds that, nevertheless, "the 'postcolonial' becomes a surprisingly elusive and slippery configuration" (52). "Rather than contend with definition when it fails,"

Bahri notes dryly, "postcolonial theorists are apt to multiply its connotative possibilities to suit *their* various needs" (52, emphasis added). Warning of "the benevolent tokenisation that replaces previous erasure," Bahri ironizes "academic gestures of acceptance of the visible difference presented by displaced Third World postcolonials" (74, 71).[34]

The essay "The Angel of Progress: Pitfalls of the Term 'Post-Colonialism'" by Anne McClintock offers an especially penetrating critique. She contends that "the term . . . signals a reluctance to surrender the privilege of seeing the world in terms of a singular and ahistorical abstraction . . . : '*the* post-colonial Other'" (McClintock, "Angel," 293). Her objection to "the term 'post-colonialism' [as] prematurely celebratory and obfuscatory" (298) has become well known. Fiercely denunciatory and intellectually probing is another challenging response to the academic prevalence of postcolonial studies, Arif Dirlik's "The Postcolonial Aura: Third World Criticism in the Age of Global Capitalism." His strong central point is that "the term mystifies both politically and methodologically a situation that represents not the abolition but the reconfiguration of earlier forms of domination" (Dirlik 331), although "it has acquired the status of a new orthodoxy" (330). Talk of a "postcolonial" condition, Dirlik believes, obfuscates the fact that we are in fact living in "the structure of the new global capitalism": "a network of urban formations, without a clearly definable center, whose links to one another are far stronger than their relationship to their immediate hinterlands" (348, 349). Because of this, he thinks,

> it is arguable that the end of Eurocentrism is an illusion because capitalist culture as it has taken shape has Eurocentrism built into the very structure of its narrative. . . . It is noteworthy that what makes something like the East Asian Confucian revival plausible is not its offer of alternative values to those of Euro-American origin but its articulation of native culture into a capitalist narrative. (Dirlik 350)[35]

Dirlik's points are important, but his suggestion that "a consideration of the relationship between postcolonial and global capitalism [is] absent from the writings of postcolonial intellectuals" (352) is an unfair, overly harsh generalization.

Aijaz Ahmad's *In Theory: Classes, Nations, Literatures* (1991) is another example of the fierce passions that the academic success story of postcolonial studies has aroused. He, too, scores some telling points against "the more recent literary theorists . . . as exemplified by Homi K. Bhabha among others," saying that "those who live . . . in places where a majority . . . has been denied access to such benefits of 'modernity' as hospitals or better health insurance or even basic literacy, can hardly afford the terms of such thought" (Ahmad, *Theory,* 68–69). He denounces a perceived "eclecticism among the politically engaged theorists" (71) as well as "the metropolitan theory's inflationary rhetoric" (69). How well such "internal fights" play into the hands of the ancient imperial strategy *divide et impera* is ironically evident when Ahmad charges that "the metropolitan Left . . . has abandoned the fundamental project of socialism, which is none other than the destruction of the imperialist character of modern capital" (317).

Although widely known as a postcolonial theorist, Gayatri Chakravorty Spivak (Marxist-feminist-deconstructionist) is simultaneously one of the cautionary critics of this intellectual movement. Her famous question "Can the Subaltern Speak?"—half taunt, half lamentation—is also the title of a substantial essay. Quoting Foucault's recognition of "a whole set of knowledges that have been disqualified as inadequate . . . or insufficiently elaborated (Foucault 1980:82)," she proposes an extension of the perception of suppression of "knowledge": not only inside, but also beyond the European centers. Foucault, she says, "locates epistemic violence . . . in the redefinition of sanity [in Europe] at the end of the European eighteenth century." To this she adds a question, "But what if that particular redefinition was only a part of the narrative of history in Europe *as well as in the colonies*?" (emphasis added). Linking the grasping of control by means of the definition of knowledge within Europe with the subjugation of non-European people, she asks, "What if the two projects of epistemic overhaul worked as dislocated and unacknowledged parts of a vast two-handed engine?" (Spivak, "Subaltern," 281). Spivak answers the question in her essay title quite firmly—"The subaltern cannot speak" (308)[36]—and her explanation is that "the subject implied by the texts of insurgency" can only gain a hearing by means of "the narrative sanction granted to the colonial subject in the dominant groups" (287).

In *Postcolonial Theory: Contexts, Practices, Politics* (1997), Bart Moore-Gilbert introduces his chapter on her writing with the remark, "The work of the US-based critic of Indian origin Gayatri Spivak constitutes one of the most substantial and innovative contributions to post-colonial forms of cultural analysis, though her essays are also some of the most elusive, complex and challenging in the field" (Moore-Gilbert 74).

Moore-Gilbert later adds a criticism of her theoretical concept by saying that "the more the subaltern is seen as wholly other, the more Spivak seems to construct the subaltern's identity neither relationally nor differentially, but in essentialist terms" (102). Perhaps ungraciously, I would add the question whether Spivak's declaration/definition of the silenced condition of subalternity does not itself constitute a "speaking for" the oppressed subject. Moore-Gilbert writes:

> While Spivak is excellent on the "itinerary of silencing" endured by the subaltern, particularly historically, there is little attention to the process by which the subaltern's "coming to voice" might be achieved. Spivak often

> appears to deny the subaltern any possibility of access to . . . (self-) liberating personal and political trajectories. (106)[37]

Although Spivak at times comes across as extremely, arrogantly dismissive of what is being done by some of her colleagues in the field of postcolonial studies,[38] her insistence on due *care* being taken by such scholars in realizing the limitations set by their own privileged position is important. So are her subtly formulated comments on the irresistible nature of "modernity": "One of the things . . . I believe one must do is the persistent critique of what one cannot not want" (Spivak, "Neocolonialism," 248).

Homi Bhabha, honored by Moore-Gilbert as the third dominant figure among the "high" theorists of postcoloniality, is widely known for his insistence that a condition of "hybridity" is not only the inevitably resulting condition of all societies that have been colonized, but that, far from being a demeaning state, it can present a strategic[39] advantage for the colonized. Bhabha is frequently criticized for the allusive, sometimes highly turgid style of his writing.[40] Bhabha can write forcefully and clearly, though, as the following lucid explanation exemplifies:

> Post-colonial criticism bears witness to the unequal and uneven forces of cultural representation involved in the contest for political and social authority within the modern world order . . . to reveal the antagonistic and ambivalent moments within the "rationalisations" of modernity. . . . Various contemporary critical theories suggest that we learn our most enduring lessons for living and thinking from those who have suffered the sentence of history—subjugation, domination, diaspora, displacement . . . social marginality. . . . It forces us to . . . engage with culture as an uneven, incomplete production of meaning . . . produced in the act of social survival. . . . It makes one increasingly aware of the construction of culture. (Bhabha, "Indeterminate," 46–47)

At the end of the same essay, Bhabha writes, "The histories of slavery and colonialism . . . [represent] an idea of action and agency more complex than either the nihilism of despair or the utopia of progress" (57), a valid and finely made point.

The study by Bart Moore-Gilbert[41] to which I have alluded several times before is important because, in addition to providing a fair-minded and elucidating account of hotly contested and intellectually intricate arguments, he places the innovations of the postcolonial theorists both intellectually and historically. Moore-Gilbert makes a rule-of-thumb distinction between postcolonial *theorists* (of which Said, Spivak, and Bhabha are his chief examples) and postcolonial *critics* (among whom he numbers Chinua Achebe, Wole Soyinka, and Wilson Harris) (Moore-Gilbert 4). He is deeply appreciative of the insights and enriching influence of postcolonial theorists, notably Said, of whom he writes: "In the reformulation of traditional metropolitan approaches to the study of the connections between both Western and postcolonial culture and (neo-)colonialism, postcolonial theory—in the shape, initially, of Said's *Orientalism*—has played a decisive (if not exclusive) role" (Moore-Gilbert 155).

Moore-Gilbert is yet one of very few writers in this field to have insisted that the supposed innovations of the postcolonial intellectual movement in fact had important precursors. It is a breath of fresh air to hear Achebe acknowledged (as Moore-Gilbert fully does—4, 173–177) in a discussion of theory for his powerful critiques of the Eurocentric vision—and to see Said, whose position is sufficiently firmly established, also by Moore-Gilbert himself, criticized[42] for his initial failure to acknowledge his intellectual predecessors. Moore-Gilbert's comment that "in seeking to defend a Western canonical figure like Joseph Conrad from the charge of racism brought against him [i.e., Conrad] by some African critics, notably Achebe, the later Said advances arguments which seem almost inconceivable from the author of *Orientalism*" (Moore-Gilbert 66). Moore-Gilbert's point can be corroborated by strategically juxtaposing two sets of quotations from Said's *Culture and Imperialism.* In the first Said writes:

> What I left out of *Orientalism* was that response to Western dominance which culminated in the great movement of decolonization all across the Third World. . . . cultural resistance almost everywhere, the assertions of nationalist identities, and, in the political realm, the creation of associations and parties whose common goal was self-determination and national independence. (Said, *Culture*, xii)

To this he adds:

> Stories are at the heart of what explorers and novelists say about strange regions of the world; they also become the method colonized people use to assert their own identity and the existence of their own history. . . . The power to narrate, or to block other narratives from forming and emerging is very important to culture and imperialism. (Said, *Culture*, xiii)

The passage with which I contrast the above is considerably briefer. It is Said's reference to what (in a footnote to what follows) he calls "the attack on Conrad" (Said, *Culture*, 413), that is, Achebe's essay "An Image of Africa: Racism in Conrad's *Heart of Darkness*" (Achebe, *Hopes*, 1–20). Here Said seems strangely condescending—especially in the first part of the comment, toward the African novelist—and uncharacteristically ungenerous:

> On the one hand, when in a celebrated essay Chinua Achebe criticizes Conrad's racism, he either says nothing about or overrides the limitations placed on Conrad by the novel as an aesthetic form. On the other hand, Achebe shows that he understands how the form works when, in some of his own novels, he rewrites—painstakingly and with originality—Conrad. (Said, *Culture*, 9)

The apparent "affiliations" (to use Said's own term) in the turns of the above argument make for interesting reading!

In his influential work *The Political Unconscious: Narrative as a Socially Symbolic Act* (1981), the critic Fredric Jameson proposed that literary works "must be read as a symbolic meditation on the destiny of community" (70), an expression both useful and profound, and certainly not ideologically slanted or limiting.[43] He also insisted, in this work, on the need to "[unmask] . . . cultural artefacts as socially symbolic acts" (Jameson, *Unconscious,* 20). Jameson "applied" and *"contracted"* the general point in his later essay "Third World Literature in the Era of Multinational Capitalism" (1986) into the contention that "Third-world texts, even those which are seemingly private and invested with a properly libidinal dynamic—necessarily project a political dimension in the form of national allegory: *the story of the private individual destiny is always an allegory of the embattled situation of the public third-world culture and society*" (Jameson, "Third World," 69).

This essay, and specifically this sentence, aroused the indignant ire of Jameson's fellow Marxist, and former admirer, Aijaz Ahmad, who sensed in it a demeaning condescension (Ahmad, "Rhetoric"). "Of course," conceded another critic, more sympathetic toward Jameson, he

> here comes close to the totalising treatment of Third-World culture as fundamentally different from First-World culture. . . . But, despite the shortcomings in [the] . . . analysis, it is useful to recall that Jameson . . . envisions Third-World literature as different primarily because Third-World societies lack the sense of a radical separation and opposition between the public and private realms that is characteristic of Western bourgeois societies. (Booker 71)

The defense is perhaps not altogether convincing.

It is, at any rate, clear that all who write in the field of postcolonial studies participate in lively mutual criticism, although moralistic and self-righteous moments do predictably mar the generally high-minded quality of the debate. For my own part I remain wary of applying the term to the work I produce, for reasons similar to the criticisms of the effects it produces mentioned earlier in this section. As will be explained more fully in the following section, the somewhat clumsy but more unassuming and precise expression "African English fiction"[44] seems preferable. In the chapter "What Is African

Literature? Ethnography and Criticism," Kadiatu Kanneh concludes by expressing ideas similar to my own:

> It is vital to resist formulations of a holistic African world, culture, or world view which can be discovered, recovered or re-appropriated. Africa, with its plural cultures and influences, has no paradigm and cannot be reduced to a single political aspiration or spiritual unity. This does not mean that African literatures should be denied their specificity, their cultural differences, the complex textures of traditions, genres and influences. African literatures pose particular and significant challenges to literary criticisms which are not sensitive to this plurality of voices. It is a relatively simple matter to attack the theoretical inadequacies of argument which insist on Africa's independence and (cultural) difference. It is a lot more difficult to incorporate, into reading practices, an awareness of the politics of resistance, the crises of representation and the layers of reference and signification which inform and form African texts. The most difficult point to accept, for Western literary criticism, might still be that Africa is not always thinking of, or speaking to the West, and that, at moments, it escapes. (Kanneh, "Ethnography," 83)

As far as "useful" theorists are concerned, another big name that must be brought in here is that of the Russian Mikhail Bakhtin.[45] His position provides, I suggest, a useful corrective to the linguistic and cultural essentialism so prevalent in much postcolonial criticism—though sometimes assumed rather than expressed. A characteristic passage is the following, from Simon During: "For me, perhaps eccentrically, post-colonialism is regarded as the need, in nations or groups which have been victims of imperialism, to achieve an identity uncontaminated by universalist or Eurocentric concepts and images" (During, quoted in Ashcroft et al., *Reader*, 125).[46]

Bakhtin's relevance to those seeking an understanding of the seemingly inappropriate, but uncommon power of African writing in the Europhone languages becomes evident if his thoughtful observations are recontextualized by applying them to African Europhone writing. Although Bakhtin's own frame of reference is almost entirely Western, his theories are sufficiently broad and generous to allow accommodation to the writings of Africans who use the languages of the former colonizers.[47] Bakhtin begins by pointing out that the novel "is the only genre that was born and nourished in a new era of world history, and therefore it is deeply akin to that era," which he describes as "the developing, incomplete and therefore re-thinking and re-evaluating present" (Bakhtin 4, 17). Such a *changing* world is certainly as African as it is European. Although (in a point on which Bakhtin "agrees" with Scheub, cited earlier) "the novel's roots must ultimately be sought in folklore," Bakhtin makes the observation that the novel is the first genre in which "the present, in all its openendedness, [is] taken as a . . . center for artistic and ideological orientation," something he calls "an enormous revolution in the creative consciousness of man" (38).

As if describing the African colonial and postcolonial situation, Bakhtin writes: "During its germination and early development, the novelistic word reflected a primordial struggle between tribes, peoples, cultures and languages—it is still full of echoes of this ancient struggle. In essence this discourse always developed on the boundary line between cultures and languages" (Bakhtin 50).

An even more pertinent comment is the following: "The novel senses itself on the border between the completed, dominant literary language and the extraliterary languages that know heteroglossia," and it is, in terms of my theme of change, also profoundly concerned with "time's shifts" (Bakhtin 67). As if he is a precursor of Homi Bhabha's notion of "hybridity" (as the consequence of colonial impact on local cultures), Bakhtin writes:

> For the novelist working in prose, the object is always entangled in someone else's discourse about it, it is already present with qualifications, an object of dispute that is conceptualised and evaluated variously, inseparable from the heteroglot social apperception of it. The novelist speaks of this "already qualified world" in a language that is heteroglot and internally dialogised. (Bakhtin 330)

And finally, Bakhtin's comments on the involvement of prose art in a world that is becoming are extraordinarily astute and apposite[48] to the present study:

> The prose art presumes a deliberate feeling for the historical and social concreteness of living discourse, as well as its relativity, a feeling for its participation in historical becoming and in social struggle; it deals with discourse that is still warm from that struggle and hostility, as yet unresolved and still fraught with hostile intentions and accents; prose art finds discourse in this state and subjects it to the dynamic unity of its own style. (Bakhtin 331)

A more distinctly, though not exclusively, political and historical study that I found highly appropriate to the perspectives adopted in my own study is the work *Empire and Emancipation: Power and Liberation on a World Scale* (1989) by the Dutch scholar Jan P. Nederveen Pieterse.[49] Pieterse is interesting because he looks at large historical interstate patterns, at the "psychology" of both empire and emancipation, and because he emphasizes the deeply intertwined nature of these two apparently directly opposed manifestations. His deep awareness of irony is amenable to the novelistic perspectives on power and change on which I focus.[50] Hence he writes that "yesterday's social struggles turn up among the platitudes of today's powers" and that "it is the routinisation of emancipation by which the humanisation of empire is achieved" (380). Nevertheless, "emancipation is often achieved at the expense of other, lesser units": "A nation's liberation may be the beginning of a minority's oppression" (Pieterse 380).

Pieterse notes that "power may be the ultimate structure of empire not by virtue of its prominence but rather by virtue of its invisibility" (Pieterse 194). Hence, "differentials of development are masked and mystified as differences of *descent* . . . aristocracy and racism are *ideologies of power*" and, says Pieterse, "essentially concerned with *transforming a temporary status advantage into a lasting advantage*" (252). Hence there is what he calls "the monotonous consistency of the European concept of order and civilisation" (318). Pieterse notes the *implication* of the colonized areas in the European process of transformation through industrialization: this huge change could come about to some extent because "the frontier was a place where class tensions were *transmuted* into ethnic tensions" (319).[51] In other words, outlying areas could absorb and cushion the social tensions which, if they had had to be contained within Europe, would have cracked the society apart. Yet Pieterse, discussing what he calls the "dialectic of assimilation itself," notes that technologies "introduced to facilitate imperial control, penetration, and exploitation, at another stage could be harnessed in resisting empire" (362). "Accordingly," he notes, "the dialectics of modernisation intersect with the dialectics of political liberation" (363).[52] "For the oppressed," writes Pieterse, "it is a strategic necessity to address the oppressor in its own language . . . indeed the point is to manipulate the self-understanding of the oppressor" (368).

I conclude this section on the theoretical contexts of my own study with a summarizing judgment of Pieterse's:

> Empires structure the world and raise standards of collective competence; they may be credited also for their dialectical aptitude in undermining themselves by means of their action. But it is not possible to be conclusive with regard to the relations between empire and emancipation. The issues involved are complex, large in scope, and ever in motion. (Pieterse 381)[53]

Choices

In one of his "Notes" (1888) Friedrich Nietzsche wrote, "No, it is precisely facts that do not exist, only *interpretations*" (Kaufmann 458),[54] emphasizing not only the relativity but also the subjectivity of human knowledge. It is on this note of skepticism that I wish to introduce a brief discussion of various choices—of subject area, framing, style of presentation, intellectual validation, and so forth—involved in the present writing project. To be emphasized initially is the point implicit in the heading here: that actual preferences—in other words, admirations and enthusiasms—led to the selection of texts and authors that form the main subject of discussion. In wishing to write about works that I experience as still insufficiently known, which means under*rated,* considering their literary merits and weight of insight, and in choosing to focus on issues that appear to me central and fascinating in my own local context and far beyond, these hunches and claims are not, finally, "provable"—except by disingenuous means. It is even impossible, I believe, to disentangle the undeniable element of cultural patriotism that I as an African feel toward these texts from my "disinterested" concern with the intellectually complex, politically engaged, and artistically achieved material they present to their readers. What the three chapters that form the body of this text do attempt to delineate are, then, "interpretations"—that is, constructs that attempt to mediate among a "real" world in my own limited knowledge of it, aspects of societies within the African continent as depicted by these authors, and the various academic renditions of the main features of life in our time and of the role in it of the texts I deal with.

To qualify the above points, it is necessary to add to the concession that what is offered here is not of a factual nature the further point that it is from its own angle a participation in the endless and huge debate about what considerations should be given precedence when people decide how to use their mental skills to cope with, or improve, the conditions of life in their time, and which intellectual methods are useful to those ends and most worthy of respect. This is rather a big bite to chew, but I raise the matter of the enormous and weighty issues involved in recognition of the intensely moralistic (in fact, frequently self-righteous and denunciatory) tone of much intellectual discussion on the quality of life—its causes as well as its future prospects—of those who find themselves in the formerly colonized areas of the world. All this is mentioned in order to reintroduce the point made before: that although this text is not untouched by theory, it is not of a primarily theoretical nature.

In the present academic climate, opting not to write within a recognizable theoretical framework and without employing an explicitly theoretical set of terms involves the risk of having one's work dismissed as un- or undertheorized (and *therefore* insignificant), naïve, or of a merely self-indulgent kind, an eccentricity. Commentary of the kind undertaken in the main body of this work is nevertheless not ultimately any riskier than heavily theoretized writing. Arguments and analyses, once available to public scrutiny, must stand or fall by the tests of validity, consistency, appropriateness, adequacy, and relevance to which all intellectual work is, and should be, subjected. Neither donning the armor of a particular theory, nor ostentatiously baring the body of one's text to intellectual assault, will protect any analysis from the slings and arrows of outraged fellow intellectuals.

At this point the present text must itself participate in a preliminary bout to explain why no single theoretical frame was chosen to guide its investigation. But because of the slipperiness of the term "theory" itself, it is of course acknowledged that *a* plan shapes this text, that *a* set of ideas and assumptions, prejudices and preferences, are at work in it—and if one contends that *that* constitutes "theory," this work employs it. However, I refer of course to the known theories of literature and politics that are prominent in the late twentieth century, and to the by now standard practice of choosing a theory or a theorist in terms of which (or in terms of whose position) other texts are discussed.

In a conference paper[55] on "Globalisation and the Research Imagination," Arjun Appadurai of the University of Chicago says:

> The modern research ethic assumes its full force with the subtraction of the idea of moral voice or vision and the addition of the idea of replicability. . . . Research in the modern, Western sense, is through and through a collective activity. . . . For most researchers, the trick is how to choose theories, define frameworks, ask questions and design methods that are most likely to produce research with a plausible half-life. (Appadurai 15)

He speaks of scholars being trained "in developing this faculty for the life-long production of pieces of new knowledge which function briskly but not for too long" (Appadurai 16). This depressing, frightening scenario is, of course, an exaggeration, but it helps to explain the present writer's distaste for an approach to academic writing that requires the painstaking application of a famous scholar's ideas, and terms, to one's area of interest, and that to some considerable extent curtails or discourages the urge to develop ideas freely in a discovery process unhampered by the lumpy passport-and-baggage of a known theory. For the present, the stream of theory-centered reading practices flows very powerfully[56] and, despite the amount of internal bickering among postcolonial theorists, it is the distinctly dominant mode in literary criticism in the area in which I work.

Postcolonial studies have gained ground for the interests of the world's previously colonized peoples in incalculable, but also unmistakable and enormously valuable, ways. This is a political advance in what may be a slow global emancipatory process. At this point in my own argument, however, my preference for a somewhat different reading strategy needs to be validated, which I shall begin to do by means of illustrating what I see as some of the inadequacies of postcolonial theorists' approaches to literary texts[57]—which function in both theory-centered readings and studies like my own as the main "body of evidence."

A core text here is the influential—generally acclaimed, although also frequently criticized—representative "compendium" *The Empire Writes Back: Theory and Practice in Post-Colonial Literatures* (1989) by Bill Ashcroft, Gareth Griffiths, and Helen Tiffin. As a broad summation of postcolonial theory and literature, this work has stood the test of time and is an excellent study in its own right. If for my own purposes I here concentrate on what I see as a few of its flaws, this should not be taken as proof of blindness to its achievements. A point on which I concur with its authors, for example, is their identification of the reception of the texts that are most widely read as an index of power distribution in the world at large—which is how I would paraphrase their identification of "a canon" as "not a body of texts *per se,* but rather a set of reading practices" (189), paralleled with the remark that "post-colonialism is more than a body of texts produced within postcolonial societies, and . . . is best conceived of as a reading practice" (193). "However," they write elsewhere, "the term 'post-colonial literatures' is finally to be preferred over the others because it points the way towards a possible study of the effects of colonialism" (24).[58] Not only does the latter quotation testify to the ready-made conceptual traps of homogenizing, essentializing and a vague universalization inherent in such a definitional approach, *but* it perpetuates the centralization of the Western incursion into other societies as the single most significant event in those regions and their histories, while purporting to look beyond it, as signaled in the prefix "post." In my own terminology, only one (albeit major) form of power and type of change is granted real importance in their work—namely, colonization. My point is also that there is in this approach a subordination of indigenous, local realities.

The three authors of *The Empire Writes Back* confidently identify as "an all-pervasive feature of post-colonial texts" what they call "the gap which opens between the experience of place and the language available to describe it" (9). This seems a reasonable point—until the linguistically deft and supple English of such texts as those in the center of the present study are considered. The problem, I believe, arises from an unstated assumption that human beings are inherently monolingual.

In *The Empire Writes Back,* reference to "the linguistic displacement of the pre-colonial language by English," and to "those *whose language* has been rendered unprivileged by the imposition of the languages of a colonizing power" (10, emphasis added) implies in its choice of the singular form that monolingualism is the natural condition of humanity, and that the acquisition of articulation skills in an "alien" language necessarily replaces the mother tongue[59]—whereas, more often, different linguistic spheres are involved for the local inhabitant and may well remain simultaneously accessible to such a person. The disjunction between the Europhone writer's *practice* and the postcolonial academic's *theory* is well illustrated in a reference, in K.A. Appiah's acclaimed *In My Father's House,* to the Congolese writer Sony Labou Tansi's writing in French—according to Appiah, "a language he *ought* surely to hate—a language literally shit-stained in his childhood—[to] use in the project of postcolonial literary nationalism" (Appiah, *House,* 53—emphasis added). The "political and cultural monocentrism" (Ashcroft, Griffiths, and Tiffin 11) of which postcolonial critics complain may sometimes be unconsciously practiced by themselves!

Ashcroft, Griffiths, and Tiffin mention that "recent *theories* of a *general* post-colonial discourse question essentialist formulations which may lead to nationalist and racist orthodoxies" (emphases added). Although they then acknowledge that the actual practitioners—the authors of the type of text about which they as theorists write—do conceive of themselves and their work in terms of "the idea of an 'African' literature," such a notion is briskly dismissed by the three theorists because, they argue, "it has only limited application as a descriptive label" (17).[60] The concentration on theory and the preference for a "theoretical" vocabulary are also to blame, perhaps, for a solecism in a passage in which the three authors quote from the foreword to Raja Rao's novel *Kauthapura* (written in English) the words "One has to convey in a language not one's own the spirit that is one's own," and then immediately afterwards label "such writing . . . an *ethnography* of the writer's own culture" (61, emphasis added).[61] Within a few lines of the above, Ashcroft, Griffiths, and Tiffin say that the "post-colonial writer . . . is *not* the object of an interpretation, but the first interpreter" (61, emphasis added).

By quoting a longer passage from *The Empire Writes Back* I can point out a few other examples of their theoretical analysis that I find unsatisfactory. It is the passage that concludes the introduction to the series of "symptomatic readings" of postcolonial novels that they offer:

> It is not always possible to separate theory and practice in post-colonial literature. As the works of Wilson Harris, Wole Soyinka, and Edward Brathwaite demonstrate, creative writers have often offered the most perceptive and influential account of the post-colonial condition. Accordingly, the analysis and exegesis of a specific text may be one of the most crucial ways of determining the major theoretical and critical issues at stake. Such analyses are not directed towards totalising "interpretations" but towards symptomatic readings which reveal the discursive formations and ideological forces which traverse the text. As a result, readings of individual texts may enable us to isolate and identify significant theoretical shifts in the development of post-colonial writing.
>
> The symptomatic readings of texts which follow serve to illustrate three important features of all postcolonial writing. The silencing and marginalising of the post-colonial voice by the imperial centre; the abrogation of this imperial centre within the text; and the active appropriation of the language and culture of that centre. These features and the transitions between them are expressed in various ways in the different texts, sometimes through formal subversions and sometimes through contestation at the thematic level. In all cases, however, the notions of power inherent in the model of centre and margin are appropriated and so dismantled. (83)

To begin with, the gesture of respect toward the insights of "creative writers" in the second sentence of the quoted passage follows hard on the heels of a passage that comes close to accusing Chinua Achebe of playing the role of a *comprador* in his writing. In the earlier passage, the three theorists refer first to the role of a type of cultural mediator in the contacts between colonizer and colonized: "The interpreter always emerges from the dominated discourse," they say, and this role "functions to acquire the power of the new language and culture in order to preserve the old, *even whilst it assists the invaders in their overwhelming of that culture*" (emphasis added). Some few lines down, the theorists say, "The role of the interpreter is like that of the post-colonial writer," just before quoting from an Achebe essay about his having lived "at the crossroads of culture." Shortly after this, Ashcroft, Griffiths, and Tiffin pronounce Achebe "unable to confront his role as interpreter/post-colonial writer" (*Empire* 80).[62] The "outsider's arrogance" in such a passage is, to my mind, remarkable, and, unfortunately, perhaps not unrelated to ancient ethnographers' habits.

On the whole, however, the first paragraph in itself sounds as if it described the present writer's convictions and methodology. Only in the final sentence of that paragraph is the priority of theory and the subjugation of the novelists' texts again made clear, along with a fairly typical theoretical assumption that earlier literary texts are (probably, or invariably) less sophisticated than later ones. And from the beginning of the second paragraph of the passage quoted from *The Empire Writes Back* the totalizing perspective of the three theorists is made clear: "*all* post-colonial writing . . . *the* post-colonial voice" (83, emphases added). The very expression "symptomatic readings" is rather odd, as if a medically certifiable state were being diagnosed, given that the three theorists openly announce that the literary works are consulted merely in order to serve the establishment/confirmation of the theory.[63] In defense it may be said that all interpretations (like the present one!) are reductive to some extent, but it seems jarring to the present writer to have that feature of one's text presented in so coolly "colonizing" and unapologetic a fashion. The justification seems to be sought in the declaration embodied in the final sentence of the quotation, with its (surely unlikely) claim that *all* the novels they proceed to discuss manage not only to "[appropriate]," but even to "[dismantle]" what the three theorists call "the notions of power inherent in the model of centre and margin" (83). Can it really be that easily done?

At the end of the section in which Ashcroft, Griffiths, and Tiffin offer their most detailed comments on a number of novels, they say: "Symptomatic readings of this kind are not concerned primarily with evaluating one text against another . . . nor with 'discovering' their essential metaphoric meaning: but rather with identifying and articulating the symptomatic and distinctive features of their post-coloniality" (*Empire* 115—emphasis added).

This, too, openly proclaims a practice that I would in a disgruntled description refer to as making the literary texts mere grist to the theory mill. If this is a legitimate and merely "procedural" denigration, it nevertheless seems to lead to and link with the following section of Ashcroft, Griffiths, and Tiffin's conclusion:

> Thus the rereading and the rewriting of the European historical and fictional record is a vital and inescapable task at the heart of the post-colonial enterprise. These subversive manoeuvres, rather than the construction of *essentially* national or regional alternatives, are the characteristic features of the postcolonial text. Post-colonial literatures/cultures are constituted in counter-discursive rather than homologous practices. (*Empire* 196)

Such a description oscillates uneasily, I suggest, between ascribing a merely reactive role to postcolonial literature, and yet allowing it an oppositional stance—while refusing to grant it an actual authenticity, difficult as that notion may be. Moreover, the above passage apparently freezes the cultures of the formerly colonized regions in a condition of dependency that can be clearly contrasted with the words of Amilcar Cabral (already quoted) in which he refers to a formerly dominated people "return[ing] to the upward paths of their own culture" (Cabral 42).

In a passage from his work *In My Father's House: Africa in the Philosophy of Culture* (1992), Anthony Appiah writes that "(as many critics complain) contemporary theory has often sponsored techniques of reading that yield somewhat homogenous results. Our modern theories are too powerful, prove too much" (Appiah, *House*, 65). I think that he here misses the point of the reductive effect of much theory-centered writing—that it "proves," on the contrary, too little. I agree with his expression of a preference for "a more political style of reading," which "may be more attuned to the distinctive circumstances of composition of postcolonial literatures" (65), as I do with his recognition that "African writers in the colonial languages . . . normally conceive of themselves as addressing a readership that encompasses communities wider than any 'traditional' culture" (70). However, Appiah subsequently writes: "The relation of African writers to the African past is a web of delicate ambiguities. If they learned neither to despise it nor to try to ignore it—and there are many witnesses to the difficulty of this decolonization of the mind—they have still to learn how to assimilate and transcend it" (76).

Here the unwarranted note of condescension at the end of this quotation to my mind shows the theorist whose theory blocks him off, who has failed in sympathy and due respect. It does not seem unlikely that it is Achebe's writings of the Nigerian past that Appiah has in mind in this somewhat dismissive comment (by far the most famous examples of this category of African writing are those written by this novelist, after all)—especially since Appiah elsewhere alludes in guardedly disparaging ways to Achebe's work:[64]

> Part of what is meant by calling, say, Achebe's *Things Fall Apart* "anthropologising" is that the narrator tells us so much about the culture that could, in this way, have been shown. I have already suggested [that] . . . "the gesture of writing for and about oneself" is not simply a matter of creating texts addressed to a European Other. For those of us raised largely with texts that

> barely acknowledged the specificity of our existence, each work that simply places before us the world we already know . . . can provide a moment of self-validation. . . . To offer such explanations of Achebe's metanarrative is surely not to engage in negative criticism. . . . If Achebe sometimes tells us too much (and in this there are many worse offenders), he is a skilful shower too. (Appiah, *House,* 67)[65]

Not only does the contrast between Appiah on the one hand according *Song of Lawino* a pat on the back and on the other hand damning *Things Fall Apart* with faint praise suggest an insufficiently attentive reading of the novel, but the whole passage above illustrates a tendency I refer to as "the arrogance of theory." In literary studies, theory—a rubric that admittedly covers a large number of approaches—does tend, I believe, to foster an illusion of encompassment and control and to prefer (in the sense of giving greater weight to) the general rule above the specific instance. In terms of an ancient distinction in logic, its methodology tends to be deductive—whereas it is my contention that an *in*ductive type of approach, illustrated in my three central chapters, is more appropriate to the study of literary texts and more likely to allow one access to the cultural wealth and sociopolitical insights that such literary works of genius contain.

It is because of the deeply inductive nature of his thought concerning the condition of colonization and its aftermath, especially in Africa, that the Martinican Frantz Fanon's writing (especially in *The Wretched of the Earth,* first published as *Les Damnés de la terre* in 1961) remains unsurpassed among theorists of that both political and psychic condition. Fanon was both a scrupulous witness and a sort of visionary concerning the decolonization process and its difficulties. Usually thought of as a liberationist political philosopher and strategist, it is because he is (especially in "The Pitfalls of National Consciousness," a chapter in *The Wretched of the Earth,* 119–165) so astute a critic of the neocolonial, or postcolonial, condition that his work is useful and helpful to the understanding of the full spectrum of prose writing discussed in the present study.

Fanon's *Les Damnés de la terre* was published more than thirty-five years ago—yet in his ability to see both colonialism and its aftermath in an adequately nuanced[66] way, and in his recognition of the shifts and disguises of power in the aftermath of colonialism, he transcends many of the presently prominent postcolonial theorists or anticipates points made in their own writing *and* in critiques of their work by other scholars.[67] Much postcolonial theory and even many critical assessments of it betray (perhaps partly because of the name "postcolonialism" given to these studies?) a fixation with the transnational, Western, form of power and, probably because the scholars involved in the field are anxious to defend the victims of colonization, remain to a greater or lesser extent silent about the power malformations evident within the postcolonized societies—*unlike* Fanon, and unlike the novelists whose works I discuss in the following chapters. Fanon sees, in other words, as the novelists do, that the struggle for democratization immediately succeeds the battle for decolonization. He also understands, as the creative writers do, how complex and deep a healing process is required in the aftermath of colonialism, and how easily this can go wrong.

Fanon has himself been criticized for such flaws as exaggerating the extent to which precolonial culture is destroyed by colonization and for underrating "the people" (Lazarus 77–78); for blindness to gender issues (Loomba 162–163);[68] for ignoring the artificiality of African national borders (Christopher Miller, quoted in Lazarus 72). But his grasp of the complexity of issues of power and of change under circumstances of the kind that Marechera, Achebe, and Head depict makes his work a natural choice as related reading for a study such as this. Especially important, to my mind, is Fanon's grasp of how very carefully organized and responsibly undertaken the process of national recovery needs to be, to prove successful and lasting.[69] Like a good physician he pays as much attention to the convalescence period as to the emergency operation.[70] Although his insistence that "the national consciousness . . . is the most elaborate form of culture" (*Wretched* 199—cf. 187) has laid him open to much criticism at a time when nationalism has been widely denounced as a misleading ideal, Fanon's sense of nationalism has been misunderstood and his careful distinction of it from chauvinism (126), tribalism (127, 147), embourgeoisement of a small profiteering class among the formerly colonized (131), domination by a party (132), consumerism (158), neocolonialism (78, 81, 115, 122),[71] and racism (170–174) has not been as sufficiently analyzed by his critics. What Fanon seems to have in mind when he invokes (as he does, over and over) the notion of nationalism is closer to the ideal of meaningful democracy than to the naïve territorial triumphalism some of his critics imagine him to be touting.[72] He denounces colonialism with as much fierceness as he castigates the small, corrupt, parasitic elites that all too often, as he shows, succeed formal liberation[73] from colonial powers. Fanon's nationalism, as I would put it, is a form of *localism* (see, e.g., *Wretched* 119).

Fanon minutely delineates the different stages of colonialism, as this particular power form shifts shape and adapts to the changes in the relationship between the West and the subjugated regions. Underlying it all and deeply persistent is, in his view, a racial dichotomy: "What parcels out the world is the fact of belonging or not belonging to a given race" (*Wretched* 31–32). Well known is his pronouncement on the starkness of the color bar: "The colonial world is a Manichean world" (32). From his understanding of colonial power as a form of violence, Fanon drew his insistence on the both psychic and military necessity of liberatory violence: "Colonialism is not a thinking machine, nor a body endowed with reasoning faculties. It is violence in its natural state, and it will yield only when confronted with greater violence" (*Wretched* 48).[74]

At a later stage he delineated an ironic, *apparent* change—a new form of the same old domination: "The colonies have become a market. The colonial population is a customer who is ready to buy goods" (51). Fanon's phrasing catches the "slyness," the cunning in the disguises of and the alliances between different forms of power. As he puts it, "Between the violence of the colonics and that peaceful violence that the world is steeped in, there is a kind of complicit agreement, a sort of homogeneity" (63–64). Especially arresting is Fanon's presentation in the 1960s of a point often made by contemporary theorists, but seldom in so literally uncompromising a fashion:[75]

> The European states achieved national unity at a moment when the national middle classes had concentrated most of the wealth in their hands. Shopkeepers and artisans, clerks and bankers monopolised finance, trade and science in the national framework. The middle class was the most dynamic and prosperous of all classes. Its coming to power enabled it to undertake certain very important speculations: industrialization, the development of communications and soon the search for outlets overseas.
>
> In Europe, apart from certain slight differences (England, for example, was some way ahead), the various states were at a more or less uniform stage economically when they achieved national unity. There was no nation which by reason of the character of its development and evolution caused affront to the others.
>
> Today, national independence and the growth of national feeling in under-developed regions take on totally new aspects. In these regions, with the exception of certain spectacular advances, the different countries show the same absence of infra-structure. The mass of the people struggle against the same poverty, flounder about making the same gestures and with their shrunken bellies outline what has been called the geography of hunger. It is an under-developed world without doctors, without engineers and without administrators. Confronting this world the European nations sprawl, ostentatiously opulent. This European opulence is literally scandalous, for it has been founded on slavery, it has been nourished with the blood of slaves and it comes directly from the soil and from the subsoil of that underdeveloped world. The well-being and the progress of Europe have been built up with the sweat and the dead bodies of Negroes, Arabs, Indians and the yellow races. We have decided not to overlook this any longer. (Fanon, *Wretched*, 75–76)

For, adds Fanon, "the apotheosis of independence [for the formerly colonized regions] is transformed into the curse of independence . . . : 'Since you want independence, take it and starve'" (76–77). He does, it is important to emphasize, also add a further recognition: that what he calls the "traditional weakness" of the middle class of "underdeveloped countries," after decolonization, "is not solely the result of the mutilation of the colonized people by the colonial regime. It is also the result of the intellectual laziness of the national middle class, of its spiritual penury, and of the profoundly cosmopolitan mould that its mind is set in" (*Wretched* 119).

That type of "cosmopolitanism" is the sham form, as Fanon sees it, of the eventual ideal of a true internationalism, a healthy or honorable globalism (161, 190–199)—what Fanon calls "a new humanism" (198).[76] He describes the vocation of the artist or intellectual in a way that fits individuals like the three authors whose work is discussed here (given the necessary "gender corrective"): "The responsibility of the native man of culture is not a responsibility vis-à-vis his national culture, but a global responsibility with regard to the totality of the nation" (*Wretched* 187).

What such writers produce, says Fanon, in a way that aptly honors and links the work of artists like Marechera, Head, and Achebe,[77] is "a literature of combat because it assumes responsibility, and because it is the will to liberty expressed in terms of time and space" (193). What they participate in is not a battle for political power or of a military kind, but a far subtler struggle for human recognition both within and beyond their countries' borders. For, writes Fanon,

> national consciousness, which is not nationalism, is the only thing that will give us an international dimension. This problem of national consciousness and of national culture takes on in Africa a special dimension. The birth of national consciousness in Africa has a strictly contemporaneous connexion with the African consciousness. . . . The most urgent thing for the intellectual is to build up his nation. . . . Far from keeping aloof from other nations, therefore, it is national liberation which leads the nation to play its part on the stage of history. It is at the heart of national consciousness that international consciousness lives and grows. And this two-fold emerging is ultimately the source of all culture. (*Wretched* 199)

As many of the above examples show, Fanon is that rarest of analysts who achieves a style both poetic and analytical; passionately exhortatory, densely reasoned, and utterly lucid. The sheer vanity that, unfortunately, colors so much intellectual writing is utterly absent from Fanon; few political writers make so deep an impression of their honesty.[78]

Even in English translation, Fanon has enriched the language with numerous profound and unforgettable sayings, ranging from the oracular, such as, "It is not enough to try to get back to the people in that past out of which they have already emerged; rather we must join them in that fluctuating movement which they are just giving a shape to, . . . this zone of occult instability where the people dwell" (*Wretched* 182–183), to the wryly earthy, such as, "Everything can be explained to the people, on the single condition that you really want them to understand" (152), and "the people must understand what is at stake. Public business ought to be the business of the public" (157). Almost everything he writes assists the understanding of the sorts of conditions out of which arose the societies depicted in the prose works I discuss. In conclusion: Fanon exhibits, in a passage like the following, his ability to speak in the simplest of words, without falsely denying his philosophically learned background, when the real concern is with the achievement of meaningful liberatory change:

> To educate the masses politically does not mean, cannot mean making a political speech. What it means is to try, relentlessly and passionately, to teach the masses that everything depends on them; that if we stagnate it is their responsibility, and if we go forward it is due to them too, that there is no such thing as a demiurge, that there is no famous man who will take responsibility for everything, but that the demiurge is the people themselves and the magic hands are finally only the hands of the people. (*Wretched* 159)

This vision of Fanon's is profoundly commensurable, in my reading, with the vision that the three novelists offer to their readers and to their compatriots.

Not even Fanon's work, though it is both admirable and apposite, is used as a theoretical frame in the present study, however. The chief consideration in making this choice was one of *appropriate methodology*. In a theory-centered approach, literary texts like novels are inevitably relegated to the position of illustrative material or corroborative data and are, by the mere logic of this method, not given the full and complex scrutiny such works require when they are allowed to occupy the center of attention. The presumption or assumption and even, most basically, the mere preference, on my own part, which this methodological choice expresses, is that these African novels are more adequate and more interesting accounts of the types of societies and conditions that postcolonial theorists *also* describe than most of the theoretical descriptions produced by the latter. Moreover, the present trends in academic writing create in me the impression that theorists' work is overshadowing the work of creative writers, perhaps because of an underestimation of the analytical, intellectual, and politically sensitive skills of novelists like the three here discussed.

The high value and sense of superior validity ascribed by myself to novels of the kind discussed here are tied up with the point that all these works can be seen primarily as *localizations* of the author's ideas; in theoretical writing, on the contrary, the trend is toward generalization, as the choice of the term "postcolonial" quite clearly testifies. Novels of the kind studied here do present (to borrow Anderson's famous expression) "imagined communities" in a very particular way; in being communities constructed by the writers, they can only faintly approximate the full complexity of *living* communities and are, like theories, abstractions. Yet the African settings or African characters depicted in the novels do, I argue, tie them "down to earth" in a way that theory often fails to achieve. The imagined actuality of prose literature works toward qualities of vividness, immediacy, and the convincing force of something more akin to testimony than it is in the nature of most theoretical writing to be.

It would have been inconsistent with the preference expressed here for the *particularizing* qualities of literary (over theoretical) prose if the novels chosen had been discussed in a bundle, or in clusters, in terms of perceived connections in theme, or style, or through the author concerned. It can be acknowledged, however, that it is probably also a preference for giving recognition to—even paying tribute to—the complexity and subtlety of the individual literary work that led to the choice of discussing the fifteen texts concerned here individually and serially. Certainly, discussions that cross-refer among a number of literary works can yield fascinating results, as the different works help to highlight particular qualities in one another. In this case, however, where most of the primary texts are not sufficiently widely known and discussed, it seemed appropriate to allow each one undivided attention in its turn.

The choice of discussing each work in terms of its depictions of power and of change involves, admittedly, a type of theoretical presumption: that these "realities" are significantly present in all of the chosen texts and are worth discovering, while—inevitably—excluding numerous other features of these texts. The selection of this focus might be termed the willingly incurred risk of the present undertaking, which presented itself as worth attempting because the large categories of "power" and of "change" are probably present in all human endeavors—textual or actual. Hence, looking for articulations of these notions as "presences" in the prose texts would, it was presumed, be less limiting and distorting of what these works achieve than a more customary thematic enquiry.[79] The approach taken to the texts is, moreover, appreciative rather than critical; an attempt to discover, and articulate, a presumed richness of meaning by means of which these works appealed to me as powerfully as they did in the first place. This is also why the novelists' work is here made the main object of attention, with the commentary in a type of impresario's, or emcee's, role, *serving* the texts.

Achebe's archetypal story-about-storytelling—the account of the encounter between the devouring leopard and his legend-making victim, the tortoise (*Anthills* 128)—expresses an idea found also in the poem "Puella Parvula" by Wallace Stevens. In this poem the telling of "the human tale" by "the dauntless master" is the one saving act in the midst of extreme dislodgement, horror, and disaster (Stevens 456).[80]

It may be the case, I believe, that the richness of African literature is at least partly the fruit of the forms of devastation with which most of those who live on the continent have had to contend—onslaughts of power provoking energies of change. Stories and literary works, in their most sophisticated form, are "personal" but, in a historical setting like that of these three authors, I suggest, especially *social* coping mechanisms. The Caribbean novelist

George Lamming recorded an impression of the nature of the West Indian novel, specifically, that is highly applicable to African novels of the kind discussed in this text. He refers to "the discovery of the novel . . . as a way of investigating and projecting the inner experiences of the . . . community" (Lamming 37).[81] The novels discussed here project, as I see it, the anguish of the actual in a way that the theoretical discussion of the same issues cannot achieve, making possible a kind or even a degree of understanding not to my mind accessible by other means—something *akin* to a "participatory" understanding is what I have in mind here, characterized by qualities like density and complexity and by the irresistible sense (in the case of a "committed" reading) that the issues raised in the novels matter.[82]

To access this sort of perspective, to practice what I have called "committed reading," the reading mode adopted in the chapters to follow is an exegetical and empathetic approach (earlier called an inductive methodology). Many African novels—even the best and the most famous—are, I think, still being read far too superficially, partly because of the predominantly theoretical bent in much contemporary scholarly criticism, and partly because of a still-persisting underestimation of the sophistication of African artists.[83] Remarks made by the African-American critic Henry Louis Gates Jr. are worth reiterating here. In his ironically titled essay "Criticism in the Jungle" Gates writes, "Mimetic and expressive theories of black literature continue to predominate over the sorts of theories concerned with discrete uses of figurative language" because the texts are so often used to back other/others' arguments about conditions in the areas from which they emanate, instead of commentators recognizing the literary skills involved in producing the texts:

> Because of this curious valorisation of the social and polemical functions of black literature, the structure of the black text has been *repressed* and treated as if it were *transparent*. The black literary work of art has stood at the centre of a triangle of relations (M.H. Abrams's "universe," "artist" and "audience"), but as the very thing not to be explained, as if it were invisible, or literal, or a one-dimensional document. (Gates, *Black Literature,* 5–6)[84]

Such an approach "reads" the African writers' texts as if they were mere unreflective recordings of social circumstances, instead of recognizing that they are (in Jameson's apt terminology) "symbolic meditation[s] on the destiny of community" (Jameson, *Unconscious,* 70).

Ever since Benedict Anderson used the catchy expression *Imagined Communities* as the title of his work on nationalism (1983), scholars and others have become much more alert to the extent to which people are inclined to devise mental images of human units to which they can feel affiliated. Anderson also drew attention to the role of novels in such imaginings. Some novels, such as Nuruddin Farah's *Maps* and Michael Ondaatje's *The English Patient,* have been written that express warnings against the possible restrictive consequences of such imagined "nation-identities," but the three novelists whose work I discuss here can be described as "area-based,"[85] although their vision is not in the least chauvinistic. The "nation-ness" they imagine indicates a circumference of social responsibility rather than any encircling authoritarian purpose—deeply aware as they are of malignant and exploitative forms of power-mongering in the societies they depict. All three novelists, moreover, show a distinct concern with and an awareness of the shared fate of Africanness—which is not an experience or an expression of power, but a continentwide need for empowerment and cultural, as much as economic, recuperation.

In contrast with a work like K.W. Harrow's *Thresholds of Change in African Literature* (1994),[86] although I do treat each writer's work chronologically (as composed), I make no attempt to outline a "process of development," because the earlier texts of *each* of these authors do not seem to me to be any less sophisticated or complex, either thematically or stylistically, than the later writings, whatever the other differences among them. In the preamble to his book ("Acknowledgements"), Harrow himself records his expression of what happens to be my own reason for not adopting the "chronologizing" approach that he chooses to employ: "We may learn a great deal about African literature," he writes, "by seeing its patterning as a series of stages, but we may also be turning a blind eye to *that which stands outside the pattern*" (Harrow xiii, emphasis added).[87] Later he writes (again expressing the point I would make) that "the problematic term here is *stage*" (3). The construction of *the* African novel as proceeding in "stages" is, of course, a fairly common one[88]—from a supposedly nationalistic or idealistic early phase, using a realist style, to one of disillusionment and antinationalism, to a contemporary postcolonial and antirealist style—a way of conceptualizing this by now vast and varied body of writing that I have always found problematic because it simplifies so unscrupulously *and* because of the implicit, and unconsciously naïve, assumption built into it that the earlier works are more naïve and the latter more complex in their vision. But then, we remain in the field of rival perceptions—of whatever reality lies "out there," foolishly assuming it to be homogeneous or "ours."

The terms to express what I hesitantly call "presences" in all the texts discussed, that is, "power" and "change," were chosen in the first place because in considering my own reading experience of these, and other, texts, these two words appeared to name something with which all three authors seemed to be greatly concerned—although obviously these exact terms might not have been the authors' own way of expressing what they were describing. The usefulness of the terms seemed to lie as much in the way they could express an interrelationship, since there is a sort of dialectical link between the two notions. As novels are one of the most inclusive strategies yet devised of rendering (in the sense of "approximating," or mimicking) the process of life, or time, or history, such texts probably invariably register change(s), whereas the factor(s) causing or resisting change can (usually) be thought of as power(s). I have conceived of "power" and consequently used the term in a quite conventional way, to refer to the sort of presence that can markedly affect, that is, direct or control or change and—especially—dominate, other realities or beings. Power does not necessarily work through a human incarnation, although perhaps we tend, as I did in the descriptions that follow, to use it especially for that sort of manifestation.

Also fairly conventionally, I have tended to talk about power mainly as something restrictive and overwhelming, an oppressive presence. Ever since Gramsci provided the world with the useful term "hegemony," it has, of course, become easier to talk about pervasive and disguised and dispersed forms of power, but I have not consulted his writings in detail or employed a Foucaultian frame for this project—partly because of the presumption that these three novelists themselves show, and should be "allowed" independently to demonstrate, their profound recognition of the working of various forms of power.

Equally, the term "change" is used here in a quite ordinary way to discuss the ways in which one type of thing may become another, of a very different order, or be transformed by means of a gradual process we usually term "growth." The type of change effected by power tends to be of a violent, disruptive kind, and that which moves "from within" to be more gradual, like an unfoldment. I do not intend here to catalog and am not able exhaustively to define "change" and "power." Part of the pleasure of the present project was to allow the novelists (by means of their texts) to expand, or more clearly to focus, my understanding of these notions. If the main power forms in the late twentieth century seem to be beyond reach—inaccessible to the "accountability" demand—it is yet probably the case that someone, or some few, on the ground, hold the strings of the huge kites pulling us all along in directions that we did not choose and that may well work to our detriment. That even such power is somehow and by some persons "inserted" into our local scene(s) is a notion that all three of these novelists can be shown to share.

It will also be evident in what follows that I use the two central terms flexibly, though not intentionally merely *loosely*—and that there is not only an interplay, but also occasionally an overlap, between them in my usage. By this I mean that the energy that changes things can be thought of as a power form, and that power to be effective obviously requires energy. In the main, though, I have thought of and sought instances of power as tending to stasis, and encompassment, and control—whereas the energies of change that I describe, although sometimes merely becoming new forms of power, are mostly those that are intent on greater freedom and that function in pursuit of fulfillment and growth; therefore "life-seeking" rather than death-directed. Moreover, the notions of power and change are invoked not only in describing what happens "inside" the prose texts, but also to indicate something of the conditions of production and reception of these texts.

In my understanding of the functioning of change and of power, I conceptualize that which constrains, contains, and crushes as power, and that which expands and *empowers* as the energy of change. The word "power," even if we think of ourselves as possessing or possibly achieving it, expresses the human understanding that the world endangers us, indeed threatens our very lives, whereas notions of energy indicate the belief that we can grow, can rise to challenges, can "reply" to power, and can foster life even beyond our own ends.

The three writers—beyond my sense of each of them as a figure of exceptional integrity, of both honesty and originality—were selected because of the substantial body of fascinating writing that each of them has produced, but also because of the interesting diversity in their visions and writing styles and the sense of profound understanding of both change and power that they convey. I have quite deliberately eschewed an intertextual approach, although I hope that in the future such studies will be undertaken, not only because cross-referencing among these fifteen texts, and many possible others, would have enormously complicated the present study, but also because I wanted to "center-stage" each text in turn. Perhaps the present discussion can help set the scene for later studies interrelating and/or contrasting texts like Marechera's, Achebe's, and Head's. I do not see these texts or the societies they depict as isolated and hermetically sealed compartments, but as a variety of ways of experiencing and coping with both power and change—in social, personal, and political contexts, *variously* African.

As far as the style, design, and presentation of argument in this text are concerned, I decided to write roughly twelve to fifteen pages of main text on each work discussed, imagining this length to represent a natural span of attention. Because I wanted to keep the central argument uncluttered, the text bristles with endnote numbers. These endnotes represent ideas and information that are in my perception usefully or organically connected with the points from which they arise, like fingers splaying off from a hand. Use of extensive annotation allowed space to pursue related polemics, to give backing to or to extend arguments, and to give fuller information or "densifying" details and references—to both the main texts and others. Clearly I did *not* discuss the full oeuvre of any of the three writers, although I studied and bore their other texts in mind. The glaring omissions—Bessie Head's short story collections *The Collector of Treasures* (1977) and *Tales of Tenderness and Power* (1989) and her social history *Serowe: Village of the Rain Wind* (1981); (most of) Marechera's poetry in his *Cemetery of Mind* (1992); Achebe's short stories (*Girls at War,* 1972) and his poetry collection *Beware, Soul Brother* (1972)—were made in the first place in order to balance the number of texts discussed in each case—answering to an aesthetic sense of design rather than any scholarly consideration. The omitted texts are themselves permeated with issues of power and change, but an already bulky study would have become inelegantly unwieldy with their inclusion. There is surely much else that is "incomplete" in a work like the present one.

The style of analysis adopted in the three central chapters relies on thorough prior acquaintance with the texts discussed. Though the discussions may serve an introductory purpose in some ways, they are written on the distinct understanding that a great deal else is "happening" in these texts that readers of the present study are assumed to be aware of—in order to be able to judge the fitness of the choices of examples of power formations and instances of change made by this writer. In devising the present study it seemed strategically important at the present juncture (as Fanon writes in his essay "On National Culture"—*Wretched,* 166–199) to approximate an African perspective, a "continental reach," as a sort of "defensive mobilisation" (171). This identification with the continent is as carefully distinguished in the novelists' creations as in Fanon's arguments from vaguely romantic glorification of Africa or any of its local societies. Fanon's caution that "the truths of a nation are in the first place its realities" (181) is fully embedded in these texts. Although the chosen works are thoroughly and vividly indigenous, the discussion has also aimed to highlight the ways in which the authors, writing from their local perspectives, reach out with the confidence to address the widest possible audience;[89] an approach recognizing that the issues depicted, although principally, or initially, African, are topics that matter to all the world.

Purposes

By contrasting two quotations from Julia Kristeva I wish to introduce the discussion of the purposes of the present work. In the first, she begins with an anecdote in order to raise a question:

> While reading Proust's manuscript notebooks I recently noticed the following question in notebook one, leaf twelve: "Should this be turned into a novel, a philosophical essay?" Knowing how to deal with a topic that preoccupies us . . . should we treat it *theoretically or fictionally*? Is there a choice? Is it legitimate to favour one procedure over the other? (Kristeva 77, emphasis added)[90]

"The imagination," she writes in the second one, "could be considered as the deep structure of concepts and their systems" (Kristeva 78). Kristeva, herself both theorist and novelist, seems to me to be working here with an ancient and still prevalent distinction that, I contend, underplays the intellectual element in creative writing. In the *alternative* that she posits, theoretically or fictionally, she also, I believe, dichotomizes the activities of the intellect and of the imagination, but her second quotation seems to correct that.

Working on the assumption that literature is a significant way of asserting qualities of the African presence on the continent and in the world, it is my main purpose, in the chapters that follow, to show that the chosen novelists are *analysts* of the societies they depict. By this I mean that they are "primary" thinkers who concern themselves with the investigation of social, psychological, and political realities and issues, and are not mere recorders, or providers of material for the theories of scholarly writing—though the material they provide may be at one remove from raw data. Here I seem caught in a logical trap, as it may be averred that my own point is a theoretical one that I intend using the literary texts to validate. My defense would have to be, first, that readers of the chapters to follow would be in the position to judge the extent to and the ways in which the presentation of the fictional works there is itself a distortion or an elucidation[91] of the novelists' writing. Second, I point to overt declarations and to clear or subtle hints in statements by the three authors that they intend their writing, or see it as functioning, analytically.

Retelling the ancient Greek myth of the woman Cassandra who was given the spiteful gift of accurate but inevitably disbelieved prophecy as an analogy to the position of the author, Marechera says wryly and doggedly: "I tend to see the writer as a kind of Cassandra figure with all *this enormous talent to actually analyse* . . . intensively people's destinies, only to be cursed by censorship, by persecution. . . . But precisely because you have got that talent, you must continually activate it, in spite of any opposition" (quoted in Veit-Wild, *Source Book*, 41–42, emphasis added).

Marechera's terms, "cursed," "censorship," "persecution," and "opposition," emphasize (to use my own terminology) that writers incur resistance from the power centers of society to the extent that they lend their energies[92] to the laying bare of the way the most crucial dimensions of people's lives, their "destinies," are affected by social structures.

When Achebe states in an interview that "literature is one of the ways . . . available to the writer—to organise himself and his society to meet the perils of living" (Achebe, Interview, *Times Literary Supplement*), clearly thinking (among other things) of his own role, he seems to me to be testifying, similarly, to that analytical and diagnostic role that an author can play, as in his well-known essay "The Novelist as Teacher" (*Morning,* 42–45). Bessie Head formulates the notion with characteristic subtlety: "Creative writing," she says, is the "subdued communication a writer holds with his own society" (Head, *Alone,* 101).[93] Elsewhere she states that she views her "own activity as a writer as a kind of participation in the thought of the whole world" (*Alone* 95).

By calling these authors analysts I am simultaneously stressing that, without being "mere" realists—providers of anthropological data in the interpretational approach that Henry Louis Gates has castigated so effectively[94]—they yet constantly engage with the actual conditions (to some extent in the past, but mostly in the present) of the societies in which they live. Achebe's portrayals of an earlier Igboland, Marechera's surrealism, and Head's plunge into psychic depths do not avoid or seek to escape from the circumstances in which the authors and the many others who are similarly located find themselves. This is another purpose of the present undertaking: to show the texts discussed as encounters with the power forms and the energies of change located in[95] the African conditions of their settings. Implicit here is the attempt to investigate whether the novelists' depictions of colonial and postcolonial conditions are not more complex, compelling, and significant than many of the more derivative theoretical presentations of such conditions. It is my purpose to demonstrate the social density, literary richness, and subtlety of political analysis in these works, and to suggest that these qualities in their work contrast them with the under- or misrepresentations of their societies caused by political/colonial bias, by theoretical detachment, or even merely by the fact that such less adequate portrayals are the work of those who are outsiders to the experiential basis from which the novelists work.

Part of my purpose is also—evidently—the intention to prove, in the sense of *demonstrating* and of *testing,* the adequacy and the usefulness of the method of analyzing power and change that I have chosen as my interpretative strategy. To do so I have taken account of the existing body of literary critical commentary on these texts, with the intention of contrasting my modus operandi and the types of insights yielded by it, with such of the hitherto published criticism available to me as seemed to differ significantly from my own readings.[96] I attempt to show that, although they are very wide, the paradoxically related notions of "change" and "power" are given perceptual and conceptual precision in the instances chosen from the authors' works that I discuss. By doing so, my intention is to demonstrate what seem to me useful ways of understanding the methodologies of communication in the text.

Bessie Head, in a passage written as a young woman, when she was just setting out on her career as a writer,[97] said the following:

> If I had to write one day I would just like to say *people is people* and not damn white, damn black. Perhaps if I was a good enough writer I could still write damn white, damn black and still make people live. Make them real. Make you love them, not because of the colour of their skin, but because they are important as human beings. (*Alone* 6)

I use this "artless" quotation to introduce the point that (as Head indicates here) novelists' insights are not *presented* as analyses—a point that links with a further explication of my own purpose in the present work, which is to avoid as much as possible the application of a theory to the texts and to attempt as carefully as possible to "listen for" the authors' own communications of their understanding of what pushes toward change and what imposes power in a community, a relationship, or an individual person. The wandering, wondering eye of novelists like the three whose work I discuss is captured in two of Marechera's sayings. In the first, he tells how he prepares for writing by "just moving around . . . just meeting people and watching everything."[98] In the second, he says that "to see takes time."[99] I see the narrative mode itself as *inherently* complex, failing without the achievement of a contextualization, balancing, and testing of notions of state, society, or personhood. That the three novelists depict subtle gradations and hidden as well as overt forms of change and of power, and show the complex interchanges between different forms of these phenomena, has been a main source of interest in the undertaking of the present work—a delight in and a sense of the value of these writers' skills, which the present text attempts to communicate.[100] I find confirmation of such an apprehension when Achebe writes, "If an author is anything he is a human being with heightened sensitivities; he must be aware of the faintest nuances of injustice in human relations."[101] The two fluid concepts by means of which I describe their texts allow me to demonstrate, as I intend the following chapters to articulate, that Head, Marechera, and Achebe's depictions of power and change range from their delineations of mortal threats to society and psyche to the faintest intimations of hopes of life-furthering opportunities or of enduring strengths.

Scheub states[102] that "transformation is the metaphorical and mythic core of the storytelling tradition." A recent study of narrative identifies literary texts themselves as "transformational objects" (Scheub 183). Achebe calls his saying *"stories create people create stories"* the "universal creative rondo" (Achebe, *Hopes,* 162). The point that narrative is closely engaged with change is an old story. That novelists like those whose work I deal with concern themselves as much with power is less frequently emphasized.

As a tiny preamble to the depictions of power forms analyzed in the studies that follow, I cite three examples from Marechera. The first occurs in an interview and is entirely explicit in its illustration of Marechera's concern with power: "And because at that time black men were used to being the slaves of the whites, and the only slaves they had were their women. That's why women were the ultimate victims of racism in this country" (quoted in Veit-Wild, *Source Book*, 13).

The second example comes from an early story, with a reference to "Robert's side of the river where it was fenced and there was a notice about trespassers" (Marechera, *House*, 129). This little detail can be read as a cameo of the colonization process—implying a form of change brought about by a power imposition that not only excludes indigenous people from what used to be accessible, and theirs, but that subtly degrades and overtly threatens them with a new power presence. The third illustration (from a later work, *The*

Black Insider—54)[103] refers to a person: "He was of middle height, coal black, disillusioned, transfigured, damned, and as it seemed prey to his nerves"—in Marechera's terminology a "black insider": apparently allowed into the "fenced-off," "Western" world by having become a "barrister." His "transfigur[ation]" is the type of change that *more* insidiously confirms his position as outsider, and victim, to that power: hence he is "disillusioned," "damned," and "prey to his nerves."[104] I propose in the chapters that follow to display—by means of commentaries like those above—the larger networks of analyses, of both transformational energies and forms of power, out of which the novelists structure their texts.

More than a quarter of a century ago Abiola Irele wrote:

> We want now to decide whether ["modern African literature"] will for ever remain a tributary of Western literature, or a full literature in its own right with a legitimate place in the modern culture of Africa. And its only claim to this kind of legitimacy can come from its original African quality and from its relevance to contemporary African existence. (Irele, "Criticism," 22)[105]

Irele speaks of the role of "criticism," in his understanding of it, "in the defence of a living culture," to which he adds the rider, "If the critic is to guide, he must do so with competence" ("Criticism" 21). "The work of art," he says, "is an invitation to a dialogue of sensibilities" (19). "For us in Africa," writes Irele, there have been not only the vast processes of political change, but a "transformation of our mental landscape" (16). Yet "our appreciation of what an African writer does cannot be complete unless that African dimension is considered and consequently brought to light" (17). In such a concern with the articulation of the African provenance of a work of literature Irele happens to voice another of my own purposes. He says, "Criticism cannot be pure scholarship and is not simply an intellectual exercise," and in expressing his belief that "the best criticism implies an affective and intense participation in the creative act" (14), he formulates an understanding that I share.

As something of a corrective to Irele's ideas, I have used Said's both inspirational and cautionary words to indicate a final purpose: "If it is not to be merely a form of self-validation, criticism must intend knowledge and, what is more, it must attempt to deal with, identify, and produce knowledge as having something to do with will and with reason" (Said, *World*, 202).

This final intention of mine ("intend[ing] knowledge") would contrast with the purpose of producing largely imitative, mutually replicatory, and short-lived kind of knowledge, as "research," which Appadurai[106] describes so uninvitingly. Whether such an intention (like the other purpose expressed above) is approximated in what follows must evidently be left to others to decide.

Notes

1. One small detail may (synecdochically) represent the process: in 1890 the British Parliament passed the "Foreign Jurisdiction Act, which gave itself the right to proclaim British sovereignty over any part of the world *without previous treaty or agreement with the indigenous people*" (noted in Head, *A Bewitched Crossroad,* 176, emphasis added). See also such works as A. Adu Boahen's *African Perspectives on Colonialism* (1989), D.K. Fieldhouse's *The Colonial Empires* (1982), and J.N. Pieterse's *Empire and Emancipation* (1989).

2. Weber, *The Protestant Ethic and the Spirit of Capitalism.*

3. Contrast (e.g.) Anne McClintock's magisterial study of the deep and complex connections between the *domestic* situation (in Britain) and the management of the exotic possessions (the colonies, especially in Africa) (*Imperial Leather*). In *Plough, Sword and Book* Gellner does occasionally give an ironic (or sarcastic) account of the workings of "the Enlightened mind" (184–186). Yet the strangely complacent, narrowly Western perspective that is sometimes noticeable in his vision recurs toward the end of this work, as Gellner communicates his notion of the immediate future of (what his subtitle claims is) "Human History" (213). Since Gellner's work has been broadly influential and highly rated, he is used here as a representative figure.

4. In *Culture and Imperialism* (1993) Edward Said reminds his readers that the "prototypical modern realistic novel is *Robinson Crusoe*, and certainly not accidentally it is about a European who creates a fiefdom for himself on a distant, non-European island" (xiii). Later Said repeats the point: "The novel is inaugurated in England by *Robinson Crusoe*, a work whose protagonist is the founder of a new world which he rules and reclaims for Christianity and England" (83). Gellner's choice of Crusoe as archetype of Western man founding a new system is hence no accident.

5. This distinction is somewhat reminiscent of Marlow's distinction, in *Heart of Darkness*, between British and other forms of colonialism: "What saves *us* is efficiency—the devotion to efficiency. . . . What redeems [the conquest of the earth] is the idea only. An idea at the back of it; . . . something you can set up, and bow down before, and offer a sacrifice to" (50–51, emphasis added).

6. "The Scribes of Our Times" was the title of a report on this matter in a South African newspaper: *Sunday Times*, 26 July 1998, p. 13. See also "Comment," *New Yorker*, 3 August 1998, pp. 4–5.

7. In *The Western Canon* he wrote:

> As a branch of literature, criticism will survive, but probably not in our teaching institutions. . . . What are now called "Departments of English" will be renamed departments of "Cultural Studies" where Batman comics, Mormon theme parks, television, movies, and rock will replace Chaucer, Shakespeare, Milton, Wordsworth and Wallace Stevens. (Bloom 519)

8. Compare Achebe's sarcastic comment on Conrad's Marlow (in *Heart of Darkness*) as a representative of Europe witnessing African dancing and singing: "the terrible risk of hearing grotesque echoes of its own forgotten darkness, and falling victim to an avenging recrudescence of the mindless frenzy of the first human beginnings" (*Hopes,* 4).

9. In his footnote to this point Chomsky cites "Kennan, PPS 23, 24 February 1948 (FRUS, vol. 1, 1948), p. 511; Michael Hogan, *The Marshall Plan* (Cambridge: Cambridge University Press, 1987), p. 41, paraphrasing the May 1947 Bonesteel Memorandum." (Chomsky's 1998 article "Power" cites more-recent examples.)

10. These points were confirmed in an article in *Time,* 19 October 1998, p. 84.

11. This is the English translation (by K. Woods) of *L'Aventure Ambiguë*, originally published by Julliard in Paris in 1962. The Heinemann edition from which I quote appeared in 1972.

12. Scheub refers to "an extraordinarily fruitful interaction" between the African oral forms and the modern novel, and says that "to exclude the oral tradition from any influence on literature except for "residual oralism" ignores this rich interplay and the fact that the novel form, for example, is prefigured in the oral epic" (15). Scheub says that "African literature has from the beginning been involved in a complex dialogue with the oral tradition, thematically as well as formally" (34). Compare Abiola Irele's remark that "a continuity of form and reference exists between the oral literature of Africa and the modern literature written in the European languages" ("Criticism," 18).

13. Interestingly, Kane's expression anticipates by twenty years the title of Eric Wolf's famous work, *Europe and the People Without History* (1982).

14. Spivak writes of the imperialist project that it was

> the projection of one's own systematic codes onto the "vacant" or "uninscribed" territory of the other. By this process, the Other is transformed into a set of codes that can be recuperated by reference to one's own systems of cultural recognition. The unknowable becomes known; and whatever "spillage" might have occurred in the problematics of racial and cultural difference becomes stoppered by the network of textualisation that is inscribed onto the Other and then read as a "lack" or "negation" of that which constitutes the Imperial and transcendent One. (*Post-Colonial,* 1)

Said, Bhabha, and Young are other well-known theorists who have explored this point.

15. This is how Kane in his novel describes a public meeting called to discuss the Diallobé people's terrible choice between (on the one hand) economic survival and cultural death and (on the other) cultural survival and probable extinction (which is, of course, no real contest):

> All those present remained motionless, as if petrified. Only the Most Royal Lady stirred. In the centre of the company she was like a seed in its pod.
>
> "The school in which I would place our children will kill in them what today we love and rightly conserve with care. Perhaps the very memory of us will die in them. When they return from the school, there may be those who will not recognise us. What I am proposing is that we should agree to die in our children's hearts and that the foreigners who have defeated us should fill the place, wholly, which we shall have left free."
>
> She was silent again, though no murmur had interrupted her. Samba Diallo heard the sound of someone sniffling near him, and raising his head he perceived two great tears coursing down the rough cheeks of the master of the blacksmiths.
>
> "But, people of the Diallobé," she continued after a pause, "remember our fields when the rainy season is approaching. We love our fields very much, but what do we do then? We plough them up and burn them: we kill them. In the same way, recall this: what do we do with our reserves of seed when the rain has fallen? We would like to eat them, but we bury them in the earth.
>
> "Folk of the Diallobé, with the arrival of the foreigners has come the tornado which announces the great hibernation of our people. My opinion—I, the Most Royal Lady—is that our best seeds and our dearest field—those are our children. Does anyone wish to speak?"
>
> No one answered.
>
> "Then peace be upon you, people of the Diallobé," the Most Royal Lady concluded. (Kane 46–47)

How vividly a passage like this captures the *anguish* of transition may be registered if one contrasts it with a passage from a postcolonial theorist that makes substantially the same point. In his essay "Unsettling the Empire," Stephen Slemon writes of "the untranscendable *ambiguity* of literary or indeed *any* contra/dictory or contestatory act which employs a First-World medium for the figuration of a Third-World resistance, and which predicates a semiotics of *refusal* on a gestural mechanism whose first act must always be an acknowledgement and a *recognition* of the reach of colonialist power" (37).

16. It is noticeable that the condition of hybridity celebrated by theorists like Bhabha, Young, and others is here given another, tragic aspect, that of a fissure, of a psychic undermining.

17. Compare this comment by V.Y. Mudimbe in *The Idea of Africa*: "From Herodotus onward, the West's self-representations have always included images of people situated outside of its cultural and imaginary frontiers. The paradox is that if, indeed, these outsiders were understood as localised and far away geographically, they were nonetheless imagined and rejected as the intimate and other side of the European-thinking subject, on the analogical model of the tension between the being In-Itself and the being For-Itself" (xi) (the two final terms being the German philosopher Hegel's famous categorization).

18. Paul Gilroy, author of the fascinating study *The Black Atlantic: Modernity and Double Consciousness* (1993), reports that his writing (as an African-American) of this book "developed from [his] uneven attempts to show [his] students that the experiences of black people were part of the abstract modernity they found so puzzling and to produce as evidence some of the things that black intellectuals had said—sometimes as defenders of the West, sometimes as its sharpest critics—about their sense of embeddedness in the modern world" (ix).

19. This tendency—to read African narrative texts as if they provide merely sociological data—Gates calls the "anthropology fallacy" (*Black Literature* 5).

20. From the penultimate page of Fanon's *The Wretched of the Earth* (254).

21. Held at the University of the Witwatersrand in Johannesburg, South Africa, 14–18 September 1998.

22. My point and my image are to some extent derived from the poet Robert Frost, who in his poem "Beech" vividly and ironically expressed the idea that whenever truth is confirmed or discovered, the achievement comes at the cost of being "deeply wounded"—a painful reminder of the limited nature of human knowledge.

23. Reported in *The Cape Argus*, 17 August 1998. Of nine small reports of news from all over the African continent, published in *The Cape Times,* 1 October 1998, only two are positive ("EU Hails Mozambique as 'Model of Conflict Resolution'" and "Army Lifts Roadblocks" [in Nigeria]); the other seven are "Bubonic Plague Outbreak Kept Quiet" (in Mozambique); "Zim[babwe government] Denies Price Hike"; "14 Killed in Bujumbura"; "Hundreds Dead in Tanzanian Witch Hunts"; "Police Withdraw After Losses" (in southwest Nigeria); "Swazi Elections Delayed"; and "Zambia Warns Homosexuals."

24. "Now, what is Costaguana?" asks Conrad's figure of the American financier, of the "house of Holroyd," concerning the (proverbial) "Third World country," answering:

> It is the bottomless pit of 10 per cent loans and other fool investments. European capital had been flung into it with both hands for years. Not ours, though. We in this country know just about enough to keep indoors when it rains. We can sit and watch. Of course, some day we shall step in. We are bound to. But there's no hurry. Time it-

> self has got to wait on the greatest country in the whole of God's Universe. We shall be giving the word for everything: industry, trade, law, journalism, art, politics, and religion, from Cape Horn clear over to Smith's Sound, and beyond, too, if anything worth taking hold of turns up at the North Pole. And then we shall have leisure in hand to take in hand the outlying islands and continents of the earth. We shall run the world's business whether the world likes it or not. The world can't help it—and neither can we, I guess. (*Nostromo,* 96–77)

25. "Computerised dealings are estimated to transmit more than US$300 billion across national borders each day" (Adedeji 7)—at present the figure is probably much higher than this 1993 estimate. See also Chomsky, "Global."

26. He argues:

> All those . . . proposals for Africa's salvation . . . draw their frames of reference from a history which begins around the year 1900: a history which begins with dispossession. All of them suppose a total disjunction between the Africa that was dispossessed and an Africa—this other Africa—without a history of its own. . . . They all assume that useful or usable history in this continent starts from the colonial take-over. (Davidson, "Restitution," 18)

27. *Burundi: Ethnocide as Discourse and Practice* (1994) by René Lemarchand would be my own nomination as an example of such nondemeaning analysis, by an expatriate, of "African" violence. Chabal himself, in the essay from which I quote, lightly and "respectfully," but tellingly, criticizes the choice of title of the well-known study by his compatriot and fellow Africanist, Bayart (*L'Etat en Afrique: La politique du ventre* [1989], translated as *The State in Africa: The Politics of the Belly* [1993]).

28. A well-known example of this attitude occurs in Conrad's short novel *Heart of Darkness;* the speaker (Marlow) addresses his British friends in describing his African journey:

> The earth seemed unearthly. We are accustomed to look upon the shackled form of the monster, but there—there you could look at a thing monstrous and free. It was unearthly, and the men were—. No, they were not inhuman. Well, you know, that was the worst of it—this suspicion of their not being inhuman. It would come slowly to one. They howled and leaped, and spun, and made horrid faces [Marlow's description is presumably of an African dance, or ritual]; but what thrilled you was just the thought of their humanity—like yours—the thought of your remote kinship with this wild and passionate uproar. Ugly. Yes, it was ugly enough; but if you were man enough you would admit to yourself that there was in you just the faintest trace of a response to the terrible frankness of that noise, a dim suspicion of there being a meaning in it which you—you so remote from the night of first ages—could comprehend. And why not? The mind of man is capable of anything—because everything is in it, all the past as well as all the future. (96)

One can only add, to the expression of this type of early twentieth-century "racial tolerance," its own expression: "Yes, it was ugly enough"!

29. For example, he states: "I am not saying that the present process of democratisation in Africa is meaningless; rather that its agenda is largely set by the West" (Chabal, "Crisis," 47).

30. "So it is, for example," Chabal writes, "that the 'tribal' imperative is now often represented as the *ultima ratio* of African politics" ("Crisis," 48). An example of the South African equivalent of this type of knee-jerk pseudoanalysis would be the representation to, and by, many white South Africans of "inter-ethnic" clashes among

mineworkers, as "faction fighting"—as something to which blacks (but supposedly not whites) resort, "irrationally."

31. In a 1991 speech given at the University of Cape Town in South Africa, Said referred to "this extraordinary, almost Copernican change" ("Potentate," 68): the enlarging of "Western humanities courses" (67)

> to deal with non-western societies, with the literature, history and particular concerns of women, various nationalities, and minorities, with unconventional, hitherto untaught subjects like popular culture, mass communications and film, oral history. In addition a whole slew of controversial political issues like race, gender, imperialism, war, and slavery have found their way into lectures and seminars. (68)

32. Stephen Slemon, himself a participant in these debates, titles a 1994 article "The Scramble for Postcolonialism" (in *De-Scribing Empire: Postcolonialism and Textuality*, ed. Chris Tiffin and Alan Lawson). Bart Moore-Gilbert, in an important study from which I quote below (*Postcolonial Theory: Contexts, Practices, Politics*), refers jocularly to "*the Warring Tribes of the Postcolonial*" (202).

33. In a noteworthy essay, Karin Barber, for example, charges that "the 'postcolonial' criticism of the 1980s and '90s . . . has promoted a binarised, generalised model of the world which has had the effect of eliminating African-language expression from view" (Barber 25), whereas Ketu H. Katrak criticizes "the increasing phenomenon of using postcolonial texts as raw material for the theory producers and consumers of Western academia" ("Decolonizing," 158).

34. Similarly, Arif Dirlik answers Ella Shohat's question (which he quotes) "When exactly . . . does the 'post-colonial' begin?" with what he calls "an answer that is only partially facetious: When Third World intellectuals have arrived in First World academe" (Dirlik 328–329). The best-known articulation of this "crack" is probably Anthony Appiah's, in his 1992 work *In My Father's House:*

> Postcoloniality is the condition of what we might ungenerously call a comprador intelligentsia: of a relatively small, Western-style, Western-trained group of writers and thinkers who mediate the trade in cultural commodities of world capitalism at the periphery. In the West they are known through the Africa they offer; their compatriots know them both through the West they present to Africa and through an Africa they have invented for the world, for each other, and for Africa. (149)

35. Himself of Turkish origin, Dirlik is a historian specializing in China studies (Dirlik 329).

36. This point is (slightly) qualified but not retracted in a later formulation of postcoloniality: "Every metropolitan definition is dislodged. The general mode for the postcolonial is citation, reinscription, rerouting the historical" (Spivak, *Outside,* 217), although her *tone* here does sound (as McClintock would say) "prematurely celebratory" (McClintock, "Angel," 298).

37. He also adds later, "It is surely too simple to imply, as Spivak does, that by the very process of having found a voice, such figures have automatically become part of the hegemonic order or are now members of the stooge-like 'privileged native informants'" (Moore-Gilbert 107).

38. At one point Spivak refers to "this benevolent multi-culturalism [as] one of the problems of neocolonialist knowledge-production as well." She declares, "I call it the new Orientalism" ("Neocolonialism," 226)—something of an example of the ancient "more radical than thou" game played among intellectuals!

39. Bhabha's name for this type of procedure is "sly civility"—playing along with the powerful for one's own advantage (see "Sly Civility," 71–80). Parry, however, criticizes Bhabha for "represent[ing] colonialism as transactional rather than conflictual" ("Signs," 12).

40. Dirlik (in a footnote) calls him "something of a master of political mystification and theoretical obfuscation," and accuses him of "a reduction of social and political problems to psychological ones, and of the substitution of post-structuralist linguistic manipulation for historical and social explanation" (Dirlik 333).

41. *Postcolonial Theory: Contexts, Practices, Politics* (1997). Another admirably clear (though not simplifying) account is Ania Loomba's *Colonialism/Postcolonialism* (1998). See also Boehmer's *Colonial and Postcolonial Literature* (1995) for greater concentration on the "literary" texts.

42. Moore-Gilbert writes that "Said's next major work of criticism, *The World, the Text and the Critic* (1983), contains a single reference to Fanon, but it is not until 'Orientalism Reconsidered' (1985) that [Said] makes any extensive acknowledgement of the work of such predecessors." Moore-Gilbert quotes the passage, then adds: "While this is generous, if belated, recognition of the earlier critical tradition, it is only in the essays collected in *Culture and Imperialism* (1993) that Said engages in details with any of these predecessors" (15).

43. JanMohamed's excellent "Fanonian" study *Manichean Aesthetics—The Politics of Literature in Colonial Africa* (1988) is to some extent also an application of Jameson's suggestions to particular examples. However, see Parry's critique of JanMohamed (Parry, "Problems," 48–49).

44. Bhari writes of the "foundation" of "postcolonialist discourse" "in an essentialist and dichotomous binary" (53) and states: "Any developing hegemony of a postcolonial method that relies on the colonizer/colonized dichotomy should give us pause, particularly if it casts blame and self-pity" (63). He also quotes Viswanathan: "When one speaks about postcolonial literature, . . . the term becomes a kind of replacement for other literatures, like Asian [or] African American" (quoted in Bahri 71).

45. Spivak has (amusingly, and mockingly) expressed her suspicions concerning the present upsurge in Bakhtinian studies: "You know how Bakhtin is an alibi for certain kinds of work, you don't have to be anti-racist if you talk heteroglossia, then you can seem to be—well, heteroglossia is another name for pluralism," she said in an interview ("Neocolonialism," 243).

46. Raymond Williams, among others, makes a point that (to my mind) corrects During's one-sided and "unidirectional" view of the "colonial contamination" of pristine precolonial cultures, when he reminds us that "writing has always been associated with authority. . . . Historically there has been such a close association between power and privileges and the capacity to write" (R. Williams 137).

47. I term the power of these works "seemingly 'inappropriate'" in the light of During's remark, as well as in relation to the far better-known position of Ngugi wa Thiong'o, that African authors should write in their indigenous languages to "defeat" or "undo" colonialism—and that even to write in originally European languages is an act of cultural betrayal in an African author.

48. In "The Symbolic Dimensions of Achebe's *No Longer at Ease*" (a chapter in a forthcoming ALA Annual, to be titled *Multiculturalism and Hybridity in African Literatures*), I have also used Bakhtin's ideas.

49. Pieterse acknowledges the influence of the Dutch sociologist W.F. Wertheim (Pieterse 73), but takes Wertheim's ideas further in his own impressive, balanced, and wide-ranging project. One is, of course, conscious of the limits of one's own reading

circumference, yet it seems extraordinary that a work of such excellence has attracted so little reference.

50. He writes that "domination is both destructive and creative, repression and reform, while emancipation is both rejection and imitation, emulation and transcendence, modernisation and liberation. . . . Systems of domination survive by adjusting to the demands of emancipation movements. By mimicking emancipation, systems of domination attempt to forestall more fundamental change" (Pieterse 367).

51. Pieterse reemphasizes that "much of the 'social cost' of Western industrialisation and gradually rising living standards have been borne by the imperialised peoples: . . . It is the imperialised peoples of the world who have carried the White Man's Burden" (Pieterse 319). This is the same point Spivak makes vis-à-vis Foucault, above. Compare Bessie Head's expression of it, in *When Rain Clouds Gather*: "The raw materials of all the underdogs had gone into the making of those aeroplanes and motor cars, and Gilbert had been surprised to find the underdogs living in such abysmal conditions while his own country had prospered to an almost unbelievable state of wealth" (*Rain Clouds,* 134–135).

52. Ousmane Sembène's *God's Bits of Wood* (translated from French) is one prominent African novel that has this notion as a central focus.

53. What might be referred to as the *counter*dialectic of emancipation is illustrated in the historical irony of (as Pieterse points out) "Commerce, Christianity, and colonization [being] the three main elements in the *abolition* [of slavery] program" (Pieterse 344, emphasis added), emancipation (in Pieterse's terminology) hence coming about by means of new forms of imperial oppression.

54. *The Portable Nietzsche* (ed. Kaufmann, 1954, 458)—italics and second ellipsis in the original. Not quite as intellectually revolutionary as it might have seemed in its time (considering that the British philosopher David Hume—1711–1776—had propounded that all knowledge derives from impressions or perceptions) and pretty "old news" in our own poststructuralist and deconstructionist time frame, this point nevertheless seems to need constant reiteration. Compare Marechera: "What we see, being our sight, has no objectivity" (*Insider,* 32).

55. Given at the international symposium on "Globalisation and Social Sciences in Africa"—Johannesburg, Witwatersrand University, 14–18 September 1998.

56. Elleke Boehmer rightly protests: "Nowadays it seems to be an almost obligatory gesture for historians concerned to underscore the significance of their own ex-imperial researches, to make such sidesweeps in the direction of postcolonial literary theory, even while refreshing their own work with its insights, and watching carefully for its latest innovations" (Boehmer, "Diasporas," 141).

57. Ania Loomba reports that "Abdul JanMohamed (1985), Benita Parry (1987) and other critics have accused postcolonial theorists like Homi Bhabha and Gayatri Spivak of an 'exhorbitation of discourse'—of neglecting material conditions of colonial rule by concentrating on colonial representations. I want to suggest [she adds] that this tendency has to do with the fact that what is circulated as 'postcolonial theory' has largely emerged from within English literary studies" (Loomba 96).

58. Ashcroft, Griffiths, and Tiffin cite "four major models" developed "to account for" postcolonial texts: "'national' or regional models"; "race-based models"; "comparative models of varying complexity"; *and* (an uncertain distinction) "more comprehensive comparative models" (15).

59. Ashcroft et al. refer, I think, in far too heavy-handed a fashion to Tutuola's playful, mockingly "inept" English as "a striving towards appropriation, in which the cultural distinctiveness can be simultaneously overridden-overwritten" (*Empire* 68). A literary *practitioner* (yet again) articulates an attitude toward the "colonial" language

more like my own understanding of its working in the texts I discuss here: "I do not consider English to be the language of my masters. I consider language to be my birthright. I happen to have been born in an English and a Creole place, and love both languages" (Derek Walcott, Caribbean Nobel prize–winner, in an interview—82).

60. A familiar binary—the contrast between "primitive feelings" and "sophisticated, detached rationality"—hovers unmistakably in the background of this brief passage from *The Empire Writes Back,* in which the "powerful appeal" of an African identity is contrasted with its (presumably) academically "limited application" (Ashcroft et al., *Empire,* 17).

61. This passage in *Empire* seems reminiscent of something (perhaps a well-meaning, but inadvertently condescending-*seeming* quality?) in Fredric Jameson's categorical declaration of all "Third-world texts"—(as) "national allegor[ies]" ("Third World Literature," 69) in the essay to which Aijaz Ahmad responded with such indignation (Ahmad, "Rhetoric"). When a philosopher like Anthony Appiah builds a whole argument on a confident declaration of disingenuity in a novelist ("So that after all the distinctions have been drawn, we still need to ask why Soyinka feels the need to conceal his purposes"—Appiah, *House,* 78), one wonders whether the gap in sympathy or trust toward the novelist may be the result of affiliation to a different intellectual field (i.e., philosophy, rather than literary studies).

62. The allusion here is to the essay by Griffiths (one of the authors of *The Empire*) entitled "Chinua Achebe: When Did You Last See Your Father?"

63. Compare Rhonda Cobham: "Is the creative work being used to legitimise the theory? Or is the theory taken as a constant of fixed value through which we evaluate the creative writing?" (Cobham 141), as well as Ketu H. Katrak: "A new hegemony is being established in contemporary theory that can with impunity ignore or exclude postcolonial writers' essays, interviews and other cultural productions while endlessly discussing concepts of the 'Other,' of 'difference,' and so on" ("Decolonizing," 158).

64. One example (of a number of instances) is the following: "A work that, like Soyinka's plays (*and unlike, say, Achebe's novels*) takes its African—its Yoruba—background utterly for granted" (Appiah, *House,* 79, emphasis added).

65. The quoted passage is preceded by one in which Appiah heaps high praise on "Okot p' Bitek's wonderful poetic cycle *Song of Lawino*" for the way in which the cultural "information is available to us in the poem" (Appiah 66–67).

66. Here the issue of Fanon's practical participation in the Algerian war of liberation against the colonizing power France (the country where he had studied) is relevant, even though some ironic qualifications and (in certain quarters) serious criticism of limitations to that role have been offered. Fanon's position as analyst of both colonialism and neocolonialism might be said to lie between Bhabha's "upbeat" position ("festive postcolonialism"?), with its celebrations of hybridity and "sly civility," and Spivak's dark vision of the colonized/subaltern as perpetually doomed to silence.

67. In reading Appiah, Spivak, Dirlik, Bhabha, Mbembe, and Said (as well as other postcolonial theorists and critics), I am irresistibly reminded of Fanon's writings by many of their points, although their work is (of course) not necessarily consciously dependent on, or derived from, his texts.

68. It is quite true that Fanon's discourse is almost invariably male-inflected. Yet he imagines a future dispensation in which "women will have exactly the same place as men, not in the clauses of the constitution but in the life of every day: in the factory, at school and in the parliament" (*Wretched,* 163). Loomba nevertheless refers with some sarcasm to "the critical fascination with Fanon" (Loomba 180) and writes (it is unclear on whose authority, or on what evidence she does so) that "Fanon the revolutionary remained a European [?] interloper in the causes he espoused, never learning

the language or participating in the daily life of the people he championed" (147)—the harshness of which comment is matched only by its odd inaccuracy (e.g., labeling the black Caribbean Fanon a "European"). Other critical comments on Fanon can be found in H.L. Gates's "Critical Fanonism" essay and in some rather controversial assessments of Fanon's ideas in Bhabha's early work.

69. His *qualified* recognition of the difficulties of growth and of change are registered throughout, for example, in such quotes as the following: "Consciousness slowly dawns upon truths that are only partial, limited and unstable. As we may surmise, all this is very difficult." And "in the world-wide struggle of mankind for his freedom[, there] exists a brutality of thought and a mistrust of subtlety which is typical of revolutions" (Fanon, *Wretched,* 117).

70. Fanon's medical and psychiatric training shows up in his political writing—for example, in passages where compassionate concern for and acquaintance with "small people" (Achebe, *Anthills,* 136) is evident (such as on pp. 104, 110).

71. See his reference to false "development" of the formerly colonized territory as "neo-colonist industrialisation" (141).

72. For an interesting and pertinent commentary on Fanon, nationalism, and an analysis of some of the contemporary critiques of nationalism and of Fanon, see the long essay by Lazarus.

73. Not only, but especially in the chapter from *The Wretched of the Earth* called "The Pitfalls of National Consciousness" (119–165). Compare also, for instance, this extract:

> Spoilt children of yesterday's colonialism and of today's national governments, they organise the loot of whatever national resources exist. Without pity, they use today's national distress as a means of getting on through scheming and legal robbery, by import-export combines, limited liability companies, gambling on the stock-exchange, or unfair promotion. (Fanon, *Wretched,* 37)

74. Comparable with this vision is the morally impassioned (somewhat earlier) denunciation by Fanon's compatriot Aimé Césaire found in his famous *Discourse on Colonialism* (the English translation of the French original was published in 1972).

75. Noticeably, the Fanonian comment describes the same historical phenomenon as does Ernest Gellner (from whose work I quoted at the beginning of this chapter), but Fanon sees a starkly different picture from the European philosopher's. See also Davidson, *Chronicles,* 209.

76. An earlier passage can function to gloss that expression:

> But if nationalism is not . . . enriched and deepened by a very rapid transformation into a consciousness of social and political needs, in other words into humanism, it leads up a blind alley. . . . The national government, before concerning itself about international prestige, ought first to give back their dignity to all citizens, fill their minds and feast their eyes with human things, and create a prospect that is human because conscious and sovereign men dwell therein. (165—one hopes he meant women too!)

77. Soyinka and Ngugi, Farah, Armah, Mahfouz, Gordimer, Beti, Dangarembga, Mwangi, Ouologem, Aidoo, Emecheta, Kane, Coetzee, El Saadawi, Vera, Serote, Hove, Chinodya, Tuma, and many other writers of Africa could, of course, be mentioned here.

78. One quiet little sentence ("The important theoretical problem is that it is necessary at all times and in all places to make explicit, to demystify, and to harry the insult to mankind that exists in oneself"—*Wretched* 246), with its *unostentatious* humility, is to me perhaps the clue to the convincing power of Fanon's writing: committed, polemical, but free of self-righteousness.

79. Such as "Protest and Defeat in the Works of . . .," or "Profiles of the Postcolonial State in . . ." (and so on). Of course, studies conceptualized in this way (some of which I have myself written and intend to go on writing) are not *inherently* any less interesting or appropriate than the present one.

80. I would personally hold out for a dauntless mistress like Bessie Head being given her turn (to invoke another power-and-change dialectic: that of gender).

81. The ellipses reflect my extraction of Lamming's reference to specifically West Indian circumstances. Lamming's statement is similar to Fredric Jameson's well-known description of literary works as "symbolic meditation[s] on the destiny of community" (*Unconscious* 70).

82. The three closing stanzas of a poem by Wallace Stevens *called* "The Novel" (Stevens 457–459) vividly express this notion by stating that, to an absorbed reader, the protagonist in a narrative "is oneself" and that one feels, *viscerally*, all his or her experiences "as one's own."

83. I cite again Anthony Appiah's comment on the narrator in *Things Fall Apart* "tell[ing] us so much about the culture that could . . . have been shown," reiterated in the backhanded compliment: "If Achebe sometimes tells us too much (and in this there are many worse offenders) he is a skilful shower too" (Appiah, *House,* 67).

84. Compare Kanneh's comment on ethnographers' habits: "The informant is never engaged in a dialogue of cultural give and take but is used as a *resource*" (*Identities,* 10).

85. Even in the case (perhaps unexpectedly, in the light of his popular reputation as "anarchist") of Dambudzo Marechera, though more evidently in his later works—as my subsequent detailed discussions of his work outline. Compare his words in a (late) interview where, although he insists that his commitment is to his writing rather than to "Zimbabwe," he states that he intends writing a work that "would reflect in all its national contradictions and national achievements . . . what it is to be Zimbabwean today" (Marechera, "Interview," 65).

86. This work, with its somewhat similar title to that of my own text, appeared while the present project was under way. It is characterized by fine scholarship and discusses individual African novels in detail, although doing so from a clearly theoretized perspective (as distinct from my own approach). Harrow's perspective on the novels he discusses explicitly employs the "stages-of-development" notion of African Europhone novels.

87. One is reminded here of Bessie Head's Margaret Cadmore Jr., with her "attraction for the unpredictable" and "for all forms of vigour and growth outside the normal patterns" (*Maru,* 94).

88. Besides Harrow's work, two other examples (among many possible ones) are Appiah, *House,* 149–150, and Veit-Wild, "Carnival," 555.

89. In another seemingly male-centered, but surely "adaptable," saying, Fanon writes: "The responsibility of the native man of culture is not a responsibility *vis-à-vis* his national culture, but a *global* responsibility with regard to the totality of the nation" (*Wretched* 187—emphasis added to "global").

90. Compare the remark by Gerald Gaylard in a recent essay on Marechera's writing: "Marechera may initially have found the articulation of his ideas in critical

discourse but instinctively *transculturated* this discourse into idiosyncratically elusive fictional praxis" ("Marechera's Politic Body" 87, emphasis added). Although openly proclaiming the entirely conjectural nature of this (to me bizarre) suggestion, Gaylard, too, is here implying that "critical discourse" is something quite distinct from "fictional praxis," as the border-crossing term "transculturated" (italicized by me) signposts.

91. To try to avoid pressing the texts into the service of a preexisting model and to try to make the search for manifestations of change and of power (instead) enlighten the texts themselves have been a major goal of the present enterprise.

92. Marechera's terminology "continually activate" is akin to my notion of transformational energy.

93. Written in 1972.

94. See pp. 9 and 37 in my text for the relevant quotation and a brief discussion of it.

95. The texts I describe may (then) be contrasted to some extent, as well as linked with the kind of novel that the South African author J.M. Coetzee envisages in a passage like the following:

> [a novel] that operates in terms of its own procedures and issues its own conclusions, not in terms of the procedures of history, eventuating in conclusions that are checkable by history as a child's schoolwork is checked by a schoolmistress. In particular I mean a novel that evolves its own paradigms and myths, in the process (and here is the point where true rivalry, even enmity [i.e., with the recorders of "official history"] might enter the picture), perhaps going so far as to show up the mythic status of the paradigms of history, to demythologise history . . . a novel prepared to work itself out outside the terms of class conflict, race conflict, gender conflict. (Reported in the South African newspaper *The Weekly Mail,* 13 November 1987, p. 19, from a speech by Coetzee in Cape Town at an event called the "Book Week")

The link between Coetzee's position and that of the novelists here represented (and, hence, my own) is the contestation of the supremacy of "official versions" represented by means other than creative prose—for example, media reportage, historical records, or theoretical writing. The contrast between his and the other position lies, I believe, in Coetzee's dismissal of the power contestations that are, indeed, considered, analyzed, and addressed by the novelists I have chosen to discuss.

96. Certainly many available critical analyses also offer insights anticipating or complementary to my own, as I attempt to show throughout, although an academic validation process tends inevitably to lean somewhat toward contestation.

97. That is, in 1962, during the period Head spent in Cape Town. The same quotation appears also in *Tales* on p. 17.

98. Quoted in Veit-Wild, *Source Book,* 40, from a 1986 interview.

99. Quoted in Veit-Wild, *Source Book,* 362, from a public lecture Marechera gave in Harare in 1986.

100. In an interview published in 1990, Achebe is reported as saying about his own writings, with both confidence and irony, that he had a sense of their being still "underanalyzed" (if I may coin a term): "Well, I've written these novels, which are important in my view, and they have not been fully, adequately dealt with" (*Okike* 130).

101. *Morning* 79. The male-centered formulation here should of course be qualified, and evidently the work of a writer like Head does fit Achebe's description.

102. In the long (seventy-two-page) essay, "A Review of African Oral Traditions and Literature."

103. Written in 1978 when Marechera, having been expelled from Oxford, for some years led a homeless life in Britain.

104. The last expression is probably an echo from Fanon, to whose work Marechera alludes from time to time, although he here contrasts his own figure (mockingly termed a "black insider") with Fanon's figure of the "Manichaeanised" "native" within the colony.

105. Irele expresses the perception that "in the work of our best writers, a true integration of an African context with a European means of expression is being worked out" ("Criticism" 20).

106. Cited and discussed earlier at the beginning of the "Contexts: Actual" section of this chapter and near the beginning of the section called "Choices."

2

Chinua Achebe

A deep-seated need to alter things
Chinua Achebe, *Morning*

For an author who writes with so much compassionate irony, so well known for his judicious sense of historical balance, one who has himself labeled his famous first work a "sceptical" novel (*Morning* 4), Achebe's proclamation of a "need to alter things," an ethos of artistic *activism*, even of revolutionary fervor, may seem an unlikely claim. I suggest, however, that a study of Achebe's depiction of power forms and transformational energies must begin by touching on the way(s) in which his texts are themselves attempts to (re)balance international power relations through these texts' own kinetic transformation of contemporary readers' visions of the world—and of the place of Africans in that world. The proclamation occurs in a passage from the 1974 essay "Colonialist Criticism" (*Morning* 3–18; reprinted in *Hopes* 68–90), in which the usually urbane Achebe explains that "earnestness *is* appropriate to [his] situation," because that situation has been shaped by "the role and identity fashioned for [him]" by "earnest agents of colonialism" whose attitude of "resolve" he consequently needs to adopt himself, in the inevitable dialectic of this position (*Morning* 14).[1]

If the "resolve" of colonialism's agents and their heirs, "Colonialist [Critics]," was fueled by "big-brother arrogance" and by the "narrow, self-serving parochialism of Europe" (*Morning* 3, 9), the writer's "resolve" is fired, I suggest, by a profoundly moral indignation and a quest for restitution. He tells us that he feels called upon to write "because of the myths created by the white man to dehumanise the Negro in the course of the last four hundred years," with whites "talking" but not "listening" to black people (*Hopes* 23, 24). His is the commitment of a champion of the dignity of African people generally and of Igbo society in particular, though his methods are to employ the subtlest and most complex forms of verbal artistry.

Achebe's move to refute "appalling novels about Africa (including Joyce Cary's much praised *Mister Johnson*)" (*Morning* 70)[2] first necessitated a personal shift from this initially highly "Westernized" writer. He had been "named," as he said in a later essay, "for Victoria, Queen of England" (Albert was the name of Victoria's consort) (*Hopes* 30-39). Consequently, "Albert" became "Chinua" Achebe and embarked upon "an act of atonement" for his past, "the ritual return and homage of a prodigal son."[3] For the story that had to be told, he found, "could not be told for us by anyone else no matter how gifted or well-intentioned" (*Morning* 70). The statement is well known. The point to be made in this context is that Achebe is undoubtedly one of the first and one of the most effective of postcolonial critics.[4] Achebe's anger and his restitutional purpose are much more explicitly stated in his essays[5] and in interviews, but should be recognized as the fueling source of even the apparently most detachedly ironic or satirical passages or works by this author. His deeply held loyalties are the perpetual context of his writing.

To address the spheres of existence that Achebe problematizes—in the very act of re-creating them fictionally—I have throughout drawn principally on his texts themselves. I have consulted Igbo writers and commentators such as Ogbaa, Nwabara, Emenyonu, Egudu, and Uchendu along with Wren (*Achebe's World*), but they are not foregrounded in this text.

The issue of Achebe's defense of his choice of English as his major medium of writing, a question so much debated by African writers as well as critics and commentators on African writing, arises naturally at this point. Ngugi wa Thiong'o is the best-known critic of African writers' attempts at achieving cultural restitution in the colonizers' languages—which Ngugi sees not only as an irony but as a political betrayal: the essay collections *Homecoming*, *Writers in Politics,* and *Decolonising the Mind* exemplify these ideas. The issue is for many people a fraught and complex problem. Abiola Irele in the chapter "African Literature and the Language Problem" (from his *African Experience in Literature and Ideology*) explains the agonies and the difficult choices of the African-language situation in a particularly eloquent way.[6] Achebe's own defense of his choice of English is primarily pragmatic: English is a "given" (*Morning* 62),[7] the Nigerian, African, and virtually global lingua franca; if the African writer's "message" is to be heard (61), English is its most useful instrument: a powerful tool, essential in the task of transforming the conception and consequent "position" of Africa. Achebe's Igbo loyalties can hardly be questioned, or his commitment to Nigeria and to the African continent. He himself refers to "a new voice coming out of Africa, speaking of African experience in a world-wide language" (61).

Although the influential Russian critic Mikhail Bakhtin (1895–1975) does not discuss writing from Africa in his essays, some of his comments prove remarkably applicable to the language choices—which can themselves be seen as strategies or power negotiations—of Achebe and other Europhone African writers. Bakhtin speaks of the writers' use of "languages . . . [which] struggle and evolve in an environment of social heteroglossia" (Bakhtin 292). Achebe's English, one might say in application of the point, always invokes an Igbo or a generally Nigerian or an African "origin"; he is the encompassing artist that he has shown himself to be partly by showing us, in English,[8] the competing languages of many people—natives versus colonists; proletarians versus government officials; rural versus urban lifestyles; ancient versus modern (Bakhtin speaks of languages "intersect[ing] with each other"—291). In doing so Achebe empowers his people's voices to be heard in English, without homogenizing them.

"Consciousness," writes Bakhtin, "finds itself inevitably . . . *having to choose a language* . . . , orient[ing] itself amidst heteroglossia" (295). A writer's language choice is, hence, recognizable as a strategy: Achebe's use of English is no mere obeisance toward British culture, but a seizing of the "microphone" of this European language to send an African message and to tell an African story. Somewhat cryptically, Bakhtin indicates that no language is uncontaminated and no story the first—a point that helps one grasp Achebe's powerful *redirection* of the English tongue and the novel form to correct earlier "versions" of Africa. The Bakhtin passage reads: "In the novel, the 'already bespoke quality' . . . of the world is woven together with the 'already uttered quality' . . . of language, into the unitary event of the world's heteroglot becoming, in both social consciousness and language" (331).

An Achebe, had he lived in a unilingual world, Bakhtin would suggest (had he known any African writers), might not have written; the eloquent Igbo world of which Achebe writes so vividly would have remained shut into itself until a new language was brought from outside, "destroy[ing] the homogenizing power of myth over language" (Bakhtin 60). To see the multiplicity of historical disasters brought by colonialism as *also* providing new opportunities is by no means foreign to the Achebean vision. As he implicitly tells us, he is not himself an Okonkwo figure: "If you refuse to accept changes, then . . . you are swept aside" (quoted in Duerden and Pieterse 14). The destruction referred to, Bakhtin adds, created "[a] distance . . . between language and reality that was to prove an indispensable condition for authentically realistic forms of discourse," and "the creating artist began to look at language from the outside, with another's eyes, from the point of view of a potentially different language and style" (60). Although Achebe's "return path" via *falsifying* depictions of Africa inverts the Bakhtinian sequence, the notion of the fruitfulness of "disturbance" of an original language and worldview remains applicable. Especially appropriate to Achebe's use of English seems this final Bakhtinian quotation: "After all, it is possible to objectivize one's own particular language, its internal form, the peculiarities of its world view, its specific linguistic habitus, only in the light of another language belonging to someone else, which is almost as much 'one's own' as one's native language" (62).

Another theorist whose remarks contribute to an understanding of political strategy in the language choice of a writer like Achebe is Trinh T. Minh-ha, who expresses the recognition that there is a "relation," yet also a world of difference, "between [saying, in English] *we*, the natives, and *they* the natives"—between a "voluntary" and an "enforced designation" (Minh-ha, *Woman,* 48, emphases added). Calling for intercultural mingling (in somewhat convoluted prose), Wilson Harris can be seen as making a related point in his work *The Womb of Space*. He emphasizes "the need to begin to transform claustrophobic ritual by cross-cultural imaginations that bear upon the future through mutations of the monolithic character of conquistadorial legacies of civilisation" (Harris, Introduction, xv).

Africans have to mount the international stage, need to participate in the global cultural exchange if they are not to continue to be largely ignored, silenced, and exploited—a continent of victims. Achebe is undoubtedly the African artist who has most successfully—hence, to date, most influentially—entered the international marketplace without ever pandering to European prejudices in the way that he sees a writer like V.S. Naipaul doing.[9] By writing his superbly crafted African novels in English, Achebe might indeed be taken as being a champion practitioner of the strategy of "sly civility" outlined by Bhabha as an anticolonial strategy (Bhabha, "Sly Civility," 72).

Achebe is nevertheless no African chauvinist. No bucolic never-never Igboland or brave new Nigeria emerges from his pages, since he recognizes both the duty *and* the superior strategy of giving Africans their share of the blame for disasters that have happened and are occurring on the continent. As he has phrased it, "We do have our own sins and blasphemies recorded against our name . . . the very worst our acceptance—for whatever reason—of racial inferiority. . . . What we need to do is to look back and try and find out where we went wrong, where the rain began to beat us" (*Morning* 44).

This single factor of his accuracy and balance as historian of precolonial, colonial, and postcolonial Africa (thoroughly complex and difficult as its *presentation* may be) is what has earned for Achebe's writings their central position in African literature and their innumerable readers. One might at this point, then, invoke the term "realism" in its fullest resonance—for Achebe's work is known not merely for its slice-of-life vividness, its human recognizability, but also for its complex, questioning depiction of past and present aspects of the African condition.

According to the influential, visionary Caribbean author Wilson Harris, realism is, however, an inherently suspect mode; politically compromising or undermining for the would-be postcolonial author; incapable of serving a liberatory purpose.[10] Of course it is a notoriously slippery term, but Achebe has been often enough "accused" of realism[11] for the issue to demand comment in this introduction to a discussion of his works. In refutation of the suggestion that "realism" is necessarily "in league with" politically reactionary attitudes, I would suggest that Achebean realism masks subtle symbolism and carefully complex evaluation of the actual. In showing "real" worlds, Achebe never merely records or passively endorses what happened, but conveys a deeply, politically committed vision. He allows no evasions, however, since his approach to power realities and possibilities of change is investigative and diagnostic. In his refusal to manufacture a "pristine" Africa for romantic Western consumption, Achebe might be thought of as having heeded the following warning from Fanon: "In the universities the rare colonised intellectuals find their own cultural system being revealed to them. . . . The concepts of purity, naïveté, innocence appear. The native intellectual's vigilance must here be doubly on the alert" (*African Revolution* 48–49). Yet no other African author has, as effectively as Achebe, fulfilled the following injunction by Fanon:

> It is not only necessary to fight for the liberty of your people. You must also teach that people once again, and first learn once again yourself, what is the full stature of a man; and this you must do for as long as the fight lasts. You must go back into history, that history of men damned by other men; and you must bring about and render possible the meeting of your people and other men. (*Wretched* 236–237)

Against this multifaceted background, this necessarily brief *and* general introduction to Achebe's work can conclude by linking and contrasting his authorial stance with Shelley's famous rebuttal of Plato's denigration of artists; Shelley saw poets as the unacknowledged legislators of the world, powers "behind the scenes," so to speak. On at least one occasion (in Texas, at the end of 1969) Achebe abandoned his more characteristic low-keyed authorial stance and, upon being asked whether African writers have any influence in determining Africa's future, answered that "the writer's role is more in determining than in merely reporting . . . to act rather than to react" (quoted in Lindfors et al., *Palaver,* 11). It is time, he says boldly, to stop "pleading with some people and telling them we are also human . . . let us map out . . . what kind of society we want, how we are going to get there [and] what values we can take from the past, if we can, as we move along" (quoted, *Palaver* 12). In that emphasis on transformative energy Achebe makes clear that he sees "art . . . [working] in the service of man" (*Morning* 19) and that his novels, far from being nostalgic or plaintive, are intended to strike blows in the struggle for a better future.

Things Fall Apart and *No Longer at Ease*

> *to locate a people in the world*
> Chinua Achebe, *Classic*

The purpose of "locat[ion]" (of a people) may be considered in a dual sense as indicating *the staking of a claim* ("here we are"—which is tantamount to demanding recognition)[12] and as *the contextualization of a people*—historically as well as in relation to the international political and economic system. To "locate a people in the world" hence requires a careful reading of power relationships and also consideration of the energies of change at work in these interrelationships. Because this location process is "redefinitional" rather than a matter of taking up a place reserved for oneself and one's people, it requires "commitment" (quoted in Lindfors, *Palaver,* 7) and courage and involves daring—risking a challenge to vested interests and settled habits of seeing (Africa). Achebe's foregrounding of urgent social and political questions in his own work and that of other writers from the continent is an aspect about which he is entirely unapologetic. Achebe writes that "an African creative writer who tries to avoid the big social and political issues of contemporary Africa will end up being completely irrelevant" (*Morning* 78).

The popular image of Achebe, probably because of the overwhelming fame achieved by *Things Fall Apart*, is that of a writer concerned mainly with the African "tribal" past, and he is praised for writing of it in an anthropologically reliable and vivid way. Important as his concern with the precolonial past is, it is necessary to recognize that his work of "location" does not stop there and that the "long view" (Duerden and Pieterse 17) that he so values reaches both back into history and forward into the future. He is not and never was a merely nostalgic writer, which is why this section on location issues considers both the early Igbo world of *Things Fall Apart* and the more nearly contemporary urban and cosmopolitan sphere of his second novel, *No Longer at Ease*. Indeed, Achebe himself has said that his "original conception of the story was really a combination of [these two novels]. It was one story originally" (quoted in Duerden and Pieterse 16). The purpose in looking back, moreover, for Achebe is not to lament what is lost, but to equip oneself and one's people with understanding in order to cope with the exigencies of the present—and the future.

In a 1986 essay ("What Has Literature Got to Do with It?"—*Hopes,* 154–170), Achebe refers approvingly to the example of Japan as a society whose "spectacular" success in technological advances ("modernization") occurred or was facilitated (in a "gigantic paradox") because the society "was also systematically recovering lost ground in its traditional mode of cultural expression . . . to regain a threatened past and selfhood" (*Hopes* 160).[13] In other words, the cultural dignity and self-knowledge that literature of the Achebean mode can help people to (re)discover[14] are an essential empowerment affecting the whole practical world of economic survival and international political hierarchies. Put more simply, any route to a nation's future must first reencounter the past (cf. Achebe's comments in Killam, *African Writers,* 8–9).

Level-headedness and fair-mindedness—stances appropriate to a depiction of the national crises of colonisation and decolonisation investigated in these two novels—are everywhere in evidence in Achebe's texts. "We have had grovelling, we have had protest, now we must have something in between . . . so that's how I wrote it" is how Achebe puts it (quoted in Duerden and Pieterse 15).

The basic enquiry underlying *Things Falls Apart* can be seen as a number of sequential questions: What was precolonial Igbo society like? How and why did it fall to the onslaught of the European incursion? What kind of power(s) did it have, and why were its members incapable of withstanding the force of the new, the strange, and the "Western" ways? What was the nature of colonial power? Of course both issues of power (contests) and forms of transformative energy are involved here, and one does not find a simple conquest-victim scenario in Achebe's investigative "reenactment" of the colonial encounter in Africa.

In a 1967 interview Achebe stated this point, implicit in the novels, quite explicitly, saying, "I am not one of those who would say that Africa has gained nothing at all during the colonial period. . . . We gained a lot. But unfortunately when two cultures meet, . . . some of the worst elements of the old are retained and some of the worst of the new are added on to them" (quoted in Duerden and Pieterse 13).

He refers to the "unhappy . . . way things have turned out," yet recognizes that as a perhaps "necessary stage" (quoted in Duerden and Pieterse 13). Such philosophical detachment from the situation is of course highly unlike the sense of passionate involvement (or even anguish) conveyed by the novels. Like the sense of profound cultural loss *Things Fall Apart* conveys (in its title and in the entire texture of its writing), *No Longer at Ease* powerfully conveys the malaise of a dislocation process. This process is not primarily ascribed (as in the Eliot poem)[15] to the religious and ethical shift of the protagonist and society, but to the need for and trauma of belated modernization exposing inherent weaknesses in the indigenous ethos—and in the socialization of its best and brightest young people.

In *No Longer at Ease* questions investigated by the novelist include the following: What is decolonization? Why has political independence failed? What *is* independence? What new and which ancient webs of power enmesh the emerging society? Is it possible for modernization to be other than a mere dislocation or a new form of victimization of an African society? What is required for modernization to work to the advantage of an emerging nation? The issues are large and (sadly) as topical at present as they were almost forty years ago, when the novel was written (and set). In this second novel, forces of the past and of the future neither integrate successfully nor clash decisively (to produce a "victor"), but remain in an uneasy stasis, betraying the promise of a "new people" and the hope of successful modern statehood.

Things Fall Apart

The nine-village cluster of "about ten thousand men" (*Things Fall Apart* 8) (that is, households, many of these accommodating at least two wives and numerous children) that *Things Fall Apart*[16] depicts is a secure clan society considered "powerful in war and in magic" and "feared by all its neighbours" (8). The hierarchies of powers and authorities that characterize its existence are contextualized by the recognition that habitability is a condition that had to be won from untamed nature. The statement "the founder of their town engaged a spirit of the wild for seven days and seven nights" (3) presents this process metaphysically; reference to "the axe and the bush-fire" (42) does so more practically. The complex web of awe and law that orders this segment of Igbo civilization is headed by "Ani, the earth goddess and source of all fertility" (26), "the owner of all land" (13), "the ultimate judge of morality and conduct" (26). The female nature of this most potent presence points forward to the belief that "Nneka—"Mother-is-Supreme" (96) in this otherwise so blatantly masculinist society.

Ani supersedes Agbala—the "Oracle of the Hills and Caves" (12),[17] a god whose male nature is offset both by the fact that his name (when used as a common noun) is the word for "woman"[18] and by the fact that he "speaks through" his priestess Chielo, Ekwefi's widowed friend (35).

It is the Oracle (through the priestess) who pronounces on major power issues such as the validity of a military venture[19] and who reliably assesses human endeavor in terms of an ethos of labor and effort (12–13). This makes Chielo's the most powerful influence in the clan, although her power is intermittent and neither a personal nor a political "position" ("there was no humanity here. It was not the same Chielo who sat with her in the market"—76, cf. 71). Indeed, it is "the shrine of [the] great god," "this ring of hills" that "double[s the priestess's voice] in strength" (77) and makes her a source of "terror" (74) capable of commandeering a child at night from its parents' household (71–72). Chielo's is also the voice of the Oracle that decrees Ikemefuna's death (40). Something of the combination of harshness and humane decency that characterizes Igbo society is hence already evident in an examination of its theological dimensions.

Walter Benjamin's observation that every document in civilization is a document in barbarism is well known.[20] Achebe's depiction of this settled, precolonial African society recognizes its staggered benefits as well as the human cost of its establishment borne by some of its members. Both the civilized and the "barbaric" aspects of the early Igbo community are acknowledged—paralleling Achebe's balancing vision of both cruel and humane aspects to the Christian incursion that comes later. This balance cuts through the racist assumption that "barbarism" is the essential power form of "pre-Christian" Africa and "civilisation" the essential power form of the colonizing cultures.

Far from merely celebrating the masculine ascendancy that characterizes his Igbo society, Achebe analyzes this marked feature with great scrupulosity, exposing (through Okonkwo's "exaggerated" masculinism) its ironies and weaknesses as well as outlining its strengths and achievements. We are shown that the social force of the male leaders of the society is tempered by being (so to speak) theologically filtered: decisions of public assemblies are led by the Oracle's pronouncements through his priestess, and those who provide spiritual leadership and administer justice are the *egwugu*: not leading males in *propria personae*, but in their roles as "embodiments" impersonating "the departed fathers of the clan"—with whom the earth goddess Ani is "in close communion" (26). Their presence is "awesome," "powerful," and "terrifying" (64). The high court of the clan (when the *egwugu* are "in session") is a "communal ceremon[y]" (63), but it is said that "the ceremony was for men,"[21] with women placed "on . . . the fringe like outsiders" (63). These nine *egwugu,* known as the "fathers of the clan" (65), represent "the nine sons of the first father of the clan"—a theological family group as male as the Christian trinity.[22] Yet in the only case we see the *egwugu* judging, they roundly rebuke an abusive husband: "It is not bravery when a man fights with a woman" (67).[23]

Taking note of these balancings of an overwhelming male power structure is not to overlook its inherently patriarchal quality. Yet through his depiction of it, the novelist enables us to recognize that Okonkwo (whose status in his society is confirmed by the detail that "the second *egwugu* had [his] springy walk"—65) is a sort of reductio ad absurdum of this masculinism. Okonkwo's introduction (3) to the reader places him as having achieved power through physical prowess in a legendary wrestling contest (3, 36). This image of Okonkwo as wrestler figure is imbued with subtle irony, hinting as it does at the need for perpetual *re*conquest of power and prestige that so gnaws at Okonkwo's soul. (His own eldest son shows no aptitude for wrestling—Obierika's son is hailed as the new embodiment of the legend—36.)

Achebe is demonstrating—I suggest—that for Okonkwo power (like wrestling) is a continually demanding, testing, and fear-driven effort. Although he is "*not afraid* of war" (7–8, emphasis added), is considered "the greatest wrestler and warrior alive" in his clan (84–85) and "rule[s] his household with a heavy hand" (9), "his whole life is dominated by the fear of failure and of weakness" (9). Okonkwo himself is "*ruled by* passion[: the compulsion] to hate . . . gentleness and . . . idleness" (10, emphasis added). He resembles the "would be strong" character referred to in *Anthills of the Savannah* (46) and exemplified in the insecure head of state, Sam, portrayed in that novel.

Okonkwo's paradoxical role[24] is both fascinating and baffling to many readers, since he is *both* an exemplification of his people as a hero—one of the lords of the clan—*and* one of the instruments by means of which it falls apart.[25] This ambiguity is subtly established on the first page of the novel (3). Here Okonkwo's spectacular wrestling success links him with the founding father who "engaged a spirit of the wild" for an entire week. Yet that very "spirit of . . . wild[ness]," which had to be defeated to establish civilization, revives in Okonkwo himself—in his untamed "bushy eyebrows," in his (twice mentioned) habit of "pounc[ing]" on people like a fierce creature of the bush, in his impatient inarticulateness, and in the likening of the spread of his fame to a "bush-fire in the harmattan" (3).

The *gendered* quality of power distribution in precolonial Igboland lies at the heart of the analysis presented in this novel and is Achebe's major indication of the imbalance that will (*along with* the colonialist push) topple the society into collapse when "things fall apart."[26] Zohreh T. Sullivan avers: "We focus on the denial and suppression of the feminine and outcast. This fault, shared by both the hero and his culture, dismantles their coherence, hereby allowing the colonizer to possess the hero's son and the land" (Lindfors, *Approaches,* 102).

Although Sullivan gives insufficient recognition to the differences[27] between Okonkwo and the clan, she rightly notices Achebe's indicators that the nature of his hero's power is brittle, masking his inner weakness (externalized by Okonkwo in his father and in his eldest son Nwoye). The "design" of Okonkwo's nature resembles and parallels the clan's exclusion and victimization of twin children, *osu* (priestly outcasts), unachieving males, and sacrificial "gifts" like Ikemefuna, and its *relative* sidelining of women (such as their formal exclusion from public affairs).

Okonkwo's exaggerated "male chauvinism" and his neurotic need to demonstrate continually his narrow, nearly brutish conception of "manliness" are not shared by his peers: Obierika, Ezeudu, and Uchendu all criticize him for these characteristics (and Ofoedu exposes the inadequacy of Okonkwo's narrow conception of male leadership—48–49). Hence his remembered sporting triumph is referred to in power terms and linked in his mind with sex-as-conquest: "the desire to conquer and subdue . . . like the desire for woman" (30). Okonkwo's "*masculine* stories of violence and bloodshed" (37, emphasis added) are the self-stagings of an insecure person (cf. "his latest *show* of manliness"—47, emphasis added) and depict him "heroically" "overpower[ing]" "his victim" and severing his head (38). Instead of linking and endearing him to his eldest son, Nwoye, these accounts repel the sensitive youngster as almost literally "an exercise in overkill" (38).

Okonkwo's obsessive, divisive, hierarchical gendering of his world stems (as we are shown) from the lingering shame and anxiety he felt as the son of a powerless "failure," Unoka (9, 10). The term that fixes the fear in Okonkwo's mind is "agbala" (10), which not only means "woman," but also (mockingly) "title-less man" (10, 19). It is clear that to Okonkwo things fall apart when males fail to embody the harsh and violent forces that he reads as male, *or* when these qualities are themselves either disempowered or overpowered (as happens at the end of the novel). The poignancy of this character is shaped by Achebe's revelation of his largely unacknowledged capacity for the tenderness he believes himself to despise—for example in the "romantic" beginnings of his second marriage, in his love of and care for his daughter Ezinma, and in his undeniable love of Ikemefuna.

Although his complacent certainty that "the law of the land must be obeyed" (49) implicitly expresses his insider's, leader's, status in the society, Okonkwo in fact is in some respects earmarked as a transgressor against its codes. One sees this in his peers' criticism of his ruthless humiliation of a titleless clansman (19). It is a point even more evident in the series of "offence[s] against the Earth" (149) of which Okonkwo is guilty: his "unheard of" beating of his youngest wife during the sacred Week of Peace (21–23); the solemn warning (which he disregards) that to participate in Ikemefuna's killing would be unfatherly (40) and "[dis]pleas[ing to] the Earth" (47); his (accidental)[28] "crime against the earth goddess" (89) when his gun causes a young man's death; and, of course, his suicide itself—"an offence against the Earth" (149). An especially subtle hint of Okonkwo's indeed betraying the clan by his instinctual violence can be seen in the juxtaposition of his intransigence (imaged as the "man[ly]" killing of a snake) with a Christian convert's supposed "kill[ing of] the [sacred] python" (114, 115).

Thinking of himself as the supreme upholder of the clanly ethos, Okonkwo fails to realize that in rejecting Nwoye[29] (as he has always done emotionally and at last does physically by violently assaulting him for his interest in Christian teaching), *he* is overthrowing the very core of the clan's kinship code (119, 120). He does the same by scornfully dismissing the Mbanta clan as "womanly" (115) and finally, of course, by rejecting his own clan of Umuofia—including even (it seems) his best friend, Obierika. Hence the sequence of references to Okonkwo's intended "vengeance" ("avenge himself"; "my own revenge" [143]; "I shall fight alone if I choose" [144]) show him isolating himself against the clan even before the blow of the matchet (a kind of hatchet) (146) and the ensuing questions (147) that finally sever the connection—a severance confirmed symbolically by the clan's inability to bury his corpse. Okonkwo is a figure of stasis undone by the turbulent forces of change.

Ikemefuna's is the most beautiful and balanced presence in the novel. That the Oracle decrees the death of a person of whose fineness the author makes us so profoundly aware perhaps measures a degeneracy in the clan's form of power. Despite the protestations of Ezeudu (40) and Obierika (48) and in spite of Okonkwo's own finer feelings, the killing is perpetrated in a rigidly "manly" way much more awful than any killing in a war (which it supposedly "replaces"—9–11). Hence the author places the killing in a setting where "men's village[s] began to give way to giant trees" (142)—a reversion to the power of the "spirit of the wild" (3), which is now ascendant.

In the largely static society of the clan, it is Ikemefuna who breathes new life, makes new connections possible, and glows with the glamour of new vision. If anyone in the novel "embodies" the energies of transformation, it is surely Ikemefuna. He temporarily heals the breach between Okonkwo and Nwoye and makes Nwoye's "development" (37) possible, because he reconciles[30] "manliness" with imaginative sensitivity.

The image that especially vividly captures the promise and wholesomeness of Ikemefuna's nature occurs early on: "He grew rapidly like a yam tendril in the rainy season and was full of the sap of life" (37). "Yam stood for manliness" (24), we are explicitly told elsewhere, whereas the image of new growth in the word "tendril" adds to this the ideas of tenderness (which he so clearly evinces—for example, 31) as well as (tragically) vulnerability. The promise of his nature and the need for it to be fostered[31] are also subtly registered ("full of the sap of life"). The reliable commentator Obierika confirms this point with his warning that the killing "will not please the Earth" and may lead to the uprooting of "whole families" (47).

Achebe carefully and consistently contrasts Ikemefuna with Okonkwo to enable us to see that Okonkwo's rigidity and knee-jerk aggression can lead nowhere for the clan. Hence, when Ikemefuna is introduced to the new clan he is *naturally* "terribly afraid" (11), but the young boy's understandable anxiety at his displacement is juxtaposed with Okonkwo's neurotic "fear of himself" (10). Later, we are told, Ikemefuna had managed to "overcome his great fear and sadness" (20)—which contrasts with an Okonkwo whose "whole life" is "dominated by fear" (9) and who, when *he* is displaced to another clan, is seen to have "yielded to despair" (94). Evidently Ikemefuna's lovable liveliness is the sign of a psychic strength much more empowering and "saving" to any human community than the mere military, aggressive powers Okonkwo represents ("he had stalked his victim, overpowered him and obtained his first human head"—38). By contrast with Ikemefuna as a figure of human promise, Okonkwo is "son-unfriendly" (he intimidates, alienates, and eventually ostracizes Nwoye; kills Ikemefuna; and accidentally shoots Ezeudu's young son) as if severing the clan's tendrils of growth.

There is a subtle association between Unoka and Ikemefuna: like Okonkwo's father, Ikemefuna is creative, sensitive, and musical—the detail that "he could fashion out flutes from bamboo stems and even from the elephant grass" (20) reminds one of Unoka's musical skills and of his "[taking] with him his flute" (13) to overcome the fearfulness of his lonely death. Indeed, this father of whom Okonkwo was so "ashamed" (6) could, like Ikemefuna, experience "blessedness and peace" (4)—unlike the perpetually "driven" Okonkwo—and even contribute his musically expressed "sorrow and grief" (5) (at bloodshed and violence) to the clan's preparations for war ("his own flute weaving in and out of" the "blood-stirring . . . rhythms"—5). That Ikemefuna was accepted in the family to the point that he could "accompany Okonkwo, like a son" (21) hence adds further resonance and poignancy to his role.

Most important, Ikemefuna as an ideal type of clanly life incorporates and accommodates those "womanly" qualities whose suppression ultimately destroys Okonkwo—and that to some extent allow a form of survival for the clan. As Okonkwo rigidifies the masculinist "principle" of aggression, the female "principle" woven into the novel might be identified as use of the more accommodating, intercessionary skills with which certain types of crises need to be met. One vivid little moment exemplifying this necessary balance is Achebe's juxtaposition of the memory of Okonkwo's "throwing the Cat in the greatest contest within living memory" (28) with Ekwefi's "lift[ing a] pot [of 'boiling water'] from the fire" "in one deft movement" (29). If the subduing of hostile elements represents the founding of civilization (an association indicated in the novel's first paragraph), (then) Ekwefi's domestic skill indicates the arts needed to maintain it.

The recurrent detail that best focuses this balancing contrast is Achebe's focus on stories in this novel (the word "story," indicating an account, a history, or an interpretation, recurs tellingly throughout). In the very act of remembering in detail one of the tales his mother had told him, Okonkwo states that "it was as silly as all women's stories" (54).[32] Needless to say, Achebe does not share his character's masculinist contempt for such tales. An expression similar to Okonkwo's "stories of the land" (37) will recur with telling difference in *Anthills of the Savannah* (124).

In *Things Fall Apart* Okonkwo's complacent belief that the histories that matter are the "masculine stories of violence and bloodshed" (37) is indicated. But Achebe contextualizes Okonkwo's triumphalist and self-boosting accounts of his "overpower[ing]" and slaughtering his victim with the detail that "as he told [Nwoye and Ikemefuna] of the past *they sat in darkness*" (38, emphasis added). The author thus marks the supposedly "masculine stories" as lacking the energies of transformation that will be required to encounter a much more difficult "enemy," the future. No wonder Nwoye subconsciously associates this moment with his father's later killing of Ikemefuna when the Christian missionaries tell him "a story of brothers who lived in darkness and fear, ignorant of the love of God" (105, 106) and lacking "the shepherd's care" (105). Hence it is the Christians who make it possible for him to say "I am one of them" (103) as he moves into a wholly different future, whereas Okonkwo is (a new story, this, and told "unhappily") at that point "not [considered his] father" any longer (103).[33] Yet we may believe Achebe to be much more ambivalent about this severance than the "joy[ous]" Mr. Kiago ("'blessed is he who forsakes his father . . . for my sake,' he intoned"—110). The Christian triumphalism seems savage here, in contrast with the Igbo ethos that "to abandon the gods of one's father" is an "abomination" (110)—though Okonkwo (the speaker) is ignorant of his own central role in having produced that very "abomination" by his failures in fathering. Indeed Okonkwo the "living fire" has begotten "cold, impotent ash" (111), but in a much less simple, much more ironic and blameworthy sense than he is capable of grasping. Even in this comment he is again, and still, denying his son.

It is "women's stories" (54) that, Achebe demonstrates, interrogate the ethos of mindless, "manly" aggression and show awareness of the suicidal bent of this attitude (60). By foregrounding[34] the tale of Tortoise and the birds (70–71), the fascinatingly "political" story of manipulative "cunning" (69) and of cooperative, cunning resistance to it, Achebe indicates how much more complex and reflective such stories are—and how necessary to situations where the nearly unthinking taking up of inappropriate and outdated weapons (Okonkwo's "tall feather head-gear and his shield"—143) is inadequate. The detail of Tortoise's "sweet tongue" (69) links him decisively with the "sweet-tongued" messenger of the British District Commissioner (138), the D.C. who will broadcast *his* story of the events in Igboland as an admirable account of venturesome European civilization (*The Pacification of the Primitive Tribes of the Lower Niger*—150). Okonkwo's rigidity and consequent vulnerability are exemplified in the way Tortoise dupes the birds by constant references to "custom" (69, 70). The Tortoise story makes a contribution to ideas of adaptation and innovative strategy—it participates in the energies of change so badly needed in the clan's crisis.[35]

Change may be inevitable, but that Achebe measures the value of what is lost in the destruction of precolonial civilization in this novel is clear. Two brief details can be used to exemplify this focus of the writing. One is the lovely image of "each hut seen from the others look[ing] like a soft eye of yellow light set in the solid massiveness of night" (68). The other is the indicator of achieved social harmony at the betrothal ceremony for Obierika's daughter (79): "[the visitors] sat in a half-moon, thus completing a circle with their hosts" (83).

Given the vulnerability of the African civilization, change comes more as a form of destruction and obliteration than as a contribution to the growth energies of progressive transformation. The "modern world" begins here as a shattering ("fall[ing] apart"), not as a foundational or constructive act. That it *need* not have been such is lightly hinted at, for example in the missionary Mr. Brown's benignly accommodating attitude to local ways (128–130) and in his recognition that might is *not* right (128).

Achebe's assessment of colonialism as a by no means unmitigated disaster is on record.[36] In *Things Fall Apart* he uses the almost "classic" image of the colonists' coming as an invasion by locusts (compare, e.g., Chenjerai Hove's novel *Bones*) in an especially interesting and complex way. The "conventional" destructive function of the image is evident late in the text: Abame's oracle "said that other white men were on their way. They were locusts, it said, and that first man was their harbinger sent to explore the terrain. And so they killed him" (100).

Indeed Abame is left "completely empty" (100) after the punitive massacre staged by colonial authority. Earlier, the *actual* locusts' first arrival seems entirely ominous ("and then quite suddenly a shadow fell on the world" after the arrival of "harbingers"—39)—yet they are greeted "joyfully . . . everywhere" as being a rare and luxurious food, and their arrival is specifically presented as embodying glamour and force: "it was a tremendous sight, full of power and beauty" (39).[37] How much more mundane, then, and how unscrupulously hypocritical the District Commissioner's complacent words, announcing world-embracing Victorianism to the duped and captive Igbo elders: "We . . . administer justice [here] just as it is done in my own country under a great Queen. [Your administering your own justice] must not happen in the dominion of *our* Queen, the most *powerful* ruler in the world" (139, emphases added). Indeed this is a "new dispensation" (128).

The new power structure is established by the humiliation of the native institutions and authorities and by the exposure (as hollow) of some of the foundational myths of the indigenous society. In other words, the awe on which Igbo society rests is shattered. Two examples of such desecration can be cited: first there is the fact that the Christians, who "should have died" in the *Evil Forest*, survive (109); then there is the "[tearing] off" of the *egwugu* mask (literally: Igbo power is "unmasked") by a zealous Christian convert (133). The "desecrated" cultural community foresees in this "its own death" (134). By contrast, the Christian "community [is by now] self-assured and confident" (115), resting on the "unshakeable faith" (114) of its leaders and promising new life and growth. (It accommodates Nneka—the name a significant recurrence—who is a woman "heavy with child," probably expecting twins—109.)

One of the clearest signs of the transfer of authority is the "replacement" of the practice of justice by the mysterious, revered *egwugu* (63–67) by the British-run court where "justice" is practiced as a take-over strategy against the natives and in ignorance of local "custom about land" (126). The most astute analysis of the breathtaking speed of this transition is given in Obierika's account (126–127). He understands the complexity of the power that has been brought to bear upon the indigenous culture: its combination of military threat (exemplified in the extermination of Abame—126, 99–100) with a strategy of seduction and co-optation ("our people who are following their way . . . have been given power"—126). Like Okonkwo's old Mbanta kinsman (120), Obierika also recognizes that *internal* division provided the opening for the European wedge that will further destabilize and split the local community. "He has put a knife on the things that held us together and we have fallen apart" (127).[38] Most bitterly, he sees how the "benign" but insidious new faith ("[the white man] came quietly and peaceably with his religion"—127) was the stalking horse for the new "might" proclaiming its "right" not only to be in Igboland, but to take command.

There are enormously complex ironies of transition registered in the novel. Thus in *Things Fall Apart* one sees generational discontinuities (the rupture between Okonkwo and Nwoye) as well as ideological and religious shifts and (the simplest matter of the three) political takeover. Though Achebe foregrounds for us his not unsympathetically portrayed figure of the tragically flawed Okonkwo (*both* a heroic resistance fighter *and* an ironic though unconscious betrayer of his clan's central value of cohesiveness—143–149), he hints that the neglected resources of "femaleness" are the powers that will facilitate the traumatic transition toward "the new dispensation" (128). Haunting the harsh realities of the colonial incursion and the shattering of families is the shimmering image of "that land of Ikemefuna's favourite story where the ant holds his court in splendour and the sands dance forever" (25).

"If you take a long enough view" of a national disaster, says Achebe, you can recognize that "society is, in fact, adjusting [be]cause life must go on, no matter what we say" (quoted in Duerden and Pieterse 17). The world is indeed perpetually in "need of change" (*Morning* 15). Hence, the apparently finished tragedy of Okonkwo's ruin is but the first section of a much longer story, as *No Longer at Ease* will exemplify (Duerden and Pieterse 16). Achebe has said wryly that "while the African intellectual was busy displaying the past culture of Africa, the troubled peoples of Africa were already creating new revolutionary cultures which took into account their present conditions" (quoted in Lindfors, *Palaver,* 5). To catch up with his people, so to speak, as well as to "locate [his] people [more fully] in the[ir] world" (Achebe, *Classic,* 24), the author had to continue their story, "the story of the land" (*Anthills* 124).

No Longer at Ease

David Carroll has suggested that in Achebe's works "the moment of unilateral power initiates the narrative" (*Novelist* 167).[39] Aside from finding the notion of "unilateral power" un-Achebean, I believe that *No Longer at Ease* proclaims—both in its title and its opening scene—the very absence or failure of (a new) power. Obi Okonkwo, grandson of the lord of the clan whom we see in *Things Fall Apart*, is introduced on the first page as a figure of failure. One of a minority of Nigerians privileged to have had tertiary education in Britain and who was meant to take over the administration of the country from the colonists, Obi returned full of reformist idealism (17–18, 29), ready to help rid his country of corruption—but has himself succumbed to bribe taking (152–153). Although he is dressed in "a smart palm-beach suit" (1), the sign of his hitherto privileged social position (and the power that that entails), *and* despite his feigned, "sophisticated" carelessness,[40] Obi is "betrayed by treacherous tears" (2), signs of his human vulnerability and shame.

The judge (at this stage, shortly before Nigeria's political independence),[41] still very evidently British, "cannot comprehend" the failure of so "promis[ing]" and well educated a young man (2). His incomprehension is again alluded to in the novel's final paragraph (154), which adds "the men of Umuofia" (Obi's hometown) and his superior officer (60) Mr. Green to the list of those to whom so spectacular (1) and foolish a loss of power and position as Obi's makes no sense. Of course, these expressions of bewilderment (2, 154) at the opening and close of the narrative serve as indicators to the reader of the author's investigative purpose in this novel. Achebe is, by means of this novel, conducting his own judicial enquiry into the state of the nation. The broad question could be formulated as the inquiry into the causes of Nigerian incompetence, division, and corruption at a time when self-rule was imminent and when there were such "high expectations of independence" (Ezenwa-Ohaeto, *Biography,* 64).

The "surface" comedy of the novel is often scintillating, not so much satirical as wryly delighting in idiosyncrasies of behavior—yet the underlying and final impression of this "ordinary tragedy" (36) is bleak. Deep "underneath" its compassionate irony the moralist's *"j'accuse!"* can be heard. Certainly this work lacks the "intangible beauty"[42] and the evident *gravitas* of *Things Fall Apart*. It has been found disappointing by many commentators,[43] but the "earnestness" of this second enquiry into "where the rain began to beat us" is profound. To overlook it is to underrate the worth of the work and the scrupulous novelistic skill Achebe employed here.

One scene (58) measures something of the distance between the first incursions of colonialism portrayed in *Things Fall Apart* and the period when it begins to wane. Achebe inserts Obi's boyhood memory of the "huge," irascible colonial school inspector Mr. Jones, who in fury slaps Obi's Nigerian headmaster—only to be instantly "floor[ed]"—Mr. Nduka being adept at "the great art of wrestling" (58). At once recalling Obi's grandfather Okonkwo's wrestling prowess (*Things Fall Apart* 3) and indicating a welcome process of change (in inverting colonial power relations!), this little cameo is nevertheless ironized when the magnitude of the event ("*throw[ing]* a white man was like unmasking an ancestral spirit")[44] "*throw[s]* the whole school into confusion" (58—emphases added). Evidently, "replacing" the white rulers will not be easy in a society where awe has been transferred to aliens and their technology. That exaggerated concession to others is succinctly expressed by an elder in Obi's family: "Greatness is now in the things of the white man" (49). It is an attitude that has filtered into the clichés of pidgin, the everyday urban (anglicized) speech of contemporary Nigeria, and is echoed from rough soldiers in Umuofia (12)[45] to cabinet ministers in Lagos: "White man don go far" (62). To believe so continues to concede too much authority—to another world, sixteen days' sea journey away (46).

The wrestling encounter (58) "was twenty years ago" (59), but an equally bad-tempered and ill-mannered Englishman, Mr. Green, neither "rises from his seat" nor "offer[s] his hand" to the newly appointed Obi (in his "senior service" position). Although Green demands gestures of respect from his Nigerian staff, he shows very little in return—addressing the administrative assistant with humiliating scorn (59).[46] Achebe's focus in this novel is not on the colonial presence, but he shows us enough to make clear that contemptuous "liberal"[47] racists like Green are making no contribution to preparing Nigerians for self-rule, but are instead keen on contributing to their own "self-fulfilling prophecy" that the country will collapse at independence—since "the African is corrupt through and through" (3).[48]

The main theme of *No Longer at Ease* is the failure of the transformative energies required to propel the country "towards political irredentism, social equality and economic emancipation" (28), in the words of the secretary of the Umuofia Progressive Union (UPU, which paid for Obi's British education). The large "nation-building" perspective in that quotation is undercut, as the secretary's speech proceeds, by his "quoting one of the most blatantly opportunistic Igbo proverbs in support" (Achebe, *Trouble,* 57) of his argument ("Ours is ours, but mine is mine"—29) and referring to Obi as "an investment which must yield heavy dividends" (29). When Obi arrives at the monthly UPU meeting in his car for the first time, "they clapped and cheered and danced" (71), for the car is a trophy, the most evident sign of capture of the "cargo"[49] of "the *things* of the white man" (49, emphasis added).

In contrast with the secretary's grandiloquence, Obi at the outset of his career speaks soberly ("is" and "was"—29) and without power claims of the principle of selfless dedication. "Education for service, not for white-collar jobs and comfortable salaries" (29)[50]—but in contrast with his reference to "*our* great country" (29, emphasis added), the UPU chairman (and almost everyone else) refers to the government as "an alien institution" (30), from which it is "people's business . . . to get as much . . . as they could without getting into trouble" (30).[51] Hence, when Obi is eventually caught taking a bribe, the UPU laments only that the bribe was not "juic[ier]" than it was: *that* is the "shame" (5) they acknowledge. It should be clear that Achebe is registering the debasement of an Umuofian ethos—no man of title could retain the *ozo* rank if caught thieving (*Things Fall Apart* 49)—to this "comic," predatory opportunism. That Umuofians in Lagos see themselves as a small and beleaguered encampment in alien territory ("strangers in this land"—5–6, 119) is said to be a consequence of the arrival of "the white man . . . [who] levelled everybody down" (4). But that "levell[ing]" must now be dealt with.

That the huge process of modernization and the urbanization it enforces is an irresistible power shift is vividly and poignantly registered in one brief reference to Umuofia as (an example of) "a village where money was so rare, where men and women toiled from year to year to *wrest* a meagre living from an unwilling and exhausted soil" (10, emphasis added).[52] "Modernis[ation]" requires the "devotion to duty" (96) of the Conradian figure Mr. Green, but it must couple that attitude with concern and respect for Africans: *both* "the millions who die . . . from hunger and disease" (106) *and* the "educated Nigerians" (*contra* Green—95). Obi seems in some ways ideally placed to be one of the leaders[53] to point in that direction, but numerous details (even before the major crisis) undercut that "promise" (2) and hint at its eventual "betray[al]" (2).

One such detail is Obi's priggishness in the scene where corrupt police demand a small "take" from the lorry driver (39–40): although Obi is right to disapprove, he takes no action and falls back defensively on an attitude of self-righteous disdain, as alien and detached from real "local" people as anything Mr. Green might have said ("'What an Augean stable!' he muttered to himself"—before resorting to erotic daydreams—40). Even at his first encounter with corruption, on disembarking from England, his "Dear old Nigeria" (28) hardly augurs a "deep-seated need to alter things" (*Morning* 14). Similarly, he is contrasted with Clara who "choose[s her] dressmaker from the slums" (15), saving money *and* providing employment; Obi's stance is to ignore the vitality of the slum scene, concentrating disdainfully on the "putrid flesh" element (14–15).

Throughout *No Longer at Ease* Achebe plants clues indicating that the neocolonial dichotomy, the societal element on which most critics of the novel have concentrated,[54] needs to be overcome by a new integration of modernity with African realities.[55] The element of the novel most consistently overlooked by commentators is Achebe's illustration (since Obi's life is his central and carefully chosen example) that such reintegration would require discarding or overcoming some of the existing idols, *both* outdated African (Igbo) ones *and* European embodiments (58).

It has probably been noticed, but not (that I am aware) explicitly stated, that the novel contains remarkably few overtly "political" scenes. It seems that the overt power sphere is taken for granted, probably because the British are about to withdraw formally ("This no be them country"—62).[56] Since Achebe is well able to portray the Nigerian political sphere (and does so vividly in later novels) the reasons for this omission are not likely to lie in novelistic incompetence—Achebe being neither "callow" nor "nostalgic . . . about Nigeria" (14) and not having imagined [a Nigerian] community[57] for the first time "in England" (11)—as Obi has done. My suggestion is that the novel conveys throughout, but implicitly, the notion that no genuine energy of change toward "Progressive Union" (4) can occur that is not powered by a profound commitment (*distinct* from clannishness or tribalism) and that the root of any such commitment lies in (or "begins with") the personal sphere.[58] Hence the central importance (in the novel) of Clara—a figure whose significance has been so widely underrated by the great majority of commentators on this novel.[59] In later years Achebe, in *The Trouble with Nigeria,* in which he explicitly discusses "Social Injustice and the Cult of Mediocrity" (19–26), mentions that "whenever merit is set aside by prejudice *of whatever origin,* individual citizens as well as the nation itself are victimised" (Achebe, *Trouble,* 22—emphasis added). Power is lost through the waste of an opportunity to grow into a larger, more embracing commitment.

From the same work one image rings a clear bell for the *No Longer at Ease* situation: Achebe refers to "the *abortion* of a pan-Nigerian vision" (Achebe, *Trouble,* 5—emphasis added). This image is recurrent. It leads to my next point, by which I part paths from the majority of critics, who have not rated *No Longer at Ease* highly: their disappointment results (I contend) from an overlooking of the unobtrusive symbolist technique that Achebe employs so subtly but consistently throughout this text. In that sense, the abortion of the child that Clara and Obi conceived portrays—like the "cut[ting] . . . down" (126) of Ikemefuna (recalled in *No Longer at Ease*)—*both* a failure of fathering in the personal sphere (the "great wrong that a man should [allow] . . . hands to be [raised] against a child that [might have] called him father"—126) *and* the thwarting of those future-directed energies of transformation that are needed to give birth to a new nation.[60]

Omotoso, a critic who consistently underrates Achebe, believes that it is Achebe's failure as *novelist* not "to *do something for* the low caste" (*Achebe or Soyinka?* 5—emphasis added), when Clara is rejected. In saying this he fails to recognize the care and consistency with which the novelist is *exposing* Obi's, his family's, and his clan members' failure on this point. The problem of (mis)reading Achebe as if he were himself an Okonkwo (from *Things Fall Apart*) is an old one.[61] A moment of (Achebean) intertextuality is hence in order here. Toward the end of *Things Fall Apart*, acceptance of the ostracized *osu* (the "untouchable" caste of which Clara is a member) is one of the first major tests of new converts' understanding of the Christian faith (113–115). In two short stories from Achebe's small collection *Girls at War,* the wholesomeness of marital commitment *outside* the Igbo clan is expressly foregrounded. In "Marriage Is a Private Affair," it is an Igbo-Ibibio union, and in "Chike's School Days," published within a year of *No Longer at Ease*, it is explicitly the successful marriage of an "ordinary" Igbo to "an *osu* woman in the name of Christianity" (36)[62]—a telling contrast with Obi's failure to honor his commitment to Clara.

The two kinds of criticism leveled against the novel by several commentators—(a) that it merely records (fatalistically!) the fatalistic "lostness" of the Obi character and the educated class he represents ("between" two cultures) and (b) that it is stylistically flat and banal as well as fragmented[63]—can both be refuted from the text. A clear example of the complex art of Achebe's writing occurs in the crucial Chapter 14 (118–126) where Obi and his parents discuss Obi's supposed marriage plans. A power perspective is supplied in the allusions on the opening page to a "war" (of generations), "a tactical move . . . enemy . . . skirmish . . . offensive" (118). Ostensibly, Obi is going to be fighting for Clara and their marriage; however, his father's blunt "you cannot marry the girl" (120) and especially his mother's "if you . . . marry this girl . . . I shall kill myself" (123) defeat what is (and *because* it is) the absence of a real purpose: "there was *nothing in him* with which to *challenge* it *honestly*" (124, emphases added). In other words, Obi "loses" or yields to his parents' emotional pressure because there is no real power or an inadequate force of commitment in his feelings for Clara. This devastating discovery of an inner hollowness,[64] that for Obi there *is* no "*Heart of the Matter*" (36), is prefigured at the moment of his first betrayal of Clara—when his all-too-eloquent "seconds of silence" show him "disengaged" from Clara by the news of her *osu* status (64).[65]

Achebe saturates the description of these crucial family encounters with delicately symbolic suggestions that ironize and contextualize Obi's conduct. Recalling the pastor's allusion to "the days of darkness" (9), Isaac Okonkwo's lamp is "ancient" and "quite empty" (118) and with "[un]steady" hands he spills fuel when he refills it just "a little" (119). Yet Obi "idolizes" this weakening, aging man by elevating him to the inaccessible status of "a masked ancestral spirit" (120).[66] Obi (who has long ago *lost* his Christian faith—"Father, I no longer believe in your God" [51])[67]—can here only *mouth* the Christian arguments for the human worth of members of the *osu* class without real conviction. Yet when Obi contrasts the "darkness and ignorance" (120) of the tribal past from which the *osu* taboo originates, contrasting it with "the light of the Gospel" (120–121), Achebe adds the symbolic comment that "the lamp was now burning too brightly" (121), and so Obi's father (significantly) "turn[s] down the wick."

None of the novel's commentators has mentioned the scrupulously contrived irony of Isaac Okonkwo's biblical story (adapted from II Kings 5), used by him to justify the *osu* taboo, but actually invalidating the very point he intends it to prove. Naaman the Syrian leper referred to here was an "honour[ed]" man *despite* his *osu*-like leprosy and was (moreover) accepted and healed (*not* rejected) by the Jewish prophet. Ironically, *like* what Okonkwo (Isaac's own father) did to him (when he was still the boy known as Nwoye), Isaac is expressing a "curse" ("unto the third and fourth generations")—while clearly imagining himself to be "saving" Obi and his offspring from "sorrow" and "shame" (121). That Clara is "good and beautiful" (64) and (more important) a woman to whom Obi has indicated his commitment is a point raised by neither father nor son—nor, subsequently, by the mother. Indeed, consideration of the individual human reality of the woman Clara is entirely absent from these family discussions.

Significantly, it is "still very dark" (122) when Obi goes to his mother's room—a sphere where "Joy and Mercy [are] distant relations" (122)—as she tells *her* story of "a very bad dream," surrealistically expressing her revulsion at the mere idea of association with an *osu*.[68] That Joseph's "letter" (123) had earlier informed Obi's parents of Clara's *osu* status recalls "The Song of the Heart" with its advice to hold "a brother . . . to [one's] heart" (117)—advice that should presumably be as applicable to the need for fidelity to a loved one. Obi, as he did with his father, conceives of his mother as "terrif[ying]" (123) at this moment, for she (in her turn) is adding her still more potent mother's curse to the father's condemnation of the marriage. What is even more terrifying, though, is Obi's second betraying "silence" (64)—since he seems incapable of speaking up for Clara or acknowledging how far their relationship has advanced in intimacy. Obi's weakness and cowardice here lead directly to his succumbing to bribery, but it is the private failure of fidelity that "causes" the eventual abuse of "public" duty. Obi commits his first forgery ("Pity, that"—141)[69] *after* his breakup with Clara and following his "firm decision" (140) to return her "fifty pounds"—which he never does.

The final section of Chapter 14 shows Obi's father "turn[ing] the wick down, until the flame was practically swallowed up," with Obi listening to him in a position of utter apathy and defeat, "perfectly still on his back," the position receptive to "bad dreams" (124). He *thinks* of provoking another "fight" with his father, not to defend Clara or their relationship, but merely "to justify himself" (124). When Isaac tells Obi that he "went through fire to become a Christian," the reader can see that parallel courage *might* have been displayed by an Obi leaving his father and mother to make a new, symbolic bond with Clara. Instead, however, he will revert to his grandfather Okonkwo's brittle failure of nerve and "raise his hands" (in organizing the abortion) "against a child that [might have] called him father" (126).

One symbolic device that is featured throughout the text relates particularly closely to the theme of (possible) transformational energy in a decolonizing society. The central symbol of this energy is the car[70]—or driving and journeying generally, contrasted with images of stasis. Achebe gives the first clue of his symbolic use of such images when Judge Galloway (on the opening page of the novel) raises a titter with his condescending little joke about the Nigerian "problem of locomotion" (3).

The subtle flexibility with which this ubiquitous device (the car or journey image) is employed can be briefly exemplified. Its connection with the notion of progressive change is indicated when Obi, announcing his determination to marry Clara despite her *osu* status, refers to such an act as that of "a pioneer . . . someone who shows *the way*" (68, emphasis added). That this is after all merely an attitude of bravado is indicated when he undermines the "resolve" by adding "*anyway*, it is too late to change" (68, emphasis added). When Obi returns from Umuofia, having accepted his parents' rejection of the proposed marriage, he drives "in a kind of daze," "numbly," and barely escapes being killed in a crash due to one of the notoriously "reckless drivers" on Nigerian roads, exemplifying imperfect absorption of modernity.

Three times does Clara use the expression "*anyway*" (129) when Obi breaks the news of his parents' opposition to his marriage to her. The grief-filled, despairing tone of the expression is something Obi ignores—he "gave it up." It is Clara who asks, "Hadn't he better be *going*?" to indicate the end of their relationship and who (hinting at her pregnancy) says she'll "find a *way* out" (130, emphases added). That "way out" leads to the scene where Obi, having given Clara into the hands of the sinister, greedy abortion doctor, sits passively "in the driver's seat, paralyzed by his thoughts" (134), later "reverse[s] his car" and (confronted surrealistically by a barrage of "ONE WAY!" signs) "back[s] into a side street," eventually going "in the opposite direction" (135) to Clara and the child they might have brought up. Achebe caps these images when the outraged patient at the clinic denounces Obi, identified as the typically bullying "car" owner, as a "beast of no nation" (138). For the "hybrid hero" (Carroll, *Novelist,* 66) now finds himself "between cosmologies, unattached" (King and Ogungbesan 37), having *got* nowhere and taken no stand. From now on Obi's collapse is irreversible. From this point he can only justify his passivity (151).

Without elevating Clara to any superhuman status, Achebe, in describing her natural generosity (she is the only person shown *giving* Obi anything rather than only getting things from him), shrewd intelligence, professional competence, and attractiveness, indicates clearly that she would have been an ideal partner for Obi. That she is a nurse, in other words, a healer, is a symbolically significant detail—as is the name (Clara means "light") with which the author endows her. Most important, her commitment to Obi (emotional as much as sexual) is total, as even the unscrupulous Christopher, a philanderer and male chauvinist "herd man," acknowledges: "Clara had no time for any other person" (131).[71] Hence Obi's desertion and the terrible abortion leave her ill and embittered. Her blood and that of the unborn child are the primitive blood sacrifice symbolically (not consciously) demanded by Obi's mother—Obi concurs by paying "raw cash" of "thirty pounds" (the betrayer's amount!) to the abortionist. Obi's disdainful selfishness is brilliantly captured when he fastidiously observes "a pregnant woman . . . vomiting into an open drain" (143). Far from merely proving, as in the slum scene (13–14), Nigerian lack of public hygiene, the surreal dimension of the scene links the woman with Clara, the "vomiting" with the waste of their child's life, and Obi's lack of sympathy for the pregnant woman he sees here with his betrayal of Clara—"dat nursing sister" to whom he "givam belle" (impregnated) (143), in the pidgin of the "ward servants" passing by.

Finally, it should be emphasized that Obi's tragedy is a poignant one.[72] Despite his weakness, he is a much finer person than the cheerfully promiscuous Christopher (130–131). The mingling of his "sweat" and grief-stricken tears in the overheated, stationary car after his abandonment of Clara (135) is recalled in and closely linked with his humiliating "tears"—which he pretends are sweat—in the court scene (2). Achebe, by reference to these fluids, is presumably alluding to the proverbial "sweat and tears" required to make difficult personal and social advances. This detail can serve as another example of the poetic density and scrupulosity of this text's construction *and* of the profoundly probing and socially responsible vision that it conveys.

If Achebe investigates the failure of progressive energies in this text, his complex ascription of blame needs to be recognized. It is not only Obi who fails awfully as a parent—his own father, Isaac, and, especially, his mother fail to sustain Obi with the comfort of unconditional love or with the advice to honor his commitment to a woman to whom he has declared his love.[73] They, too, betray their child. So, for that matter, do the UPU tribalists and Mr. Green, the arrogant colonist, who all contribute to the complex, cumulative betrayal of Nigerian aspirations and of Obi, who embodies the hopes of a new land that could have been borne forward by its youth.

Arrow of God

[Without a] vision, the people perish.
Chinua Achebe, *Mapping*

In 1962, while discussing the setting of his first three novels, Achebe said, "*Things Fall Apart* is about a hundred years ago; *No Longer at Ease* is today; and I want to go back now to not quite the time of *Things Fall Apart*, but a little later" (quoted in Duerden and Pieterse 4). Some years later (in 1973) he said of his own father, Isaiah (to whom he had dedicated *Arrow of God*), and of *his* maternal grandfather, Udo Osinyi ("a man of note in the village"—*Morning* 66):

> There was something between those two that I find deep, moving and perplexing. And of those two generations—*defectors and loyalists alike*—there was something I have not been able to fathom. That was why the middle story in the Okonkwo trilogy as I originally projected it never got written. (*Morning* 67—emphasis added)[74]

In this commentary I will argued that *Arrow of God* is Achebe's most sustained and incisive investigation of "the crossroads of cultures" (*Morning* 67); in the novel the arrival of the massive changes that colonialism set in motion is reenvisaged as something other than a mere defeat, a mere falling apart of the indigenous culture. In other words, the suggestion here is that, although *Arrow of God* does not *center* the experience of the first Igbo converts (to Christianity and modernity), it can nevertheless be read as Achebe's most multifaceted analysis of how that huge change came about. It seems propelled by the need to help Africans understand that the acceptance of Westernization was a great deal more complex than a mere cultural humiliation, conquest, and abandonment of indigenous cultures (though indeed it has elements of all these).[75] For if the understanding of colonization (by Africans especially, but also by others) is not enlarged and "complicated" to the point where it can be seen that deliberate choices and progressive attitudes on the part of Africans played a role in the changeovers that took place on so many fronts, it is all too easy to (continue to) accept the humiliating (indeed, the devastating) role of racial and cultural inferiority, cast in concrete. That is why Achebe refers to what might be called the "aftereffects" of "the crisis of colonialism in Africa [having] reached a point where we either had to do battle—*a battle of the mind*—with colonialism, or perish" (emphasis added). This was the impetus, he suggests, of the "responsibility to create" (Chinweizu, "Interview," 29). What had to be built up was a "new fable,"[76] which could "no longer be concerned merely with the dynamics of autonomous societies, but also with the relationship between [the author's] old culture and the invading culture" (Achebe, "Uses," 12).

This "new fable" (re)stages the incursion of the new energies of technology, literacy, and industrialization as forces met and matched by indigenous processes and choices and not as mere displacements. The dignity, complexity, and viability of the indigenous culture thus had to be reestablished in this novel[77] so that colonization could be seen to be a stage in a people's progression through history—a process also developing from within that culture and not merely imposed upon it. In order to do so, Achebe had to show "that in *Arrow of God* Community is human character writ large . . . a personage of titanic proportions whose language is the symbolism of ritual and festival, and whose lifetime is . . . the endless succession of the seasons" (Achebe, "Uses," 13–14). He also had to create as his central protagonist a great leader, someone much more secure and centered in his culture than Okonkwo and capable of "see[ing] tomorrow" (Achebe, *Arrow,* 132).[78] Ezeulu is, of course, partly *at odds with* his own society, which is one of the numerous dynamic tensions of the novel and of the depicted society, but he battles with his people *because* of the completeness of his cultural confidence and his unshakable sense of personal worth. He is never culturally insecure in the way that Okonkwo is (because of *his* personal history). Ezeulu is, unmistakably, a figure of power; a *personage* within his community. That is why he can be an important force to help propel the reorientation of his society—in part consciously (in his progressive decision to have a son educated by the Christians) and in part despite himself and tragically (in his eventually adversarial role vis-à-vis his own society). That he is not unflawed is a sign of the humane depth of the author's conception.

Achebe's (unpaginated) "Preface to [the] Second Edition"[79] is of particular significance and contains (despite its unlikely location) a number of subtle but guiding clues in its last paragraph as to the way(s) in which Ezeulu functions within his society as it undergoes transition. In its oblique way, this Preface indicates the paradoxical nature of Ezeulu's role. Achebe "salute[s]" him as one of "those who stand fast" (echoing "steadfast," four lines earlier) and, accordingly, as "magnificent." Yet the imperatives of a historical process (compare "the powers of event"—230) are there, in the reference to "changes" as "uncalled for," even (more significant) "[un]justified." In the last term may be seen, then, the need to humanize or "justif[y]" process as choice, or as development. This is the end effected inadvertently ("might have come to see") by Ezeulu's "consecrat[ion]" in his role as "victim" (the scapegoat figure who suffers "agony") of his people's "defection" to the new religion, culture, and power source. Ezeulu's tragedy is, then, not a defeat, but an enormous and significant sacrifice: it is his "high historic destiny." Abandonment and betrayal ("the defection of his people") can, through him, be restructured into something that is not only *not* shameful, but indeed difficult, necessary, and maturing: "a ritual passage." It is clear how vividly Achebe here addresses issues of power encounters and of change and how centrally they are located in this densely constructed novel. The pressure and the cost exacted by energies of change (shaming and humiliation; loss; a sense of betrayal) require that that which was most valuable in the old structure ("salute . . . stand fast . . . spiritual . . . magnificent . . . high . . . raising") undergo destruction—in order to allow ("consecrate") its abandonment in the course of the process onward. The use of religious language here both hallows Ezeulu the "steadfast" *and* validates the new (which has sacrificed and betrayed the old, but is "forgiven"). Achebe too, one might say, with this novel is then "consecrat[ing]" both Ezeulu and those members of the clan who defected.[80]

A major insight underlying Achebe's presentation of Igbo society in *Arrow of God* is succinctly expressed in a later comment of his, that "our ancestors created . . . polities with myths" (Achebe, *Hopes,* 168). This idea can be linked with his more oracular statement concerning "the universal creative rondo . . .[:] *stories create people create stories*" (162). It is evident that Achebe recognizes in these expressions the sociopolitical skill made manifest in the creation of a complex communal society like that of the Igbos, which he names as "one of the major cultures of Africa" (Enekwe 129). If a people could, out of the "wild" (*Things Fall Apart* 3) of nature, develop so dense a civilization as they did, then it should be possible, from the (initial) devastation of colonialism, to rescue and re-form, by means of the cultural resources of indigenous societies, modern African states. It is from this perspective that the author's disclosure of the "invented" nature of the god Ulu is nothing like a scoffing, modernist demythologizing of the ancient culture. It is, instead, a tribute to the inventive skill of the people who needed to sacralize a necessary, but new, political union. Therefore the revelation that Ulu is not the equivalent of the Christian God (who is identified as *the creator*), but a knowingly "fabricated" deity, is a clear recognition[81] that like art, religion is "in the service of man" (*Morning* 19). And therefore Achebe can also convincingly show the profound reverence felt by Ezeulu and his people at the numinous presence of Ulu, especially at the Festival of the Pumpkin Leaves (*Arrow* 66–73), which celebrates, mythically and symbolically, "the First Coming of Ulu" (70–71). The both fearsome and sustaining power of "Great Ulu who kills and saves" (72) is shown in prayer and ritual and (mostly) in the unquestioning obedience to Ulu's will, even when (at the end of the novel) people begin to suspect that Ezeulu may be misrepresenting the god's will. (This is partly the consequence of the bitter price paid for the earlier communal transgression of Ulu's will in waging war with Okperi—6–7, 14–29.)

One of the most beautiful expressions of religious awe in this novel occurs quite early, when the narrator mentions that even "now [as] an old man[,] . . . the fear of the new moon which [Ezeulu] felt as a little boy still hovered round him . . . the fear was often overpowered by the joy of his high office; but it was not killed. It lay on the ground in the grip of the joy" (*Arrow* 2). This is a sense of a power that, though accessible to human awareness, is far beyond people's grasp (either of understanding or for manipulation). For this presence, this great sustaining energy, the *word* "power" is not even used. In deft and telling contrast with divine power, the author then juxtaposes (with the preceding quotation) the passage in which Ezeulu "consider[s] the immensity of *his power* over the year and the crops and, *therefore, over the people*" (3, emphases added), "wonder[ing] if it was real" (3). That revealing rider (the second quotation) indicates Ezeulu's sense of challenged authority and his growing rancor, which will push his "natural" arrogance, his hubristic *assumption* of personal "power," to the point of destructive (and, of course, self-destructive) "dement[ia]" (229, 222, 212–213, 191–192, 176, 131).[82]

In no other novel of Achebe's is there so strong a sense of social dynamism as in *Arrow of God.* The society is shown to be a web of constantly adjusting inner tensions and rivalries, intensely competitive by nature. But the rivalries are shown to be contained in the larger union, which is, however, never static, but consists of vital and ever-changing interlinkings. It is, in other words, a society where a wide range of forms of power and a turbulent variety of energies of challenge and change intermingle and (re)adjust themselves. Words like "challenge" and "fight" and tests of competitors' powers occur constantly throughout the text. The sites or relationships where ("among," "between," or "within" which) such contests occur make a long list. They are the three religions (serving Ulu, or Idemili, or the Christian God); different leaders and their visions of the situation (Ezeulu and Nwaka and Ezidemili; Winterbottom and Clarke and Wright and their remote superiors); siblings (Ezeulu and his brother, Ezeulu's sons, Ezeulu's younger children); co-wives; age-grades (76–77); performers (195–201); neighboring clans (Umuaro and Okperi); villages within the Umuaro union; spouses; generations (for example, Ezeulu and "young men [of today]"—1); and families.

Given Ezeulu's central role, he is a participant in or a "cause" of a majority of these tense encounters and he carries his "enem[ies]" with him in his mind even when they are not physically present (3, 159, 221–222). As paterfamilias he is irascible and often biased, but we see no family violence in his compound, as in Okonkwo's. Ezeulu's piqued and touchy vanity throughout clouds his judgment, but Achebe manages always to retain the impression of the "magnificen[ce]" (Preface) of his "haughty" (134, 229)[83] nature as a power source—drawing from deep within Igbo culture. He is compelling and worthy of compassion, a character whose Lear-like dimensions (flawed, terrible, lovable) provide the major evidence in the novel of the power and worth of the civilization he represents.

Late in the novel Achebe explicitly demonstrates that the notion of power *transference* (when energies of change are brought to bear upon old forms, which have become outdated) is a recognized aspect of Igbo culture (in contrast with the mere ambitious envy of a figure like Nwaka and his selfish machinations against Ezeulu and Ulu). The context is a discussion of the Feast of the New Yam, a festival that serves to "[remind] the six villages of their coming together in ancient times and of their continuing debt to Ulu who saved them" (201). The occasion also serves as a census of the Umuaro population (202). Both the origin and the present life of the community are hence given recognition.

> If the festival meant no more than this it would still be the most important ceremony in Umuaro. But it was also the day for all the minor deities . . . [which] stood in a line outside the shrine of Ulu [to receive gifts from grateful worshipers]. . . . Some of them would be very old, nearing the time when their *power would be transferred* to new carvings and they would be cast aside; and some would have been made only the other day. . . . Perhaps this year one or two more would *disappear*, following the men who made them in their own image and departed long ago. (202, emphases added)

This theological legitimization of change can be linked with the far-seeing, progressive-minded attitude to process, the willingness to adapt, that is manifested in Igbo society. Ezeulu's is one of the major articulations of this openness to change, this alertness to powerful new energies. "The world is changing," he tells Oduche.

> "I do not like it. But I am like the bird Eneke-nti-oba. When his friends asked him why he was always on the wing he replied: 'Men of today have learnt to shoot without missing and so I have learnt to fly without perching.' I want one of my sons to join these people [the Christian missionaries] and

> be my eye there. . . . If there is something there you will bring home my share. The world is like a Mask dancing. If you want to see it well you do not stand in one place." (45–46)

As in *Things Fall Apart*, and even more strongly (since this is a period when colonialism has made further advances), there is the recognition of foreign incursions and consequent destabilization ("the white man turned us upside down"—16). Ezeulu is, however, not alone in the clan in seeing that depredations of the old lifestyle bring opportunities as well as disruptions. The carpenter Moses Unachukwu becomes "the first and the most famous convert in Umuaro" (47) and is a figure of considerable influence and ambition.[84] Having witnessed the destructive might of British military power, Moses (the name he chose for himself) has been "taught . . . that the white man was not a thing of fun" (47).

In the aftermath of one of the central events in the novel, an event that illustrates the crude power of the colonists in their humiliation of the indigenous culture (the incident of Obika's whipping by Wright—81–83), Moses Unachukwu's is the most informed and authoritative explanatory voice. "There is no escape from the white man," he tells the group of furious but cowed young men: "he has come. . . . As daylight chases away darkness so will the white man drive away all our customs" (84). Whites have "power" (84) legitimated by their "God and it burns like fire" (85). Moses understands the *complex* power of colonialism: "The white man, the new religion, the soldiers, the new road—they are all part of the same thing. . . . He does not fight with one weapon alone" (85).

Unachukwu is an interesting figure whose successful cultural mediations contrast instructively with Ezeulu's intransigence (based finally, as it is, on an underestimation of the new power).[85] Moses can speak "with great power" (48) in the debate on whether Christian converts should openly attack the Umuarians' revered, living idol (the python), because he retains his respect for and recognition of the local culture (48–50). He can even quietly outmaneuver the overzealous new catechist, Mr. Goodcountry, by combining the powers of the old religion ("the priest of Idemili") and the new ("the Bishop on the Niger") to the advantage of both the old and the new (214–215). It is significant that he does so by employing the new technology ("got a clerk in Okperi to write a petition on behalf of the priest of Idemili"), as a consequence of which "the Lieutenant Governor" (the colonial ruler) insists in (another) "letter to the bishop to apply the reins on his boys" and not persecute the followers of the old faith (214, 215). His superiority as a strategist (compared to Ezeulu) is made clear.

John Nwodika (given that "Christian" name because his employer finds his first name "Nwabueze" unpronounceable—170) is described by Akuebue as "one of our young men [he is the first, a point that earns him fame] who lives with the white man in Okperi" (135). He, too, is a pioneer and a mediating figure.[86] By the end of the novel he has "left Winterbottom's service to set up a small trade in tobacco" (229–230). He had announced that he did "not aim to die a servant" (170) in the discussion (in the Okperi guardroom) during which Akuebue discovers a progressive like-mindedness between Ezeulu and "Nwodika's son" ("*their thoughts are brothers*"—170). It is John Nwodika who voices the urgent need for economic advancement as an opportunity and not a closing of doors for their people: "Leave dancing and join in the race for the white man's money" (169). He encapsulates this go-getter attitude with an Igbo proverb: "If the rat could not run fast enough it must make way for the tortoise" (169).[87] He is concerned because Umuofia has "no share in the market [and] . . . no share in the white man's office"; Nwodika explains that he escorted the Court Messenger sent by Winterbottom to Ezeulu's home (135–140) because he believed that that was a "chance to bring our clan in front of the white man" (170) and not as an act of betrayal.

Even Nweke Ukpaka, who can give "a new and irreverent twist" to an ancient dirge and turn it into "a half familiar, half strange and hilarious work-song" (81), is another such transitional clan figure. Although the previous quotations show the ambiguous emotional balancings between the tragic sense of desecration and the wryly felt need for adaptation and opportunism, Achebe shows Ukpaka to be a person of influence and insight. Like Moses Unachukwu, Ukpaka warns of the dangerous power of the whites and of the need for great circumspection in a situation where open confrontation would merely be an opportunity for the colonial power to crush them. In his memorable speech and the sage advice it contains (85–86), one homely proverb stands out: "The white man is like hot soup and we must take him slowly—slowly from the edges of the bowl" (85). The interesting suggestion here is the recognition that sustenance *may* be derived from even so initially harmful a source.

How is it, then, that colonial power does not only penetrate Igbo society, but actually breaks it apart? Over and over again Achebe brings the ancient imperial axiom *divide et impera* (divide and rule) to one's mind. The fissures and faultlines in indigenous society emerge once it is subjected to the unprecedented force of the colonial incursion. It is not so much a case of the imperialists' dividing the locals as of their presence revealing the existing divisions among indigenes. Early in the novel Ezeulu laments the "division" in the clan (6). "Umuaro was *divided* in two" (27, emphasis added) long before the interference of "the white man." Even before the ill-timed war with Okperi, against which Ezeulu warned the clan, an unnamed Umuarian refers to the way in which Igbo wars create for the colonialists the powerful, cunningly masked role of "pacification" (32, echoing the title mentioned on the last page of *Things Fall Apart*): "The white man . . . says, like an elder to two fighting children: You will not fight while I am around" (20).

Ezeulu's role changes from his initial attempts to prevent division to his eventual, major contribution to the clan's weakening by near-starvation and division, as he exacts his selfish and indiscriminate vengeance on it. Hence, the proverb that he uses early on ("When two brothers fight a stranger reaps the harvest"—131) is eventually quoted in criticism of him (220). Numerous other proverbial sayings and allusions[88] indicate the Igbo awareness of the need to unite against an external threat (a point that was, after all, the founding principle of the clan and the origin of Ulu himself).

The combative language[89] that Ezeulu uses when thinking resentfully of the clan's supposed "desertion" of himself should be contrasted with the expressions betokening recognition of the need for Igbos to overcome petty divisions in the face of the major challenge of colonialism ("even a hostile clansman was a friend in a strange country"—162).[90] Clearly this is strategically more appropriate as well as more in keeping with Ezeulu's role as high priest of Ulu, who is known as "the saver" (207).[91]

It is on the distinction between the letter and the spirit of Ulu worship—or between rigidly upholding Igbo custom versus adapting it to unprecedented circumstances—that Ezeulu's later, dangerous role depends. Ezeulu and Akuebue had at one point (132–133) discussed how both Ezeulu's grandfather and his father (both *as* high priests of Ulu) had abolished aspects of clan custom due to humane considerations.[92] When the clan leaders come to appeal to Ezeulu to devise a strategy to permit the violation of ritual in eating the uneaten yams (to bring the agricultural year "up to date" with the high priest's timekeeping and to prevent famine), the same point is made: "customs . . . had been altered . . . when they began to work hardship on the people" (209). Ezeulu's position has, however, now hardened to that of the rigid primordialist—in order to rub in the point of Ulu's (and his own!) preeminence. It is, in other words, a half-unconscious power game. Ezeulu remains intransigent in order (perversely) to assert his personal status and authority—though, as Achebe vividly illustrates, at this stage the vengeful pride of the high priest has been internalized to the point where he believes himself to be fulfilling the will of Ulu ("'Ta! Nwanu!' barked Ulu in his ear. . . . 'Who told you that this was your own fight?'"—191).[93]

Ezeulu's announcement that Ulu will not countenance any adaptive strategy "spread[s] . . . alarm"—it means "that the six villages would be *locked in the old year* for two months longer" (210, emphasis added). The highlighted expression here recalls a parallel phrase from much earlier in the novel—when the python imprisoned by Oduche left Ezeulu wondering "whatever power his son had imprisoned in a box" (44).[94] That vivid phrase now sums up the encapsulation of the old culture by the new system—showing that

Ezeulu, too, has come to contribute unknowingly to the process that devalidates the clan's ancient life values and customs.[95]

In *Arrow of God* we are made aware of the nightmare of colonialism that overtook Africans. This perspective is shown in the surreal recurrence of certain details in the course of the novel. Ezeulu may confuse his personal prestige with his clan's power and forget that "no man however great can win against a clan" (131),[96] but his instinctual sense of endangerment and challenge is a discerning *reading* of his and his people's changing position. Colonialism recontextualizes the Igbo in a new "wild."

Ezeulu's first nightmare shows his fear of not only a personal displacement, but also of cultural power loss: "What is the power of Ulu today? . . . he cannot save us from the white man . . . [you are] the priest of a dead god" (159). The *ex unitate vires* motif—that is, the point that the clan can maintain resistant "power" (189) only if unified—is raised by "Ofoka, one of the worthiest men in Umuaro" (187). Momentarily Ezeulu is shown recognizing not only that unity is a requirement on "his people [to sing] their support behind him," but that it simultaneously requires *him* to "confront danger," not in piqued resentment against the clan, but as "the responsibility of his priesthood" (189). Moreover, to see *his* "priesthood" in competitive contradiction with Ezidemili's is an attitude he slowly, albeit subconsciously, recognizes as a diversionary war—where a far greater, predatory, outside enemy is looming over them all.

His children's disrespectful song ("Python run! There is a Christian here")[97] may make him laugh (204–205), but its recurrence (221) in Ezeulu's second and far profounder nightmare (221–222) shows him at last acknowledging that Idemili (whose god the python is) represents the clan's (and his own!) cultural self[98]—whose crushing will displace him as well. This thought brings the first sign of that desolation and "madness" (222) that will overcome him eventually.

When the tragedy of Obika's death—the death of the finest in the clan[99]—strikes Ezeulu, he registers it as the "[sudden] . . . desert[ion]" of "power" (228). He feels betrayed by Ulu, abandoned by the clan, and has now lost his favorite son. Ezeulu's agony lends him great dignity, though. He has been struck down, partly as a register of his stature,[100] by a mysterious, "implacable assailant" (229). This could be any or all of the following: the clan; a "powerless" but treacherous Ulu (229); his own insanely extremist pride;[101] or "the powers of event" (230), a huge historical process. Ezeulu's awesome end, in "demented" and "haughty splendour" (229), is no simple affair, but a central knot in the many threads that run through Achebe's depiction of this crucial period in his people's history. He makes of Ezeulu and his fate an account of profound significance, one that distinguishes among but also contains in its complexity a personal tragedy,[102] a people's defeat, and the story of their survival.

A Man of the People and *Anthills of the Savannah*

that there shall not be misrule
Chinua Achebe, *Mapping*

Achebe's concern with matters of government and issues of justice and social improvement grows more overt in his later novels, as his sense of the urgency of the Nigerian crisis of rule intensifies—along with actual developments in his own country. *A Man of the People* was first published in 1966 and *Anthills of the Savannah* in 1987. During the two intervening decades, Achebe lived through a number of crises. The first military coup in his country occurred in 1966; he witnessed growing enmity against Igbos (from other Nigerians), which eventually took on genocidal proportions; he also experienced the Biafran War (1967–1969) and the secession of Biafra (in the administration and international justification of which he played a not inconsiderable part). The defeat of the secessionist state was followed by the reunification of Nigeria (1970). Most of Achebe's English poetry and a number of his short stories were written, and both collections published, during this period (in 1971 and 1972 respectively).[103] The essay collection *Morning Yet on Creation Day* was published in 1975, the political pamphlet *The Trouble with Nigeria* in 1983; he coedited (with C.L. Innes) *African Short Stories* in 1985. His second essay collection, *Hopes and Impediments*, appeared in 1988 (first U.S. edition was in 1989). All in all, it is clear that the "gap" of twenty-one years in this author's novel-writing career was filled to the brim with both other forms of writing and participation in public affairs (as well as by his academic and editorial[104] duties).

Qualities of rule and of the administration of justice are matters both of national concern and intimately affecting individual lives. In these later novels, *A Man of the People* and *Anthills of the Savannah,* Achebe continues to concern himself with the way uses of power (in the administration of people's affairs) both impinge upon and are affected by the quality of the participation of a range of persons in their country's *national* life. Impetus toward (necessary) change is shown to require individual effort and commitment. Social and individual life are (still) perceived and presented as inextricable, although the more cohesive clan life portrayed in earlier novels is now something of the past. The scope of experience depicted in these texts has enlarged "geographically" and the sense of the pressure of the present[105] is more evident than in earlier works.

The Trouble with Nigeria (1983) is an important indicator of the author's concern during this period with (what he perceives as) the close link between a flawed national morality and national failures in economic and political matters. In this text, the author identifies and criticizes national faults in political and social conduct and names and criticizes (and occasionally praises) living and known political figures. The well-known opening sentence of this tract reads, "The trouble with Nigeria is simply and squarely a failure of leadership" (*Trouble,* 1). Other chapter headings list tribalism; "false image of ourselves"; [lack of] patriotism; social injustice and the cult of mediocrity; indiscipline; corruption; and the "Igbo problem" as the concatenation of social sins that have brought Nigerians to the brink of a national disaster.

The sharp focus on the responsibility of leadership in this political commentary of Achebe's was called for at the time when and in the light of the purpose for which he wrote *The Trouble with Nigeria.* It is, however, necessarily a considerably simpler composition than either of the novels and should not (as some critics have allowed it to do)[106] overshadow the more nuanced and complex, balanced evaluation and analysis of similar issues in the novels. Both *A Man of the People* and *Anthills of the Savannah* are read (in the individual discussions that follow) as indeed containing examinations of leadership (among other things), *but* leadership is itself presented and analyzed by the author as a far more complex phenomenon than an individual's personal traits and style of public conduct. Power in the form of leadership is shown in each novel to be a function of a society in its entirety; power is *conferred* upon (usually) the few (usually) by the many in a sociopolitical *context*, and overt manifestations of power are themselves immersed in intricate contexts: in webs of personal, familial, social, and political relationships. These generalizations are vividly concretized by Achebe in his depictions of actual situations and of role players in the two novels.

A Man of the People

The 1966 publication of *A Man of the People*[107]—which ends with the description of a military coup—was succeeded so soon by an actual military takeover of rule in Nigeria that Achebe was naïvely suspected and openly accused by many of having had a hand (or a thought) in the execution or planning of this major political event. Although a "tribute" of sorts to his prescience, the absurdity of the accusation (and its suggestion of political bias) afforded the author some irritation.[108] Another problem with this linking of the novel with actual events is that it led to an interpretation in which the author is thought to endorse military rule as a "solution" to political problems—whereas the final section of the text clearly indicates that the coup is an index of the failure of politics (that is, of civil government). Instead of the making of superficial "political connections," it should be recognized that "the endemic weaknesses of civil society have . . . added to the historical and political burden of the writer in Africa, foist[ing] immense responsibility on [such a] writer and ma[king] his duty principally political" (Adebayo Williams 361).

A Man of the People ends with Odili's discovery that "in the affairs of the nation there was no owner" (148).[109] My argument here will be that this vision of the postcolonial state is, in fact, inherent in the novelist's implicitly analytical rendition of such a state—*from the very beginning of the novel.* Achebe's authorial stance retains throughout his oeuvre a critical distance from the protagonists—this distance ensures the efficacy of the depiction of protagonists' experiences as a tool of analysis of a whole society.[110] Achebe is here examining the social permeation of a particular "style" of power throughout a political community—a form of power that offers very little hope of social transformation, because the location of political accountability is indeterminable.

One clear, small sign in the novel that the focus is not mainly on the self-styled "Chief the Honourable" Nanga is the fact that he fades almost unnoticed from the narrative (147). Had he been an example of a leader determining the quality of public life in his community instead of merely an indicator or consequence of it, his "disappearance" would have been far more noteworthy. The narrative focus—*despite* what the title seems to indicate—is not principally on Nanga as the "*Man*" of the title. He is, instead, a phenomenon indicative of the nature of "*the People*"—of the whole society. The preposition in the title *("of")* is thus especially significant: Nanga is much less a leader than he is an expression of what his people allow "leaders" like him to be.

If "populist power" is the appropriate term for the social condition depicted here, Achebe might be said to be showing us that such a form of power is here not merely a swindle of the supporters by the power holders (even if that aspect is by no means absent). It is a far more intimate relationship between a "big man" and his "people"—in fact, a collusion.[111] Hence Odili can at the end of the novel identify as "the real culprits," not the man who orchestrated the death of his friend and party leader Max (that is, Chief Koko—Nanga's colleague and counterpart), but "*the people* who had *led* him on" (148, emphases added). And *these* "leaders" (though they may include the foreign backers—"the Americans" and the firm "British Amalgamated" being those most frequently referred to in the novel), who are identified in the same paragraph, are the local "praise-singers" of the formerly mighty ones as well as the "newspapers, the radio, the hitherto silent intellectuals and civil servants"—in fact, "everybody" (148), the populace as a whole. No one is free of blame for the social disaster.

Late in the novel Achebe employs as an apparently small "side-show" a village scene of children playing at conducting "a real, dangerous Mask" (96–97).[112] It is, in fact, a vivid little allegory of how power should be held in check by vigilant "attendants." An image of privilege that recurs throughout the novel (the "stuffed pot-belly"—which the children in their song call "bigi bele Sunday") is used here.[113] The threat of power, however, is exemplified in the "outsize matchet" that the Mask "brandish[es]." The danger of uncontrolled power is described as "a wild rampage and loss of life and property"

(97). Yet the "laws" (148)[114]—represented by the way the Mask is "held in restraint by his attendants tugging at a rope" (96), which he himself helps "retie" when it comes "undone" (97)—are, in the *children's* masquerade, effective enough to contain the (image of) power, in sad contrast with the realities of the national political scene. There, the "laws" and restraints have been allowed to become "powerless" (148).[115]

"The people themselves," Odili realizes toward the end of the novel, "had become even more cynical than their leaders" and consequently quite "apathetic" about leaders exploiting and abusing their power (144). This is the attitude that Ikem (in *Anthills of the Savannah*) terms a "diseased tolerance" (138). If "the people themselves" care only about survival and are, like their leaders, profoundly opportunistic (merely "Minus Opportunity"—12), then a particularly pernicious form of laissez-faire, from "the people" *toward* "the leaders," results; inverting—or preventing—even *that* far from ideal style of government. Odili describes it, disgustingly and disgustedly, as "the fat-dripping, gummy, *eat-and-let-eat* regime" (149, emphasis added).[116]

By the time Odili comes to this conclusion, he is a chastened (proverbially a "sadder and wiser") person, but the tragic tone of the novel's finish is not the voice of a merely disillusioned person. Odili's growth in political understanding in the course of the novel is, in fact, one of the few hopeful signs in the society depicted. His words and his attitude have that "moral force" (126) of whose importance he slowly *and* suddenly becomes aware, midway into the novel.

Achebe, by means of a few deft intertextual touches, draws attention to similarities as well as dissimilarities between Odili and Obi (of *No Longer at Ease*). The similarities are indicated not only in their names (Odili is sometimes called Odi) but also in what *might* very likely have been Odili's career path ("I had gone to the University with the clear intention of coming out again after three years as a full member of the privileged class whose symbol was the car"—109)—an evident parallel with Obi.[117] When Odili drives the car made available for his use—paid for from party funds—he registers the temptation of such privilege ("I hoped I was safe"—109). Yet Odili's growth, as depicted in the whole course of the novel—a growth in both moral and political understanding—contrasts clearly with Obi's private and professional collapse as shown in *No Longer at Ease*. Although the broad social outlook in *A Man of the People* and Odili's final pronouncement on it offer little hope of improvement in public morality and political health, (at least) Odili's own nature and the outline of his social participation embody a small, though vivid, instance of hopeful, transformational social energy (144, 148–149),[118] as does Edna, and Odili's commitment to her—in contrast with his initial desire for the "shimmering" (68) Elsie.

Odili is sufficiently self-interested and susceptible to the temptations of "advancement" to be a thoroughly credible character. His moral-political outlook oscillates somewhat, until toward the end of the novel it steadies at a position that is neither cynically uncaring nor naïvely hopeful, but both principled and realistic. He is, in fact, snobbishly cynical when the novel opens—whereas, by its end, he has come to measure the horrific consequences of the cynicism of "the people."[119] He takes their measure *then* not merely as a naïvely disdainful young class snob, but from a position of moral, political concern.

Odili's relation to Nanga (with the latter as a power symbol in this society) is particularly interesting. He starts out as a more-or-less unthinking, satisfied supporter of the party in power ("very active in the Students' branch of the People's Organisation Party," taking "pride" in his ex-teacher Nanga's role as M.P.—3). His first disillusionment with the party, with the government, and with Nanga is caused by the discovery of their collective opportunism and lack of political morality—their determination to hang on to (or to increase) *power,* setting them up against the principled, the intellectual, and the properly trained members of government (3–7) at a time of political "crisis" (3). It is when Odili witnesses at first hand (*and* sees its misrepresentation in the newspapers) the ugliness of the anti-intellectual scapegoating in Parliament, in which Nanga takes the role of the "[leader of] the pack" (5), that the young man first realizes the "dangerous and sinister" (4) route that political affairs are taking. "The whole country was behind the leader" (4) and "what mattered was loyalty to the party" (4) are quotations emphasizing the fascist trend in this society, with its typical primordialist strain ("speak the language of the people"; "ancient culture"—4). In contrast with the highly educated Minister of Finance's "complete plan for dealing with the situation" (3),[120] merit and skill are made suspect by Prime Minister, press, and populace. What becomes manifest is the merely primitive[121] reliance on the lowest common denominator, which governs this society: the casually accepted belief "that the mainspring of political action [is] personal gain" (114),[122] as even Odili's father holds.

It is, of course, the hope of "personal gain" that inspires the pseudosophisticated, disdainful Odili ("personally I don't care too much for our women's dancing"—1) to join the "danc[e]" around Nanga (cf. Mbembe, "Provisional," 20, 25, 29). Odili disingenuously denies the hope of a further ("post-graduate"—12) scholarship promised by Nanga ("without any godfather's help but purely on my own merit"—17), though he is quite content to allow Nanga's request—on Odili's behalf—to Chief Koko, Minister for Overseas Training, to proceed (32). The aspect of the offer that proves the most seductive, however, is Nanga's "guest-room with everything complete," where (in the minister's broad but eventually unfulfilled promise) Odili (and, as he intends, Elsie) can supposedly "do *anything* [he] like[s]" (18).

Read as an image, the reference to Odili's rooming in Nanga's "mansion" (75), one of the scandalously opulent "ministers' official residences"

(36), is an early occurrence of the novel's central image of (state) power as a building or construction (37).[123] It is seen, significantly, not as an institution erected by indigenous skill and effort, but as "the one shelter our former rulers left," for which "a handful of us . . . hardly ever the best—had scrambled" and in which the new (local) rulers at Independence "barricaded themselves" (37)—a brilliant image of isolationist, parasitical power use. The absence (from this type of state occupation) of any transformational energies is indicated by the "extension" of the metaphor (but *not* of the "house"!) in the reference to communication "through . . . loudspeakers"[124] of the demand for political quietism—"all argument should cease and people speak with one voice," since "dissent" will supposedly "subvert and bring down the whole house" (37). The peculiar resonance of this "shelter" image and its tragically apt portrayal of a common postcolonial condition has been frequently noted. That Achebe here attributes the metaphor and the insight it conveys to Odili is a mark of this character's relative reliability as political commentator and social observer, despite his temporary yielding to the "hypnotis[ing]" (36) enticements of ill-gotten power (compare "smothering me in his voluminous damask"—8).

The suspect, *adroit* quality of Odili's rationalizations of power misuse while Nanga "accommodat[es]" (39) him is shown up in many details, such as Achebe's wicked little pun when Odili refers to "the insight [he] got into the *affairs* of our country" (39, emphasis added) during his stay with the minister. Given that the only "performances" on Nanga's part of which we hear are his baying for the blood of the worthy in Parliament and displays of his sexual stamina, Odili is inadvertently confirming the absence of meaningful attempts to make progress to the benefit of all ("our country's lack of dynamism and abdication of the leadership"—39).

Odili's own corruption by the unearned benefits of association with power is registered in his "substituting" for Nanga both socially and sexually (at Jean's party and in her bed); at his open-eyed justifications of Nanga's corrupt practices (42–43, 65); and in his lazy, indulgent lifestyle at this time.[125] It outlasts even the (obviously revealing) point when Nanga installs Elsie in his wife's suite (67) as a first sign of the "*droit de seigneur*" that the minister is about to assert—so humiliatingly to Odili. That it is *power* which Odili lacks here is shown in the effects that the shock of the sexual dislodgement has on him: "paralysis" and "pressure"; "revulsion and hatred" (70). Although saying that "action" is needed, all he can do is to pack his clothes. He exits from this "shelter" (37) of privilege and corruption, however, and now, unlike when he was being driven around "Bori at night" (53) "sightseeing" and embarrassed at the exposure of his country's inadequacies, he begins to *identify* with "beggars sleeping under the eaves of luxurious department stores" (71). His noticing such social outcasts clearly recalls the central image (37) contrasting those inside the "shelter" of power and privilege with those excluded from it. That this is a moment of insight is confirmed by the comment that follows: "my head began to clear . . . and I saw Bori" (71).[126]

Strangely enough, Odili's inability to articulate[127] the monstrosity of Nanga's sexual greed is almost itself a form of power or resistance: it has "moral force" (to use Odili's later expression—126). The outrage he now feels at Nanga's behavior replaces Odili's earlier rejection of criticism of the minister, when he began to think that such objections stemmed from a "delicatc [rcfincment] that belonged elsewhere" (11). Nanga's pathological greed has now come home to Odili in an unmistakable way. From his indignation and shock come the power of Odili's contempt for the sheer vulgarity of the politician—the "bush" man (73) who will never again intimidate or impress him.[128] Unlike in *No Longer at Ease,* with its progressive disillusionment and corruption of the main character, Achebe gives us here a protagonist's disillusionment, which is an advancc in moral and political understanding. It might begin merely as a thirst for a tit-for-tat type of vengeance, but it grows rapidly into something much more real and worthy. That it can become a genuine energy of transformation (compare "nucleus of activity"—77) is made possible largely by Max, who (along with his friends) not only offers Odili alternative accommodation ("Max's house"—76) but also a "political home." On his own, though, Odili understands that his sexual ousting by Nanga encapsulates the broader scene of gross political and social inequalities of a community in the grip of corruptly used power (76).

If "ultimately . . . what literature is about [is] that there should not be misrule,"[129] then *A Man of the People*—not only up to this point, but beyond it and until its close—creates no illusions that the abolition of "misrule" is imminent or even likely in the kind of political community depicted here. The founding of the "Common People's Convention" (as the new opposition party is called) is intended to initiate the eventual political restitution of power and political say to "the worker, the farmer, the blacksmith, the carpenter . . . [a]nd the unemployed" (78), whom the "vanguard" of "professional[s]" and intellectuals is intended to "draw in," once they "are ready" (78). Yet how very difficult *this* will be to achieve, given the political attitudes of "the people," is vividly illustrated at the launching of the party in Odili's own village of Urua.

Initially, the boycott of the corrupt trader Josiah by the combination of forces in the village of Anata (84–86) seems (to the somewhat bemused eyes of Odili) a hopeful sign. It *seems* to show that common people can successfully organize resistance against exploitation and greed[130] when such selfishness eventually overreaches itself. Achebe's standard figure of "a kind of Christian and a carpenter" (see 107–108) as a reliable index—one that effectively combines old and new moralities—recurs here. The carpenter is given the summarizing, proverbial statement explaining the matter: "Josiah has taken away enough for the owner to notice" (86). Odili adds, "And the owner, I discovered, is the will of the whole people" (86), which acts effectively against one who robbed them. "Within one week Josiah was ruined" (86). He will, however, be resuscitated on the national political stage ("mounting the altar of the new shrine in the presence of all the people to whisper into the ear of the new celebrant," in Odili's bitter and memorable words) at the end of the novel (149).

The launching of the Common People's Convention is full of the exhilaration of youthful energy, enthusiasm, and a will to change things for the better (121–123). Odili's father allows and accepts these political "rivals" because he holds (in terms of the ancient Igbo proverb) to an ethic of tolerance: that "the hawk should perch and the eagle perch" (122)—a morality that the village as a whole will end up rejecting fiercely, under the pressure of Nanga's blackmail ("they knew one man, and one man alone—Chief Nanga"—134).[131] That the village people are *not* receptive to the morality of political vigilance and demands for justice is evident from the start, however, in the "dialogue" between Max and the village audience. The worst sign is their "slack, resigned laughter" (124, 123) in response to Max's expression of indignation at "Government swindling and corruption" (123). The "ex-policeman" (fired for accepting bribes) "put it very well" (says Odili): "We know they are eating, . . . but we are eating too" (124). What governs here is, in other words, a *general* ethic of profiteering, as entrenched in the governed as it is in the rulers—or perhaps even *stemming from* "the people." Even Max, to Odili's dismay, begins to show some signs of yielding to this permeating pressure when he uses self-interested arguments in his speech (125) and reveals that he accepted Koko's bribe without any intention of fulfilling the undertaking he made to him (126).

Early in the novel one of Odili's apparently artless[132] "diversionary" anecdotes quietly inserts a symbol of the only way in which parasitical, *preying* power forms can be combated (by vigilance, exposure, and vigorous, concerted action). It is his little story of how the rats who "emerged to eat the grains while we sat around the . . . fire" "flew" "as you entered the room with a lamp," how he and his friends "decided to go hunting" and would "plug the holes." "It worked very well," he concludes (41).[133] Max uses a similar image in the most impassioned part of his village speech ("his hands and his voice began to shake"), when he speaks of the "two vultures" who consume the hunter's kill, whereupon the hunter proceeds "to wipe out the dirty thieves" (124). "That hunter is yourselves," he tells the people (124). The failure of this appeal to activism and vigilance is prefigured early in the novel, however, when the members of the seldom-seen Anata "hunter's guild" show up "in full regalia" (1) to honor the opulent, corrupt Nanga with a "warrior's salute" (2). More tellingly, "they wielded their loaded guns as though they were playthings" (2). This image of the irresponsible use of voters' power is capped when the hunters "let off their last shots, throwing their guns about with frightening freedom" (7).

The overall picture of "people" and leadership in this society is (as indicated), despite the surface vitality and cheerfulness, a dismaying one. The jovial, ebullient Nanga is also *superficially* attractive (61–65). As Achebe is particularly aware, however, that "where there is no vision the people perish" (*Mapping* 25),[134] his portrait of his people includes some signs of hope (of what has here been termed energies of change) at the individual level—not only in Odili and in Max and Eunice, but also (for instance) in Odili's father and in the distinct improvement of the paternal-filial relationship in the course of the novel. That the general tone of rural or village life has irretrievably lost its culturally pristine quality under the pressures of capitalist modernity and neocolonial politics is made amply evident. The most vivid illustration of this "degeneracy" is Edna's father's pretense that he lacks a kola nut with which to welcome Odili on his first visit to their village home (89, 92).[135] But Odili's father, in his refusal to "deny" the welcome he had extended to his son and his son's friends and political associates (132, 135), at least shows the survival of some essential Igbo values. He makes an ambivalent, but finally appealing, impression on the reader as well as on Odili. This is perhaps possible because Odili maintains a healthy independence from his father (30—in contrast with Obi's submission—in *No Longer at Ease*—to *his* parents). Odili's father might be seen as a sort of "recovered" Nanga, perhaps—in his days of power as court interpreter he gathered profit and was feared and hated by many (28–29); in his old age he is innocuous, but not without some moral authority. This trait is displayed with some courage and at some risk to himself ("I received your friends in my house and I am not going to deny it"—135). It is telling that in this novel, at last, there is no expression of a paternal curse (30–31) and, at last, a united father-son front—a "compound" (136).

Odili's growing appreciation of Edna is also significant. Though he generally underrates her maturity, he does feel the effect—one could certainly term it the power—of her purity of being. Odili registers this (although he could not be said to understand it) when, on his first visit to her at her home, her appearance causes "all [his] composure [apparently] to leave [him]" (90). Thus the young woman who was supposedly to be a mere instrument[136] in his campaign of vengeance against Nanga is shown to have affected and "reached" him *immediately* at a far deeper and uncontrollable level. The accident during the bicycle lift episode (93–94), also originally a ploy ("she was obviously the trusting type"—93), creates an opportunity that shows their attitude of mutual concern and sensitivity to each other's feelings (94). That Edna is the very opposite of Elsie is shown when she rejects Odili's first physical overtures ("she swung round and pushed me away in one alarmed movement"—98). She literally brings out the best in or "empowers" him[137] when he courageously defies her father's threat of assault ("I saw his matchet gradually descend"—105). Edna can also effectively castigate Odili with the force of moral denunciation ("Her tongue . . . stung. . . . I recoiled, tongue-tied" clearly illustrates this—129). But when Nanga and his henchmen assault Odili on the dais, Edna's loyalties are made clear as she attempts with self-forgetful courage to insert her body protectively between Odili and his assailants (140), who represent corrupt, punitive power. The young couple's eventual reconciliation and intended marriage mark a further, hopeful advance—it is an alliance that augurs well.[138] Edna is clearly contrasted with almost all the other women in the novel and their profiteering alliances with Chief Nanga.[139]

By inserting certain key passages (108, 130), Achebe endorses the reality of Odili's twin commitments—to Edna and to political change. That this young man's personality and his actions remain colored[140] by a degree of youthful vanity and naïveté is certain. Yet it is "out of" the cheery, often mischievous or arrogant tone in which most of his story is narrated that we reach the outraged *authority*, the "moral force" (126) of its conclusion (148–149). Like Max's poem for the "black mother," Africa, the "highlife rhythm" of Achebe's text is also a "dirge" of national lamentation—recalling "Rachel weeping for her children" (80–81).

Anthills of the Savannah

By the time Achebe came to write *Anthills of the Savannah* he had witnessed—in Nigeria and elsewhere in Africa—situations considerably more appalling than "the gargantuan disparity of privilege"; "the institutionalized robbery of the common people . . . by their public servants"; "the thrusting indiscipline" (of the society) and "official thuggery" (Achebe, *Trouble,* 22, 23, 29, 35)—descriptions that seem applicable to the bad government depicted in *A Man of the People*. One might say, though, that *Anthills of the Savannah*[141] has proved as unfortunately prophetic as its predecessor, or (more appropriately) that the kind of awful tyranny in whose grip[142] Nigeria found itself until 1998 was the appalling confirmation of the depth of Achebe's understanding of the political ill-health of his own society (and others like it).[143] In *Anthills of the Savannah* we see how military government may spawn actual tyranny when power contorts the familiar (even the innocuous, as Sam initially is—11–13, 49–53, 59–60) into the terrifyingly "strange" and "poisonous" (1); when a "game" or a "play gets out of hand" (146). This novel is a study of power by terror. It is the author's most inclusive analysis of a modern authoritarian African state and the society that it harms and frightens. The prevalent perception of the state of the nation can be given in the sorrowful words of Ikem's neighbors, who witness his kidnapping by members of the so-called State Research Council (the country's secret police): "This our country na waa. Na only God go save person" (This, our country, is in trouble/chaos. Now only God can save us) (166).[144]

In this novel, the distinction between the entrenched and increasingly tyrannical forms of power[145] (on the one hand) and the stubborn, but besieged or crushed, energies of change (on the other) is a stark one. Each relates "the story of the land" (124) in a tellingly different way.[146] Power tells stories that "blind" society,[147] whereas those in whom Achebe makes us see energies of change at work produce and participate in "stories" that can "escort" the society beyond the horror of the present, to apply the terms of this novel's central passage (124–126).

The official radio broadcast announcing the shooting of Ikem (168–169) can serve as an example of a "story" circulated to "blind" the people of the country to what has actually occurred. The frantic enquiries Chris makes about his kidnapped friend are blocked by the blanket phrase he hears from his former friends and others in government, an all-male group: "a matter of state security" (168). This sphere of government is hence supposedly beyond the reach of mere citizens, whereas in truly "secure" states the citizenry keeps watch over a government that acts as a protector. In *not* telling the story of what has been done to Ikem, Major Ossai and the President take what Chris calls "a quiet *line*" (168, emphasis added), the term indicating his perception that theirs is a strategy of obfuscation. In response, he recognizes the urgency of telling the story[148]—and after Major Ossai's statement is broadcast, Chris will also set about telling *on* the power abusers (170–173). That this happens after Ikem's death does not make such broadcasting of a countering truth irrelevant.

By the time, deep into the novel, that readers encounter the recorded radio broadcast, they are in a position to decode the profoundly sensationalized and distorted "information" it contains—and to enquire into the roots of this particular story of the land. The voice of power that is so loud here is signposted by the capital letters that mimic the tone of "Authority" (41)—a "Special Announcement from the Directorate of State Research Council" (168)—and the exaggerated emphasis, the "protest[ing] too much" quality of the communication, indicates something of its basis in falsehood and fear. From the first occurrence of the words "Special Announcement" (168) to the second (169), the radio report is studded with terms and expressions claiming legitimacy, exploiting the status of officialdom,[149] and, mainly, displaying (supposedly entrenched) *power*. The one expression that encapsulates the claim (also in the sense of a *demand* on the citizenry to "hear and believe—and obey") is the recurrent phrase "security of the State" (168). Exactly like the ubiquitous expression "*Kabisa!*" (which is not even in a local language, but was taken over by Sam "from old Ngongo," the "President-for-Life," or aged dictator, in another African country—52–53), this phrase is merely meant to put a stop to all discussion, all questioning (1, 53). Its deepest irony is that it masks its origin in the very opposite of the "security" of Kangan and its citizenry. It originates from the most serious threat to their collective well-being, which is the deep *in*security of the President, personally as well as politically. Because Sam was never trained to be a politician and (more important) was never elected to his post, he is a deeply anxious man (5, 9, 14–25, 44–46, 49–53, 119, 143–245, 147)—open to the worst elements in his government,[150] who prey upon and manipulate his fears and turn him against the very people who might have helped (5, 14–25).

The bogus "conspiracy" outlined in the radio broadcast about Ikem's death is the threat that Sam in his paranoia (first fed by "President Ngongo's advice"—23—and further intensified by Okong, the Attorney-General, and Major Ossai) has imagined, feared, and wanted, and that Ossai has at last fabricated to "HE"'s satisfaction. That it also (ironically) creates the opening for Lango (in due course) to engineer both *their* downfall and his own power seizure (213, 218–219, 221) confirms that the elaborate displays of power grew from weakness—that Sam's government was a house of cards. The quality of posturing that characterizes Sam's personality and political regime[151] is what is being placated in the debased, James Bond/CIA thriller vocabulary (such as "key link"—169) of the official statement. It is meant to excite, with its combination of melodrama, reassurance (that all is "under control" now) and the titillation of "danger"—creating "villains" and "heroes." A ritual of appeasement is being concluded: Ikem is the first of the scapegoats whose slaughter Sam has been craving in order to "validate" (even more than to alleviate) his fear, which springs from unacknowledgeable self-doubt. Without Ikem pointing out the application, it is Sam who is the most extreme example in the novel of the "would be strong" in contrast with the "truly strong" (46). (Beatrice is the really "strong" person in this novel—230.)

Almost every detail in the broadcast calls to mind the "opposite" (truth), which is being belied here: the words, by their very inversion of Kangan realities, inadvertently call the ugly facts to mind. The masquerade of power is—simultaneously—an unintended self-exposure. Thus the accusation against "unpatriotic elements," supposedly "working in concert with certain foreign adventurers to destabilise the . . . country" (168), reminds the reader of "the Kangan/American Chamber of Commerce" (116) and its shady multimillionaire chairman, Alhaji Mahmoud, "ruthless" and "prince of smugglers," who is known to be "fronting" for the President himself (117)—as it does of the attractive American Lou Cranford ("of the American United Press"—74), who may be a CIA agent and whose exposure and exploitation of the "Mickey Mouse," neocolonial quality of Kangan and its President so incense Beatrice (78–81). Similarly, "incit[ement]" of students to "disaffection and rebellion" is what is done by the falsifying newspaper report (162) of Ikem's speech at the university and by the hooliganism and violence ("orgy of revenge") of the Kangan Mobile Police (173). Achebe uses what may be termed "syntactical sarcasm" to highlight this point, by having the broadcast statement end on the inadvertent absurdity of the reference to the country's "chosen path of orderly progress into renewed bloodshed and anarchy" (169).

So persuasive is the voice of power, though, that the reader needs to juxtapose the actual behavior of Ikem and his associates (as depicted elsewhere in the novel) with the plausibility of the ascription to them of all sorts of dastardly deeds—in order to *see* the distortions involved. The "plotters in Kangan" mentioned here (169) are Ikem, Chris, Beatrice, Elewa, and the Abazonian delegation; the "foreign collaborators" are the jolly, kindly MM and his effete British visitor Dick (54–62); Ikem's supposedly rabble-rousing speech was his urging of his student audience to examine their own lives as well as all assumptions and orthodoxies (153–162); and the supposedly "disgruntled and unpatriotic chiefs in . . . Abazon" are the benign, visionary old man and his supplicatory attitude to the power holders of the moment (122–128).

As Chris notices, the expression "fatally wounded" (169) is calculated to confuse, buying time for the tyranny to obscure the fact that Ikem is in fact dead and not merely injured. As he takes steps to counter this particular piece of disinformation (170—"make sure that people underst[and]"; 172–173) we see that this is a broader battle against "officialese" (36) in general, which legitimizes oppression and crime as the maintenance of social order.[152] Most personally and passionately, it matters to Chris "to counter the hideous lie" (170) with the truth about Ikem's integrity and commitment to improving the quality of national life in Kangan. As in *Things Fall Apart* with the killing of Ikemefuna (a youth whose name probably links the two figures), Ikem's shooting is a wanton deed damaging the communal psyche—a severing of the life of one of the brightest and most promising members of a society, a curtailment of its growth energy.

Ikem, BB, and Chris form a trio of friends and thinkers whom the novelist contrasts with the all-male "troika of proprietors who [imagine they] own Kangan itself" (202),[153] Sam and Chris and Ikem (cf. 66–67). For, of course, Sam soon decides—due to his jealous insecurity—that the other two are power contenders who need to be "shed." First Ikem, then Beatrice, and ultimately Chris experience rapid spurts of mental growth in the months or mere weeks of intensifying crisis in their country. That their advances in personal, social, and political understanding are forms of growth energy, wholesome and badly needed for the healing of this ravaged society, is shown in the way it extends their sympathies to people who had been, formerly, in one way or another, "beneath" their notice (or whom they had not encountered as full human equals from whom they—the educated ones—could learn).[154] All three become rapidly or gradually more attentive to spheres of social life with or within which they can form new alliances—a dimension of the experience of the three chief protagonists that Achebe maintains to the very end of the novel, without sentimentalizing these new connections or being naïvely blind about the obstacles that they have to surmount. A somewhat didactic, more overtly moralizing, trend is perhaps discernible from time to time in *Anthills of the Savannah*,[155] compared to his other novels, yet on the whole Achebe makes the discoveries—intellectual, even spiritual—of his three main characters *exciting* to his readers, as to those who are experiencing these advances in understanding.[156]

As an example of one such "transformation . . . in process" (said to be "of the man he was"—204—i.e., reaching to the depths of his being), some details of the description of Chris's fateful bus journey could be examined. The title of the bus (company?), "*Luxurious*" (200), marks it as an embodiment of relative social privilege in so poor a country[157]—yet so much better off than most is Chris that he "had never been inside a *Luxurious*."[158] The atmosphere he had lived in was that of farcical "cabinet meetings" (1–8) and the "hollow rituals" of cocktail parties—spheres of power for all their "vapidity" (204). Now, dwarfed by "The Great North Road" and its gigantic surrounding landscape, Chris becomes accessible to "the story of the land" (124) of a much more ancient and rugged kind—as it becomes possible for the landscape through which he is traveling to tell its own story. Even here, in transit between "the massive buildings of the new-rich down the coast" (206) and "the burning desolation" (209) farther north, Chris notices that what is being "told" by the landscape is the "*story* of two countries" (205, emphasis added). The "cushiony" sphere of wealth and abundance gradually wears away, exposing "the brown underlay." As the brittle cosmopolitanism of presidential parties is left behind, a kind of archaeology returns Chris's awareness to the mere "reddish earth" (206) of the walls of "thatched huts." It is not merely a sphere of "African simplicity" that now emerges, though, but an area of rural squalor dependent for water (which must be bought) on "tankers [which] have not come" (208). Sam's resentment against the Abazonians for voting against his longed-for "life presidency" led to his victimization of the area's inhabitants (by ordering the digging of boreholes to be suspended). This adds political insult to the injury effected by the drought—so the memory of the political victimization prompts Chris's sense of the outrageous absurdity of "security forces" at the border post. Now he asks (like Ikem earlier, in his denunciation of the Presidential Retreat—73): "Who or what were they securing? Perhaps [they are there, he adds sardonically] . . . to prevent the hungry desert from taking its begging bowl inside the secure borders of the [more prosperous] South" (209).[159]

This is one of the central images and insights of the novel: that power is threatened by need. Ikem's "Pillar of Fire: A Hymn to the Sun" (209, 30–33), which Chris now rereads, establishes the link between natural devastation and political oppression—only to end with the recognition that in a continent no longer empty, where crisis can no longer be "exported" by moving one's settlement to prey on strangers, "government" becomes the court of last resort, to which survival problems will be brought (33). Yet the worst, unfortunately *real* danger in an embattled society is of a power gone so insane that its subjects' very survival is disregarded. Such madness is illustrated in Ikem's pregnant phrase: "silt[ing] up the canals of birth in the season of renewal" (31). Sam has done exactly that in vindictively ordering a stop to the digging of boreholes in the drought-ravaged Abazon (127) and in imprisoning (and no doubt ordering the torture of)[160] the delegation from that province. The battering of the landscape by the sun, which brings these ideas to mind, links back not only to Ikem's analysis of oppression in his "Hymn" (30–33) but also to early details in the novel that first establish the symbolic link between Sam and the sun.[161]

The only things in the landscape that can withstand the devastation of the sun or the "brush fires" (31) are the anthills (31, 209, 211). That this is the novel's central symbol is signposted by its title, but the image also mediates so skillfully between the novel's two central myths[162] or "Pillar[s]" ("of Fire" and "of Water"—209, 102) that it needs to be recognized as Achebe's sign of a very particular alternative power (or alternative *to* power, its counter). The anthills indicate the stubborn earth; the quality of endurance that resists the assaults of power and its fierceness, being the merely basic element—so devoid of extraneity that it seems beneath the notice of power and its threats. The cunning skill of the novelist endows the symbol with another, more significant aspect, though. In his early reference to these earth fingers, Ikem writes of the "anthills surviving *to tell* the new grass of the savannah about last year's brush fires" (31, emphasis added). Beyond mere endurance, then, the anthills signify the powers of commemoration, linking them directly with the old Abazonian's ethos that "Recalling-Is-Greatest" (124). They "store" the knowledge of how ruination came about and stand to warn the next generations—they *are* "the story of the land" (124), expressed in the very earth of which they are made.

There is (still) more to the meaning of the anthills symbol: since they are small pillars of earth, these anthills call to mind the power and wonder of metaphor and of hope; both needed to (en)counter the horror and despair caused by the depredations of oppressive power use. This further reference can be traced in the chapter called "Daughters,"[163] in its first subsection, "Idemili," where the narrative voice is discussing the universe's only alternative to brute power, the Almighty's "daughter Idemili," sent to "bear witness, to the moral nature of authority."[164] Although her true incarnation is "the resplendent Pillar of Water" (102), humanity's need of this alleviation of Power is so intense that it has to

> ritualise [the] incongruity [between the vision of Idemili and her mere earthly embodiments] and by invoking the mystery of metaphor . . . hint at the most unattainable glory by its very opposite, the most *mundane starkness*—a mere stream, a tree, a stone, *a mound of earth*, a little *clay* bowl containing fingers of chalk.

> Thus it came about that the indescribable Pillar of Water fusing earth to heaven at the navel of the black lake became . . . *a dry stick rising erect from the bare earth floor.* (103, emphases added)

These "mound[s] of earth" clearly (like the other emphasized details) call the anthills symbol to mind. In the suggestion of the way the human imagination must transcend the ordinary or the dreadful to make living bearable, we are simultaneously reminded of the doomed, defeated Tortoise's brilliant, cunning, and tragic overcoming of mere obliteration by his leaving the marks of a titanic struggle before succumbing to defeat (128). The leopard of power will consume it, but the record is there, the creatively established[165] history that will "tell." Achebe's own sense that, despite defeat, another kind of power is involved (or achieved) even at a time of ruination, is captured in his resonant phrase, "the potency of lost causes" (218). The anthills tell, simultaneously, of the fires of destruction and of the waters of redemption.

That "telling" is not merely a "[comforter]" (65), however, any more than Beatrice is (or women are, despite the tendency in most societies to relegate them to secondary positions, as Ikem comes to realize—96–101). The words that signal BB's survival of thc suffering caused by Chris's and Ikem's deaths express the most intractable question of the novel—and of societies (like many in Africa) where a seemingly almost complete civic breakdown has occurred: "*What must a people do to appease an embittered history?*" (220, emphasis added). *This* seemingly implacable power (203, 220) looms hugely beyond the merely incidental, replaceable power mongers of the moment:[166] it presents the terrifying notion of a doomed nation caught in the downward spiral of social breakdown.

Yet, into that very question Achebe has built a sense of the possibility of revival.[167] First, it marks the "slow thawing" (219) of Beatrice's dull, frozen grief into the emollient tears of eventual understanding and appreciation of the "message" in Chris's death (232–233). That "coded" (231) insight (the last grin/green—230) itself conveys the message that defeat must be transcended. Chris himself, dying in great agony, *achieves* the insight by making the effort (for his friends' and the future's sake) to overcome pain. He sends his wry, self-forgetful, and ultimately "beautiful" message (233) to Beatrice and beyond. It is a reiteration of the point all three main characters had been learning, that "this world belongs to the people of the world[,] not to any little caucus"—not only a warning (232), as BB initially sees, but also an encouragement (he "died smiling"—233).

Second, Beatrice's portentous question ("What must a people do to appease an embittered history?"—220) recognizes a national task, an assignment to be undertaken (as the verbs "do" and "appease" indicate). Some of the modalities of such a task are indicated in the novel as needs and also as tentative achievements. What was in Ikem's experience a "rare human contact across station and class" (136) has become something much more definite (and, it is suggested, lasting) in the association of the small "band" (218) of survivors gathered around Beatrice (217) and under her "captain[cy]" (229).[168] In the quality of their association there are strong suggestions of participation in further struggle to counter the lies and cruelties of the powerful. Achebe also highlights, in many details in the last section of the novel, the sense of "furthering," of creative energies reemerging.

Elewa and Ikem's baby and the name she is given ("Amaechina: *May-the-path-never-close*"—222) form the novel's most vivid symbol of an enduring energy with the potential to achieve eventual transformation. It is, in fact, the thought that this "living speck" of Ikem (184) and Elewa's must be given the recognition of a name that first fills Beatrice with an influx of new energy (a "sudden inspiration"—217).

A parallel image of hopeful energy is captured in the references to a "defensive *pact* with a small *band* of near-strangers" (218, emphases added) who are "like *stragglers* from a massacred *army*" (217, emphases added) after their defeat by brutal power. Yet this is the "*remnant*" (cf. "residual"—217) which "shall-return" (222), the anthills still standing to tell the lessons of defeat to the future. Achebe highlights the idea of a regirding of the loins as an elevating, progressive energy[169] in details like the description of Beatrice ("one morning she *rose up*"—218, emphasis added); in the way her "return" "lit up" (220) her friends' faces; and in her "improvis[ation of] a ritual" (222). Beatrice chooses as a name for the baby the Igbo version of "hope that *springs* eternal" (222, emphasis added)—a description that is one of the "echoes from a bottomless *pit* of sadness" (270, emphasis added), since the deep well of BB's suffering has produced renewed concern and compassion. The burgeoning energies of the moment also find expression in the "ecumenical" dance of the women (224).

But Achebe adds a further, entirely unexpected influx of energy to the scene, in the arrival of Elewa's disreputable (224) uncle. Told that the naming of the baby, the task assigned to him as "surrogate father," has been fulfilled by BB and her "company" (229), he "explo[des]" into laughter, "dragg[ing] them all into his *bombshell* of gaiety" (226, emphasis added). He, too, is an anthill figure or a "remnant," come "[*to*] *tell* you people something" (226, emphasis added). His approving words register his understanding of the "company's" employment of the adaptive strategies of transformation—and the "powerful current" his presence generates (227) is a further image of energy. His wonderful prayer illustrates and expresses the morality of communal responsibility that lies at the heart of the novel.[170] The repeated injunction "May" (228) expresses a yearning or hope—yet it also lays down a duty (as BB understands).[171] In fact, the old man summarizes the postcolonial *malaise* as a diseased parochialism ("mak[ing] plans for themselves only and their families"—228), which could manifest itself in power cliques, class arrogance, or tribalism. Hence his prayer ends on the expanding circles of "Everybody's life!"; "The life of Bassa!"; and "The life of Kangan!" (229).

As representatives of modern, educated Africans near the top of the social ladder of their country, Ikem, Chris, and Beatrice are particularly appealing figures and in themselves hopeful signs that there *are* transformative, progressive energies at work even in countries like theirs, seemingly in the death grip of monstrous dictatorships. Perhaps the most interesting dimension of *Anthills of the Savannah* is, then, the subtle, underlying, but constant suggestion that even the finest members of society contribute in various ways to "the birth and grooming of . . . monster[s]" such as Sam becomes (10). That is why Chris's barely acknowledgeable indications of "responsibility" (10)[172] for Sam's transformation from imitation British gentleman to African dictator are picked up again in the ominous bus inscription ("*Ife onye metalu*—What a man commits"—202)[173] as he attempts to flee the wrath of the state on his doomed journey to Abazon. Similarly,[174] Ikem's rather self-congratulatory sense of being a man of and for "the people" in his "crusading editorial[s]" (43), although partly confirmed by the taxi drivers and the Abazonian delegation, is also called into question by his inability to recognize the taxi driver into whose face he had so officiously shone his torch (36–37, 135). He, too, is *in*sufficiently "connect[ed]" to earth and earth's people" (140–141).[175] Beatrice self-righteously and most uncharitably condemns her "paid help" (in her own snobbish phrase—83) for (supposedly) having "no single drop of charity in her own anaemic blood" (183), for being "desiccated" (183); yet when the memory of Ikem's appeal to "*you women*" (184) resurfaces in her mind, she, too, can offer a surprising, generous apology and be rewarded "through the mist of [Agatha's] tears, [with] a sunrise of smiles" (185).

Although the main focus in the novel seems to be on the elite, the depiction of the "small people"[176] (in the telling pidgin phrase—136, 150) of the society makes it a rich and dense work. The "heart" of the society is contaminated by what Ikem calls the "diseased tolerance" (138) it shows toward the privileged and the mighty.[177] One kernel of health it retains, though, is that "stubborn sense of community" (142), that solidarity of the lowly that Ikem notices, connecting Elewa and the taxi drivers. For "to succeed as small man no be small thing" (194), the privileged learn. The novel's final word goes to Elewa (233), encouraging Beatrice not to yield too far to grief.

Here, too, Achebe's sense that tragedy and devastation must be surmounted is brought to mind. The vision without which the people will perish is the aspiration "that there shall not be misrule" (Achebe, *Mapping,* 25). If this remains a hope, they live, but without it they will indeed die, reverting to that "red sunset" (216) into which Chris's murderer betakes himself. Without a "story," history is meaningless and induces despair. The last words in this chapter (spoken by the author shortly before the publication of *Anthills*) may go to Achebe himself. In contrast with dangerous, political power there is, he says: "another kind of power. The power of creation . . . the force that enables one thing to create another" (quoted in Petersen and Rutherford 161–162).

Notes

1. Compare his answer to a question given at the end of 1969: "Well, according to my own definition of protest, I *am* a protest writer. Restraint—well, that's my style, you see" (quoted in Lindfors, *Palaver,* 7).

2. Compare Achebe's essay "An Image of Africa: Racism in Conrad's *Heart of Darkness*" (*Hopes* 1–20) and his scornful quotation from what he terms "a colonialist classic, [John Buchan's] *Prester John,*" from which he takes the complacently racist statement: "That is the difference between white and black, the gift of responsibility" (*Morning* 11).

3. See also the first part of Ezenwa-Ohaeto's *Biography* of Achebe, on this point.

4. He is at last being given some recognition for this role, being named (in a field dominated by theorists) a prominent "postcolonial [critic]" in a 1997 work (Moore-Gilbert 4, 172–180).

5. For example, "Colonialist Criticism" of 1974 (*Morning* 3–18; repr. *Hopes* 68–90); "An Image of Africa: Racism in Conrad's *Heart of Darkness*" of 1975 (*Hopes* 1–20); and "Impediments to Dialogue Between North and South" of 1980 (*Hopes* 21–29).

6. See, for example, *Research in African Literatures* 23, no. 1 (Spring 1992), a collection of articles devoted mainly to the language-choice issue.

7. See the whole essay "The African Writer and the English Language" (*Morning* 55–62).

8. Compare Achebe's example of his evocation of Ezeulu's thoughts in English (quoted from p. 55 of the 1964 edition of *Arrow of God*) with the alternative, stilted, "un-Igbo-like" English version he concocts to make the point (*Morning* 61–62).

9. Achebe approvingly quotes Naipaul's "fellow Caribbean" Van Sertima's reference to Naipaul as being "overrated by English critics whose sensibilities he insidiously flatters by his stock-in-trade: self-contempt" (*Morning* 12), and at a later date Achebe refers to "the growing corpus of scornful work which Naipaul has written on Africa, India and South America." He also refers sarcastically to Naipaul as "this literary guru, a new purveyor of the old comforting myths of [the European] race" (*Hopes* 28).

10. He asserts:

> The narrow basis of realism, as an art that mirrors common-sense day or pigmented identity, tends inevitably to polarize cultures or to reinforce eclipses of otherness within legacies of conquest that rule the world. In so doing it also voids a capacity for the true marriage of like to like within a multi-cultural universe. (Harris 55)

11. For a recent example, see Veit-Wild, "Carnival and Hybridity," 555.

12. Compare: "Even those early novels that look like very gentle recreations of the past—what they were saying, in effect, was that we had a past. . . . There were people who thought we didn't have a past. What we (African writers) were doing was to say politely that we *did*—here it is" (Achebe, quoted in Lindfors, *Palaver,* 7).

13. Achebe's fellow Nigerian Kole Omotoso, who now lives and works in South Africa, has published a whole book *(Migration)* in which he explores essentially the same issue at some length.

14. Achebe refers to the "revolution" of assisting his society in "regain[ing] belief in itself" as combining his own and his people's "deepest aspirations" (*Morning* 44).

15. "The Journey of the Magi" by T.S. Eliot (Eliot 109–110)—primarily the lines "But no longer at ease here, in the old dispensation, / With an alien people clutching their gods" (110).

16. All page references to the 1986 Heinemann edition.

17. The landscape reference ("Hills and Caves"—12) presumably links Agbala with Ani, the earth goddess, or makes him a special part of her.

18. A further symbolically significant detail is the fact that the clan's most powerful protective "medicine" (8) is "called agbadi-nwaye, or old woman" and is supposedly *made from* "an old woman" (8–9).

19. It is made clear that mindless aggression is not likely to be approved and that ethical discrimination is applied (9).

20. "There is no document of civilisation which is not at the same time a document of barbarism." See Benjamin 248.

21. Contrast p. 79 ("really a woman's ceremony") as well as p. 97 ("when a woman dies . . . *there is no-one for whom it is well*") and p. 95 ("All the other men stood outside the circle, watching").

22. See the mocking discussion of the "absent mother" in the Christian trinity in the last three paragraphs on p. 105.

23. The victim's male relatives have intervened to protect her and bluntly warn the wife-beater that "if he ever beats her again we shall cut off his genitals for him" (66).

24. Compare Egejuru: "Okonkwo does not function as a singular hero or antihero (quoted in Lindfors, *Approaches,* 63; see 58–64: "The paradoxical characterization of Okonkwo").

25. Achebe himself said, "Okonkwo's extreme individualism leads to working against the will of the people and to self-destruction" (quoted in Lindfors, *Approaches,* 63).

26. On one occasion Achebe put it as strongly: "The society itself was already heading towards destruction . . . [its] internal problems . . . made it possible for the Europeans to come in" (quoted in Lindfors, *Approaches,* 58).

27. Okonkwo both "represents" *and* "misrepresents" the clan.

28. Achebe carefully establishes that although technically an accident, there is in Okonkwo a disposition toward such conduct. Earlier he "luckily" misses his wife Ekwefi at whom he fires his gun in fury. The fact that the dead youth is the son of the elder who had warned him against killing Ikemefuna "poetically" links the "accidental" with the deliberate killing. Thus, it *is* his own "chi" which has defeated him (in terms of Igbo cosmology—94, 110), but not (as he believes) unfairly. I thus strongly disagree with A.A. Elder's reference to the accidental killing as one of a number of "inexplicable misfortunes" (Lindfors, *Approaches,* 60). *At the symbolic level,* the event is no accident.

29. His references to Nwoye are memorably ugly and redolent of Okonkwo's gender neurosis: he calls Nwoye "degenerate and effeminate," "a woman for a son" (110).

30. Juxtapose his using authority to preserve family peace (31) with Okonkwo's knee-jerk "desire to conquer and subdue" (30).

31. Traoré provides the information (from Shelton) that Ikemefuna's name means "let my strength not become lost" and makes interesting comments on Ikemefuna and Okonkwo (in Lindfors, *Approaches,* 71–72).

32. Compare Traoré: "The mythic stories . . . offer variational paradigms of Okonkwo's gender imbalance and govern his abominable and nonepic acts" (Lindfors, *Approaches,* 69).

33. Nwoye's story of disaffiliation is matched by Okonkwo's telling his other sons that Nwoye "is no longer [his] son or [their] brother" (124).

34. The story is told at some length and in detail and placed almost exactly at the center of the novel.

35. Compare Achebe's pronouncements that "change was inevitable . . . [a] new force[, whereas] . . . Okonkwo just saw his duty to . . . stand against the assault. So he failed." Yet "as long as people are changing, their culture will be changing. The only place where culture is static . . . is the museum [which, he says] is not an African institution" (quoted in Lindfors, *Palaver,* 8, 5).

36. Compare Achebe's comments, e.g., quoted in Duerden and Pieterse 13 ("we gained a lot") and in Achebe, *Morning,* 65.

37. Compare the "stories about the white men" of "*powerful* guns" and "*strong* drinks," and the power to "[*take*] slaves away across the seas" (101, emphases added).

38. Yet Achebe earlier establishes a prior or additional cause of disintegration in Nwoye's shock at Ikemefuna's killing (43–44)—as he does in describing Okonkwo's "[leaving] hold of Nwoye" (109)—Nwoye having been (instead) entangled by the "chords" of Christianity (105). To be contrasted with Obierika's tragic awareness (126–127) is Okonkwo's shallower and more selfish perspective on the clan's "falling apart" (131).

39. Carroll silently omits *No Longer at Ease* from his list, without acknowledging the exception!

40. "He . . . *appeared* unruffled and indifferent. The proceeding *seemed* to be of little interest to him" (1, emphases added).

41. The novel was published in 1959. Nigeria gained independence in 1960. Numerous references in the text indicate its author's concern that its contemporaneity should be recognized. (References throughout are to the 1963 Heinemann edition.)

42. G. Adali-Mortty, quoted in Ezenwa-Ohaeto, *Biography* (69).

43. E.g., Killam, Carroll, Palmer, Gakwandi, Irele, Omotoso.

44. This "unmasking" (the revelation that *white* power can be overthrown) "inverts" a key event near the end of *Things Fall Apart* (133), suggesting that change requires the shattering of awe at old power forms.

45. "If you see a white man, take off your hat for him. The only thing he cannot do is mould a human being" (12). Compare the English influences permeating Umuofia (7, 45).

46. "You are not paid to think, Mr. Omo, but to do what you are told. Is that clear?" (59).

47. So identified by Wren, I think correctly (*Achebe's World* 38).

48. Green propounds his theory while being served efficiently by African waiters (3). See also his sneering "And you tell me you want to govern yourselves" (139) and his tirades against "educated Nigerians" (95, 106).

49. At a later time Achebe would refer more explicitly to "one of the . . . manifestations of under-development . . . [as] the *cargo cult* mentality that anthropologists" mention (*Trouble,* 9—cf. also 11, 13, 59, 63).

50. Contrast the Umuofians' acknowledging that "it is money, not work" that brought them to Lagos (72—cf. 106).

51. His question to Obi is, "Have *they given* you a job yet?" (29, emphasis added). Compare "Colonialism produced the state structure and nationalism; but [such] nationalism . . . merely reproduces . . . (neo)colonialisms" (Ogundele 130). As Wren noted, *No Longer at Ease* "becomes a parable of modern Nigeria" (*Achebe's World* 38).

52. The beautifully unobtrusive echo of the wrestling image should be noted.

53. Compare: "selfless leadership . . . will radiate . . . through . . . national life" (Achebe, *Trouble,* 17).

54. For example, Carroll, Innes, Ravenscroft, and Gakwandi, to name only a few. Gikandi's chapter on *No Longer at Ease* in *Reading Chinua Achebe* is by far the most sophisticated. He refers to "Achebe's generation" attempting "to invent a Nigerian nation and a Nigerian national consciousness from amorphous and unstable entities arbitrarily yoked together by the coloniser" (Gikandi, *Reading Chinua Achebe,* 80). Obi, says Gikandi rightly, "cannot completely dissociate himself from the colonial culture which he has inherited from his father, nor can he totally identify himself with the Igbo culture of his ancestors" (*Reading Chinua Achebe* 98).

55. The Onitsha traders' Igbo song (42) proclaims a disintegrating society of which "English[ness]" is the marker; in contrast, "The Song of the Heart" (117), sung by the young village women in Umuofia, in English, enshrines the integrative principle of loyalty, articulated by the educated (literate) members of the clan. The second song seems to point the (right) way.

56. When Obi stays with Joseph in Lagos before leaving for England, "political meetings" are mentioned (12), though none portrayed; on his return visit after just under four years he finds out that Joseph no longer attends any. In the cabinet minister Okoli we see someone well "dressed" and "eligible" (33) and vulgarly nouveau riche (61–62), but politically shallow-minded.

57. To adapt Benedict Anderson's famous phrase.

58. As distinct from the public, institutional sphere of formal "politics."

59. Gikandi is the one critic who begins to touch on Clara's significant role, but he does not develop the point, leaving it a critical "hunch" (*Reading Chinua Achebe* 92 and "Location" 10–11). Thus he notes, "And yet there is a sense in which marrying Clara would have been the apotheosis of Obi's desire for a Nigerian space," but undercuts the idea by adding, "At the end of the novel, we come to realize that these are not real options" ("Location" 11).

60. Obi's second poem about Nigeria (94, 136) is, though still naïvely idealistic, considerably more aware of Nigerian political and even geographic realities than his vaguely "romantic" first one (14–15). Tellingly, the second poem, with its overt reference to the need to "build" "unity" in the "noble fatherland" by overcoming divisions of "region, tribe or speech," alludes delicately but unmistakably also to intratribal (one might say "class") divisions such as the ostracism of the *osu* members of the Igbo people. Obi rereads the poem on both occasions after breakups with Clara, crumpl[ing] it the second time (137), when the abortion has occurred.

61. Contrast Achebe's (pressured!) confession, in an interview, that "there is something of Obierika [from *Things Fall Apart*] in Achebe," because Obierika is, in contrast with Okonkwo, "more subtle" (quoted in Jeyifo, *Resilience,* 57).

62. Both stories appear in the 1972 Heinemann collection *Girls at War and Other Stories* (20–28, 35–40). Innes (*Chinua Achebe* 121–133) is one of the few critics to have mentioned the connection between the short story (about Chike) and the novel (121–123), though she makes less of it than I do.

63. See especially Gikandi's *No Longer at Ease* chapter (*Reading Chinua Achebe* 78–100) for an eloquent and learned presentation of these arguments. On being told by

Achebe (in an interview) that the author thought *No Longer at Ease* "better, technically" than his first novel, the critic Lewis Nkosi demurred: "Most of us," he said, consider "the texture of the writing [of *Things Fall Apart*] . . . so much more . . . syntactically finished" (quoted in Duerden and Pieterse 4).

64. See "nothing in him"; "the periphery and not the centre" (124).

65. Compare the scene where Obi manages to blot out the thought of his "responsibilities" *to his parents* with sensual memories ("shapely"; "succulent") of Clara, which both ignore his responsibility *to her* and reduce her human worth to the level of mere gratification (55).

66. Contrast the earlier suggestions of social change achieved by the overthrowing and unmasking of "ancestral spirits," both in *Things Fall Apart* (133) and in this novel (58).

67. If we consider T.S. Eliot's "The Journey of the Magi," from which Achebe took the title of this novel, it is relevant at this point to recall that the "[un]ease" of the returned magi is caused by their enduring commitment to Christianity in a context where their own people are still "clutching their [old] gods" (Eliot 110). Obi, by contrast, does not dare tell his father (who yet no doubt senses it) that he is no longer a Christian believer and is "faith-less."

68. Both parents seem to have subliminally feared that Obi might have found a "white" wife in England (see 48), as his father's leprosy analogy (121—compare *Things Fall Apart* 53) and his mother's dream details of "white cloth" and "white termites" (122) indicate. That Clara is, then, a "fellow" Igbo and African exposes the fierceness of the rejection as all the more "uncharitable" (130) in terms of their Christian morality.

69. Contrast Obi's very "English," coolly detached tone here with the anguish in the voice of another African, Shakespeare's Othello, who also betrays his beloved: ". . . yet the pity of it, Iago! O Iago, the pity of it, Iago!" (4.1.191–192, Arden ed.).

70. See, e.g., 33, 60, 61, 84, 90, 127–128, 134–135, 137—ending with the first briber's "new model Chevrolet" (151) and finally the "police van" (154) in which Obi is driven away. The expression "greatness is now in the things of the white man" (49) is clearly recalled when the "shining élite" is referred to as "an exclusive club" of "car" owners (90).

71. In this she contrasts, of course, with Obi, who has his little flirtations "on the side."

72. I disagree with Gakwandi's (not uncommon) position that Obi's "dilemma does not move us deeply because the author fails to convey any deep human anguish or struggle" (35).

73. As they know from Joseph's letter (123).

74. The allusion in "defectors and loyalists alike" is to the fact that the grandson (Achebe's father) "joined the missionaries" as one of the early Igbo converts, whereas the grandfather (who had brought up the orphaned Isaiah Achebe) remained true to the faith of the clan—although the old man "raised [no] . . . serious objections to the younger's conversion to Christianity. [For, adds Achebe,] perhaps like Ezeulu he thought he needed a representative in their camp" (Achebe, *Morning,* 66). This quotation clearly suggests some parallels between the supposedly unwritten part of the Igbo story and events in *Arrow of God*, as I argue below. The terminology ("defectors and loyalists") also clearly links with Achebe's Preface to the revised edition of this novel, discussed in detail later in this section. For a reading rather different from mine (of the same allusions), see the piece by Griffiths ("Chinua Achebe: When Did You Last See Your Father?"). In a later interview Achebe identified his father's guardian as the fa-

ther's "uncle [not grandfather] on his mother's side . . . a very powerful man who had taken some of the highest titles in the community" (G. Lewis 186–187).

75. Compare Achebe's reference to how "control and stability were totally smashed, and African people steadily lost the ability to control and sustain their world" (Achebe, "Uses," 12).

76. In the same interview Achebe refers to "our legitimate distinctiveness" (i.e., that of African literature), which lies, among other things (he believes), in being "more ready [than the average European or American writer] to assume a social purpose without embarrassment" (Achebe, "Uses," 9).

77. An authoritative anthropological account like Victor Uchendu's richly confirms the accuracy of Achebe's depiction. Even a detail like the use of dogs to maintain hygiene in a hut where there is a sick baby (*Arrow* 90–91) is confirmed by Uchendu (31, 61).

78. "Ezeulu . . . is a different kind of man from Okonkwo. He is an intellectual . . . so he goes into things, to the roots of things, and he's ready to accept change, intellectually. He sees the value of change and therefore his reaction to Europe is different, completely different, from Okonkwo's. He is ready to come to terms with the new—up to a point—except where his dignity is involved. This he could not accept; he is very proud. . . . The tragedy is that they come to . . . the same sort of . . . end. So there's really no escape. . . . But if you take a long view of society, you will see . . . that society is, in fact, adjusting. Because life must go on, no matter what we say" (quoted in Duerden and Pieterse 16–17; compare also Lindfors, *Palaver,* 8–9). The relevant passages from the novel are *Arrow* 45, 84–85.

79. Because this 1974 edition was revised by the author, it is the text used throughout this section.

80. Achebe's father (to whom this novel is dedicated) can be seen as a figure akin to Oduche (Ezeulu's Christian son)—to link with the quotation cited in note 74. Achebe himself there links Ezeulu with his own father's grandfather (the guardian who raised Achebe's father).

81. This humanist perspective of course contrasts with many presentations of Jewish and Christian belief, though some Christian theologians do acknowledge that people make gods in their own images and in order to serve their own purposes, afterwards claiming preexistence, eternity, or omnipotence for their gods.

82. In an interview, Achebe refers to Ezeulu's "priestly arrogance" as "show[ing] from time to time, like when he's confusing his thinking with the thinking of the god" (quoted in Lindfors, *Palaver,* 9). Another interesting interpretative comment by the author on *Arrow of God* (focusing on its ending) is reprinted in Ezenwa-Ohaeto, *Biography* (178–179).

83. Compare Clarke's fury at "the proud inattention of this fetish priest" (174) and Captain Winterbottom's "rage and frenzy" at the reply he gets from "the self-important fetish priest" (149)—both descriptions combining "intended" contempt with unwilling respect.

84. Achebe's fascination with and appreciation of this form of Igbo opportunism and advance are shown in the recurrence of "carpenter Moses" (*No Longer at Ease* 118) from the previous novel *and* in another vague echo in the author's most recent novel (*Anthills of the Savannah* 109), which mentions "a certain carpenter/comedian" and refers again to "barely literate carpenters . . . mak[ing] straight [Beatrice's] way" in later times. See also *A Man of the People* 87–88.

85. After his release from the guardroom in Okperi, Ezeulu believes that he has "settled his little score with the white man" (175) and that "for the moment his real

struggle [is] with his own people," even that "the white man [is], without knowing it, his ally" (176). Compare the later exaggeration of these misconceptions (192).

86. He features early in the novel but is initially identified only as "Winterbottom's [efficient] servant John" (30–31). He tells Winterbottom of the whipping of Obika by Wright (106), but that information is overridden by the lie in Clarke's report, that "there was no truth in all the stories of Wright whipping natives." Hence the British "club" (32) together despite the evidence of "a native of Umuaro," with Clarke absurdly claiming the authority of "the man on the spot" (106).

87. Uchendu confirms Achebe's suggestion that this ambitious attitude is "typically" Igbo and precedes the incursion of "Western" capitalism: "If you ask the Igbo why he believes the world should be manipulated, he will reply, 'The world is a marketplace and it is subject to bargain'" (15).

88. Such as the references to the incursions of strangers by means of "internal" assistance (98–99, 132, 137); the image of bringing ant-ridden faggots into the home (59, 132, 144); the image of assisting an enemy's demolition of a house (85, 213); and the proverb of the lizard ruining his own mother's funeral (230).

89. Such as "thought of his revenge"; "now the fight must take place" (160); "I want to wrestle with my own people . . . strip him of his anklet" (179)—compare also 175–176, 182, 191–192.

90. Compare the "tying of the blood-knot between Edogo and John Nwodika" (168).

91. Compare "Ulu who saved them" (201) and "it is for you, Ezeulu, to save our harvest" (207).

92. His grandfather stopped the practice of facial scarification (as a test of manliness) and his father the custom that children born after their father's death were declared slaves.

93. Contrast the bellicose tone of the words here ascribed by Ezeulu to Ulu ("the saver"!), with the strategically placed "song of responsibility" (186–187; first printed on p. 124), sung by a child in a caretaking role. Compare Achebe's own comment quoted in note 82. In the novel, details on pp. 182 ("elation") and 204 ("glowed with happiness") show Ezeulu savoring a private triumph at the expense of his people.

94. It is emphasized that the box is one of the new artifacts characteristic of the new religion (43, 50).

95. Early in the novel Ezeulu comments sardonically that *if* the Christian bell is saying, "Leave your yam . . . and come to church" (42), "then it is singing the song of extermination" (43)—ironically this will be the "song" *he* "sing[s]" toward the end of the novel. The deftly inserted parallel between the clan's situation (or Ezeulu's strategy) and the Russian peasants' self-destructive boycott strategy against a new regime (180) is to be noted.

96. Like Akukalia (16–24), Ezeulu feels himself taunted with "impotenc[e]" by Nwaka—and like Akukalia, Ezeulu resorts to a form of desecration to get his own back, (also) getting himself destroyed in the process.

97. The children's song evidently recalls the "irreverent twist" given to the ancient funeral dirge by Nweke Ukpaka (81).

98. Ezeulu here implicitly acknowledges the point made by Ezidemili, "that Ulu was made by our fathers long ago [as a political founding myth]. But Idemili was there at the beginning of things. Nobody made it" (41). Idemili represents the originary *identity* myth of the people.

99. Obika's is distinctly a sacrificial death: he undertakes what he knows to be an overtaxing assignment to protect his father's name (224–225).

100. Achebe contrasts Ezeulu clearly with the uncomprehending and unscathed Winterbottom: "The gods and the powers of event . . . had used [Winterbottom] and left him again in order as they found him" (230).

101. Compare: "When a man as proud as this wants to fight he does not care if his own head rolls as well in the conflict" (213).

102. Ezeulu's protest against the suggestion that *he* is desecrating the clan should be remembered: "Who brought the white man here? Was it Ezeulu?" (131).

103. The poetry collection *Beware, Soul Brother and Other Poems* was first published in 1971. A revised and enlarged edition was published by Heinemann in 1972. Heinemann first published the short stories as *Girls at War and Other Stories* in 1972.

104. As general editor of the Heinemann African Writers Series and as editor of the scholarly journal *Okike*, which concentrated on the publication of African writing. For an interesting and comprehensive documentation of this period in Achebe's life, see Ezenwa-Ohaeto, *Biography* (105–265).

105. Gikandi *(Reading Chinua Achebe)* makes much of this; Wren is good on linking *A Man of the People* with Nigerian circumstances at the time.

106. Such as Niven and Maughan-Brown in their essays, both published in the 1991 collection *Chinua Achebe: A Celebration* (Petersen and Rutherford 41–50, 139–148 respectively).

107. References throughout the discussion are to the 1988 Heinemann edition of the text.

108. See, for example, Nwachukwu-Agbada (119–120); or Achebe, *Hopes,* 104; or Lindfors, *Palaver,* 8.

109. In a recent review by a political scientist of four books that discuss "the contemporary African state," this comment of Odili's is quoted as summarizing the "pathologies deriv[ing] from the . . . exogeneity of the state . . . [such as p]atterns of predation" (Englebert 768).

110. Even the most sophisticated of Achebe's critics sometimes seem to miss this crucial point. Hence Gikandi writes of commentaries on *No Longer at Ease* that "critics of the novel have not always found mechanisms of engaging Obi as subject"—the same being largely true of Odili in *A Man of the People*—whereas earlier in his chapter this critic himself writes that "this novel does not arouse any passion for meaning; the tone adopted by the narrator . . . is one of boredom or cynicism" (Gikandi, *Reading Chinua Achebe,* 97, 91). On the contrary, Achebe continually challenges his readers to find the subtle clues to his complex, balanced evaluations of societies and of individuals' roles in them.

111. Achille Mbembe in a recent essay sees this issue in terms reminiscent of Achebe's 1966 presentation: "In Africa and elsewhere . . . [p]ower and servitude . . . exist as an ensemble of socially sanctioned . . . superstitions" ("Prosaics" 144–145). In an earlier essay he writes that "an intimate tyranny links the rulers with the ruled" (Mbembe, "Provisional," 25).

112. Compare a similarly allegorical use of the same image in *Arrow of God,* where the attendants on the "Mask . . . [which] stood for the power and aggressiveness of youth," "did not leave the Mask free too long" (199).

113. Compare a detail from Achille Mbembe's essay "Provisional Notes on the Postcolony": "the mouth, the belly and the penis constitute the classic ingredients of *commandement* [authority] in the postcolony" (23). Compare also *The Politics of the Belly,* the subtitle of J.-F. Bayart's *The State in Africa* (first published in 1989).

114. These would include actual legislation, rules of social conduct, and the alertness to measure the conduct of power holders against such norms.

115. Terence Ranger, in *Postcolonial Identities in Africa*, quotes a commentator referring to central Africans living in "a world that is falling apart" and then wryly highlights the Achebean echo—which has continued its relevance from "the coming of colonialism" even into "post-colonialism" (273).

116. Images of eating (to represent greed, opportunism, or parasitical attitudes) recur throughout the novel. Associated with Nanga are "the meaty prize" (7); the cliché of the "national cake" (12, 134); "flesh-pots" (74); and "eat Nanga's wealth" (88). Associated with Edna's father are the reference to his "enormous, shining stomach" (89); his words "I will eat until I am tired" (91); his "prayer about bringing and eating" (92); and his tick and bull anecdote (106). From "the people" we get "we are eating too" (124); "eaten . . . reach the plate" (125); "let them eat" (144); and Odili's description of an "eat-and-let-eat regime" (149).

117. Compare also on the same page (as if the author is making sure the point is not missed): "bourgeois privileges of which the car was the most visible symbol in our country" (109). One other (among a number of examples) occurs early on, when Odili's father urges him "to leave 'this foolish teaching,' and look for a decent job in the government and [to] buy [him]self a car" (31). Another relevant quotation is Nanga's deliberately ambiguous reference to "a *strategic* post in the civil service" (12, emphasis added).

118. Since Odili has been read as an altogether unreliable and even unpleasant protagonist (see especially Palmer, also Carroll, as examples—and to some extent Gikandi, *Reading Chinua Achebe*), it is worth recording Achebe's own express(ed) approval of him at this point. He refers to Odili as "basically honest" because he "admitted that [his] motives were not very pure" and says he "suffered in this kind of society because it was very cruel, very ruthless. But he was learning very fast, and . . . improved his chances of being of service" by the end (quoted in Lindfors, *Palaver,* 9–10).

119. The people are, as we saw, "even more cynical than their leaders" (144).

120. In the contrast between this attempt to *cope* economically and the prime minister's mere swindle of having "fifteen million pounds" "print[ed]" (3), there may well be an ironic reminder of the moral contrast highlighted in the Scouts' motto, "*Not what I have but what I do is my kingdom*" (3).

121. Primitivity is conspicuously emphasized by Achebe in the animal images employed by Odili ("pack of back-bench hounds," "yelp," "hungry hyena"—5) as well as by the booing, stoning, and violent attacks—on the targeted ministers—to which the mobs resort (5).

122. For example, "'That's all they care for,' he said with a solemn face. 'Women, cars, landed property. But what else can you expect when intelligent people leave politics to illiterates like Chief Nanga?'" (76).

123. Besides the main, pointed image (37), the title of the "Minister of Public Construction" (42) draws attention to the nation-building idea (he allows, of course, shoddy construction—42–43); "a new cement factory" is "built with American money" (47); "the Minister of Construction" profits by renting houses to embassies (54); Max's poem proposes to "rebuild" the "black mother['s] house" (81); Nanga builds a "new house" of "four storeys" in the village—"a 'dash' from [a] European building firm" (96); he also "built out of his gains three blocks of seven-storey luxury flats" (99); whereas Odili is "barred" from the Anata school hall (101). By contrast, Nanga's political "platform [is] solidly built from new timber" (136). On Odili, blows fall like "rain" (140), and Max's shade would, but for Eunice, have "been waiting still, in the rain and out in the sun" (148).

124. Compare the "loudspeakers" (35) urging the people "to support [the] great national effort" of buying "Our Home Made Stuff" (35)—whereas the ministers mer-

rily continue luxuriating by means of imported goods (ironized in the "poisoning" incident—33–35).

125. Compare Odili's justification (under the "influence" of luxury): "We ignore man's basic nature if we say, as some critics do, that because a man like Nanga has risen overnight from poverty and insignificance to his present opulence he could be persuaded without much trouble to give it up again and return to his original state" (37). Even Nanga now justifiably calls Odili "lazy boy" (38). He "reads about" the city's bucket-borne sewerage system "from the cosy comfort" of Nanga's "mansion" (40–41), describes himself as "bravely doz[ing] in [his] chair" after overeating (43), and sits back in Nanga's Cadillac "with a proprietary air"! (58).

126. The comment recalls and contrasts with the earlier moment when Odili first "fell for" Nanga's blandishments: "I was dazed. Everything around me . . . became . . . unreal; the voices receded" (9), a description that emphasizes the *spell* of power.

127. Compare his earlier "Good Heavens" and "My word!" (70), which hardly constitute a flood of condemnation.

128. Contrast Jalio the author who, despite being insultingly criticized by Nanga (62), "[says] many flattering things about Chief Nanga" and adds bogus praise (63), even asking Nanga for a copy of his speech (65). The newspaper editor (65–66) behaves even more nauseatingly in his combination of placation and blackmail toward Nanga.

129. To quote more fully the statement from which the epigraph to this section was taken (Achebe, *Mapping,* 25).

130. "Some people's belly is like the earth. It is never so full that it will not take another corpse. God forbid" (85–86) is one expression of outrage, though from a slightly suspect source.

131. Odili points out that this is a parody of "the will of the whole people" (86): "If the whole people had taken the decision why were they now being told of it?" (124).

132. Odili's occasionally "wobbly" English has often been noted and understood (e.g., by Innes and Gikandi) as a sign of the great care of the author's portrayal of this protagonist.

133. I suggest the seemingly irrelevant reference to a "worm expeller" (26) could be linked with the symbolic working of these images. There is a comic but also symbolic equivalent in the anecdote of Nwege (representing corrupt and inefficient rule) "cascading down a steep slope [recalling Odili's reference to 'those who had started the country off down the slopes of inflation'—2] that led to a narrow bridge at the bottom of the hill," on a direct collision course with a "lorry." The only "solution" in this situation is expressed in the cyclist's cry: "Push me down. . . . Push me down" (13)—that is, expel the bad leaders.

134. Achebe refers to an "aura of cosmic sorrow and despair," which he feels characterizes Armah's famous 1969 novel, *The Beautyful Ones Are Not Yet Born,* as "foreign," "scornful, cold and remote" (*Morning* 25–26).

135. Even this man's *prayer* is "avaricious" (and brusquely "short") (92)!

136. "I realised that I must go back, seek out Nanga's intended parlour wife and give her the works, good and proper" (76).

137. Not that he quite understands the source of his upsurge of courage! For he says, "It was as though I was drunk—with what I couldn't say" (104).

138. Not least because Edna notices and protests against Odili's lingering condescension, shown in his (revealing and ill-considered) reference to her as "a little girl" (146).

139. Mrs. Nanga (see her "let her come and eat Nanga's wealth"—88, and the detail of the "luxury flats" registered in her name—99); Mrs. John (15—to be linked with 99, where we learn that Nanga had been minister of foreign trade); Elsie; and "Barrister Mrs. Akilo" (47 and 127).

140. One such "coloring" is Odili's decision (147–148) to use the C.P.C. party funds left in his hands to "buy off" Nanga's claims to Edna (in which he may *seem* to be following Edna's father's advice—106) and in his plan "to found a school" (which may make him seem another Mr. Nwege). Yet the similarities are superficial and the differences profound.

141. All references to the 1987 Heinemann edition, published in London.

142. Wole Soyinka in 1996 (after the execution of Ken Saro-Wiwa and others) wrote in an impassioned plea to the international political community of conditions in Nigeria under the Abacha regime, which he saw as characterized by "blatant, unrepentant defiance of civilised society"; "a national haemorrhage"; "leadership dementia"; and "the death-knell of that nation" (Soyinka, *Open Sore,* 152–153). Compare the reference, toward the end of *Anthills* (1987), to "the deepening crisis in the country" (219), or Ikem's choice of the word "cannibals" (150) to refer to Sam's security forces.

143. The setting of the novel in Kangan and (mainly) Bassa is not merely a thinly veiled allusion to Nigeria and its capital city, Lagos, but suggests that Achebe draws our attention to the way events like those depicted in his novel occur elsewhere in Africa as well.

144. Contrast the jeering Afro-cynicism expressed by the rapist police sergeant in Abazon—"A whole President de miss. . . . This Africa na waa!" (A whole President gone missing. . . . This Africa is a crazy place!) (213).

145. Some of the "monst[rosities]" (10) of Sam's reign by terror are illustrated or alluded to in details dispersed throughout the narrative (14, 39–42, 57, 70, 72, 106, 107, 119, 127, 147, 163, 165–166, 173, 176).

146. Achebe distinguishes between those "fictions" that are beneficent and those that harm people (such as the "fictions" of racism and of sexism) in his essay "The Truth of Fiction" (*Hopes,* 95–105).

147. The irresponsible, drunken police sergeant (later a would-be-rapist and a killer) is called a "story-teller" on p. 212 as he justifies the theft (the "commandeering") of the beer on the delivery truck.

148. He says he "must embark on a massive publicising of the abduction." Chris first mentions the resource of "foreign news agencies." Although Kangan radio, television, and the *National Gazette* are (all now) in the hands of the oppressors, he knows that locally he can rely on the enormous *potential* of that great network he nicknames "VOR, the Voice of Rumour, the *despair of tyrants* and shady dealers in high places" (168, emphasis added). Here, then, expression of public opinion is a resource *against* tyranny, uncontainable, opposing "the cheapening of cruelty," in Gordimer's fine phrase (79).

149. See "duty . . . safeguarding . . . lawful government . . . government-owned . . . top security officers of the SRC . . . the government and the life of His Excellency the President and the peace and security of the State . . . security officers effected the arrest . . . official . . . Government Reservation . . . military vehicle . . . SRC headquarters . . . His Excellency . . . appointed a high-level inquiry . . . headed by the Chief of Staff, Major-General . . . directive . . . report . . . proceeding . . . uncover . . . bring to book . . . chosen path of orderly progress . . . Republic of Kangan . . . Colonel . . . Director of the State Research Council" (168–169).

Compare Prof. Okong applying the term "Rebellion" (18) to the vote of no (to Sam's bid for life-presidency) brought out by the Abazonians. Okong is given a key cabinet appointment because Chris initially believes that his "cliché[s]" and "phrasemongering" (11) will stand Sam's government in good stead and help to "sell" it (11–13). How soon such a "talent" will turn poisonous under a dictator's pressure is shown on pp. 14–20. Compare Achebe's own comments on the dangers of debased language, quoted in the second half of note 152.

150. Compare a passage in which Fanon writes with great scorn that "the ranks of decked-out profiteers whose grasping hands scrape up the bank-notes from a poverty-stricken country will sooner or later be men of straw in the hands of the army, cleverly handled by foreign experts" (*Wretched* 140).

151. See "game"—1; "disguising"—2; "on the cover of *Time*"—15; "*it's not done*"—49; "basically an actor"—50; "mask-face"—523; "his act"—53; "play"—146; "*appearing*"—147.

152. See "orderly" (169); "properly and constitutionally" (143); yet again "the security of this state" (143); and what Chris later terms Sam's "threat to do things constitutionally" (145).

In a 1981 interview Achebe said: "The language of a man is . . . the best guide . . . to his character. If you don't listen carefully enough, then all kinds of charlatans and demagogues will steal the show, which is . . . happening not only in Nigeria" (quoted in Innes 173).

153. This is a slightly distorted echo of Beatrice's way of pointing out the blasphemous arrogance of power by referring to "the trinity who thought they owned Kangan" (191).

154. Compare Ikem's talking over Elewa's head and packing her off home (where she is unlikely to have a bathroom) while he luxuriates in a hot shower (34–36); BB and Chris ignorant of Elewa's surname (167), as Chris is of his steward's (192), as well as Beatrice's condescending attitude toward Agatha.

155. Might one say, the novelist as preacher? In the opinion of David Carroll: "This is the least successful part of the novel. They have to learn too much too quickly" (*Novelist* 184).

156. Compare the use of interventionist narrative devices such as "and do you know what?" (184), or references to "elation" (136) and "exhilaration" (140), to "the lifting of his spirits" (206) and to "the prodigious passions of that extraordinary day" (232).

157. It is referred to (by Chris) as a "termagant," "recklessly" "bullying every smaller vehicle" (205)—a clear image of oppression.

158. Many details in the novel function to link the idea of the isolation (from the mass of humanity and the deprivation of their circumstances) of the privileged, with their ownership of technology (e.g., the "Flit" Braimoh's family cannot afford—200; the taxi driver's reference to the "big man" who "put him air conditioner and forget we"—136; Ikem's "hot shower"—38; and the "smooth, precious carapace" of the "owner-driver['s]" car body—29). The culminating passage occurs in Ikem's impassioned denunciation of "the Presidential Retreat": "Retreat from what? From whom? . . . From the people and their basic needs" (73). Compare Fanon's reference to "the national middle class . . . disappear[ing] . . . shocking[ly] into the . . . traditional bourgeoisie" (*Wretched* 120–121).

159. Clearly recalled here is the delegation of Abazonians who arrive at the Presidential Palace during the cabinet meeting, when the opening of a window allows the "surg[ing]" in of "a violent wave of heat and the sounds of a chanting multitude," resembling a "storm" (8–9).

160. The reference in the horrifying television broadcast to their having made "useful statements" (151) to the secret police clearly hints at this.

161. For example, "the fiery sun retires temporarily" (3); "the sun in April is an enemy" (despite what radio broadcasters say!—27); "you will not relent . . . from compassion" (30); "government" (33); "the sun's heat came down so brutally" (39); and the reference to "the sun's routine oppression . . . [becoming a *directed*] vindictiveness," a "reprisal" against those who fail to act as "decreed" (181).

162. "Ikem's male myth of the sun, . . . 'The Pillar of Fire: A Hymn to the Sun,' . . . is a myth of the arrogance and cruelty of naked power. . . . Against it is set the female myth of Idemili, 'The Pillar of Water,' . . . reminder of 'the moral nature of authority'" (Innes 156–157).

163. For quotes from and comments on Boehmer's essay, see note 168. Gordimer, in her essay on *Anthills of the Savannah,* expresses deep appreciation of the depiction in it of the role of modern African women (86–93). In contrast, both Sougou and Ezenwa-Ohaeto in their essays mention and give full references to critiques of Achebe's placing of women in his fiction generally and of what is thought to be a not altogether successful attempt at "atonement" by his centralizing of Beatrice in *Anthills*; Sougou drawing attention to Amadiume's criticism of Achebe's "subjugating" the goddess Idemili to a he-god father (Sougou 5–54; Ezenwa-Ohaeto 29–31, 34). It might be pointed out, though, that Achebe is deliberately both echoing *and changing* the Christian figure of Jesus, the male savior, to a female intercessor in his, partly reoriginating, mythology. It is notable that in *Arrow of God* (see "*his* priest," 41, emphasis added) Idemili is gendered male by Achebe. For Amadiume's political and theological centralization of Idemili, see her *Reinventing Africa* (e.g., 18–19).

164. Again the importance of "telling," of proclamation, articulation, expression; communication of ideas is brought to mind—a central energy of change.

165. The expression "*benign mischief*" (125) used by the Abazonian elder not only tolerates, but approves, the exaggeration of heroism in (hi)story telling (125, 128) and its "harm[less]" "lies" (125). In the face of death or obliteration, such "lies" are heroic. The old Abazonian's talk—a benign tale of defeat, yet of dignity, of humble appeal to persecutory might—is at the heart of this novel. The struggle Achebe depicts is not that of military resistance to oppression, but the postcolonial battle to regain authority for humane perspectives in communities brutalized by power abuse. Anderson's expression for nations as "imagined communities," now so well known, can be linked as well as contrasted with Achebe's wider conception and urgent insistence on the political-moral imperative of actively and arduously broadening the mind by imagining a national *community* into being, in order to counter the people-oppressor dichotomy that characterizes the dictatorial state.

166. As Sam has been ousted and replaced by Lango (218) and as Nigerian dictators have succeeded one another.

167. Achebe himself has said that "there is more of looking into the future" in this novel, since "artists should not be the ones to offer despair to society" (quoted in Gikandi, *Reading,* 126, 147). Gikandi comments that in *Anthills*, the author "seeks a narrative that speaks about, but also transcends its historical imperatives" (130).

168. Boehmer's essay is a particularly articulate and clearly argued critique of Achebe's "recentering" of women in this novel. Referring to the "strategic gender configurations of his characters" (102), Boehmer expresses doubt whether this is "a new radicalism" or merely "emblematic" (103) and suggests that the novel may reenshrine "woman's conventional position as inspirational symbol—the mentor who is never a full political actor" (106), but who merely (still!) incarnates the ideals and the desire of men" (108). See "Of Goddesses" 104–105. Acknowledging the validity of such a critique, I direct my own argument on the whole at other aspects of the work.

169. In contrast with this slow process, we are shown the mushrooming of a deadly new power in General Lango (see "suddenly surface," "revulsion," "his pledge to the nation"—218).

170. Beatrice recognizes how close in meaning the old man's words are to the "coded message" (231) of Chris's dying words (232).

171. "It was a pledge. It had better be better than some pledges we have heard lately" (232).

172. Chris says that Okong "perhaps . . . has more responsibility than any other individual *except myself* for the remarkable metamorphosis of His Excellency. But, *perhaps* like me he *meant well*" (10, emphases added), and exclaims "to think that I personally was responsible" (2) for the appointment of almost half of the sycophantic cabinet. Ikem begins his "Hymn" by asking: "What hideous abomination . . . have we *committed?*" (30, emphasis added).

173. The verb links with Chris's ministerial title of "Commissioner" (215).

174. Sougou refers to the "specular structur[ing]" of the novel (37).

175. It is not only the "rulers" (as Ikem believes), but all privileged members of society, Achebe indicates, who need "to re-establish vital inner links with the poor and dispossessed" (141). Ikem, too, is prone to "passing the buck"! The limitations of his supposedly "democratically inclusive" vision are well analyzed by Innes (especially Ikem's sexism). See also Gikandi (*Novelist* 144–145).

176. Such as the taxi drivers, Abazonians, a servant and a "shop-girl," marketeers, Elewa's dirty old uncle, soldiers, and orderlies. Ngara and Boehmer consider the presence in the novel of these characters rather inadequate, though, as if they are a type of tokenism (Ngara, "Achebe as Artist"; Boehmer, "Of Goddesses").

177. In eschewing sentimentalization of "the common people" and establishing clearly what he sees as dangerous weaknesses and faults among them, Achebe seems to be in step with Fanon's recognition that "the truths of a nation are in the first place its realities" (*Wretched,* 181).

3

Bessie Head

a broader question than mere protest
Bessie Head, *Index*

The short statement[1] by Bessie Head from which the epigraph is taken opens with a startling claim whose reasonableness the author subsequently proceeds to demonstrate:

> I believe that people *cannot protest* against evil social systems. The people who create it merely laugh in your face, and . . . pass two more repressive laws to liquidate your gain and you end up by increasing the suffering of the people in the country. . . . It involves a broader question than mere protest—it is a question of evil as a whole. We are likely to remove one horror and replace it with another. . . . We . . . need [instead] new names for human dignity. (Head, *Index,* 23—emphasis added)[2]

Considered superficially, the line of reasoning here may seem striking confirmation of the supposedly apolitical or even antipolitical quality of Head's vision, which an influential South African critic, Lewis Nkosi, saw in her writing.[3] The statement used as an epigraph above clearly reflects South African political realities of the time, as well as briefly mapping the nature of this author's *broadly* political and literary aspirations. Head's particular origins—a South African classified "Coloured" whose very conception was a transgression, as she was the product of "miscegenation"; "illegitimate"; orphaned; adopted; daughter of an "insane" white mother and an entirely unknown black father; a stateless "refugee" for fifteen years in Botswana—brought political and social structures heavily to bear upon her, especially in the form of *displacement.*

The *Index on Censorship* statement can be read to indicate Head's notion that "finding a place" is the most profoundly significant redefinition strategy for the oppressed. Since it avoids the trap of (counter)power politics, it prevents either (A) becoming what one detests (should one "win") or (B) intensification of oppression (should one "lose")—both counterproductive ironies of which Head was especially conscious. Finding a place means (re)naming the self. Oppression in its bureaucratic power forms (as Head experienced and described it) denies worth by withholding selfhood, legitimacy.[4] Daring to (re)name the self, to take up a socially useful role (i.e., a social "place") chooses a space and assumes (a) being. All Head's major protagonists—Mouse and Johnny in *The Cardinals*; Makhaya in *When Rain Clouds Gather*; Margaret in *Maru*; Elizabeth in *A Question of Power;* and Khama III in *A Bewitched Crossroad*—can be construed as illustrations of this strategy. It is the liberatory energy, the form of change to which they contribute. The confidence to articulate this idea and to act upon it had to be arduously won and constantly reachieved both in Head's work and in her life: it could never be a comfortable "assumption."

In one of her early autobiographical essays[5] Head writes: "Though I am as African as everyone, yet am I a fragment, a thing cut off and *apart*" (quoted in Cullinan, "Edge," 5—emphasis added). The last word in the quotation is italicized here because of its special significance and poignancy. Though it unmistakably echoes or subliminally refers to South Africa's apartheid system, within whose horror Head had lived for twenty-seven years, it was written in and of her Botswana (re)location where, it is clear (as many of her other writings—and most clearly the Vigne letters—confirm), she felt still un- or even mis-*placed.* "I am a stranger in a continent that is my home," she states later in the same autobiographical essay, "I, comic, with the strange-painted face, am unreal, because unrecognisable. . . . I do not know who I am or what I am except that I live in Africa" (5).[6] What makes Head a *writer*, an author of profound importance (whose stature is being increasingly recognized), is that she turned all this personal anguish into an opportunity for the analysis of oppressive power and the careful plotting of routes to bypass futile power contestations. The misery of a condition of unbelonging was not merely to be overcome to improve her own lot, but was a cause she saw as central to the "huge view" she preferred to take as "mankind's storyteller" (MacKenzie and Clayton 13, 12), whose "loyalty [lay] only with the future" (quoted in Cullinan, "Edge," 5).[7]

Head reiterated her distrust of political "solutions" and "kingdoms" in 1979 when she wrote that "the horizon of African liberation has been narrowed down to horrific power struggles that destroy one country after another" (*Alone* 73). Civil wars, military coups, tyranny, and genocide have (since) horrifically confirmed her prescience and the validity[8] of her attempt to help Africans to "move into the future" by means of the types of "alternative choices" (73) that her works demonstrate. "It was consciously in my mind," Head wrote in one of her last essays, "that African independence had to be defined in the broadest possible terms" (85).

One can begin to recognize at this point that Head's discovery of broadly humanist principles arose from personal suffering and need and that she came to give a central position to the lowly, the powerless, and the poor (especially in Africa)—speaking for those who do not have the resources to participate in protest politics. Yet a world of power systems that disregards and cannibalizes such people needs to be changed to accommodate them—and it is to the work of propagating recognition of the overlooked and brutalized people—of whom she knew herself to be a part—that Head bent all her novelistic resources. Since being African was the one "place" or identity she could claim, it became a main thrust of her work to write of this continent and of the majority of its people—the poor, bare lives that she saw as so rich in human worth. She named "a reverence for people" (*Alone* 99) as one of the main themes of her writing. To quote from her short story "The Old Woman":[9] "Tell them too. Tell them how natural, sensible, normal is human kindness. Tell them, those who judge my country, Africa, by gain and greed, that the gods walk about here barefoot with no ermine and gold-studded cloaks" (*Tales* 43).[10]

Yet not even "Africa" had automatically afforded Head a place—a cause of anxiety expressed in an early piece called by the name of the continent, in which she conceives of Africa as a baffling, elusive (male) lover, to whom she says: "You are ashamed of me as the thing of nothing from nowhere. Nothing I am, of no tribe or race" (*Cardinals* 141). This fear of rejection even by "Africa," politically experienced first under apartheid and then in the long withholding of her Botswana citizenship, led to the breakdown described and explored in Head's central work, *A Question of Power*.

This book was the final eruption of Head's sense of precarious placelessness, of being unaccepted by a "place" itself unhonored and unknown. Politics and personal experience intertwined and mirrored each other, in turn reflected in her writing—or as Wilhelm puts it, "individual and collective experience . . . are . . . suggested as analogues of each other" (Wilhelm 1). Needing the shelter of acceptance and respect, Head saw how this mirrored the need of countless others. For her to "find" a space for herself in Africa, it was necessary that Africa be recognized by the world as a place deserving respect for its dignity, however hidden and disguised by its powerless indigence. All Head's early pieces express this "precarious"[11] identification claim:

> I have taken an advance on what I have not earned in any battlefield—human dignity. As there is a convulsion of change in Africa, so in similar fashion has there been a corresponding convulsion in my own life. . . . Without the liberation of Africa it would have been a super-human impossibility to release the energies, potentials and possibilities of my individuality. (*Cardinals* 146)[12]

Detesting the second scramble for Africa among power-greedy politicians, resenting and resisting being "claimed" merely by "men who would control every part of my life, yet care nothing about me," she nevertheless knew that she "need[ed to claim] Africa[:] I need to identify myself with it for the human pride and dignity it alone can give me," she wrote at the time (*Cardinals,* 148, 155). How much more arduously she would experience this anxiety and its hard-won alleviation in the "gesture of belonging" she at last manages to make, *A Question of Power* (206) would later testify.

Although the parables of liberation Head wrote in her first three novels could be thought of as partially undercut by this terrifying work, Elizabeth (the main character) also eventually fights her way back to acceptance of herself and her Botswana neighbors and neighborhood. Though a sense of isolation was never permanently absent from or overcome by her, Head's tribute to *Serowe: Village of the Rain Wind* (1981—which records the voices and realities, past and present, of this huge "village") and her short story collection *The Collector of Treasures* (1977) articulate the appreciative understanding and the courageously expressed strictures of "one who has put down roots" (Head, *Alone,* 62). Her final work, the "historical novel" (Eilersen 236) *A Bewitched Crossroad* (1984), is itself the profoundest gesture of belonging (and the best celebration and analysis of African "belonging") that she could offer Botswana. Simultaneously it restores African history,[13] placing her adoptive country on the map of the past from which Africans had been so harshly obliterated. For, wrote Head, "I think we are as desperate as anything to make Africa the black man's land because I see no other place on earth where the black man may come into his own, with dignity" (*Alone* 27).

Because of the intensity of Head's experienced conviction that a locale must accommodate the people who find themselves in it,[14] she construed South Africa as possibly "the unholiest place on earth" (*Alone* 27).[15] Here again her sense of the intertwinement of ultimately "religious," political, social, and personal matters is illustrated. Because she writes that South Africa (in the 1970s) causes in the majority of its inhabitants "a *shattering* sense of anxiety," we see how ideas about evil, displacement, and power abuse converge in her analysis. Conversely, she wrote that, although in 1975 still "a stateless person," she had made the village of Serowe "[her] own hallowed ground" (*Alone* 27, 28—emphasis added).[16]

What Head referred to as "the questions aroused by my South African experience," which she lists as "refugeeism, racialism, patterns of evil, and the ancient South African historical dialogue" (*Alone* 67), are essentially questions of placement—or of its denial. From this perspective she identifies the barrier-creating apartheid system as essentially a form of "primitiv[ism]" (97). Only if an "invader has given himself up to the spirit of [a] place . . . [can there be a] civilisation," she writes (79). Head's image of the ideal civilization is African and historical, quoting the image of an embracing, nurturing pharaoh figure, with the essence of civilization defined as nonexclusivity (50).[17]

The liberation toward which Head's writings are intended to contribute is thus something much larger than political enfranchisement (which it yet includes as a consideration, as earlier quotations have shown). In 1984 she wrote: "I have worked outside all political and other ideologies . . . but always fighting for space and air . . . in order that I retain a clarity of thought [and fluency of] sympathies" (*Alone* 95).[18] "I deal in human grandeur as a writer," she stated in the same piece, but added that its achievement could only be the result of "a collaboration of many great minds" (99)—thus "democratizing" greatness and progressive aspirations in her concept, as well as dispersing power and position. Grandeur, moreover, was for Head never a question of accoutrements, but of human generosity.

Writing, Head suggested in a 1972 essay ("An African Story"), is not so much "a nationalistic activity" as "the subdued communication a writer holds with his own society" (*Alone* 101). In her view the author's role is not the initiation or fomenting of political change and power participation, but the offering of envisioned alternatives. She wrote:

> It is impossible to guess how the revolution will come one day in South Africa. But in a world where all ordinary people are insisting on their rights, it is inevitable. It is to be hoped that great leaders will arise there who remember the suffering of racial hatred and out of it formulate a common language of human love for all people.
>
> Possibly, too, South Africa might one day become the home of the storyteller and dreamer, who did not hurt others but only introduced new dreams that filled the heart with wonder. (*Alone* 103)

Though her warnings still require heeding, perhaps Bessie Head's dreams and stories can begin to come home even in, and to, South Africa—at last.

The Cardinals

> *The Cardinals . . . are those who serve as the base or foundation for change.*
>
> Bessie Head, *The Cardinals*

The epigraph for this section is the one that Head chose for *The Cardinals.* That she gave it such prominent placing serves as the clearest indicator of the novelist's concern, in this work, with the "necessary possibility" of transformation (seen at the time)[19] of even so hugely powerful and intransigent a sociopolitical system as South African apartheid. About the possibility of transformation she said in 1965: "In spite of what the politicians say people are not going to be destroyed" (*Alone* 31), and she articulated on the same occasion the sense of the frightening power of the system: "There are huge armies prepared for war against unarmed people and we are all overwhelmed with fear and agony, not knowing where it will end" (31). That particular form of power (apartheid in its socially compartmentalizing and subjugating effects) is demonstrated in the opening paragraph of this highly unusual (first) novel,[20] a passage that deftly and disconcertingly foregrounds not a person, but a place—yet paradoxically, eerily, "It" (*Cardinals* 1) is a location[21] that *dis*places "discarded people":[22] its inhumane and unaccommodating qualities highlighted by the details of the setting among death (the graveyard), refuse dump, and the very edge of the land (the beachfront) (1). The adjectives in this paragraph add to the impression of bleakness ("bounded" and "separated" both calling apartheid legislation to mind), whereas the sense of the socially outcast quality of life in this slum is borne out in the third paragraph.[23]

The overwhelming disempowerment of those who dwell here makes the "dump[ing]"[24] of the baby (who will become Mouse) by her own mother, Ruby—whose fastidious shrinking from the township conditions is highlighted (1)—seem especially brutal and irresponsible.[25] The "*wrenching* agony" (60, emphasis added) that Ruby feels at the thought of her inability to nurture the baby[26] confirms that the separation of the child from its parent, though caused most immediately by the mother's "moral coward[ice]" and failure to "acknowledge" socially her love for its father (56–57), has a further and more powerful cause in a huge and intricate system of separating[27] social categories by which South Africa is ruled at this time. Johnny refers to the system as having "machinery" designed to effect "the perpetual suppression of the oppressed" (106), and Mouse sees it as a "trap[ping]" (107) of human beings.

Johnny and Ruby's short-lived, but intensely pure love (48–60) presents one of the early instances in the novel of instinctive disregard of the social strictures and structures of apartheid.[28] Their love begins, however, in the socially isolated and uncharacteristically tolerant setting of the fishermen's sleeping area, where it is not exposed to the pressures of social conformity (to class and race separation) to which Ruby will later yield (57). Her weakness *then*, however momentarily, shows that the "foundation" of the love is devastatingly "insecure" (54) and Ruby herself guilty of a "hollow[ness]" and "superficial[ity]" (57) that will "fling [her and Johnny] miles *apart*" (54, emphasis added). Ruby is not a cardinal, but her reaching out to Johnny will give birth to a person with enough "courage and complete sincerity" (113) to become one.

The much younger Johnny who was Ruby's lover had shown his refusal to yield to forms of power and oppression first in his unwillingness (even at the risk of his life—42) to be dragooned into joining a township gang,[29] instead freely "join[ing] a small group of . . . hermit men" (48) who fish for a living. A further sign of his instinct for freedom is his determination to seek "refuge" here, however "temporar[ily]," from "crushing poverty" (49). This will to liberation[30] in Johnny, which manages an escape from an unsheltering social environment, parallels and prefigures the account of the child Miriam's "walking" and eventually "stumbling" (9) away from sexual abuse and ignorance (in her first foster home), until she can at least (and from the first) [stand] her ground" (13)[31]—even when the superconfident, professional male, Johnny (in her first encounter with him), "approache[s] menacingly" (13).

Head juxtaposes the potential energies of change and the pitiless structures of the apartheid state, using three individuals (rather than social movements or dogmas) and their relationships (beginning almost "at first sight," but of brief duration in the case of Ruby and Johnny; of agonizingly slow growth, but more lasting[32] in the case of Johnny and Mouse). This focus on the three individuals is not an advocation of apolitical withdrawal (by the novelist),[33] though. It is, rather, an astute and analytically based recognition that in apartheid South Africa, what is "political" has penetrated and lays siege to the very intimacies of the most private and personal aspects of people's lives[34]—the sexual and passional dimensions of individual lives and relationships. It is, hence, in this sphere of intimacy that Head seeks and shows energies of change at work.

In Ruby, such energy (though present) is weakest. Her characteristic "long, swift stride" (49) is an expression of the energetic confidence of a socially privileged and sheltered person.[35] Yet this is the woman who "walk[s] swiftly" (2) away from the baby she is abandoning (certainly not merely heartlessly, but as the first stage of her suicide),[36] and who will, as an act of moral justice defying the moral conformity and hypocrisy that her mother and her would-be husband Paddy represent, walk "with her long, swift stride" (60) to the taking of her own life. In Johnny, the "vital and beautiful power" (49) that attracted Ruby so irresistibly to this innocent young man has been harshly scarred by her betrayal,[37] leaving him with "the restlessness of a caged animal" (13) and a "neon-like vitality" (16)—an anarchic, defiant intensity and energy that are simultaneously "destructive" (115) *and* his protection against the "despicable . . . sly and secretive" social conformity of a man such as his colleague James (46) and the politically compromised lifestyle of a PK.[38] Mouse has the most difficult, clamped-in situation of the three ("year by year she had become more and more silent . . . almost to a point where no living being could reach her" 10 11). Her doggedness[39] in moving out of the "muck" (28) of her childhood circumstances is, hence, the most admirable and difficult achievement of the three, although her efforts to extricate and to educate herself[40] leave her, still, "all clamped up and petrified" (66), an apparently incurably "withdrawn" (67) and emotionally stunted person. This is due to her unsheltered, traumatizing upbringing as an "unwanted stray" (10), "undernourish[ed]" emotionally (29), who "knows for a fact that no one cares one hell about her" (67).

It is Johnny who realizes very soon Mouse's abundance of potentially liberating and passional energy when he states with characteristic flamboyance that she is a "powder-keg" hidden under an "iceberg" exterior (21). Although his perception certainly includes his intense awareness of her capacity for sexual passion, it is carefully contrasted with the crudely salacious "interest" in her of their colleague, James[41]—especially in its *linking* of her condition of "dumb[ness]" with its cause in the political "clamps" of the apartheid system (21). "Anyone who has a mind to change the system will have to change you first" (21) is a crucial declaration of Johnny's. It indicates (again) how the sexual and emotional life of people is in this novel seen to be intertwined with and affected by political circumstances.[42] As he says to Mouse on a later occasion, "you cannot feel like the underdog and at the same time feel that you belong to a country" (72). Johnny's "project," as far as Mouse is concerned, combines sensitive and humane concern—his generous desire to rescue a brave and worthwhile person teetering on the edge of emotional "disaster" (29)[43]—with an inner need to escape his own sexual devils and "restlessness" (15) in a lasting emotional commitment to a partner, *and* with his sense that the two of them need to combine forces (both in loving and in writing). To do so, they would have to make a "home" (136) together and to assume a vantage point (134–135) from which to analyze and resist the "mess" (87) that is apartheid power politics.

The novel ends when Mouse has discovered and begun to articulate the true purpose of human society: though it contains in its "structures" the petrified "expression of power," human society is the product of some "working harmony in the minds of many men," she finds. Its "interweaving patterns" demonstrate the functioning of cooperative social energies that continuously "[expand]," proving that "its purpose is to sustain human life" (135) and not to degrade and stifle it (as exemplified in the slum scenes in the novel, e.g., 1, 80–81).

Mouse has, with Johnny's aid,[44] traveled far in social, artistic (and, implicitly, political) confidence by the time she is able to write this. Although her impending sexual union with Johnny still leaves her nervously afraid, the suggestion to the reader is that here, too, some of the tight emotional clamps that have hampered her access to full life are beginning to be removed. The *partnering* of the two cardinals, unwittingly father and daughter, after a slow and difficult wooing, runs deep and suggests how "supreme [an] effort" South Africans "need to make in order to allow [them] to find a deep faith to live together" (*Alone,* 31). Head absolutely (and deftly) inverts the shock value, the *taboo* quality, of incest[45] by turning it into a metaphor suggesting that social taboos (like apartheid's branding of racial "mixing") need to be reconsidered and overcome in order to reunite the broken family of humanity in South Africa. If an (unwittingly) incestuous love can be as healing and creative as Mouse and Johnny's relationship, the obscenity of "Immorality" legislation[46] is highlighted by contrast.

What links Mouse with Johnny from the start is their experience of suffering (78)[47]—this links them also, inextricably, with the whole South African community of "branded" sufferers of whom, despite their partial escape and minimal privileges,[48] Johnny and Mouse remain inextricably part. They belong to this community also in the kind of writing they do, of which Mouse's final description (135) is one example. An early instance of Johnny's journalism can be cited here as another example:

> Townships
>
> How long is it all going to last? Recently, 80,000 people were moved out of the slums of the Cape into new homes. Another government township was established.
>
> With the township the government built:
> 1 Butchery
> 1 Dairy
> 1 General Dealer
> 1 Barber
> 1 Beerhall
>
> The township is miles and miles away from any shopping-centre. In this ghetto 80,000 people have only:
> 1 Butcher where they may buy meat
> 1 Dairy where they may buy milk
> 1 General Dealer where they may shop
> 1 Barber where they may cut their hair
> 1 Beerhall where they may drink
>
> Dominating the scene is a large police station and barracks to maintain the "efficient management" of the township. The township has a stark, naked look. The roads are dirt roads. The houses are like those square boxes you see at a loading-zone, empty of imagination or style. The only soft, light colourful touches in this atmosphere of doom are the pink, yellow and red dahlias outside the police station. (19–20)

Johnny's journalism[49] is contrasted by careful juxtaposition with James's stories "about the happy little Coloured man and the colourful Malays" (17)—writing far more deserving of the label "sentimental junk" (18) than Mouse's socially conscious and sympathetic, but "unsuitable," rejected reports (to which PK does append the label). Despite his superficially pleasant qualities, PK exposes his profoundly irresponsible cynicism in his editor's creed: "This paper is paying you only to write a dirty story," and in his not wanting to know (or to report) the real driving forces of social conduct (18). "*The public should have no sympathy*" (18) is a line in the report that sums up his perhaps not entirely conscious endorsement (or spineless acceptance) of the repressive sociopolitical system.[50] The alternative "story" (20) with which the editor attempts to supplant Johnny's report (19–20, quoted fully, above) is, as Johnny bitingly tells him, "support[ive] of the government" (20). PK's mind-set is that of an evasive personality,[51] unwilling to confront ugly truths. By contrast, Johnny's forthright (*and* factual!) reporting (19–20, quoted above) springs discernibly from a profound, humane indignation. However straight-faced, its muted but unmistakable insistence (discernible, for instance, in the words "ghetto," "only," and in the quotation marks around "efficient management" indicating the inadequacy of the "new homes" (provided for the slum-dwellers) fills the report with fierce sarcasm, which implicitly and sanely denounces[52] such social "insanity" (115). In a way characteristic of Head's vision, the focus falls on the *unaccommodating* aspects of the new location—to which 80,000 people are deliberately subjected.

That conventional political resistance or protest will be ineffectual to bring about change at this time is suggested by Head's touching on three areas or aspects of South African social life. She makes clear that the socially degraded circumstances, the mere precarious sordidness of life in most ghetto communities, makes organized resistance quite unlikely to arise here. Mouse (and Johnny) are indeed exceptional in having managed to extricate themselves, by means of a combination of inner strength and some luck,[53] from under the "crushing" (10, 49) effect of poverty (itself a consequence of power abuse). Aside from this large underclass (the conventional term perhaps unthinkingly indicates that people who have been suppressed over a long period become repressed—or "silent" and "dumb," as Mouse is described as being—11, 27), the section of the community classified "non-white" who achieve middle-class privileges tends to become (as Johnny sees) "stooges" and sell-outs (106–107)—perhaps the greatest obstruction to the achievement of liberation from racist oppression. Johnny sees them as "cunning" and as "prostitute[s]" to power (107), whereas in Mouse's eyes they exemplify but another form of victimhood.[54] Most agonizingly, there is the futile martyrdom of those who "pit" their "unarmed violence . . . against armed violence" (81) in a grotesquely unequal power contest. Fully empathizing with the way "suppressed rage" at the "humiliati[on]" (80) of the pass laws forces an outburst from time to time, the sense of such tragic waste[55] nevertheless leaves Johnny "depressed" and "confused" (81)—because such a triumph of brutal immorality is (in his eyes) anachronistic and itself a mere misuse of energy: "It completely distracts us from more useful occupations" (80), he says.

The deep sincerity of Johnny's commitment to the liberation of humanity from political, social, and emotional shackles is an *achieving* energy of change, which seeks (and finds) in Mouse an answering energy—hidden and badly damaged though it is, itself in need of freeing. He begins his approach to her by expressing his confidence in and his admiration of her "creative gift[edness]" and by suggesting that a type of duty[56] is attendant upon such talent: "It is a great responsibility to be a writer at this time" (72). "Work" is to be done[57] with the writer's talent, which is worthy of (and appropriate to) the specific location in which they find themselves (71).[58] Here, Johnny declares, "a new way of life is emerging" (71), and to contribute to that process they "can [perhaps, he says:] help to throw some of those imposed standards [which oppress and separate people] overboard" (72). In Johnny's words, "We need a country the way we need food and clothes" (71). Head's familiar preoccupation with the "belonging" urge is expressed here. But it is astutely and with authorial integrity adapted to the speaker and the situation. Belonging, Johnny explains, cannot be felt by those in whom a sense of oppression is paramount.[59] It follows, hence, that the writerly project in which he is inviting Mouse to participate will be *writing to free* (themselves and their compatriots) *by writing to "belong"* (writing to confute the denial of belonging to those whom apartheid entraps in exclusion).

This paradox[60] is exactly paralleled by Head in Johnny's inviting Mouse to liberate herself (both her creative talents and her sexual, emotional being—75) by joining him in his home (72). Johnny seems to struggle to articulate to Mouse that the elemental power of attraction, the final commitment he imagines occurring between them, is not his to control. He has a "fixed idea" that Mouse "belong[s]" to him (83) in "a kind of commitment from which [she—and evidently he also] can't ever be free" (84), knowing nevertheless that he cannot and will not enforce this by exercise of power: "I want all of you to be in agreement with me" (84), he says. Though he is utterly "dependent on" Mouse, this is the only alternative to his dislodging sense of "insecurity" (88). These ideas may sound Romantic, Lawrentian,[61] or simply like the voice of the patriarchy to a modern reader, yet Head's plural in her title suggests that a partnership of equals, a combining of forces, is what she and her character Johnny have in mind. It is to be contrasted, as a principle of a humane and natural order, with the falsely "tidy" South African mosaic of color-coded living spaces. In the compartmentalization of its citizens, the ruling power has made a "mess" (87—compare "chaos," 117), which the writer needs to "see *through*" in order to "correlate . . . impressions into a definite pattern" (75), recognizing "that the real [person] is alive *under [her or his] skin*," in the range of their "complexities" (76, emphases added). In the same way the anarchic and promiscuous lifestyle by means of which Johnny has attempted to fend off political encampments and the unassuageable "unhappiness" of his loss of Ruby (54) seem "meaningless and empty" against the possibility of "correlat[ing]" (88)[62] his life in a committed union with Mouse.

In order to distinguish Johnny's love of Mouse from an uncaring power drive,[63] to see it (in the terms of this investigation) instead as a form of progressive energy, one must recognize how scrupulously and yet subtly Head presents this love as Johnny's taking progressively intensifying responsibility[64] for Mouse as a woman, a partner, and a writer. He resorts to slapping her when the "monster . . . despair" (89), to which she is prone—a suicidal tendency that he regards as utterly irresponsible in its negation of her human and artistic worth—threatens to "[engulf]" (89) her. Though it may seem brutal, it is a desperate, life-saving strategy on his part, fundamentally different from wife beating. Taking responsibility is not related to taking possession or taking power over another person (as in political tyranny or in an abusive relationship). Yet Head shows herself deeply aware of the play of power in an intense relationship, which is never merely "safe," as Johnny says.[65]

The risks that both Mouse and Johnny take in building their relationship originate from the damage that their society inflicted upon them; Head shows that both have "shells" in which they have been hiding their inner selves. She links (throughout the novel) the creative energy necessary to make a love commitment—to heal their damaged selves—with the social caring and courage required to address a sick society. Further risks and self-exposure are involved, once the first step has been taken—rather than the attainment of a haven that will be passively occupied.

The poignant "outsider" figure in the novel, the unnamed man who helps Mouse (unsuccessfully) search for a wheelchair, fatalistically interprets himself as "helpless against [the politician's] power" (120). Although this seems reminiscent of Mouse's fears concerning her position in her relationship with Johnny ("his personality is too strong for me"—120),[66] she here says quietly and with conviction (to her friend), "Somehow we must survive and fulfil ourselves" (120), evidently knowing in her own way the duty or hope of fulfillment that Johnny is trying to teach her. Her statement is important as an indication that she, like Head, *knows* (so quietly emphatic is her tone) that individuals can build a (small) wholesome social environment around themselves, given some assistance and a little luck, despite the larger, deadening political and social forces that would deny this.[67] If in no other way than by "storytell[ing] and dream[ing]" (*Alone* 101), creative energies "survive"—since people cannot be stopped from yearning for "fulfil[lment]" (120).

When sexual passion eventually begins to surge up, irresistibly, in Mouse, Head's image for it is an elemental, "pulsing" energy—a "*forward* rushing" (133, emphasis added). The repetition of the term "rushing" in this paragraph, indicating an inward sensation of emotion, makes Mouse's hanging-back complaint to Johnny ("You just rush me into everything"—137) somewhat disingenuous (by this stage). Such "rushing" is indeed dangerous, but it is a life-giving, vital compulsion utterly opposite to the inhibiting and exploitative effects of power misuse. Although natural and wild, it is no mere chaotic or selfish choice. "Nothing can be *right* until a man and a woman make all things *meaningful* through each other" (152, emphasis added)[68] is a comment of Head's that seems precisely fitted to the Johnny-Mouse relationship. The liberation that the novel advocates as a condition worth striving for (even when it seems unattainable) is not merely political freedom, but the personal *and* social conditions that will make fuller life possible.

Head's constant distinction between "inner" liberation, which matters more (in her view) than outer, social, and political freeing (to which it should contribute and on which it is to some extent dependent), is stated in a challenging question written not long after the novel: "We may liberate ourselves from alien oppressors, but when do we come alive to ourselves?" (152).[69] In

The Cardinals, Head seems to imply that self-fulfillment is not achievable in isolation or by withdrawal from oppressive power structures, since, in the quest for fulfilment, such bastions will be *encountered* by the energies of change and growth. The small "explosions"[70] of "private" passion may yet serve to undermine the might of falsifying structures.

Head was not—any more than Mouse—writing "sentimental junk" (18) when she composed this strange love story. Nevertheless, her image of the couple as the necessary ideal of human belonging[71] would later be discarded, as her own isolation intensified.

In nothing as much as in their unremitting honesty are Mouse and Johnny linked with each other—and with their creator. Wicomb calls Johnny's "the voice of truth in the novel" ("Postcoloniality" 8), but Mouse's is no less so. Her voice needs coaxing into the open from its initially "inarticulate, dumb" (21) condition until it can pronounce with the authority that Mouse manages in her writing toward the end of the novel (110–111, 135). Like Head's, Mouse's writing fulfills several of the criteria that Njabulo Ndebele would in later years mention as needed for South African writing to move beyond the "protest literature" category: "clarity of analysis"; a fresh angle; and the "radical substitution of that emptiness [of the "manipulative culture"] with reconstructive content" (Ndebele 58, 25, 65, 142).[72] Neither Head's nor Johnny's (or Mouse's) writing could (in itself) "get rid of governments and systems for good" (31). Yet the novel educates the reader concerning another possibility—that of both living in a way that is somehow "beyond" social cells and compartments,[73] and pronouncing on the inadequacies of such categories by exposing the untruths they enshrine.[74] That Head managed to write a tender, surprising, and vividly erotic love story without ever falsifying the ugliness of the South African social scene (or suggesting that the "small white-washed house" in District Six where Johnny and Mouse are about to fulfill their love physically can eclipse or compensate for the huge social tragedy within which it is set) shows her to be depicting (like Boris Pasternak in *Doctor Zhivago*, which she so much admired) two "human heart[s] . . . [in a] secret conspiracy against all the insanity and hatred in mankind" (*Alone* 58–60).

When Rain Clouds Gather

Discovering "the man with no shoes"
Bessie Head, *When Rain Clouds Gather*

The emphasis in *When Rain Clouds Gather,* the first published[75] novel of Head's, falls distinctly on growth energies rather than on restrictive power manifestations. Nevertheless a constant dialectic, a perpetual *engagement* between both these presences is depicted in the text's field of play. Though it may seem likely that the emphasis arises from the author's personal relief at having escaped from apartheid rule,[76] Head's letters reflecting her early days in Botswana in fact indicate traumatic experiences of rejection and exclusion.[77] It seems more appropriate to argue, then, that Head should be thought of as having (on the one hand) an "inspirational" intention with this (clearly future-directed) work,[78] while (on the other hand) in her strong, constant commitment to the everyday and the real,[79] she makes the threats and troubles in even "a free country" (10) (although outbalanced by gains) terrible and real. As in *The Cardinals*, the "fairytale" or "romance" elements[80] are not merely naïvely used or indicative of an overall utopianism in the author's vision.[81] The wry expression (on the opening page of *When Rain Clouds Gather*) describing Makhaya's ironic awareness of his proceeding "to whatever *illusion of freedom* lay ahead" (7, emphasis added) and Head's depiction of the perpetually arduous nature of her characters' lives in Botswana are indications that an author intent on hope-giving can (and should), in her own words, retain "a sturdy sanity" (Sarvan, "Letters," 14).

The major metaphor that Head employs to indicate the workings of progressive energy in the social situation that she depicts here is that of growth[82]—especially regenerative growth; a process of recovery. An early passage illustrative of this feature occurs at the beginning of Chapter 3 (36–37, 39). That the land in this area has been devastated is illustrated in the heavy fall of the past participles: "overstocked and overgrazed and overpopulated" (36). Yet the promise and hope of regeneration are perceived by Gilbert to lie in an insignificant, apparently unpromising, yet plentiful kind of plant ("the carrot-seed grass"). The reference to its leaves as "impoverished" (36)—like the later reference to its occurrence in "impoverished soil" (37)—links it with the poor of the land, with whom Gilbert, Makhaya, and Head are so much concerned in this novel, and in whom they see the real hope of progress. "It had the ability to build up the humus layer" and was a "tough pioneer which paved the way" (37) are passages that show a similar "double vision" (botanical and human).

The careful, subtle, and unobtrusive way in which Head's *socializing* imagination can be seen functioning in such an excerpt (36–37) binds her vision to the earth and to survival issues and gives her vision its persuasive power. What Gilbert is discovering is the earth's ability to recover and the strategies people can employ[83] to seek out and harness such energies for their own regeneration. "Had all this strange new growth lain dormant for years and years in the soil?" (37) indicates that devastation[84] need not be permanent or damage as irrecoverable as people fear.[85] Most especially, the cherishing *and* scientific attentiveness in the passage gives recognition to the unrecognized potential of the ordinary and the everyday, portraying both Gilbert's cast of mind and the inclusivity of Head's vision[86]—with her special focus on the condition of lowliness[87] as the human basis from which all social life grows. Hence, here, the hardy carrot-grass provides for and shelters the "frail . . . lush, sweet grass" (36) and among it can appear "stars," "sprays," and "whorls" (37) of the more delicate and playful plant forms. In his fascination with "the speed with which the natural grasses of the area *recovered*" (39, emphasis added), Gilbert, the white foreigner,[88] is contrasted ironically with the indigenous Chief Matenge. The chief's destructiveness is indicated in adjectives such as "fuming" (37) and "violent" (38), whereas "lucrative" (38) indicates his parasitism, in contrast with Gilbert's "ability, though educated, to live under the same conditions as the poor" (39).

This is one of the early instances in the novel of Head's critique of tribal traditionalism as a form of progress-inhibiting power. Ancient African socialism, benign in the original intention ("ownership of the land was vested in the tribe as a whole . . . to prevent the land from falling into the hands of a few rich people"—38) may in practice, she shows, allow cunning manipulators of hereditary chiefly power to profit at the expense of the poor *and* to block their advancement out of envy, greed, and power insecurity (23, 44, 145). Initially (and superficially) Gilbert is suspected of having capitalist intentions ("freehold tenure . . . barbed-wire fencing"—38), whereas his project is a form of communalism—an adaptation of tribal practices with the aim of common gain (99). Head calls this (expressing Gilbert's vision) "change . . . as the outcome of the natural growth of a people" (45).

Matenge is the most vivid power figure in the text and, although aligned with tribalism (which is his power base), he is more than a tribalist (45). He is Head's study in compulsive power seeking, the lifestyle of the man not quite on top. His power props (e.g., the "royal purple gown" and the "kingly chair"—62; the "huge cream Chevrolet"—44) do not make him a mere buffoon, though. He is too menacing a presence for that.[89] He *invades* people spiritually, because he has "an extremely cunning and evil mind, a mind so profoundly clever as to make the innocent believe they were responsible for the evil" (31). This chilling description probes further than the average psychological thriller, though—because Head makes Matenge's (albeit perverted) humanity and the political likelihood of such a power form seem convincing.[90] Matenge is unmistakably evil in his persecution of others ("an African oppressor, . . . exploiting his own people"—183), and Head's claim that "you couldn't ever forget Matenge" (183) rings true even for the reader. Something in him complicates easy condemnation; some unwilling, "terrible pity" (182) is generated by the sense of how tormented[91] a person he is (or was). Because he is not simple, he is no merely dismissable cartoon character. Head here first (before her major study in *A Question of Power*) links a reader *into* the abusive power phenomenon. Her most memorable description of Matenge, as convincing as it is startling, is of the tears slowly coursing "down the rutted grooves of his cheeks" (176)[92] as he stands watching the villagers gathered outside his house. The "great unseen shadow" (182) that he casts outlives his death. He is subtly associated by Head with the gathered, gorging vultures who [reign] supreme" in "desolation" (159, 165)—the "claws" that he "[keeps] . . . in a people's heart" (175) being an image reflecting not only active preying by a living oppressor, but the lingering fear, the ever-present possibility of such an exploiter[93] arising among them.

Head suggests that a tribal lifestyle may lend itself particularly readily to the propping up of a tyrant of Matenge's ilk, since it establishes as tradition the profiteering position of a single leader (or ruling family, or favored group) at the expense of a whole people. Head was entirely deliberate in her unfavorable depiction of this type of communal traditionalism—she said in a 1978 interview that "tribalism is a narrow, exclusive world and there is a strong anti-tribal theme in *When Rain Clouds Gather*" (Marquard 53).[94] Although the carefully balancing quality of her vision is apparent in her depiction of the brother (and superior) of Matenge, Chief Sekoto—who is shown as a generally benign ruler, though cunning and joyously sensual—he, too, is contemptuously dismissive of "commoner[s]" (180). She nevertheless devotes a long passage (50–53) to a vividly moving description of Chief Sekoto at his most "charming" (49), using his presidency at the *kgotla* (tribal court) to rescue an old woman from persecution by the villagers among whom she had lived. If the villagers' fierce, communal injustice is an instance of the "chilling group attitudes" (101)[95] of tribalist people, this section also illustrates the "kindly heart" (51) and the carefully responsible role of the chief, made possible by the venerable tribal institution of the *kgotla*.

It is the deep conservatism of tribal "diehard[s]" (44) and the irrational blocking out of literally life-improving knowledge and skills that arouse Head's wry sense of the stultifying effects of this form of social power. Intent on "ke[eping] out anything new and strange" (100) and on maintaining the "feeling of safety" (42) about the familiar, this conservatism actually enshrines "strange prejudices" (41) against the consumption (and even the growth) of food types ideally suited to the harsh local climatic conditions. Even Paulina, as lively minded as she generally is, has set ideas about rigid, prescribed gender roles (139) and social habits (142)—on which Makhaya comments that "all these rotten customs are killing us" (162). Tolerance of autocratic behavior, ignorance (assuming that prejudice is a form of this), and male power exploitation[96] are (hence) the constellation of attitudes characterizing a society as tribalist.

The form of power abuse (South African racism in the complex sociopolitical system of apartheid) by which Makhaya has been harmed does not magically disappear from his mind once he crosses the border into Botswana. In a way that Head was to explore much more fully in her third published novel, *A Question of Power*, racist victimization is shown to haunt the mind of someone who has formerly been its butt. The author centers her exploration of the psychic recovery process (her major theme) in the consciousness of Makhaya, the most ravaged personality among the six main characters.[97] The hurt of racism's degrading technique of *misnaming* is threaded throughout the narrative, and Makhaya's psychic progress can be signposted by juxtaposing an early passage from the novel with one occurring near its end. Early on, Makhaya's "reasons for leaving" South Africa are explained in a "simple" but profoundly indignant statement: "He could not marry and have children in a country where black men were called 'boy' and 'dog' and 'kaffir'" (16). Toward the end, an attitude of confident dignity is ascribed to Makhaya: "The world would not rid itself of African men. He would always be there, but not any longer as the white man's joke, or his 'mundt' or his 'kaffir' or his 'boy'" (171).[98]

Makhaya is "released" from the confines of his natural bitterness and distrust of people (as a refugee from South Africa) through his encounters with all five of the other main characters: Dinorego (who first takes him in); Paulina (who falls in love with him); Maria (his twin soul of loneliness); and Mma-Millipede (whose humane wisdom heals and enriches him). One might describe him as unusually or unconvincingly lucky in having such friends and opportunities—or say that Head is depicting how arduous the process of recovery is for someone who has been as deeply hurt as he has been, by the psychopolitical terrorism of apartheid. It takes the combined energies of all these influences, as well as his own determination, to "come to terms with his society" (164) as an "ordinary" person (171) and (perhaps) a "future millionaire" (165).

It is the abusive power of apartheid that turned "the quiet, reserved young man" (126) into a "Black Dog" (128), a "mad dog" (129)[99] with "a violent torrent of hatred" (129) boiling inside him. This frighteningly intense urge to retaliate against the violation of (his) human dignity measures (in balance) the fierce predatoriness of apartheid's racist power. *When Rain Clouds Gather* is no soothing little pastoral romance, but has "an edge of harshness" (Head, *Alone,* 97), and this is nowhere more apparent than in the central section where Makhaya analyzes and exposes the apartheid power conspiracy. Once "captivated by the doctrines of Christianity" (134), black people had had to "[watch] their lives overrun and everything taken away,"[100] reduced to a situation where "they had no life apart from being servants and slaves" (133). The sheer predatoriness of this power form is measured in this passionate account of the human wreckage it causes: an inner "inferno" (128) of frustrated, helpless "hatred" (133); "the living death of humiliation" (125);[101] and an unbearable "strain" (133). The "hollow feeling inside" that is "driving [him] mad" (129) is caused by the sense of "life [being] . . . soiled and tainted" (130) and by the "powerful accumulation of . . . centuries . . . of silence" (133) threatening to burst out in a howl—to the amusement (129), perhaps, of the oppressors, but not for long.[102]

Yet Makhaya is endowed by Head with a sense that *oppositional power politics* is not the road to take. This strategy is described dismissively by Makhaya as "a whole new set of retrogressive ideas and retrogressive pride" and as a "bandwagon," while "the very real misery was still there" and "people in southern Africa were still oppressed" (80). That is why (in Head's quaint formulation) "Makhaya turned to agriculture for his salvation" (81)—the point being that his personal recovery will be sought in the attempt to help provide for people in this impoverished continent, seeking (with Gilbert) "practical solutions" (81) rather than political positions. He is also enabled to overcome his inclination to attack the "Matenges everywhere [who] get themselves into . . . position[s] over the poor" by Mma-Millipede's gentle reminder that power is in some sense an illusion, since, "whether good or bad, each man is helpless before life" (131).

A nonpolitical form of power with which the whole society is confronted in *When Rain Clouds Gather* is the force of nature—the harsh, hot climate and the devastation brought by prolonged drought. When Head began planning the writing of this book, she declared her intention to write "a saga about the elements" (Eilersen 85), which the novel to some extent is. Deeply conscious as Head is of the life-giving, beautifying effect of the sunlight,[103] that combination of power and energy, she shows us no less how terrible a "barren earth" can be, when "the great stretches of arid land completely [stun] the mind" with the thought of such emptiness as a threat to survival. Here, too, her descriptions fabricate no utopia.[104] We are, instead, told and shown "the terrible story of the bush" (161) in which "hundreds and thousands of cattle had died" (147). It is this drought, the poverty it intensifies and the starvation it causes (43), that snuffs out the bright young life of Paulina's son Isaac, who dies of tuberculosis (121) in the "desolation" (159) of the cattle post in the bush (150–151).

Having understood before, concerning the Botswana landscape, that "this expansive ocean of desert" causes a type of "mental flight" in which people seek refuge in the smallest and most risk-free ventures of mere "subsistence farming" (115), Gilbert knows that the decimation of the herds, tragic though it seems to be, can provide an opportunity for people to change their vested, but "ruin[ous]" (35) farming habits to methods more appropriate to this land (154–156). Yet he, too, is shocked and grieved at the terrible cost nature has exacted as they drive to find the little boy's body (159).[105] The energy to create a better life than this harshness is propelled also in Makhaya,[106] who joins Paulina at last in a sexual and emotional commitment, because he cannot let her face the tragedy alone (157).

Makhaya's instinctual fleeing from "the painful knots" (8) and the "barbed-wire fencing" (7) of apartheid's prison land aligns him from the first with the energies of change. His premonition of psychic liberation is subtly shown in the sight of the "dust of the mud floor [which] rose up and shimmered and danced in the sunlight" (8). Late in the novel, he will look bemusedly at how "huge quantities of earth and rock [are] hurled high into the air"

(137) in a joyous image of constructive energy.[107] One of the most delicately complex passages in the novel (employing similar symbolic indicators) occurs when Paulina first attempts to get to know Makhaya (77–78). This passage is preceded by the information that she had "soon recovered" from the disaster that ended her first marriage and had "set out to build up a new life in Golema Mmidi" (77).[108] She is thus clearly associated with regenerative energies. Her "gaudy-hued skirts" are the outward signs of her generous, passionate nature, which Head links with the "sun" itself (77).

That Makhaya's own "recover[y]" is beginning is signposted in his sensitively appreciative response to the Botswana sunsets, when he sees the "gold shafts" of evening light "retreat[ing] quietly" as if a huge flower were "folding into itself"—an image of majesty and serenity. The "engulfing wave" of "pitch black shadows"[109] that follows (77) carries, hence, no threatening overtones of "engulfing" power, but is, instead, a reassuring image of sustained and sustaining energy.[110] Sunset is to Makhaya a miraculous "transform[ation]" (78) of the earth,[111] itself now gloriously "gaudy-hued" (77, 78).

> One evening, Makhaya walked right into a great drama. The thornbush was seeding and it did this in a vigorous way. One spray of seed struck him on the cheek, and on a closer inspection, he noticed that all the branches were profusely covered with beanlike pods. These pods twined tightly inward until they were coiled springs. Once the pod burst, the spring ejected the seeds high into the air. He stretched out his hand, broke off a pod and pressed it open. A few minute kidney-bean-shaped seeds slithered on to his palm. He stared at them in amazement. Could this rough, tough little thornbush be a relative of the garden bean? He decided to take the seeds back to the farm and question Gilbert.
>
> Paulina, meanwhile, had watched these comings and goings at sundown with avid curiosity and at last, being unable to contain it, had sent the little girl to Makhaya with a message. This particular evening Makhaya stood just a stone's throw away from her yard, and being absorbed as he was in the popping, spraying drama around him, he did not at first notice the child standing near him. And even when he did, he looked down rather absent-mindedly into a pair of small beady black eyes.
>
> "Sir," the child said. "My mother says she sends you her greetings."
>
> "Who is your mother?" he asked.
>
> The child pointed in the direction of the huts. Makhaya glanced up briefly, was struck in the eye by a vivid sunset skirt of bright orange and yellow flowers and momentarily captivated by a pair of large bold black eyes. He looked down at the child and sent back a cruel message.
>
> "Go and tell your mother I don't know her," he said.
>
> He turned and, without looking either left or right, walked back to the farm. Paulina, on receiving his message, flamed with confusion and humiliation. So distressed was she that she rushed over to her friend Mma-Millipede.
>
> "Mama," she said. "I've make a terrible blunder." (78)

Vitality and liberation are the main themes of this beautifully contrived yet entirely natural-sounding passage, delighting as it does in the marvels and amusing oddities of nature and humanity, so closely aligned here with each other. Head's "grounding" imagination, which sees the liberatory strivings of people ("seeking [their] own living life"—136) as both individually and socially salvific[112] forces, is skillfully at work in such writing. She focuses on the natural "vigorous[ness]" of the scene of the thornbush seeding, transforming this ordinary occurrence into something as exciting as a fireworks display—a "popping, spraying drama" (78). Especially arresting in this description, however, is the parallel—presumably "invisible" to Makhaya himself—between him and the seeding plants, whose "pods twined tightly inward until they were coiled springs." This is strikingly reminiscent of the bitterness and mistrust that have driven Makhaya's basically warm, passionate, and sensitive personality into an aloof, self-withholding strategy of withdrawal.[113] The fending off of intimate contact is illustrated within the passage by the "cruel" message Makhaya returns to Paulina's first overtures of friendship. Yet at the same time, certain subtle touches prefigure the eventual development of a passionate and sexual relationship between them.

One such touch is the parallel between the Botswana sunsets (which Makhaya loves) and Paulina's personality and garments (already mentioned).[114] Another is the parallel between the way Makhaya is first "struck . . . on the cheek" (as if with a little admonitory, alerting slap!) by a "spray of seed" and later "struck in the eye" by Paulina's bright skirt, as well as "captivated" by her "bold black eyes." The sense of the naturally *rising*, arousing energies at work here is indicated in the way the seeds are flung (as if joyously) "high into the air" (78).[115] Paulina's being "unable to contain" her curiosity is like the "burst[ing]" forth of the seed from the pod. Mainly, perhaps, the behavior of the seeds is a reminder of human sexual desire as a transformative energy and of its beauty and importance as a life-giving force (perhaps, since Makhaya is at center stage here, with a special focus on his still-withheld *male* potency). The most remarkable achievement of the writing here is, however, its suggestions of the close alignment between natural, physical satisfaction and the profoundly spiritual, aspirational urges of the human soul that find expression in the building of relationship and society, though based on bodily needs and the earth's own energies. The celebratory trend of the whole passage is deftly qualified, and enhanced, by the momentary setback Paulina experiences at the "humiliating" rejection of her greeting. Even this is made humorous, and finally "promising," though, since her "flam[ing]" embarrassment and "rush[ing]" movement (78) still link her with life-giving vigor—which will eventually transform Makhaya's hard-bitten conduct and open up the tough shell in which he has isolated himself.

Dinorego with his wise kindliness first teaches Makhaya that "allowance" can be (sometimes must be) made for evil, "though we don't like it"

(27).[116] This means perhaps that justifiable hatred and bitterness can consume victims of evil power (a danger Makhaya is aware of in himself). If such resentment is to be transcended, a psychic effort will be required to place the former victim on another, nonconfrontational route in her or his world.[117] Mma-Millipede consolidates this idea to a point where Makhaya can begin to understand (though not quite accept) it, in the taxing, probing conversation she has with him in what may be labeled the "Black Dog" section of the novel (126–134). No doctrinal, conventional Christian message would have persuaded Makhaya,[118] but he cannot contest the validity of Mma-Millipede's suggestion that life is a "great burden" (130) to everyone, even to the perpetrators of oppression or other evildoers, and that their "helpless[ness] before life" (131) makes all people—finally—pitiable. The "deeper" and uncontrollable "mystery" to which she refers seems an inaccessible and final power, since it is not "control[lable]" by anyone—perhaps her way of referring to the animating energy we call life, since she is avoiding religious terminology in order to "get through to" Makhaya.[119] It is this "accepting" attitude that seems to affect even the turbulent spirit of Makhaya when he is (at the end of the novel) confronted by the still, hanging body of the "gruesome"[120] Matenge (178, 185–188).

Mainly, though, Makhaya discovers that "something ha[s] to be done about" the "thousands and thousands of people who [walk] around with no shoes" and that "voices ha[ve] to be raised in Africa too" by "men like Makhaya who deeply [crave] a better life"[121] for themselves and their fellows (123).[122] Gilbert, to whom "life meant love and work . . . [and] getting out of the rut" (86),[123] is the person who, both by example and as his intellectual instructor and partner, teaches Makhaya "this love and care for the earth" (135) in order to begin to provide for those who are "starving" (43, 123).[124] Head performs a subtle and judicious balancing act in her presentations of poverty in this novel. Poverty devastates, she shows—most awfully in the death of Paulina's son Isaac. Yet her complex apprehension of life simultaneously registers and emphasizes the unexpected, unrecognized "wealth of poverty"—an expression most particularly applicable to Dinorego, whose beauty of nature can be exemplified in his invitation to Makhaya to join him: "A poor person like me can still be hospitable" (21). It is evidently Dinorego that Head has in mind when she speaks of God's being in evidence in Botswana "in the expressions of thin old men in tattered coats" (185). This theme of inner riches, or hidden wealth, is central to *When Rain Clouds Gather* as a whole. It is expressed most explicitly in Maria's words of comfort to Makhaya, devastated by the sights of the drought-ravaged landscape and the memory of the pathetically curled-up skeleton of the little boy (Paulina's son) in the cattle post hut. Though perhaps "not a cloud appears in the sky," "we keep the rivers inside us," she says (168).[125] "Human generosity" (61, 132)[126] is the essential growth energy without which life cannot prosper. In this dry land, that merciful quality can make life bearable and beautiful and inspire "all the hard work [that has] to be done" (187) to fulfill aspirations.

Golema Mmidi as an imagined community is indeed "a dream [that Head] evoked out of [her] own consciousness . . . to help make life tolerable" (137).[127] But, as she adds, "if it [is] a dream, it [is] a merciful one" (137). It is also an injunction.

Maru

the strength to build a new world
Bessie Head, *Maru*

The epigraph, a quotation from *Maru*, can serve[128] as an initial hint of the extent to which, in this work, ideas and impressions of power(s) and of energies are shown to coincide from many sources to make possible the *initiating*[129] breakthrough against the confining power of racial prejudice in an African[130] society. That breakthrough is, simultaneously, the union of a Motswana ruler and a Mosarwa[131] woman in a startling marriage, and the "open[ing]" of the "door" on the "dark airless room" of racial prejudice that had trapped the Basarwa in a conviction of their supposed subhumanity (126–127).

The style[132] of this text, the second Head was to publish, is unusual and strikingly different from the continuous narrative mode she had employed in *When Rain Clouds Gather*. It is a brief novel, but taut and vibrant, rich in paradoxes and sudden shifts of perspective that can startle the reader into the considerations and reconsiderations Head seeks to arouse. Neither naïve nor childish, for all its borrowing of the quest-and-reward pattern,[133] *Maru* has the stark, clear lines of myth—and its power and rhythm in the telling. Though the title foregrounds Maru, he is no solitary hero, but acts within a field of forces where there is a complex interplay between characters and conditions and their powers and energies. Margaret Cadmore, the Mosarwa teacher, artist, lover, and friend, is the major catalyst[134] that sets off the sequence of interrelated events—for several of which the image of a bomb going off[135] appropriately indicates the shock of suddenness and the displacement of entrenched social arrangements.

The novel opens on a skyscape that presents a highly complex and ambiguous image of the coming of the "new world" of Margaret's imagination (108), which has become[136] Maru's "vision" (7). It reads:

> The rains were so late that year. But throughout that hot, dry summer those black storm clouds clung in thick folds of brooding darkness along the low horizon. There seemed to be a secret in their activity, because each evening they broke the long, sullen silence of the day, and sent soft rumbles of thun-

> der and flickering slicks of lightning across the empty sky. They were not promising rain. They were prisoners, pushed back, in trapped coils of boiling cloud. (5)

Since this is the preamble (one soon learns) to the supposedly happy-ever-after situation of Maru and Margaret (in terms of the fairy-tale paradigm), it is the first, carefully placed indication that Head's imagining of the founding of future, humane communities takes full cognizance of recalcitrance, obstruction, and delay—and that such qualifying, "realistic" considerations are not "illegitimate meanings percolat[ing] through ['fissures in her discourse'] and so undermin[ing] an overt [hopeful] message,"[137] but indeed a fully *intended* effect of the author's. No social change as huge as the eradication of racism, one of the great cornerstones of the social construct (10–12), will or can occur overnight—and despite Head's private expressions of satisfaction[138] with the beauty, importance, and liberatory potential of this novel, within the text itself she places careful markers[139] that indicate how entrenched racism is—and how difficult to dislodge. Yet it is exactly because the power of racism is so terrible and so immense that gestures as unexpected in their generosity as Maru's and Margaret's marriage (*and* what such an event requires for it to become possible) are needed to initiate the social and political, as well as psychological, "surprise"—that people called names like "Masarwa" are "as human as everyone else" (126–127).

The unexpected shifts in the opening paragraph (7, quoted above)—a "pattern of disconcertions"—work as follows: after an opening sentence that registers disappointment or frustrated expectation, the longer second and third sentences seem to offer a countering reassurance, only for the short penultimate sentence to cancel hope, a letdown seemingly exacerbated by the flat finality of the last statement. Yet so deeply paradoxical is Head's style that the image of impending, life-giving, though delayed, rain (when the "storm" finally breaks—8), which the first sentence establishes, overrides the insistence on its delay in the two concluding statements of the paragraph. Huge and vital energies are *present* here—though for the present unreleased.[140] Maru's "prepar[ation of] his fields" (7) is both appropriate (cf. "seasonal" 5) *and* proof of his depth of conviction and faith despite the evidence—or the odds.

Depicting Maru as she does in these opening pages, at work with his friends in the "fields," planning the yellow daisy garden for Margaret and "construct[ing] . . . vegetable beds" (5–6), Head seems to have forestalled critics' misgivings that in surrendering the paramount chieftaincy Maru has merely opted out of society.[141] Such readings fail to pay attention to the distinctly "construct[ive]" (6) and innovative activities depicted here and to the description of Maru as one who "*accept[s]* . . . and *fulfil[ls]*" (5, emphases added) not only one, but "many destinies." He continues to introduce "new" ideas (6) and "beginning[s]" (7)—energies of change that challenge the powerful, viciously defended[142] fixities of society.[143] The strange turn in the sentence "he did not need any kingship *other than* the kind of wife everybody would loathe" (6, emphasis added) indicates how far Maru's "vision of a new world" (7), through his love of Margaret, takes him. Rejecting power, the one goal most people greedily, desperately pursue, as trash in comparison with the creative energies of a love relationship,[144] he is acting in accordance with the logic of liberation—psychic *and* political. Not only is he leaving an indelible "message"[145] behind for his people—however hard they "pretend" his death (6)—he is also dislodging a power pyramid that ultimately rests on (and requires) slavery, as all hierarchies have their bases in the lowest tier of society (11; cf. the top of 69).

A "born leader" (5)—in the sense of Maru as one who inherits dynastic power—is, hence, an outdated meaning that the text crosses with the dawning realization that his inborn leadership qualities are actually shown in his deliberate, inspired *transgression* of conventional expectations (5–7).[146]

Yet, has Maru not merely shifted from the position of paramount chief, ruling thousands of Batswana and Basarwa, to that of a mini-tyrant commanding his three Batswana friends and enslaving, holding captive, and erasing the creative genius of his Mosarwa wife—whom he "kidnapped" and manipulated[147] into marriage? During her own lifetime Head was made aware of difficulties readers had with the figure and role of Maru,[148] and some more contemporary critics have expressed clear misgivings about power relations within the marriage as Head depicts it.[149] The highly cryptic quality of the style; the "strange,"[150] idiosyncratic behavior (5) depicted; and the author's refusal to present unproblematic solutions or situations are probably the three main factors that have contributed to the dissatisfactions[151] with this outcome-at-the-beginning (since Head places part of the narrative conclusion here in the opening pages—the other part being reserved for the novel's closing pages).

Because of these difficulties, it is possible to read *Maru* as an indication of secretly phallocratic, fascist tendencies in the author.[152] To do so may, however, be not merely legitimately deconstructive reading, but an actual violation of carefully balanced effects in the text. Initially baffling and unappealing impressions can be read as authorial challenges to careful (re)appraisal. Here, too, issues of power and of transformative energies that link (and divide) writer, reader, and specialist critic are at stake: "authority" is always an interchange.

One crux[153] is Margaret's "[fearful]" response to the unexpected return of her husband (8). Does this depict a dominant, terrorizing spouse? Extremely careful, contextualizing writing has gone into this passage (8–10). The morality of Margaret and Maru's relationship is a deeply intricate matter, as Head describes it—but the thread to follow (the clue of liberatory energy as distinguished[154] from popularity-based power) is always provided (9–10, 58, 67–68). Roles are not straightforward or static in this text, and Moleka is no mere villain, but a "co-hero" to Maru and, indeed, Margaret's *initial* savior from racist obliteration. Yet Head early on makes a definite separation between them (later again changed, complicated, and ameliorated as new relationship configurations begin to form), casting Moleka as a power figure *opposed* to Maru as a figure of gentle, salvific energy (who uses "power methods" to other ends).[155]

Indeed, decontextualization of the detail—Margaret's looking up "fearfully" (8) when Maru walks into their home—blots out the extent to which Head casts him (in the marriage) in the role resembling the one most feared by the "macho" male: that of the emotionally dependent husband in whose wife's love life "there is someone else" (see 8–10). That Maru's position in the marital relationship is not that of power preponderance is shown in the repetition of the adverb "fearfully" (8), the second time to describe Maru's and not Margaret's reaction. Clearly, a balance of emotional and sexual power is established at the same time as Head insists on the continuation (or even intensification) of human vulnerability in a relationship so very intimate and committed[156] that one partner understands what the other dreams (and forgets) (8–9). The expressions "dark shadow," "completely undone" (8), and "helpless victim" (pertaining to Maru) establish Moleka's continuing, haunting presence (and influence) as a power restriction on Maru—and as an anguishing yet empowering influence on Margaret. Head indicates here, also, the continuing entanglement among the main actors and others in the society that she depicts. As Maru haunts his people's minds, so does Moleka haunt his (and Margaret's), and they his.

Head seems to present in this novel some tentative, exploratory answers to the question of how socially transformative energies may become powerful or efficacious, remedial, and liberatory.[157] Much of the narrative is focalized through Maru, and Head does indeed assign to him a "directing" role. Both his gender and his inherited power—phallocracy and autocracy—provide him with power bases whose social reality Head recognizes. Maru ruthlessly employs and exploits those power bases in order to transcend them eventually. Yet a central feature of Head's vision is that the daunting task of social change is no single person's (or even lone leader's) responsibility or within the capacity of their energies.[158] Her particular complication of the obvious point of the need for cooperative social action is the sense that she conveys that these multiple forces for change need not and will not necessarily function in the shape of conventional political structures and organizations—or even consciously (intentionally). The key statement of this point occurs late in the novel: "In this strange tangle[159] of secret events, secretly they all assisted each other" (116). The sense that life-*giving* energies are involved is registered in the verb "assisted."[160] Head indicates additionally that some transcendent powers (whether these are powers to be termed historical, natural—that is, "earth-energies"—or spiritual, is immaterial) are involved, by making Maru himself the instrument of "the gods . . . in his heart" (73) and by referring to Margaret as needing to learn to control "the power machine of [creative] production" (101).[161] Moreover, transformative energy is depicted in the novel as bounding or transferring from one point or person to another, as is appropriate to the notion of a kind of social electricity that never stands still, working against those (deathly) influences that merely want "to keep the world the way it was" (7).

The initiating, "electrical" moment in the novel is the *recognition* by the British missionary Margaret Cadmore[162] of the spiritual status of the reviled, dead "Masarwa" woman, the younger Margaret's mother. That this is a transformative moment is measured in the fact that the caption to the elder Margaret's sketch inverts the conventional social pyramid: a "dog" (42, 14) Lesarwa becomes a god/dess (67).[163] And because the elder Margaret "for the first time" now "[sees] human suffering, close up," its (neglected) dignity exerts sufficient power upon her to "[frighten] her into adopting" the "Masarwa" baby (15). This "adopti[on]"[164] will, in turn, make possible the startling, transforming effect, on Moleka, of the "soft fluctuations" and "plaintive cry" (32)[165] in Margaret's cultivated voice. Indeed, both she and he experience this transformative moment[166] as a small explosion.[167] In accordance with their vastly different social status, the effect on each of the two is diametrically opposed—and balanced. The despised "Lesarwa" is "made [to] feel . . . the most important person on earth" (30), whereas the "savage, arrogant Moleka" (57) is softened and "humbled" (57)—or apparently so.[168]

Head carefully prepares the reader to receive the idea that despite the importance of this "love at first *hearing*" between Moleka and Margaret, Maru is the person more fitted to be her partner, the one who has a true kinship with her and whose alliance with her will have greater creative consequences. This occurs through careful juxtapositions like the back-to-backing of the details that Maru (*before* he meets Margaret) has "towards everyone" the manner of "courteous informal respect" (50)—whereas Margaret "ha[s] dignity and respect for everyone" (51). Maru's "common touch" and Margaret's "royal dignity" bridge the gap of conventional status distinctions between them and show both of them exhibiting a socially inclusive mentality. It is also significant that Maru "falls in love with"[169] Margaret on hearing her conduct and her transformative effect on people (merely) described—and decides to marry her, knowing that she is a Mosarwa, whereas Moleka could not have grasped this fact (her "Masarwaness") by seeing her or by hearing "the near perfect English accent" (23) at the moment that he makes his "connection" with her.[170]

Nevertheless, the link established between Moleka and Margaret plays a crucial role in both their lives, continues to connect them after they are separated, and affects the larger sphere of their society. One might describe the connection between them as having an "energizing" effect. For Moleka it begins with the "unbalanc[ing]" experience (32) of some power greater than his own[171] ("strange . . . beyond his control"—30). It creates "a new Moleka" (32, 38), "a changed man" who has acquired courtesy (54) and who becomes a slave liberator and social reformer (55).[172] Delicacy of feeling and nobility of conduct become possible to Moleka because of Margaret's influence on his "secret heart" (82), just as he inspires and sustains Margaret with his unspoken love like "half suns glowing on the horizons of her heart" (93, 113). This, too, functions like a transmitted energy, since it "freed her to work and live with vigour" (99) and enables her to link imaginatively into the village life around her (31, 112–113). The "radiant energy" that is Moleka's formerly hidden core can later (through Maru's maneuvering)[173] find its "true complement" in the deep, creative peace that is Dikeledi's being (83). More mundanely, it is suggested that loving and losing Margaret is what makes it eventually possible for Moleka to become "a real husband" (125) to Dikeledi. Moleka's and Dikeledi's encounters and suffering during this period will contribute to making the two of them the "living dynamo[s]" in the practical role of rulers who can progressively transform a "future" Africa (70).

Maru thwarts any development of a relationship between Margaret and Moleka because of his conviction that the latter has "a public eye" (9). This cryptic expression means that Moleka is one to whom popularity and image matter. This Maru analyzes probingly and convincingly (9) as a sign of a "weakness for power"[174] in Moleka and an indication that this friend would have been unable to withstand the long-term pressure of racial prejudice ("ridicule" and "malice") exerted by the "public" on a "Masarwa" wife (9). This realization touches on a discovery Maru articulates elsewhere, about an illusory aspect to political and social power: that the powerful one may be merely a tool to the basest and most backward mob instincts (which are prejudices and entrenched habits) in any society (67–68).[175] The way Maru imagines that Moleka would in the future have buckled under the relentlessness of racial ostracism leads directly into the presentation of Margaret's memories of racist abuse directed at her, as a child (10ff.). We are being shown why racist social persecution is seemingly ineradicable: the weak, the "low," and the powerless may have only the one power advantage to press—that of racist denunciation (10). When Maru subjects first Moleka (55–64) and then Dikeledi (65ff.) to a testing of their loyalty to Margaret *as a* "Masarwa" woman, even these two, the most enlightened members of his society, yield to the pressure of the (pretended) racial prejudice he exhibits in his capacity as powerful ruler.[176] The power issue of racialism eats into the commitments of love and friendship in all but the most rare of individuals—whose task to challenge it is commensurately intensified and made more difficult.[177]

Since racism is a function of power (compare 109), Maru's actual, eventual *dis*sociation from power is (symbolically appropriately) a resounding antiracist act: his and Margaret's marriage. His selfhood is not that of the sort of ruler whose *subjection* to power is exhibited in the pursuit of popularity[178] and in the signs of ambition. Contrastingly, he is himself psychically a subject, since he is the instrument of the "gods in his heart" (or of "something" mysterious—a propelling force—55) to which he is (in Head's carefully chosen term) "subjected" (37—cf. "subjection," 73).[179] The unfolding energy in Maru's soul (which is then socially dispersed) is not like Moleka's "sun" (31, 58). It is instead likened to an "evolution" and to a gentle growth propulsion: "the way the rain made the grass and flowers bloom" (73).[180] Yet the arduousness of such growth is also recognized in Maru's indignant comment on most people's failure to recognize their duty and their need to "make [the] effort to become a god" (36).

Margaret lacks the power of being able to announce an identity as a power base, which most other members of the society can wield. Identified by (most) *others* as either a "Coloured" (39, 51)[181] or as a nonhuman "it" (40), depending on whether they have heard her quiet statement that she "[is] a Masarwa" (24, 40), her unashamed self-identification nevertheless has power to startle. People with "decent" (19, 47) instincts (like Margaret [Sr.], Dikeledi, and Moleka) immediately move to protect her from what they perceive as the dangerously challenging, provocative effect of her statement of ethnicity. Others (like Seth, Pete, Morafi) take steps[182] to persecute and to oust her (e.g., "Either the Masarwa teacher goes or I go"—89). It is only Maru who grasps instantly that she is a "goddess," Margaret having made a "god" of a mere arrogant man such as Moleka used to be (67). Yet Maru's "recognition" of Margaret's status[183] is preceded by a series of other "recognitions" that she achieves in Dilepe. The lorry driver's punctilious kindness toward her (21–23), Dikeledi's instant respect and generous friendship (23–28), Ranko's devotion (51–55), and Moleka's self-humbling love (29–33) are all proof of Margaret's "hidden power" (71, 112) and her ability to elicit people's finest feelings. These precedents to his own meeting with her serve to alert Maru to a sense of her ability to empower *him* to act in a socially transformative way.

In some ways disconcertingly "identityless" (15)[184] or even "beyond" identity (20, compare 16),[185] in other ways indelibly branded a despicable "Lesarwa" woman (10, 17, 94), Margaret (Jr.) is also (by her "experiment[ing]" foster mother—15) endowed with a responsibility toward "[her] people" (17, 18, 20ff.) that presumes an identif*ication* with them. She is never shown meeting any of them and has been effectively severed from "Masarwa" society through no choice of her own. Yet both symbolically and in a way politically (given the effect her marriage has),[186] Margaret fulfills the destiny of being a savior of her people. She does so in the way that Head favors: as an independent, visionary artist rather than as a political organizer or ruler.[187] The author's thinking on this point (as the text illustrates) is (still) neither nonpolitical nor an advocation of passive withdrawal from the power distortions of society, but instead it advocates a form of social participation by the creative person through the communication of transformative impulses to the larger society.[188]

The poignancy of Margaret's undefensive, unaggressive response (in childhood) to vicious abuse by peers is something Head conveys both beautifully and convincingly as a response entirely distinct from mere weakness or capitulation. Margaret thinks and analyzes,[189] in contrast with the unthinking and "beastly" (18) fierceness of those who persecute her.[190] She has to negotiate a social space for herself.[191] In her later life, although convinced that Moleka (who, she knows, is in love with her) "will never approach [her], because [she is] a Masarwa" (94), she is nevertheless able to draw on his unspoken support (30–31, 99) to express her sense of the interconnectedness of all life in her paintings. In expressing that powerful insight with all the "vigour" (94, 99, 101, 108) of her deeper self, she is taking her place in "the tug and pull of the spider-web of life" (Head, *Alone* 35). Although that place is a seemingly detached one at the time, it is at the quick of fuller life for all sections of society. She is a center of transformational energy. That is so because Margaret's art envisions and then demonstrates the possibility of bringing a "new world" (7, 50, 108, 68–70) into being—a world where richer, freer life will result from people's acceptance of mutual and separate powers in order to weave a "tapestry" (cf. *Alone* 30) to beautify their single existences. Such a "new world" will be the opposite of the "hierarchy of contempt" by which society is presently constituted (68–69, 109, 11).

It is not only,[192] but especially through her painting that Margaret imagines and then "images" (gives shape to) what such a "new world" might be like. It is not a never-never land. It depicts "ordinary" (107) people and creatures doing ordinary things, but *seen* as magically vital and noble. So powerful is her vision that the energy can be relayed to Maru with the "message" (107–108, 109) that the people endowed with the powers to construct the space where all can be humanized and recognized[193] are the lowliest members of society (108–109). But the lesson of "decency" must be taught first (47), as Dikeledi earlier observes.

Margaret's paintings are one such lesson—Maru's relinquishing of kingship[194] for a "Lesarwa" woman's love is another. The third one may become necessary in due course, when "it [will] no longer [be] possible to treat Masarwa people in an inhumane way without getting killed yourself" (127).[195] On this austere note of stern warning, which is simultaneously exhilarating and encouraging in its vision of future[196] freedom, Bessie Head concludes this novel.

Maru, which Head herself considered a "magical" work,[197] is not such in any tinselly, sleight-of-hand fashion. It is a scrupulously constructed and politically challenging[198] text—as well as being a "beautiful" one (Head, *Alone* 68).

A Question of Power

knowledge of evil
Bessie Head, *Alone*

A Question of Power, a deeply moving, formidably "difficult" novel,[199] is a work in which Bessie Head explores the dimensions of power far beyond the personal and sociopolitical arena, to delineate its metaphysical dimensions: she suggests in it that evil is the ultimate, hidden form of power.[200] The pattern of reasoning that informs the novel—though in part extremely complex and intricately allusive to the point of inaccessibility—is in the end both lucid and terrifying. Since power is essentially evil[201] and since power is—by earning the name of power for itself—recognized as that which is stronger than anything else, it will and can *overpower*—that is, invade, hurt, possibly destroy—*anything* else. Evil is stronger than good(ness). Evil is that which conquers. Evil is power. This is an appropriately circular definition, as it functions by entrapment—as an "inescapable" truth. Elizabeth's report on her experience sums up the above: she "was never to regain a sense of security or stability on the question of how patterns of goodness were too soft, too indefinable to counter the tumultuous roar of evil" (159).

Elizabeth finds that certain widely accepted notions by means of which people attempt to protect themselves against the onslaughts of power (whether thought of as oppression or as evil) are actually exposable as delusions: these forms of protection or salvation from power *cannot exist.*[202] For, if goodness adopts the defensive strategy of a counterpower, it loses the nature of goodness.[203] In *A Question of Power*, this insight is illustrated in the ambiguous form of "Sello," who in being powerful includes evil in his past and in his manipulation of Elizabeth.[204] The same insight[205] is conveyed in the shape (preferable to Elizabeth) of ordinary, loving human decency, which is humbly nonpowerful and preoccupied with sharing. It is really the latter that is the true opposite of the triumphant, exclusive cruelty of "Medusa" and "Dan"—in not being powerful. Elizabeth's philosophical generalization of this point is the cryptic, italicized statement by "Sello" from which the novel's title is taken: "*If the things of the soul are really a question of power, then anyone in possession of power of the spirit could be Lucifer*" (199); her own experience of the point is her "rediscover[y]" that "the soft flow of life . . . include[s] all mankind, and . . . equalise[s] all things and all men" (202).

Long before the writing of *A Question of Power* (in 1968), Head wrote to Randolph Vigne: "The truth is that this mental torture will have to lead me to some conclusion more powerful than I have now. *I have always hated soppy, wishy-washy love and truth*, . . . but it is first one's mind that has to be sharpened up. You can only do so by putting it into fire" (*Gesture* 67, emphasis added). The italicized words can serve as a warning to readers that although the novel ends on the protagonist's release from a period of torturing anguish and demoralization, as well as the philosophically important discovery that the only alternative to power is a connected "ordinariness" (1, 39, 196, 206),[206] this is no easy option[207] or sentimental platitude—the road of discovery toward it is too "excruciating" (15) and taxing. Nor is it a sanctuary, a safe place. For the ordinary are also those who are utterly, perpetually vulnerable to the depredations of power–"how easy it was for people with soft shuffling, loosely-knit personalitics to be preyed upon by dominant, powerful persons" (12) is one of the eerie insights qualifying and setting off Elizabeth's "gospel" of the godhood of humanity[208] from those "lofty statements of mankind's great teachers" (12)—as is her even more frightening discovery that the victim and the meek may herself or himself "*personif[y* evil], in vivid detail, within themselves" (12). The source from which power draws lies within every individual soul. Power *preys* on the innermost self.

When Elizabeth begins to analyze the "ghoul[ishness]" (13, 197) of power (recognizing that "the power people . . . lived off other people's souls like vultures"—19), she feels that "some of the answers lay in her experiences in Botswana" (19), but the question(s) of power are subtly signposted as having originated in South Africa. There Elizabeth experienced racial discrimination outwardly as a "back-breaking life," but also inwardly, "like living with permanent nervous tension," as one of those who are the inexplicable butt of "hate" and "loath[ing]" (19). Head links *that* harrowing, South African exclusion with "Dan's brand of torture,"[209] as "something that could go on and on and on" (19). That evil "c[an] be a powerful invasion force from outside" (145) testifies to an irresistible contamination process. Head traces—poignantly, harrowingly—the route by which a person oppressed by racial abuse in South Africa can flee to a Botswana sanctuary and yet end up herself yelling racial abuse at a Motswana (51), as well as the process that leads a person terrified by mercilessness to end up assaulting an innocuous, kindly European (173).[210] The desperation of her condition is in both cases illustrated in the *subsequent* "scream" (51, cf. 174).[211]

One of the possible reasons why Head was reluctant to identify herself as a feminist in her writing is her intense awareness of and her deeply compunctious criticism of *all* forms of oppression and exploitation. In South Africa Elizabeth's experiences of racism (as a person classified "nonwhite") and of sexism (as the wife of an indiscriminate philanderer) are somewhat distinct, but this changes when she reaches Botswana as a single, mixed-race woman.[212] Hence in the novel, *both* "Medusa" and "Dan" are shown persecuting Elizabeth in ways that are both sexist and racist,[213] although perhaps "Medusa" harps more on the racist and "Dan" on the sexist string. Nevertheless, "Dan was simply the extension of Medusa" (168), as all forms of dignity-violating power are interconnected. Power is a continuum and power mongers cooperate.[214] Head may also be intimating that sexism is the more degrading and devastating, because more intimate, form of violation. Power rapes, as Head indicates by means of the detail that "Dan" "attacked [Elizabeth's] head the way he had attacked the vaginas of the nice-time girls" (180).[215]

"Sello's" power is less crude than racism or sexism: his is really a manifestation of spiritual arrogance. Yet in his reliance on and claim to a female partner (whose power greed he underestimates or overlooks), "Sello," too, exhibits elements of sexism, which a late passage explicitly indicates (199, quoted below). Before his "disappearance," "Sello" assures Elizabeth that their "friendship will never end" and she herself comments that, "funn[ily]" enough, "she really adores [the humbled] Sello" (200)—yet because she warily (or as she says, "cunningly"—201) wants any future relationship between them to be that of equality,[216] she clearly recognizes the element of disingenuity of the claims in one of his last speeches:

> It wasn't power that was my doom. It was women; in particular a special woman who formed a creative complement to me, much like the relationship you and I have had for some time. She was captivating and dazzling. I liked slaves. I could never say goodbye. I could never accept a rejection. I was too important. I tried to break her. She had your power. She broke free and unleashed centuries of suffering and darkness. Nothing stood in the way of her prestige and self-esteem; she was God. She was like Dan with a terrible will, with magic rituals and all kinds of tricks. I saw the story repeating itself because, once he saw his power, he wanted to be God on the strength of his power, irrespective of the fact that his heart is filth. What he showed you was all that he had in his heart. . . . He thought you might not fall in with his plans. That's why he took you on, to remould you in his own image. I gave him a free hand because I wanted to study, completely, his image. And I thought you needed the insight into absolute evil. I'm sorry it was so painful. (200)

Since "Sello" isn't an ordinary person, this remarkable passage does not exhibit character defects, but is an analytic depiction of the cunning of power[217] and of the way it inserts and inveigles itself even into the best of intentions so that it begins to wreak havoc. Despite the denial in the opening sentence of the speech, every sentence that follows exhibits the greed, jealousy, and dishonesty of the power principle, with strong sexist overtones. The ancient pattern of "blaming it on Eve" is here; the inability to admit the evil of arrogance ("Sello's" declaration is permeated by the unspoken, arrogant claim of natural or "deserved" supremacy); the blindness to the aspects of projection and contradiction[218] in a state of self-righteousness.

Head herself indicated that she thought the proclamation, in this novel, of the deep ambivalence of, and "about," power (an ambivalence that in her estimation and experience is an attribute shared by all human beings)[219] was its central insight. In writing that "you don't realise the point at which you become evil" (96, 145—cf. *Alone* 69, 77), she shows the insidiousness, the *tempting*, enticing quality of the thought (a misleading hope or a false dream) that power can be put to benign use. Even more important (even heroically, in the brave exhibition[220] of a whole period of inner degradation and contamination), Head acknowledges throughout this work one of the most unpalatable or even unacknowledgeable of realities: that power lust is inherent in every individual—including victims of power.[221] That is probably the core meaning of the fact that even though power is on the one hand described as an invasive force, "Sello," "Medusa," and "Dan" are simultaneously products of or emanations from Elizabeth's own inner mind. The expression "knowledge of evil" (Head, *Alone* 63), chosen as epigraph to this section of my text, can legitimately be adjusted to proclaim Head's "[ac]knowledge[ment] of evil" (and of power lust) through Elizabeth. "The roots of evil, as a creative, propelling force, had become as close as her own breathing" (85–86)[222] is a central expression of this terrifying, shameful[223] idea. Another is the theological notion of someone being "both God and Satan at the same time" (161), which indicates a combination of huge powers (each "invalidating" yet propping up the other) *or* a statement of the ambivalence of (all) power.[224] Power confuses—its nature as well as its effects are confusing,[225] baffling, "mind-boggling."

Clearly, as the title signposts, the focus of this novel is on forms of power rather than on forms of transformative energy. After writing her more "cheerful" or "hopeful" earlier works, Head seems to have encountered the need to delve further back (into history) and deeper (into the psyche) to establish what the (transformative) process of "humanization"[226] is *up against*—as it were, confronting its enemies and taking the measure of the dangers involved.[227] *A Question of Power* is *dis*comforting because of the insistence on how harrowing the process is. Without invalidating anything Head had written earlier, it balances those visions of society and its possible destiny.

Almost the entire collection of Head's letters to Vigne (*A Gesture of Belonging*) can be read as a continuous commentary on and as accompanying evidence for the *Question of Power* experiences.[228] Concerning the issue of where the growth points for transformative energy are located in *A Question of Power*, a few pointers may be drawn from the letter collection. The concern with food growing and productive efficiency[229] in the novel is reflected in a comment from 1968: "The practical will change the world at the right time" (*Gesture* 69).[230] In the novel, this is reflected in "Ditamati, Dionions, Dispinach, Dibeans, Dicarrots" (204)—plants in her and Kenosi's vegetable garden that, like the "Cape Gooseberry" associated with Elizabeth herself, have "settled down and bec[o]me a part of the village life of Motabeng" (153), growing "with shimmering, green leaves in the intense heat" (124, 72). They originate from the "beautiful dreams" (150) of a man like Eugene (another ex–South African in Motabeng), but they produce rooted, edible, life-enhancing results.

In the novel Head conveys the notion that destiny earmarks certain individuals to "prepare the ground," by the experience of anguishing spiritual quests, for the possibility of future growth and the eventual advancement of all humanity. "Boldness and wisdom," she wrote to Vigne in 1969, "are spiritual qualities," and the "growth and unfoldment [of the spirit] is slow and gradual"—yet she felt that "the process of suffering creates something big" (*Gesture* 74–74—cf. 75–76). In *A Question of Power* Elizabeth tells Tom, after her discharge from the lunatic asylum: "I seem to have been born for this experience. . . . Someone weighed up my soul . . . I have to attend the trial" (192). Exceptional suffering and a terrible testing period such as Elizabeth is made to undergo are seen as a sacrificial contribution to the possibility of human progress.

The novel is no triumphalist account of certain victory; the hovering presence of evil powers (embedded in social structures, lurking in the psyche, or "taking over" what is benignly intended) is presented with too awful a vividness for the achieved relief to be the overriding impression.[231] Head wrote to Vigne in 1970: "the causes are too far ahead . . . but we work all the same. . . . One is never sure the world will change" (*Gesture* 125). Commenting (in 1978) on her own writing, Head nevertheless wrote later: "What has driven me is a feeling that human destiny ought not to proceed along tragic lines, with every effort and every new-born civilisation throttling itself in destruction with wrong ideas and wrong ways of living" (*Alone* 63).

Some of the "wrong ideas" from which *A Question of Power* attempts to rescue people, in order that a "proce[ss] along [more hopeful] lines" might become possible, are Elizabeth's refutation of the idea that (a) God will come along to "put things right";[232] the notion that divinity is a power "out" or "up there," beyond humanity; and naïve ignorance of the dangerous fact that love itself may harbor and facilitate evil. Comments from the Vigne letters that are parallel formulations of these ideas in the novel are (in the same order as above) the following: "There is no such thing as saying: God help me. I don't want to die. I don't want to go mad. You just do" (105–106). "Divinity seems to suggest an untouchable holiness. I distrust that. There is no such thing" (135).[233] "Now I question love and am deeply afraid of it because its other face is evil. You can come up against a sort of love so vehement and cruel that it is hardly fit for human society" (145–146).[234] These "wrong ideas" are seen as mental or spiritual impediments to growth. They are clearly exposed as such in the novel, though not merely in intellectual argument, but in bleak and terrifying experience. In the novel, Elizabeth's being "thrown to the wolves" ("Medusa" and "Dan," obviously; "Sello," more insidiously) illustrates the first point; the conclusion of the novel with its dispersal of divinity into "the brotherhood of man" (206) illustrates the second; and Elizabeth's "relationship" with "Dan" (as well as "Sello's" with "Medusa"), the third. In 1971 Head commented to Vigne in a letter: "I was suffering from a form of insanity not yet known on earth. . . . I knew nothing until I went right through the mill and now I wonder if some years of suffering pay for centuries of hell and that it was well worth it" (*Gesture* 147).[235]

In *A Question of Power*, "the everyday life [is] deliberately juxtaposed against the interior narrative for contrast and a choice between two worlds; one of death and destruction and the other which promotes life."[236] On a strict line count, the passages in the novel dealing with the "promot[ion] of life" may exceed those exhibiting "death and destruction." Yet the gentle, low-keyed energies of growth[237] presented in this text are humble and modest in contrast with the deafening "roar" (36, 159) that represents the malice and the *overwhelming* effect of the power sphere.[238] By assaulting, undermining, and seducing Elizabeth, power enforces a stasis[239] of deep doubt, terrifying anxiety, and profound sadness[240] in her. She cannot progress along "the elegant pathway of private thought" (149, 206) while this is the case. Mostly, the novel depicts an extremely precarious holding action on the part of its chief protagonist in showing the "reduction" of "Sello's" status as well as Elizabeth's two major breakdowns. How much energy will be absorbed in encounters of this kind, with power, Head testifies to in a 1978 interview in which she repeatedly employs the term "work-out" (Marquard 53)—which suggests not only a complicated intellectual disentanglement process, but something of the arduousness of the experience. Mere endurance of the great soul storm that Elizabeth undergoes hence precludes and precedes possible future growth. And Head's insistence on the massiveness of the power danger would not have been as convincing as it is had there been a quicker, easier "recovery" in Elizabeth.[241] Head depicts destructive, humiliating power as *itself* an incandescent energy, for instance in the "terrible thunderbolt" with which "Medusa"[242] "str[ikes Elizabeth's] heart" (39) with humiliating ideas, and in the "spectacular display of soul-power," in the shape of "an atomic bomb of red fire" (104—cf. 198), with which "Dan" impresses and intimidates Elizabeth.[243] The end of the novel probably presents a very tentative new beginning, still beset by many dangers, rather than any final triumph or safety for Elizabeth.

Yet the existence of the book itself is testimony to the function of creative powers employed by the author to address the power situation in which she found herself a victim—a situation that she nevertheless *ends* in the role of commentator.[244] The split between Elizabeth the protagonist and Head the author-narrator proves that a kind of transformation has occurred. Elizabeth's reference to her (past) role as "Blabbermouth" (40) points to a collaborator-victim becoming a narrator and an analyst of power: she *tells on* power, which is to sever herself from it. In structuring *her* tale[245] (of the experience of subjection to power domination and the paranoia that it engendered) by *beginning with its ending*—the exposure, unmasking, and release that followed that period—as well as by interspersing her account of the frightening insanities to which she is prey during this period with lucid, warm, and humane moments and encounters, Elizabeth/Head is retaliating *creatively*.[246] She changes roles from victim-patient to therapist, counseling others about the illusory and poisonous qualities of the yearned-for and powerful, supposed savior they tend to turn to in distress. That is merely another form of abjection.[247] Instead, she opts out of the clutches of power by reenvisioning a world of related equals who mutually sustain[248] each other. For this, the Motabeng garden project—a tiny, unlikely, re-created Eden—is the appropriate metaphor.

In response to her "shattering" (109) by power (into "Sello," "Medusa," "Sello in the brown suit," "Dan," and the seventy-one "girls" of his harem), Elizabeth restructures her self by means of the shaped and coherent (though complex and nonlinear) narrative or epic that has become the novel.[249] She does so also by reintegrating herself into the human community[250] of which she is a part, but from which the overwhelming intensity of her feelings of fury, mistrust, and horror (aroused by power abuse) had detached and fragmented her. She does not suppress the "lava" (83, 98, 136, 140, 171)[251] of her natural resentment at the goading she has undergone—yet she begins and continues to rechannel those energies creatively into the communally beneficial and interlinking activities that her roles of food supplier and loving person[252] make possible. The novel itself is proof of the working of transformative energy, because there is an emergence, an account, an analysis, and a "history" in it: it is a faithful record, yet a reinvented past. No longer the merely passive screen for "Sello's" historical pageants or "Dan's" porn shows, Elizabeth paints and re-creates her tale—which is riveting and harrowing, yet interspersed with many scenes of gentleness, deep trust between people, and endearing humor.

If love[253] and creativity are integrative energies, power is seen to work by "shattering" (109) and "aparting."[254] Its effects are those of dislodgement and displacement. Once this "dark, evil" feeling of "unbelonging" and unworthiness has lodged itself in the mind (as was first done to Elizabeth at the vulnerable childhood stage, in South Africa), it "set[s] down roots deep into [the] soul and [eats] and [eats] and [eats]" (43).[255] It is what makes Elizabeth, supposedly leaving a racist society behind, in South Africa, so defenseless against experiences of racial discrimination directed against her (in her mind) in Botswana. It seems to leave her nowhere to go. Yet Elizabeth does manage to retain, or rather to revive, the dream of (or faith in) African society—as the opening and closing pages of the novel clearly testify. In what she considers the "African" desire for all people to be "ordinary" lies the alternative to the enslaving, hypnotizing effect of power.[256]

The power forms analyzed in the novel are not the predictable incarnations of power (such as governments, rulers, authority figures, or social institutions) of the usual political novel. Head's strategy avoids these obvious targets. She depicts power in surreal, but intensified ("concentrated," distilled) form[257] in order to get to its roots. How risky the undertaking is, she testifies when Elizabeth tells Tom: "I'm going insane" (161). "Sello," "Medusa," "Dan," and his harem of "girls" are all *imagined* power forms[258]—but they are neither illusions nor hallucinations. They are mechanisms allowing Elizabeth to study[259] (as she experiences it) the concentrated onslaughts of power on the soul. The deep feelings of unworthiness with which she is overwhelmed—that as a "Coloured" she is not a "true" African,[260] that she is a sexually inadequate woman—are externalized in the display of African xenophobia (mainly this is what "Medusa" represents) and in an imagined relationship with an African man who entraps her in a supposedly great love *while* humiliating her sexually (this is "Dan").[261] ("Dan" represents the type of gloating male sexual power in which women are often complicit—hence the seventy-one "girls.") The gesture expressive of a sense of "belonging" on which the novel ends marks Elizabeth's release from both these "enemies within," which are reflected from her outward circumstances.

The reason that the "gesture of belonging" (206) that Elizabeth makes at the end of her period of agony is so significant is that it enacts an alternative to attitudes both of power *wielding* and of *victimization* by power.[262] A person who can make such a movement is (as Elizabeth says elsewhere of Tom) "tentative yet secure" (122). A sense of self-worth (as distinct from the power form of personal arrogance) is implicit in the "gesture," which simultaneously recognizes the worth and equality of others, because the gesture is in the mode of dedication. Without being abject, it is humble[263] and (in Elizabeth's special sense) humanly "ordinary" (206). It is the "underground water" in "the place of sand" (19).

A Bewitched Crossroad: An African Saga

restoring the "broken sense of history"
Bessie Head, *Alone*

One of Bessie Head's most memorable comments (published midway into the ten-year period it took to produce *A Bewitched Crossroad*)[264] reads:

> The social and political life of the country [i.e., South Africa] was becoming harsher and harsher. A sense of history was totally absent in me and it was as if, far back in history, thieves had stolen the land and were so anxious to cover up all traces of the theft that correspondingly, all traces of the true history have been obliterated. We, as black people, could make no appraisal of our own worth; we did not know who or what we were, apart from objects of abuse and exploitation. (*Alone* 66)[265]

The striking effect achieved in this passage derives perhaps from the way Head combines the sense of a huge injustice and power loss (being deprived[266] of a resource as basic, as much taken for granted, usually, as one's own history) and of the bewildering and even eerie effect this has, with the stunning aftereffect of the realization that it was precisely the land annexation (in Africa) by Europeans that required and propelled the indigenes' deprivation of even "a history." It was, hence, not merely "*as if* thieves had stolen the land" (emphasis added). In fact, those who had taken it, and who had justified the theft with the lying claim that it was theirs by right, were practicing their deception in order to dislodge Africans, not only physically, but psychically. The expression "as if" registers their success in the *bewilderment*[267] of the locals, and the whole passage is a succinct analysis of the international invasive power practice that we call colonialism—seizure of land followed by and providing the footing for seizure of rule and the colonization of the minds of those whose land has been taken. *Crossroad*, Head's culminating work,[268] can be read as a major act of reclamation.[269] It is a text that works throughout by recognizing all those rights and dignities that were denied by the colonial sneer and the settlers' brutal greed. It does so without producing a fairy tale or a romantic inflation of African lives. Head was, in fact, conscious of the temptation of what might be called "reactionary glamorization" of African history[270] and was, instead, determined to insist on the deep human worth of the actual people and the need to portray their lives accurately. She wrote accordingly of the need to "[reclaim] that humility that has been trampled on and abused" (*Alone* 79).

Despite or, rather, in conjunction with her act of recognition, or empowerment, of such "humility," Head was also determined—in the process of writing from a continent almost indelibly associated in the average "Western" or "Eastern" conception of the world with notions of general primitivity, and of especial savagery in rulers as the typically African forms of power—to draw attention to the existence of a type of leader who could achieve the rare combination of benignity with power, *using* power to humanize his society.[271] It was as important to her to demonstrate that such leaders were not mere unlikely "accidents"—hence her insistence that "only a basically humane society could have produced Khama" (*Serowe* 3) *and* her illustration that the humane style of rule for which Khama III is renowned has an illustrious predecessor in the leader of the (South African) Sotho people, Moshoeshoe, an "unconverted" African leader (25–28). In other words, she is implicitly refuting both the claim that Khama is "un-African" and that his humanity came to him from his conversion to Christianity, as missionary writings other than those of MacKenzie tended to imply.[272] If it was the "image" of Khama III that provided the major salvific power (56–57) rescuing the area that became Botswana from the depredations of the colonists, Head was intent on illustrating the African rootedness of that image. Hence her preoccupation, throughout the text, with the contrast between Khama's rule and the forms of European power (Cape Colony expansionism and authority; British imperial intervention; the Transvaal republic's and other anarchic demonstrations of Boer land greed and racism) with which he had to contend, and her insistence on the contrasts between Khama's management of his situation and the way internal dissensions among other African leaders could be exploited by the Boers (88–93)—the most obvious contrast she draws being that between his (and his people's) society, on the one hand, and the "Matebele" power, on the other.

In a piece published in 1979 ("Social and Political Pressures That Shape Writing in Southern Africa"), Head referred to "Khama, The Great [i.e., Khama III—the nickname was commonly used], and his son, . . . [as] men distinguished for their personal integrity and *the power with which they articulated the hopes of their people*" (*Alone* 70—emphases added).[273] The italicized expression indicates the vicarious, unselfish quality of such power—that it is used on behalf of their people—as well as the leaders' role as mediators between their own people and a much greater power. In the term "articulated," moreover, it is not only the use of power to communicate and to intercede that is brought to mind, but the command of literacy, documentation skills, and modern technologies of communication. In his seeing the usefulness for his people of these techniques and in courageously accepting and discriminatingly employing them, Head recognized the brilliance, far-sightedness, and essentially progressive attitude of a man who was himself barely literate.[274] It is perhaps one of the aspects of Khama III that especially struck Head, as herself a writer intent on serving humanely liberatory and enlightening energies by means of her communicative skills.[275]

The culminating passage exhibiting Khama's superb negotiation skill (i.e., his ability to "read" the virtually world-governing power of British imperialism, with which he has to deal, and to avoid the brute, incommunicative power of the Boers),[276] first articulated no doubt in Tswana but, by means of the presence of MacKenzie (115–116), shown translated into and documented in English—and to be dispatched hence to the main political center of the time (Queen Victoria's court)—occurs in Chapter 8 (102–121, especially 117–119). From the "bare statement" (illustrated on p. 113) delivered with the "brisk curtness" (115) of the British military messenger, Warren, is developed the marvelously eloquent and moving expression (in reply) of African hopes and dreams of surviving, as an intact nation and land, the stormy season of colonialist land grabbing. In the previous chapter Head noted that "of all the foreign invaders, to only Britain had been extended an essentially African courtesy, that of seeking the protection of a greater power, with an implicit trust in the humanity and justice of that greater power" (108).[277] This attitude toward the superpower (especially the careful appeal to its national honor) is most vividly illustrated in the lengthy document that Head quotes in full

(117–119), for the reading of which she has prepared *her* text's reader by careful contextualization.

The document itself testifies to (it *documents*!) Khama's capacity for harnessing and combining "resources" (115) in a synergizing manner, creating channels for progressive change. She describes how he "huddled in private interview *with* Warren and MacKenzie, sensitively *working toward* a complete *control* of the astounding event" and how "he and MacKenzie went into final and deep consultation *out of which* was *produced* a voluminous document" (115, emphases added), one that combines the cooperative vision and foresight of both men (115–116).[278] Other forms of technology (than a command of writing skills and of the English language), for example, mapmaking, are also available as "resources in Shoshong" (115), because Khama has won the respect of resident Europeans.

The delicate rhythms and patterns of the document reflect a combination of courtesy, innate dignity, and diplomatic skill.[279] The Protectorate, states Khama by means of the document, "has been established by the desire of the Queen and . . . has come to help the land of the Bamangwato *also*" (117, emphasis added). Apparently conceding to Victoria the right to rule the Bamangwato people, he adds a double and delicately paced qualification: "Nevertheless I am not baffled in the government of my own town, or in deciding cases among my own people according to custom; but again I do not refuse help in these offices" (117).[280]

Especially, he insists that "the lands of the Bamangwato are not saleable"—that is, acceptance of Protectorate status neither "sells" his country to Britain nor does it allow the British to buy or sell portions of it.[281] The same point concerning the territorial integrity of the land is made delicately in another comment: "My country has got known boundary lines" (117), a statement refuting arrogant refusals by Europeans (at this time) to respect African national self-awareness and historical knowledge, and implicitly protesting against a merely Eurocentric purpose and perspective. The point is quietly reiterated: "I propose that a certain country of known dimensions should be mine and my people's" (118).[282]

Head's "contextualization" of the document (earlier referred to) can be illustrated from Khama's astute reference to the possibilities of progressive change (in order "to go forward and improve"—119) "if we are *wisely connected* with the English . . . adopting *some of*" their "ways" (119, emphases added). For it is notable that this chapter, with its powerful focus on the achievement of Protectorate status "up to latitude 22 degrees" (121), registers in the quoted words the refusal of the British to consider any but their own imperialist interests—thus an implicit refusal of Khama's request that his "country [should *not* be] cut in two" (115). Hence the ironic balance in the first sentence of the paragraph on which Head concludes this chapter: although "the expansion of the land-grabbing, cattle-grabbing Boers was halted," this is done in order that "the interior of Africa [would now be] open to British penetration" (121). The arid and (at this stage, apparently) resourceless Botswana area is simply not desirable to imperial eyes. What is to Head's vision a "hallowed land" (196) is in British dispatches described as "a god-awful country" (195). Yet that very material-minded blindness of the imperialist is presented by Head as resulting from the "bewitched" (196), magically elusive nature of the area she so reveres—its "powerless power," like Khama's own.

The central placing and full quotation of the Protectorate document (115–116) can also be contextualized by linking it with Head's reference to "the story of the manner by which the land was wrested from the people and their leaders during the scramble for Africa" (143), when the "illitera[cy of the] African chief[s]" was one of the main weaknesses on which imperialist power and other forms of land greed could prey (143—cf., e.g., 144–147, 150–155, 104, 89, 190) in the obtaining of chiefly "signatures" to fraudulent documents. It is in the end, of course, military power as the instrument and expression of commercial greed (a "land hunger," not for a home, but for profit and possession) that transforms mere pieces of paper into maps indicative of containment and border expansion. During the period of her composition of *Crossroad*, Head wrote to Benson of her "struggle to pull together the whole Southern African experience at that time[, mentioning that she was] mainly concentrating on the land question" (quoted in Eilersen 260). The abyss on the edge of which the "hallowed land" (198) of the Bamangwato teetered was the fact that "most of the tribes of South Africa were landless by the 1830s when foreign invasion reached the southern tip of Botswana . . . [and, as Head documents in *Crossroad* and elsewhere,[283] enormous] suffering . . . ensued. [Head hence saw t]he land question and almost every other question relevant to the black man's destiny [as] converg[ing] in Botswana" (*Alone* 70–71).[284]

The most fully documented instance of land loss in the novel, the breaking of the Ndebele people, occurs mainly by means of Cecil John Rhodes's awful combination of power, guile, and greed. It occurs also, most certainly (Head illustrates), with the collusion[285] of British political power, Cape expansionist appetites, and the bribable "conscience" of a British Christian missionary (149–151, 155–156). In Rhodes, she suggests, the Ndebele nation had "finally" met its match (156). Head indicates that the nature of the "Matebele" power structure contains a brittleness, in contrast with the flexible, adaptable, diplomatic skills of a visionary leader (like Khama) of a people who enshrine humane values (like the Bamangwato people)—as she characterizes them.[286] As a novelist she has the freedom to pronounce her perception of Ndebele culture as differing fundamentally from that of "Khama's people" (54) in being "informed" by "an inhuman brute force . . . almost a kind of dull illiteracy" (156). In "the inner totalitarian structure of the Ndebele nation," seemingly so strong in its "unyielding," impenetrable resistance to Christianization and (initially) to colonial penetration,[287] lies (according to Head's analysis) the "weak[ness]" (148) that will end in the virtual obliteration of these people. Yet the delicate pendulum of authorial sympathy swings to the side of Lobengula and the Ndebele nation in Head's documentation of the buildup of forces against them—human forces to whom they (the Ndebele) are not people, but mere obstacles and instruments: a more brutally inhumane power, thus, than even the "Matebele" in their heyday (see "breaking up" and "broken up" in Moffatt's letter—155). Its pitilessness is unforgettably recorded in the parable of Lobengula's that Head records for its perception of power relations: "England is the chameleon and I am that fly" (161).

All of *A Bewitched Crossroad* could be read as the careful juxtaposition of a variety of power manifestations for comparative (analytical) purposes. Head uses her novelistic skills and her moral sensitivity (as well as her "African loyalty") to *read*, reinterpret, and rearrange histories that had been differently deployed, and to other ends. Especially interesting is her tracing of the convolutions of British imperial power at this time. Clearly, nineteenth-century Britain is, *on the whole*, a power form of which she approves *in comparison with* the Boers' mere brutality (as she sees it), "Matebele" savagery, and Rhodes's undiluted, harsh "arrogan[ce]" (151). But she carefully traces the unreliable, erratic effects of a "culture" that she refers to as "a confusion of evil and good" (160), now championing humanitarian causes and then allying itself with the most naked land greed, linking these extremes often with inevitable maneuvers of profound hypocrisy or blatant callousness. Hence Moshoeshoe finds that a "succession of treaties signed with various British [Cape] governors . . . gradually reduce[s his] territory in favour of Boer encroachment" until "British influence in the area" is withdrawn, leaving the Basotho "entirely at the mercy of the Boers" (34). Later, the Colonial Office, appealed to (by MacKenzie) to assist Chiefs Montshiwa and Mankurwane upon the "seizure of [their] lands," blandly acknowledges the event as "a most miserable page in South African history," adding "but as we shall not attempt to coerce the Boers, Montshiwa and Mankurwane must face starvation as best they can" (105).

Where there is no British self-"interest," there is no commitment, merely the determination to do "as little as possible by way of administration" (122). The ugly side of that focus on (only) Britain's "interest" emerges during the period when the British government countenances and covertly assists Rhodes's "dirty work," tainting them with the same "ruthless rapacity and cynicism" (151). As Rhodes notes, "The objects are the same" (152). MacKenzie's eloquent, *moral* sarcasm and fury at plans resulting in a person being prevented from "hav[ing] . . . citizen rights, because he is a native African in his own country of Africa" (157), prove powerless. When their appeal *has already* been outmaneuvered, the Ndebele delegation requesting Victoria's help and advice is "magnanimously welcomed in London" (158) and given outdated, useless advice in the Queen's letter (159). For "the British government and Cecil John Rhodes had become one indivisible whole" (174).[288] The astounding culmination of naked imperialism is registered in Head's reference to "the Foreign Jurisdiction Act, which gave [the British Parliament] the right to proclaim British sovereignty over any part of the world *without previous treaty or agreement with the indigenous people*" (176, emphasis added). It is perhaps no accident that this coincides with the use of "the newly invented Maxim gun[289] which fired 620 rounds a minute [and] sliced the [Ndebele] warriors down like corn before a scythe" (182). Head records without comment, but in telling juxtaposition, the following sentences: "By 1895 it was clear that [Rhodes's B.S.A.] company was unfit to govern people and that too much power had been placed into the hands of lawless bandits. But by 1895 it was widely known that the British government had determined to hand the Bechuanaland Protectorate to the company" (185). By the "accident" of the Jameson raid fiasco, the British government "postponed the transfer" (191), and in 1966 ("with a sigh of relief," says Head) "they handed over independence" (195) to the country that became Botswana.

In analyzing the various power forms that dominate the historical and geographic landscape, Head works implicitly with the concept of a "basic (group) ethos," displaying these powers as if they are characters interrelating. After showing us the serene courtesies of the Banyai (or Shona) court and subcourt (10–13) through Sebina's eyes, disruption sets in—first, through the anarchic rule of Tumbale (13–14), then when the "Matebele" arrive to disrupt and shatter all civilized ways (14–18)—since they are a people "roaring like lions" (15, 17) and preying fiercely on all others. The "Matebele's" raiding, "annihilat[ing]" attitude (19) leads eventually to the establishment of another "military state with a standing army" (19), like the culture of Shaka (19–23) from which it sprang like a side shoot, Shaka having established "the precedent of the military state" (23) in Africa.

Like the "Matebele" are the Boers (in Head's portrayal), sometimes considered *as* and sometimes seemingly *more* "terrible" (91, 92) than the Ndebele warriors. Although they are like the "Matebele" in the depredations that they practice on other nations, Head suggests two particular dimensions of their culture that are displayed in their interactions with other peoples in the area and that distinguish them from the "Matebele." The first is their practice of guile, shown especially in the exploitation of power rivalries among African leaders (37, 39, 88–89) and in what is called "chicanery" (92) by the disapproving Africans. The second is the overt, ideological (religiously based) racism that is used to validate all their incursions—the distinction between the European "mensch" (person) and the non-European "schepsel" (creature) (31)—an attitude Head describes as "fanatic" (31) and as colored by the same awful, "fierce exultation" (39) that she associates with the other main predatory presences on the scene—Rhodes and the "Matebele." The emphasis in Head's portrayal of the Boers falls insistently on a single, main aspect of their role: "land grabbing" (30). This expression or its equivalents ("encroachment"; "seizure of . . . lands"; "dispossessions"; "depredations")[290] surround all their reported activities like some awful miasma. It is not a nuanced portrait and no individuals emerge from it, but it is a starkly condemnatory limning of what Sol Plaatje had referred to as "a gigantic plundering raid" (quoted in Head, *Alone* 82).[291]

It is in her depiction of Rhodes that Head portrays the ugliest "personal" embodiment of power greed she ever examines. Even the awful Matenge in *When Rain Clouds Gather* is touched with some humane compassion and some sense of his inward suffering, but in Rhodes Head finds no single redeeming touch. Her portrayal of him is perhaps of this kind because he retains his quality of triumphant, inhumane, *gloating* power to the very end,[292] and although Botswana is saved from him, he suffers only temporary and not devastating setbacks in his pitiless advances over Africa. Rhodes is introduced in Head's *African Saga* when he replaces the upright MacKenzie as a "more suitable"[293] deputy commissioner for southern Bechuanaland (109), the appointment measuring the preponderance of land greed over humane considerations in the ranks of the colonial power. Rhodes's power of drawing together[294] people motivated by a spirit similarly ruthless to his own, or otherwise corrupting them by offers of bribery from his immense fortune (110, 149–152) to serve his cause, seems like parody or inversion of the benign nation-builders depicted in this history—Mambo of the Banyai, Moshoeshoe of the Basotho, and Khama III of the Bamangwato. Head introduces Rhodes twice over as "representing the unity of British and Afrikaner Boer interests in the Cape" (149, 110). It is an alliance of brute force, devastatingly powerful and yet devious in deployment (149–155).

The fierce greed of the man is so gross and extreme that it is almost unbelievable; hence Head's careful documentation of his awful, "[ugly] utterances" (151, 156, 184) and his "violent combination of exploitation and abuse" (151). Rhodes is in himself (as Head portrays him) the extreme, naked expression of European rapacity. The one saying of his (reported by Head) that articulates this most bluntly is his "If you want the black man's land, take it" (151; repeated 184). He does just that. Because he can buy allies and overpower opponents, he establishes a vast, corrupt network of men throughout the colonial service and in British government circles. Head lists the shameful catalogue of the men who assist Rhodes's work of devastation in deliberate detail. Just as (in her vision) "integrity" or "human grandeur . . . [is] achieve[d] not [by] the effort of a single man but a collaboration of many great minds" (*Alone* 99), so too is corruption the product of a number of people cooperating to evil ends, as she indicates. Head exposes the full sordidness of both the true motives for, as well as the methods used in, the war that destroys Ndebele power (180–183). The gestures of Rhodes's on which the war is concluded (his "[need] to squat on Lobengula's possessions"—182) sum up the (ad)venture in vivid and morally telling images (182–183).[295] The indigenes are turned into "squatters" (184) on and in their own land.

Bessie Head has three main criteria for the identification of benign power forms: they are accommodating, sheltering, and progressively adaptive.[296] The leader she presents as Khama's model, Moshoeshoe,[297] has all these qualities. It is he who can cut across the devastating, demeaning conflicts of the Wars of Calamity with the words: "Men cannot eat stones. Let it all be forgotten" (27)—words that, like an "Open Sesame!" open a new route to the nations of this region. It is the discovery of nation-building.[298]

Although he acts decisively in politics and in battle,[299] Khama's is primarily a *civic* leadership, and *even as* he enacts his role of a major social reformer, he maintains the African courtesies (116) of consultative rule—though broadening the base from which he draws inspiration and advice to include Christian and technological features. Head draws attention to the negotiated, careful gradualism of Khama's reforms.[300] Throughout, his major purpose is to negotiate space for his people, and his embrace of the Christian faith and the associated skills (the "new learning" referred to so copiously in the text) is the careful, considered choice of an enlightened leader. He knows the threats[301] besetting the Bamangwato and that, for his small nation to survive, an alliance with the international power of Britain is necessary.[302] The alliance is an empowering link that he, through his fame as a principled African reformer and his careful use of European allies, achieves[303] for his people.

This Head contrasts explicitly with the way "the land was wrested from the . . . illiterate" (143). It is because Khama lays his dignified claim, as an African, to the skills and techniques of modernity[304] for the Bamangwato that he can lead his people into the large, international sphere of the future, without their suffering the devastation and cultural humiliation caused by land loss.

Not himself a major innovator or initiator of change, the figure of Sebina is nevertheless another of Head's major challenges to the negative stereotype of the "primitive," xenophobic, change-resistant, dour, fierce African. In the character of Maruapula she does insert a figure of this kind into the narrative, yet she makes us understand and humanly respect him—as Sebina does. Sebina himself is, in his capacity for appreciating intellectual vision as well as the need to maneuver a place for African society within an international context, the embodiment of the joyous, gentle openness of mind and generous adaptability that Head consistently admires. Sebina's receptivity to change and his appreciative recognition of the importance of timely social reform are the attitude that the innovative leader needs among his people for change to be successful. Sebina humanizes—for the reader—the rather remote figure of Khama and enables us to see the lovability as well as the grandeur in this apparently aloofly austere leader. In depicting the invented, grandfatherly figure of Sebina, Head achieves for herself the freedom to imagine how Khama's major changes might be received, and the circumstances of this period be experienced, while retaining her scrupulously trustworthy documentation of Khama's life and works.

Sebina's wondering eyes, wise yet open mind, and warm generosity form the perfect filter by means of which Head allows the steady calmness, "compassion" (50), and intellectual vision (121, 168–169) of "Khama, the Great" its full recognition—it is an African, profoundly humane perspective.[305] Within the serenity of his own nature and of the Bamangwato culture, for Sebina even death is not a terror or a devastation—a living, expanding energy is passed on to new generations and new developments. As the aged Sebina begins to die, he reads in the glowing face of his educated grandson, Mazebe, the comforting and cheerful message: "I'll see the sunrise for you tomorrow, grandfather!" (195). If a "future . . . of dignity and compassion" is to be "shape[d]" in Africa (*Alone* 64), Head shows, through Khama, Sebina, and Mazebe, how that might be achieved. Our considerations of the past, Head knows, have everything to do with[306] how we deploy our energies toward the future.

Notes

1. The statement was her "Reply" to a questionnaire that the periodical *Index on Censorship* sent out in 1975 to a range of (especially South African) authors, to canvass their opinions concerning the strategy of a cultural boycott against the South African apartheid system.

2. Compare her words about evil here with a 1978 statement of Head's: "If all my living experience could be summarized I would call it knowledge of evil, knowledge of its sources, of its true face and the misery and suffering it inflicts on human life" (*Alone* 63) and one she made in 1982: "I perceived the ease with which one could become evil and I associated evil in my mind with the acquisition of power" (77).

3. Nkosi's on the whole highly appreciative assessment of Head's writing (*Tasks* 98–103) is offset by remarks that come across as denigratory: "For most of the time Bessie Head seems politically ignorant. She has only this moral fluency" (99); "Bessie Head is not a political novelist in any sense we can recognise; . . . she is generally hostile to politics. . . . This lack of precise political commitment weakens rather than aids Bessie Head's grasp of character . . . the author's own confusion whenever she enters the realm of political ideas" (102). Contrasting Head with the avowedly Marxist writer Alex La Guma (her compatriot), Nkosi seems to be writing here not only from a rather patriarchal perspective (for which critics—e.g., Ibrahim, *Bessie Head,* 77, 79; Matsikidze 105; and Ola 4, 63—have taken him to task), but to have confused a consistently held critique of the inadequacies of political dogma and the dangers of power politics with mere lack of knowledge, whereas Head understood politics both experi-

entially and intellectually. "Power relationships, as they inform and are informed by exiled identities who seek to subvert the social and individual institutions of the nation, are the particular concern of her novels" (Ibrahim, *Bessie Head,* 3); and "Head's stance on syncretism has implications for contemporary debates on multiculturalism as she seldom loses sight of relations of power . . . her gift for rediscovering the turbulent powerplays within . . . rural society" (Nixon, *Homelands,* 116, 119) are two more-recent assessments that may be contrasted with Nkosi's.

4. In Head's experiences this denial was illustrated with particular intensity: birth in an asylum for the insane; being bandied about among prospective adoptive parents due to the baby's evidently racially "mixed" origins; the trauma of sudden removal from her supposed mother in early adolescence; the cruelty, crudeness, and suddenness of the "news" of her origins; a short-lived, unsatisfactory marriage; departure from South Africa on a one-way exit permit because she was considered politically "suspect"; refugee status; withholding of citizenship status by Botswana authorities. See Eilersen's biography (*Bessie Head*) as well as Head's own frequent references to her stressful origins. Sadly, even in 1983 (she died early in 1986) Head was still saying, "but I find that in reality I'm more and more isolated" (Mackenzie and Clayton 27).

5. Like several others, an only recently "recovered" piece, this was written soon after her arrival in Botswana. Patrick Cullinan recounts the sleuthing required because of the present obscurity of the original publication. The whole piece and the accompanying plea (in a letter to the periodical) are reprinted in *The Southern African Review of Books* 4.1 (January/February 1996): 4–5 (from the original in *The African Review* 1.1 [1965]: pagination unknown).

6. In the first part of the *Southern African Review of Books* piece, Cullinan quotes from a letter of Head's in which she had written to him that "one PAC fellow from South Africa attacked [her 'Edge' essay (which Cullinan quotes fully in the second part of the same piece) by saying:] 'she's just writing that way because I think she's a Coloured and neither fish nor fowl'" (quoted in Cullinan, "Edge," 4). Compare Nkosi's similar (unfortunate) reference to Head's "vision of a 'power hungry' and 'exclusive' Africa" (his scare quotes seeming somewhat naïve nowadays!): he inadvertently confirms the validity of the fears he scoffs at by referring to Head's supposed "obsession with this theme" as being "rooted in her insecurity as a mulatto" (Nkosi, *Tasks,* 101).

7. Compare a later (1978) restatement of this claim: "I have always reserved a special category for myself, as a writer—that of a pioneer blazing a new trail into the future" (Head, *Alone,* 64).

8. Compare a comment from a 1982 essay of Head's: "There was a fear in me that monsters would merely change roles, that black faces would simply replace white faces of cruelty, hate and greed" (*Alone* 77).

9. From the little series, "Village People."

10. On "normal," note Head's insistence on and interest in those she named "ordinary people" which could be taken to prefigure the urgent plea, at a later time, by the influential South African intellectual Njabulo Ndebele (author, academic, and critic) that South African writers should eschew the politically "spectacular" to write of the "ordinary" (*Rediscovery of the Ordinary* 37–57).

11. Head, *Cardinals,* 146. Compare "A Personal View of the Survival of the Unfittest," from the same collection: "I know myself to be cut off from all tribal past and custom, not because I wish it, but because I am here, . . . between nothing and nothing, and though it is a cause of deep anxiety, I cannot alter the fact that I am alone" (147). Virginia Ola says that "no writer . . . can claim a deeper experience or understanding of loneliness than Head" (Ola 87).

12. Compare: "this concept of individual liberty. It would seem the only answer to the master/slave relationship. . . . I seem to think in terms of two different kinds of liberties and yet, if Africa had not in part become liberated, I might never have been able to confront this individual self of dignity, and power" (quoted in Cullinan, "Edge," 5).

13. An important, deeply resonant comment of Head's is the following:

> A sense of history was totally absent in me [because of the upbringing a nonwhite person was given in South Africa] and it was as if, far back in history, thieves had stolen the land and were so anxious to cover up all traces of the theft that correspondingly, all traces of the true history have been obliterated. We, as black people, could make no appraisal of our own worth; we did not know who or what we were, apart from objects of abuse and exploitation. (*Alone* 66)

The working of oppressive power to displace people by *deculturizing* and *dehistoricizing* them is brilliantly analyzed in this passage. So Head understood that "one of [her] preoccupations [had to be] a search as an African for a sense of historical continuity, a sense of roots" (*Alone* 86).

14. Such a locale would not only be physical/geographical. Of the author of the work *African Religions* (J.S. Mbiti), Head writes in a review that his ideas appeal to her because "they are wide and generous enough to take in all the humble" (*Alone* 51). Here, an idea (a book) *accommodates* people.

15. Compare her prophetic remark: "Southern Africa isn't like the rest of Africa and is never going to be. Here we are going to have to make an extreme effort to find a deep faith to help us to live together" (*Alone* 31).

16. Correspondingly, she says of her writings that "everyone *had a place* in my world" (*Alone* 28, emphasis added).

17. In the same piece she writes: "For largeness of heart is what we need for a civilization and big, big eyes, wide enough to drink in all the knowledge of the heavens and earth" (*Alone* 50).

18. The inadequacy of dogma is similarly articulated in one of her early pieces: "We may liberate ourselves from alien oppressors, but when do we come alive to ourselves?" (*Cardinals,* 152). Her relevance as a *postcolonial* commentator is evident over and over in her writings. Compare her reference elsewhere to "wonders and things, which will be more important than our revolutions" (*Alone* 67).

A typically cryptic, profound passage from Fanon's writings comes to mind as the expression of an insight parallel to Head's vision:

> Before it can adopt a positive voice, freedom requires an effort at disalienation. . . . It is through the effort to recapture the self and to scrutinise the self, it is through the lasting tension of their freedom that men will be able to create the ideal conditions of existence for a human world. (Fanon, *Black Skin,* 23)

19. Comments collated in *A Woman Alone* suggest that she later decided that the South African environment was so brutalizing that it was impossible to write about—"How does one communicate with the horrible?" (*Alone* 103—cf. also 14, 62, 64, 101). *The Cardinals* was not published in Head's own lifetime.

20. Written during 1960–1962 while Head was living in the District Six area of Cape Town and working as a journalist for the *Golden City Post*, the novel was not published until 1993 (Daymond vii–viii), a number of years after her death.

21. Head refers to it here, blankly, as an "area." The term "location" was the commonest one at the time for the ghettos set aside in South Africa for urbanized black South Africans. Here Head is describing the sort of squalid township set aside for "coloured" citizens, found at the time (before the "slum clearances" referred to in the novel) along the beachfront main road leading into Cape Town, where the entire novel is set.

22. *The Discarded People* was the title chosen by Father Cosmas Desmond for his (later banned) book exposing the effect and realities of the policy of forced "mass removals" of African people in South Africa under the apartheid government.

23. In which the cumulative effect of the terms "makeshift . . . stifling . . . struck . . . steeled . . . small . . . junk crammed . . . stuffed . . . faded . . . old, cracked . . . torn, stained . . . battered . . . small, shaky" (*Cardinals* 1) is notable.

24. Johnny says of "[this] hellhole" (27) and "swamp" (28) that "everyone knows it's the *dumping ground* for illegitimate babies" (28, emphasis added).

25. The sum of five shillings given with the child confirms the impression of betrayal, commented on by the township woman: "What kind of woman is it who will sell her child for five shillings?" (2).

26. Who "appeared to look at her possessively" with "its great black eyes" (60).

27. One of the common (justifying) political euphemisms for apartheid was the term "separate development," with the accuracy of the adjective always clashing with the lie in the noun. In several of her essays Head analyzed and commented explicitly on the apartheid system and its effects—for example, in her Introductions to works by Sol Plaatje and Ellen Kuzwayo (Head, *Alone,* 79–82, 88–91) and in some of the pieces in the *Tales of Tenderness and Power* collection (e.g., 19–27, 116–140).

28. That theirs is not only a cross-class (57), but also a cross-*race* union is not emphasized by the author—yet a sufficient number of indicators is given to show that the novelist's linking of the erotic and the political (throughout the work) is manifest in this "foundational" relationship as well. The privileges and "refinements" of Ruby's upbringing, in so strict a pigmentocracy, make it unlikely that hers is not a "white" family (49–60). Moreover, Johnny's eventual sexual vengeance against Ruby's betrayal is in short-lived relationships with "high society" (94) women (like Mona—96–108—who is signposted as "white") and sleekly predatory specimens like Liz (108–114), to whom Mouse is a "maid" (109), that is, a domestic servant. For agreement on this point, see Ibrahim (*Bessie Head* 48–49) and Kossick (36); for disagreement, see Driver (17) and (with qualification) D. Lewis (76).

29. The encapsulating power of this particular social structure is emphasized in Head's choice of terms to describe it: "control . . . order . . . power and dominance . . . subjects . . . unquestioningly . . . orders . . . threat . . . power . . . prestige . . . control . . . powerful" (48). Compare Johnny's later comment: "The crudest expression of the power drive is in the gangster; the most subtle and disastrous in the politician. Evil, too, because in that field it affects many more people and creates more suffering" (87).

30. Which is here read as a form of transformational energy.

31. Compare the way Mouse's honesty deflects the smooth hypocrisy and smugness of Mona (96–97), without the white woman having sufficient sensitivity to recognize this—or Mouse's human worth.

32. "Until eternity," Johnny says (80).

33. Contrast Dickens's ending of *Little Dorrit* (the title character somewhat resembling Mouse), where the "inseparable and blessed" couple (895) seem much more isolated from "society" than Mouse and Johnny are depicted as being.

34. See also, for example, Mouse's and Johnny's comments on the "Immorality" court cases (which prosecute the practice of interracial sex) (110–111, 114–115). This is, of course, an issue that permeates the entire fabric of the novel.

35. Compare a reference to her "purposeful" walk (49). Her upbringing as a treasured child, so starkly in contrast with her daughter Mouse's, is reflected in the name her father gives her (50).

36. We are told that "the life within her was already cold and dead" (60) at this stage.

37. The long-lasting consequences of this are noted: "eating you up" (45); "knock . . . gripe . . . messing up" (46); and "an unhappiness that could not die" (54).

38. PK shuts his eyes to many social and political realities—half naïvely and half cynically. The novelist aligns him with the sort of woman Mona is, whose social protests seem essentially frivolous (96–99). Compare PK's words (81) with Johnny's (82).

39. See "struggled desperately" and "only a silent, stubborn will-power kept her feet moving" (9).

40. "For the next four years of her life she *sat up* educating *herself*" (12, emphases added).

41. "I know your type. They're real hot mamas in bed. . . . You just need a good rape" (94). I suggest that Head wishes the reader to contrast such awful, crude sexism with Johnny's very rough-and-ready, but profoundly sensitive, responsiveness to Mouse, evident from the start.

42. Johnny's "powder-keg" image (21) for Mouse is to be linked with his desire to "put a stick of dynamite" under the stultifying social system (29, 106, 115).

43. See "I wish I didn't care" (66) as well as "to put it right" (22); "have to reach" (67); and "I can help her with this writing business" (68).

44. "Johnny, I'm indebted to you" (135) is Mouse's acknowledgment of the extent to which his coaching, cajolery, and encouragement have helped her in her writing (and in her sense of herself as a writer—a person with worthwhile things to say).

45. Compare Daymond's Introduction to *The Cardinals* (xiii). Much in Mouse's biography clearly resembles Head's own experiences—*without* the work being in any simple way autobiographical. I have discussed the issue in my essay on the novel (Gagiano, *Cardinals*). Daymond, Driver, and D. Lewis do so as well, in their commentaries, in different ways.

46. See Daymond's Introduction to *The Cardinals* (ix–xiv; xviii) on the history of these laws. It is a theme that moved a number of South African authors (see, for example, my listing of some of them in my essay on this novel—*Cardinals* 59—as well as Lewis's).

47. Johnny contrasts "suffering" with "hypocrisy"—the rotten basis of the false "laws and rules of society" (78).

48. Perhaps the fact that their cottage in District Six is described as "whitewashed" (136, 72) is an indication of relative privilege; when Head wrote the novel, she probably did not know about the impending razing of District Six by the South African government (an act of racial "cleansing").

49. Compare Bessie Head's own thoughtful, forthright essays (written during her Cape Town sojourn) on the political passivity and manipulability of the Western Cape coloured people (*Alone* 8–15). Although she was strongly aware of (and admired) their warm "sense of belonging" (10, 7) and felt welcomed by them (9–11), at a later stage she wrote that she had been made conscious of being "not fully grounded in the colour brown" and "excluded" (extract from an otherwise unpublished interview with Cecil Abrahams—quoted in C. Abrahams 4).

50. As the shopkeeper Mohamed tells Mouse, "No one want to buy AFRICAN BEAT from my shop anymore. They say it make out that the non-Whites bad" (34). PK's despicable wheelchair "stunt" (32–37, 43, 61–64) is fiercely criticized by Johnny for its multiple irresponsibilities ("How typical of secluded White mentality," he observes—63).

51. His "I haven't got time for a political conference" (20) sums up how lacking in "cardinal"-type energy and commitment he is—he can refer breezily and unfeelingly to "the gruesome details like burnt-out bodies" (22) after a township fire. See further comments outlining his position (25, 81, 100).

52. In a later discussion of this "slum clearance" policy, PK says tamely that "the government is trying to clear it up"—a naïveté to which Johnny responds in a probing *analysis* of this "move" (in two senses of the term) (28).

53. Exemplified in Johnny's encounter with Ruby and in Mouse's with the old man who teaches her to read and write—as well as in the job offer to Mouse from the *African Beat* editor (49–54, 4–8, 12).

54. "Everybody is trapped. They are trapped too" (107), she says.

55. In that the "riot" is quickly quelled—the "people . . . driven back . . . surrounded by barbed wire . . . encircled" and besieged (80–81), their solidarity finally a solidarity in defeat and suffering (81).

56. "Destiny" has chosen Mouse to write and Johnny to mentor her, he believes. Although Johnny is a writer, Mouse's teacher as well as the major commentator on the craft of writing in the novel, he seems to have a sense that hers is the greater talent—he believes (13, 19, 135) that she should stop being a journalist at *African Beat* for the sake of this duty (of being a creative writer).

57. Near the end Johnny praises Mouse's latest piece of writing by saying, "That is how your creative powers will become *dynamic*" (135, emphasis added).

58. Compare the remarkably similar points (to Johnny's), though the difference in diction is great, in the following, more contemporary passage: "The necessarily fictional nature of this process [of 'narrativization of the self'; i.e., identity-formation] in no way undermines its discursive, material or political effectivity, even if the belongingness, the 'suturing into the story' through which identities arise is, partly, in the imaginary (as well as the symbolic) and therefore always, partly constructed in fantasy" (Hall, "Identity," 4). The extent to which Head's thinking was ahead of her time is continually striking.

59. "You cannot feel like the underdog and at the same time feel you belong to a country" (72) is how he puts it here. On a later occasion he declares:

> It's just fools like me who have headaches about the freedom and rights, of the individual. I doubt if any political party can ever really guarantee that. It is a matter above the petty manipulations of politicians. It is intensely personal too. I would like to know of one man who does not consciously or subconsciously strive for the freedom to live as he wishes; move as he wishes and think as he wishes. To me the history of the world is the history of man's search for freedom. (87)

60. Compare Johnny's describing a true writer as "uncommitted," but no "fence-sitter"—"stand[ing] for non-commitment" (116–117).

61. Head's admiration for the writing of D.H. Lawrence is known (see MacKenzie and Clayton 9). Compare, in *The Cardinals*, "possessive . . . closely knit unit . . . never allow you to live free and *apart* from me" (103, emphasis added). There may be a clue in the emphasized word of Johnny's sense that the force of passion binding them is a counter to the power of the political system in South Africa.

62. Head's own carefully correlating imagination is evident in the significant recurrence of this term. Compare Johnny's sense (to some extent acknowledged by Mouse) that she is like a "shambles of unfocused atoms" (127) that, like the *form*-giving imagination at work in her sketches and written description of the city, needs "compact[ing]" *in order to* be "dynamic" (135)—rather than desiring her to be encapsulated in an Ibsenian *Doll's House*. "I love you because you are the living symbol of freedom to me" (87), Johnny tells Mouse.

63. For which critics like Driver and Lewis have (I believe) mistaken it. Johnny's desire for Mouse is combined with feelings that are neither patronizing nor patriarchal, but that have a "paternal" aspect (131).

64. The unnamed "other man" in Mouse's life (34–37, 120–121) is used to articulate this principle; Johnny's flamboyance is carefully contrasted with boasting or self-righteousness (34–37, 120–121).

65. Compare Head's comment (in a 1977 essay): "Between two living human beings there is always Truth and Truth is like that double-edged thing and is constantly expressing itself as Fireworks" (*Alone* 46). With this, compare Johnny's term "gamble" (83).

66. Mouse reiterates this remark to Johnny himself (130) and then adds that she feels he "overwhelm[s]" her. "I could get lost like that" (130), she says. "I have to know I have the strength and independence to live too" (130). He assures her that her psychic integrity is beyond his control ("Oh Mouse. Your strength and independence is something I cannot interfere with. You will achieve it"—130). Balancing these tender, cherishing words, he does, however, warn her *also* that no one in an intense relationship is "safe" (137).

67. Contrast Head's later sense of South Africa as "unhol[y]" and inimical to dreaming (*Alone* 27, 100).

68. From a piece written only slightly later than *The Cardinals*, presumably (no date is supplied by the editor of *The Cardinals—with Meditations and Short Stories*). The quotation is from one of the essays Head composed soon after her arrival in Botswana (she had left *The Cardinals* with a friend in South Africa when she left the country to seek publication for it). The statement quoted itself compellingly combines romantic and socially aware attitudes, much like *The Cardinals* does, throughout.

69. For the dating of this quotation, see the previous note.

70. Johnny's early desire to "blow this status quo to bits" (29) can be linked with both his erotic promise to Mouse to "explode" her (134) and his encouragement to her that her "creative powers will become *dynamic*" (135, emphasis added).

71. "Belonging" is, of course, a concept deeply compatible in Head's usage with (even essential to) freedom, rather than being its opposite.

72. These quotations are taken from Ndebele's essay collection *Rediscovery of the Ordinary*, published in 1991 (though some of the essays were written in the 1980s). Compare Mouse's preference for reading "Darwin's theory of evolution" rather than well-intentioned "protest literature" (11) with Ndebele's position.

73. As Mouse and Johnny do. Contrast Head's keenly observed portrayals of the unconscious hypocrisies and inconsistencies in the conduct of the "white liberals," PK and Mona, who only play at defying the system.

74. In line with my point here is Head's sharp contrast (in an art review she wrote at much the same time as the novel) between a vulgarly "escapist," but successful artist, and the challenging, truthful one who "reminds people, who would rather forget, that townships are nasty places" (*Alone* 15–17).

75. *When Rain Clouds Gather* was first published in 1968, three or four years after Head's arrival in Botswana. The edition used here is that published by Heinemann in 1987.

76. As expressed in a passage like the following:

> When I first arrived in Botswana in 1964, I was entirely dependent on what the people of the country communicated to me. The major talking point at that time was a terrible drought in which 300,000 cattle died. The other issue was the first general election for independence. I think only a South African–born black person could fully appreciate the situation. It meant that here, if black people were faced with a national calamity that affected them deeply, they could form little cattle co-operatives to resolve their distress; a co-operative of any kind in South Africa would cause a riot of hysteria among the white population—their wealth and privilege are dependent on the poverty and distress of black people. It meant that here all the people could vote for a government of their own choice, which would presumably care for their interests and welfare. (Head, *Alone,* 64)

77. See Head, *Gesture,* 9–16, 27, 30–31, 65, 85–86. Makhaya's quickly granted residence permit contrasts clearly with the years the author had to wait for Botswana citizenship.

78. In the same essay in which Head expressed her feelings about the first general election for independence, she wrote (showing how conscious Head was of the public purpose of her writing):

> So Makhaya's entry into Botswana, as a refugee, was like sending a message back to his own home; this is what we really ought to have. . . . It would seem as though Africa rises at a point in history when world trends are more hopefully against exploitation, slavery and oppression—all of which has been synonymous with the name, Africa. I have recorded whatever hopeful trend was presented to me in an attempt to shape the future, which I hope will be one of dignity and compassion. (*Alone* 64)

79. Head ascribes this quality in her writing to "the inspiration of Bertolt Brecht" (*Alone* 98–99—see also MacKenzie and Clayton 8–9, 20–21). "Everything that is related to the everyday world [she said at a later stage] is much more lovely than anything else" (MacKenzie and Clayton 24). Head's scrupulosity as a witness is confirmed by her biographer ("An agricultural officer checked everything she wrote"—Eilersen 100) and her reliability about local conditions is borne out by the fact that this text is given to foreign aid workers in preparation for their stay in Botswana (compare E. Campbell; Simonse).

80. Such as the apparently "happy-ever-after" future promised for Paulina and Makhaya and the "convenient" suicide of subchief Matenge.

81. Ibrahim characterizes Head's vision in this novel as exhibiting qualities of "nostalgic reminiscences" (*Bessie Head* 52); "utopian nostalgia" (53); "a lack of racial or economic tensions between people" (69); even "a Walt Disney level of conspiracy of good people and goodness" (71), which she ascribes to "the necessary euphoria . . . for negotiating an ontological space where an exile can function and heal after the apartheid experience" (71). She avers that "for Head, 'old Africa' consists not so much of traditional Africa but rather [indicates] a habit of desire" (57). This makes Head seem naïvely wish-fulfilling in her writing (which she is not) and is too one-sided in its comments on a complex interplay between the life and the work of the author.

Although Head could refer to the "inner release" (*Gesture* 17) she had felt on arrival in Botswana and testified that she "learnt tolerance, love, brotherhood" there, "because that is what is in the air here" (44) (these experiences being evidently embodied in Makhaya in the novel), she could say with right: "Some of my writing had nasty things to say about Africa. There are ways of thought and life that have to be broken down" (18)—"and the book doesn't say pretty things about tribal people.

Those at the top" (51). See also her nuanced discussion in *Gesture* 58–60 as well as 21 (bottom of page).

82. When Head had begun to think of writing the novel that would become *When Rain Clouds Gather,* she wrote to Vigne: "There's all this awakening and movement towards a new destiny. I know I can catch hold of the vitality; the newness. . . . so that I may *grow* too" (*Gesture* 25, emphasis added).

83. Compare Gilbert's words: "The farm itself . . . should not progress beyond the living conditions of the people of Golema Mmidi. Both have to *grow together*" (99–100, emphasis added).

84. Illustrated in "abandoned villages" and "sandy wastelands," "eroded and uninhabitable" (37).

85. Compare Makhaya's question to Mma-Millipede: "Can you look on life again with trust once it has become soiled and tainted?" (130).

86. "Machinery, agriculture, progress go hand in hand with spiritual knowledge," Head wrote to Randolph Vigne (*Gesture* 59).

87. See, for example, MacKenzie and Clayton, 9, 13; Head, *Alone,* 39–40, and *Gesture* 58–59. Head thought that "poverty has a home in Africa—like a quiet second skin" (*Alone* 39). Her comments on this issue in MacKenzie and Clayton (9) are especially interesting.

88. Head's description of a "volunteer" who "brought [her] around to accepting the fact that the white man is human" (*Alone* 45) might be compared with the portrayal of Gilbert in the novel.

89. Another instance of sinister chiefly power occurs in the forced marriage of Mma-Millipede (68–69).

90. Similar exploiters of a political system lending itself to autocracy were evident at the time in the shape of South African "homeland" leaders such as Chief Lucas Mangope. Head commented astutely in later years on the role of Chief Buthelezi (*Gesture* 219). A fictional parallel is the homeland leader Chief Lerato portrayed by M.W. Serote (74–79).

91. Compare "devil that drove" (23); "hate" (45); "tormented hell" (65); "lonely" (146); "forlorn and lonely" (177); "terrible private hungers" and "victim" (180).

92. The image indicates both how many years of suffering have worn these lines on his face and how closely associated it is with his commitment to the "rut" of hereditary privilege, power, and isolation. (Contrast Gilbert's orientation toward "getting out of the rut and the habitual way of doing things"—86.) The rut in which Matenge lives is that of the thwarter of others' advancement, in order to ensure his own materially "advanced" position ("he said no, no, no to everything they wanted to do"—175).

93. Head shows the possibility of one such future exploiter in her unattractive (72), warning depiction of the both sinister and foolish "Pan Africanist" politician, Joas Tsepe, who finds in Chief Matenge his natural ally. These future power seekers are sarcastically depicted as starting parties "to liberate the Botswana people from a government they had elected" (47) and as having "little or no membership among the people but many under-secretary generals" in their "Botswana National Liberation Party" (46), as Head shrewdly observes. They speak in "conference table terms" (63), but "[act] like spies against the new government" (67). Most sinister of all, they are (the author hints) probably the instruments of foreign backers (their "secret financier[s]") who aim to gain power over African societies, for exploitative purposes (48).

94. Compare Makhaya's thoughts on tribalism (124). Head even suggests that African tribalist social organization facilitated the colonial takeover of the continent: "For everyone from the chiefs down to the colonial authorities had lived off the poor

in one form or another" (40). Compare also Makhaya's similar comment: "Black men as a whole had accepted their oppression, and added to it with their own taboos and traditions" (125).

95. Causing "misery, suspicion, and fear" (53). Persistent reports of "witch burnings" in South Africa's northern parts and in parts of Nigeria confirm the enduring pertinence of Head's portrayal of this event. Head's later work of oral history (or socio-historical testimony), *Serowe: Village of the Rain Wind*, "confirms" the balanced evocation of Botswana village life in *When Rain Clouds Gather*. She did portray a "ghoulish" (186) "witch-doctor" (11) in "Jacob: The Story of a Faith-Healing Priest" in *The Collector of Treasures*.

96. An awareness of what is presently termed phallocentrism is quite literally illustrated in the conduct of the "loathsome" old woman Makhaya encounters on his first night in Botswana. When she sends her ten-year-old granddaughter to him for sex (for money), Makhaya's thoughts are that

> such evils . . . were created by poverty and oppression. . . . It was the mentality of the old hag that ruined a whole continent—some sort of clinging, ancestral, tribal belief that a man was nothing more than a grovelling sex organ, that there was no such thing as privacy of soul and body, and that no ordinary man would hesitate to jump on a mere child. (15)

See also the following passage: "It was as though a whole society had connived at producing a race of degenerate men by stressing their superiority in the law and overlooking how it affected them as individuals" (93). In her short stories (*The Collector of Treasures*)—culminating in the title story (especially the long paragraph 91–92), but permeating the collection as a whole—Head would analyze this phenomenon more fully and in more detail.

97. "The terrors of rape, murder and bloodshed in a city slum [had created in Makhaya] . . . a horror of life, and it was as though he was trying to flee this horror and replace it with innocence, trust, and respect" (97). See also: "He was attempting to reach up to a life beyond the morass in which all black men lived. Most men were waiting for the politicians to sort out their private agonies" (166). Head was later to refer to this novel as her "only truly South African work" (*Alone* 68) (since she could not have known that *The Cardinals* would be published posthumously).

98. Thanks to African women like Bessie Head as well as to African men (and some others), this prophecy is at last beginning to come true.

99. See "it begins to drive you crazy" (34), as well as "he lived on a touch-and-go line with his sanity" (125) and "tormented and broken" (133). Hence "inner friction . . . propelled him . . . along a lonely road" (124).

100. Compare the tone of the passage by Plaatje that Head quotes in her Introduction to his *Native Life in South Africa* (Head, *Alone,* 79–82), as well as other commentaries on and analyses of apartheid that she wrote at various times (e.g., *Alone* 89–91; *Tales* 116–143). Head's expression "flaming power and energy," which she applies to Plaatje's book, is equally applicable to the "Black Dog" section of *When Rain Clouds Gather* (122–137).

101. Makhaya thinks bitterly that "black men as a whole had accepted their oppression, and added to it with their own taboos and traditions" (125).

102. "White people," Makhaya believes, "must know, somewhere deep down, that one day all those millions of unarmed people would pitch themselves bodily on the bullets, if that was the only way of ridding themselves of an oppressor" (133–134). Head's position is thus a *qualified* pacifism.

103. See the exhilarating description of Makhaya's first "free," Botswana sunrise: "Suddenly, the sun sprang clear of all entanglements, a single white pulsating ball" (16), which makes the "vast expanse of sand and scrub . . . somehow bewitchingly beautiful" (17).

104. Ibrahim speaks of "the desire to escape to a 'perfect little village' (*Bessie Head* 59—quotation unidentified, if it is one) as characterizing the "exile's consciousness," but Ibrahim's description seems to me to fit neither Head (the author)'s conception nor Makhaya's.

105. The "terrible" sight of the newborn calf about to be devoured by the jackal obscurely prefigures Isaac's death (159).

106. Makhaya believes that "many a future millionaire must have had a dead child in his life who had died from lack of proper food" (165).

107. Contrasted mentally (by Makhaya), somewhat self-mockingly, with his South African sabotage plans (as political activist) (137).

108. The "tragedy" was the suicide of her Zimbabwean husband on being falsely accused of embezzlement, as well as the confiscation of their property. The name of the village Golema Mmidi itself means "to grow crops" (22).

109. See Head's brief early piece "My Home," with the refrain "and the wind don't blow," and her use of images of blackness and darkness to signify peace and sustainment (*Cardinals* 145).

110. See "plunging"; "threw up"; "afterglow"; "sparkling" (77).

111. Compare: "Makhaya found his own kind of *transformation* in this enchanting world" (122, emphasis added).

112. Earlier, Makhaya's choice of the "road . . . lead[ing] to peace of mind" (20) might have made him seem selfish in his withdrawal from oppositional political activism. Indeed, he himself is afraid that "because he needed to save himself" (135) and had "decided to strike out on his own" (80), he is "guilt[y]" of being "a traitor to the African cause" (81). Yet Head makes clear that such self-salvation is the necessary first step to enable an individual to be of service to others. As Makhaya tells Paulina later, "poor people stick to me" (143), and self-improvement will have to benefit those around him, as well. See also the "jackal" passage (164–165) with its reference to his "new life *with* Paulina" (emphasis added), and Head, *Alone,* 48, 64. Rather than Gilbert's momentary plan for wholesale agricultural reform in Africa by means of social engineering through a "dictatorship" (82), Makhaya wants a democratic dispensation, even if "painstakingly slow," that will allow the continent to develop by "trial and error" (83). Compare also Head's comment on Makhaya in a 1983 interview (MacKenzie and Clayton 13).

113. See "as if no man was his brother or worthy of his trust" and "no one can invade my life" (111). See also the reference to the protective, "thick wall of silence" (128) behind which he had had to ensconce himself.

114. The point is reiterated later, but then consciously and appreciatively, by Makhaya, when he notices "that [Paulina's] skirt was the same flaming colour as the sun," "both . . . beautiful to him" (117). Earlier, too, he had seen that "the gaudy-hued skirt was familiar" (107).

115. Prefiguring the description of the dynamite blasting and also recalling the rising of the dust motes that fascinate Makhaya early in the novel (both details alluded to above) (137, 8).

116. Compare his commiserating reference (to Makhaya) to South Africa as "that terrible place." "The good God don't like it," he says. "This [i.e., Botswana] is God's country" (20; cf. 183). A detailed, comparative study by South African political scien-

tist P. Du Toit, *State-Building and Democracy in Southern Africa* (1995), more or less confirms Dinorego's contrast between the two countries.

117. In *When Rain Clouds Gather,* Head suggests that the effort itself is less terrifying and taxing than she herself would experience it as being and (in due course) describe it (in *A Question of Power*). Makhaya's *welcoming* in Botswana is the main difference between his experience and Head's own, much more ambiguous and difficult, period of adjustment.

118. I disagree with Wilhelm's reading that Makhaya's "position [she quotes p. 169 from the novel] is the most overtly *Christian* of Bessie Head's protagonists" (emphasis added). Head is quite emphatic about Makhaya's sense of Christianity as a hypocritical cloak for oppression (134)—and about his "desire to push the . . . Bible off the table" (130).

119. "She was searching around in her mind for a way to inform him of this without having to refer to the Bible . . . [which] she knew this wild-hearted man did not like" (131). Of course Mma-Millipede's usual term for the "mystery" would be "God." Yet Mma-Millipede is not sentimental (128)—she knows that "we all live in a world that is full of danger" (89).

120. Head's reference to "these grinning, ghoulish oppressors" (186) evidently brings Matenge to mind, recalling Makhaya's sense of the "ghoulish rites" of "witch doctors" (11). Makhaya's present compassion with even a (dead) Matenge is proof of "the secret development that had taken place in him" (125).

121. Head is noticeably male-centered in her terminology here and elsewhere in the novel, though of course the fact that hers is the main "voice raised" *through* the text must qualify critical anxiety about a monogendered vision of humanity—of which she is hardly to be accused. In a 1983 interview she emphasized that this novel "concentrates on . . . the fact that the women are the agriculturalists of the land" (MacKenzie and Clayton 28).

122. Compare p. 135.

123. Gilbert is said to be "intent only on being of useful service to his fellow men" (81). Makhaya echoes these sentiments on p. 103. Compare Dinorego's sense of what "[a] Batswana man" is like, emphasizing progress and "improve[ment]" (25).

124. Compare: "The man with no shoes was often too hungry to stand in the parade these days" (185).

125. Maria's words are confirmed when Paulina's and Mma-Millipede's grief at the death of little Isaac is transformed (at the sight of his collection of wood carvings and the vivid memories they evoke) into a cherishing delight—the "waterfall" image being an added metaphorical clue here (170).

126. Compare Makhaya's realization "that it was only *people* who could bring the real rewards of living" (163, emphasis added).

127. While writing *When Rain Clouds Gather,* Head wrote to Vigne that "the whole thing is set at a development project, where I actually lived for five months but I want to go beyond what was going on there which was NOTHING" (*Gesture* 46), as she stated with characteristic bluntness.

128. If its textual context is taken into account. In the edition used here (1987, 1995 printing) the epigraph occurs on p. 108. Pagination in the later (U.S.) Heinemann issue differs from this.

129. Which is how Head seems to intend the Margaret-Maru marriage to be regarded. See "Did it end there? Was that not only a beginning?" (7).

130. Head was, of course, avoiding the "expected choice" (writing of racism by depicting South African society) in favor of the more unexpected and even daring

choice of a Botswana setting to explore this topic. That she was aware of this somewhat provocative, "exposé" quality of her text is shown in certain dry comments she inserts in the text—for example, "something they liked as Africans to pretend themselves incapable of was being exposed [as] oppression and injustice" (48), and "*before* the white man became universally disliked for his mental outlook, *it* [i.e., racialism] was there" (11, emphases added).

In a 1983 interview Head made the point starkly—speaking of *Maru*, she said, "It *definitely* tackles the question of racialism because the language used to exploit Basarwa people, the methods used to exploit them, the juxtaposition between white and black in South Africa and black and Basarwa in Botswana is so exact" (MacKenzie and Clayton 11). Compare Head, *Alone,* 68–69, and a letter of Head's quoted in Eilersen (112–113). She wrote to Vigne in 1970: "It is different if a racial feeling is created by people and I mean African, who are also human to you. It is then that you really sort out the differences and life is not the same again for me, but a horror I may never forget" (*Gesture* 121). Compare also 124–125 as well as Sarvan, "Letters," 14, which explains how Head wrote her "beautiful" book against racism while feeling herself to be the butt of it—in Botswana.

131. A note on terminology: throughout the novel (appropriate for the topic of racial prejudice) Head uses the insulting plural "Masarwa" (for which the singular is "Lesarwa"). Inoffensive or less offensive words for this group of people (to whom the term "Bushmen" is also applied and the less offensive "San") are "Mosarwa" (singular) and "Basarwa" (plural). Compare "Motswana" (singular) and "Batswana" (plural).

132. Eilersen quotes a striking comment by Head on the style she adopted here: "The endless, outer, caressing snapshots are a trick to direct the eye of the reader inwards" (Eilersen 118). See also Head's comments on its "rhythm" (*Gesture* 158–159).

133. In her later life Head would refer to *Maru* as "a *kind of* fairy-tale/love-story (I do agree with the fairy-tale *element* of it)" (MacKenzie and Clayton 23, emphases added). Ibrahim's commentary exaggerates this fairy-tale element (*Bessie Head* 91–92). Head referred to the work as "a masterpiece, but certainly not for little children" (*Gesture* 97).

134. Despite her supposed "passiv[ity]" (MacKenzie and Clayton 12)—a term by which Head seems to have meant a kind of "contained creativity" and personal serenity (she also applies it in this same quotation to Maru). Head did not mean the term in a denigratory sense, since she said of both these supposedly "passive" characters that she had "put three-quarter-part of [her] own stature as a human being" into each of them (MacKenzie and Clayton 12). To these comments she added later in the same interview (speaking of Margaret) that "she holds herself together through creativity, but she's cast in this passive mould" (20). Compare the notion that Margaret's is the real transformative vision in the novel, centralized in an article by Coundouriotis (25).

135. See 35, 60, 92, 115, and 6 ("shocks"). In 1969 Head wrote to Vigne: "My short novel [i.e., *Maru*] is a bomb" (*Gesture* 104).

136. The sequence of communicated insights is significant. Just as Maru's dreams about the house in the field of daisies (his and Margaret's more "personal" future—103) seem to have been "projected" (104) onto Margaret's imagination by Maru, so her paintings of the "resilience" and "animat[ion]" of "ordinary, common" village events, people, and creatures "carr[y] a message" to Maru concerning "the eventual liberation of an oppressed people" (107–108—i.e., addressing the more political and social dimensions of the future).

137. I here recontextualize and slightly reorder a long quotation pertaining to gender issues from an article by Wicomb in order to suit my own purpose ("Variety" 43). Wicomb's own concerns are addressed in a later note.

138. Head wrote to Vigne in 1971 that "the major theme is racial oppression and a hard look at it but it is blended and blended and was written with a real glow" (Head, *Gesture,* 136—cf. "masterpiece"—97). Slightly earlier, although acknowledging that "one is never sure the world will change," she wrote to him that "*Maru* ought to liberate the oppressed Bushmen here overnight" (125).

139. One such marker is the fact that Maru's (Batswana) people prefer to suppress the knowledge of his marriage and its significance in order "to keep their prejudice" (6); that the event is recognized as being "only a beginning" (7) (since *so much* is left to be done); and that the prejudice is so intense that both Maru (7—on the narrator's authority) and Margaret (67—on Dikeledi's authority) would have been killed had they remained in Dilepe.

140. This mysterious, portentous passage contains other ambiguities. The words "secret" (5, recurring on 6 and 7) and "brooding" (5, recurring on 10 and as "brooded" on 7 and 9 in passages on Maru) point forward to a human parallel. Since the Tswana name "Maru" *means* "clouds," "weather," or "the elements" (Head, *Gesture,* 104), this character is of course called to mind here. But then, so is Moleka, with his distinctive "thundercloud brow" (*Maru* 27, 74, 80—cf. 30)—who also helped Margaret (and inadvertently, Maru) to get to this point (see the thematic statement on p. 116, elsewhere referred to). Furthermore, the image of the potentially life-giving clouds as "trapped" "prisoners" reminds one of the "shut"-in "Masarwa tribe" (126), who also threaten a liberating "storm" (127—cf. 9) and whose creative potential must be allowed to contribute to human society—as Margaret's was. Breaking the "sullen silence" is necessary, as is the potent energy of "slicks of lightning" and "boiling cloud" (7).

141. See Ibrahim's references to "the failure of the authorial desire for the possibility of the merging of dominant and marginal discourses" (93) and her suggestions that Maru "somehow wishes to become a pariah" (109) and that "his revolution is a private one" (116). She writes that Maru "takes his pariah wife and, tail between his legs, disappears from view forever" (114–115). Ibrahim considers that "the pretence of his death neutralizes the one political as well as personal gesture he makes in the entire novel" (*Bessie Head* 18). Compare Ngcobo 349 and Menager-Eversen ("The hero of the novel flees Dilepe to escape from what he has set in motion"—47).

142. A bestial fierceness is suggested elsewhere in Dikeledi's warning that "people" will "plot to kill" Margaret the minute they hear of Maru's marriage plans. Here it is indicated in "torn him to shreds" and "to keep the world the way it was" (7), the last six quoted words showing *willed* fixtures.

143. These fixities are often (despite the odd inappropriateness in the term) labeled "conservative"—since their effect is destructive, socially compartmentalizing and barren making. In contrast, Maru's insistence on "*conserving* moisture in the soil" by "*not breaking up* the clods" (6, emphases added) is notable and symbolically significant of his creative, constructive role.

144. He chooses "husbandship" (to a despised "Lesarwa"!) above kingship—the paramount chieftaincy.

145. The disturbing "message" that a "Masarwa" woman's love is worth more than the kingship—hence, that the Basarwa may be worth more than the members of the society that despises them.

146. Note the similar contrast drawn later between "the outer Maru and his earthly position" and "the inner Maru, who was a king of heaven" (35). The transgressive qualities of his "dreams and visions" is elsewhere emphasized ("stretched across every barrier"; "know no barriers") (110)—another way of indicating the creative energies of his mind. Compare Head, *Alone,* 73.

147. Compare "engineered" (120) and "arranged" (121), as well as "controlled" (72).

148. She said: "They don't like him. . . . Why do you have to have the god-man the world is waiting for?" "A lot of people have conflicts about Maru. They don't like him. He cheats." To this her response was that "they attack the small things. He *boldly* acknowledges his deceit" (MacKenzie and Clayton 19, 23).

149. Although Wicomb attempts to defend Head's supposed "antifeminism" by describing the text as (so to speak) "feminist despite itself" (in her comment that there are "fissures in [the] discourse where illegitimate meanings percolate through"), she writes that Margaret's "powerful suitor" dominates her dreams and that he "sweeps her off into marriage" (Wicomb, "Variety," 43). Ibrahim refers to Head's "[inability] to position female identity as it epitomizes oppression within the dominant discourse of the nation . . . even as it resists and subverts the nation" and says that Head (merely, or inadvertently) "succeeds in . . . inculcating total passivity in a 'bush woman'"—as if the author were the major racist and sexist at work here! Ibrahim writes that Margaret "remains barren" and that "she fits into nothing and has to be taken deeper into the dream or fairy-tale to which she belongs." Ibrahim asserts, "I believe that Margaret Cadmore remains the perfect victim of racism and sexism throughout this novel" (*Bessie Head* 91, 99, 100, 102, 104).

150. See the term "strange" on p. 5, as well as Maru's friends' shaking of their heads (6) at his "typically," progressively "adjusting" the way things have always been done, now in the agricultural sphere.

151. Such "dissatisfactions" perhaps stem from readings desirous of greater consistency or predictability in texts, whereas it was Head's conviction that "contradiction or even apparent contradiction could be called the other name of truth" (*Alone* 20).

152. Head's next novel, *A Question of Power*, addresses the excruciating issue that racism, sexism, and fascism (forms of power worship and soul enslavement) may lurk in the psyche of even the oppressed and the victims. However, Head herself understood *Maru* as a hard-won, arduous victory over assaults by racist anxieties and attacks directed at her, the author, during its writing. She wrote in a letter that she

> was trying to reply to those obscene shouts with dignity. . . . The passive, still girl was my own eyes watching the hideous nightmares which were afflicting me and all the girl's personality opposes the shouts of dog, filth, dog filth, you are a coloured dog. "No," she says, "I'm a Masarwa. I'm not ashamed of being a Masarwa." (Sarvan, "Letters," 14)

Compare also Head, *Gesture,* 125–125, 64, 71, 86.

153. Discussed as such in Ibrahim, who asks challengingly, "'Fearful' . . . of a loved and loving husband? Why?" (*Bessie Head* 106).

154. That Maru's moral analysis (and the ways in which he distinguishes between Moleka's and his own motives and basic psychic orientations) on pp. 8–10 is presented as almost agonizingly scrupulous—rather than self-serving or rationalizing—is signposted for the reader in details like the conjunction "and" and the word "brooded" (in the penultimate line, 9), in the self-scrutinizing questions that follow (9–10), and in the narratorial assurances of selfless sincerity ("his heart said"; "he would truthfully surrender" even though "it could turn the world to ashes"; and "inwardly lived out"—10).

155. Although his methods are acknowledged to be "ruthless" (73); his "true purpose and direction are creative" (58), "the way the rain made the grass and flowers bloom" (73). The "road" along which he moves is said to be "straight," directed at (and by) "gentle goodness" (37). In contrast with Maru's "*creative* imagination,"

Moleka lacks direction for his "*dizzy* energy" (58, emphases added). Yet the images of "sun" (58) for Moleka and rain for Maru (73) point forward to the social synergy between them (see the top of p. 70), just as both of them "empower" Margaret.

156. Head wrote, "But between two living human beings there is always Truth and Truth is like that double-edged Thing and is constantly expressing itself as Fireworks" (*Alone* 46).

157. In a 1983 interview she said, "*Maru's* style is: I want [i.e., she, the author, wants] a new attitude towards racialism and so I create a highly vivid and original character . . . the story is intended to linger with its lessons and reflections" (MacKenzie and Clayton 22–23).

158. Contrast Maru's sarcastic, but socially and politically astute, criticism of Moleka's demonstrative behavior (eating with his "Masarwa" slaves—53, 56): "Moleka is trying to change the world by himself" (56). Head wrote in one of her last pieces that if "greedy, power-hungry politicians" were to be replaced by "men who are God," this would not be "the effort of a single man but a collaboration of many great minds" (*Alone* 99).

159. Dikeledi feels "life . . . [as] a mystery, a deep interwoven tangle" (104). Compare also Maru's deliberately creating "a tangle of events" (72), and reveling in "tangle and confusion" (86), the repeated term indicating a complex bondedness.

160. Compare Maru's (at the time probably received as provocative and taunting) words in his farewell note to Moleka: "Remember that people quarrel but they should always make it up again" (125). Also relevant to this point is Head's (to most readers, probably) unexpected description of the novel as "glorif[ying] *friendship* between a man a woman" (*Gesture* 136). In the novel, another important passage contrasts, separates, *and* links Maru and Moleka: "When had they not worked hand in hand? They would do so again, except as enemies this time" (73).

161. It is said to be "more powerful than her body could endure" (102).

162. This is so despite the many ironies with which Head endows the description of her motives and activities (e.g., her attitude of "experiment[ation]" toward Margaret (Jr.)—15; Margaret (Jr.'s) "semi-servant" position in the household—17; her quality of "common sense" rather than "love of mankind"—12–13; and Margaret (Jr.'s) sense that "she was not good [but] . . . rich," that is, privileged—88). The farewell description of her by Margaret (Jr.) is something like a grateful tribute (20), though. For a somewhat contrasting assessment, see (e.g.) Wicomb ("Variety" 43).

163. That a transformational process is set off at this moment is also indicated in the narrator's discussion (12–13) of Margaret (Sr.'s) action in the context of the purpose of "chang[ing] the world"—even if in her case this is motivated by "common sense" (13) rather than by any visionary, inclusive "love of mankind" (12).

164. The "adopt[ion]" not only endows Margaret (Jr.) with a "cultivated" accent and manner, but exposes her (in her stepmother) to someone who "stood for all that was the epitome of human freedom"; helps her to "gain control over . . . her [own] mind and soul"; and empowers her with the "capacity . . . to survive both heaven and hell" (16).

165. Said to be "like deep sweet music . . . a new experience for" Moleka (76—cf. "Help me," same page).

166. This crucial moment is "defined" elsewhere as exhibiting the following qualities: "necessity, recognition, courage, friendship and strength" (99). It is, in other words, especially for Margaret (whose perspective is reported here), an "empowering" moment.

167. Head gives a virtually identical description of the moment as both Margaret and Moleka experience it: Margaret senses that "something inside her chest [goes]

'bang!'" (30), and Moleka also recalls that "something had gone 'bang!' inside his chest" (32) at the very moment that he saw Margaret raising her hand to her heart. The image emphasizes mutuality *and* transformation.

168. Although Moleka, so frequently referred to as "arrogant" (29, 35, 57), is now described as a "changed man" (54), Maru finds on "look[ing] . . . deeper" that a Moleka who has found a (potential) partner to unlock his formerly hidden self is actually "another version of arrogance and domination" that leaves his (Maru's) "heart cold with fear" (57).

169. In the sense that he decides to marry her, judging that she is the person who can both provide the incentive for *and* sustain his abdication of power. Significantly, Moleka senses obscurely that it is his loving Maru that has prepared him to recognize Margaret as lovable (see "someone like her" 32–33). In this novel (as in *The Cardinals*), Head is at pains to indicate how deeply politics is involved in seemingly "romantic" matters. In both these areas, types of alliance-forming occur. She could thus write to Vigne (in 1969): "If there were no love making in the world, racialism and prejudice would never die. It is the only way to break down insanity" (*Gesture* 72).

170. Of course Moleka finds out Margaret's race subsequently and attempts in his flamboyant manner to improve the social standing of Margaret and her people by the gesture of eating with his former slaves (53)—a deliberately socially shocking act in a rigidly racialized social context.

171. How used he is to wielding power ruthlessly and irresponsibly Head makes clear in describing his careless promiscuity (74), his terrifying driving habits (28–29), and his demanding, male chauvinist conduct in relationships (77).

172. Compare Dikeledi, whom Head in a careful tribute characterizes as a "drastic revolutionary" (25) because she had, long before Margaret appeared on the scene, and quietly—in contrast with Moleka's flamboyance—freed "Masarwa" slaves and recognized their rights by paying them salaries that allowed them to improve their lifestyle.

173. It is possible to describe Maru's maneuvers as personally and socially responsible *planning*, since his motives are always broader than mere selfish considerations. Head seems to present Maru's machinations as part of the "synergizing" developments occurring in her imagined society. Her presentation of him exemplifies her fondness for paradoxical, puzzling portrayals, a sense of the unobvious, unsimple quality of human endeavors—which she explores in even greater depth in her next work.

174. Head presents persecutory, privileged power (i.e., the conventional notion of political power or power of position or status) as hateful. She suggests that it is a system of terror in a sort of mutual standoff between ruler and ruled (in a passage on p. 36): "Maru had all the stuff that ancient kings and chiefs were made of. People had acclaimed those around [or?] on whom they could build all kinds of superstitious myths. Yet the fear and terror magicians inspired made them live with their lives in the balance. Who knew how many murder plots were constantly woven around the life of Maru?"

See also "thieving" (42); "shameful" (43); "ego" and "dizzy," merely "*revolving* energy" (emphasis added), in contrast with "creative imagination"—i.e., constructive power/energy (58); as well as "blood money and stolen goods" (106), indicative of power abuse.

175. See p. 67: "You think of me as they all do . . . [as] public property to be pushed around and directed."

176. Moleka denies knowing "any Masarwa who is a teacher" (59—contrasting with Margaret's unashamed acknowledgment of her racial identity) and fails to defend

Margaret from the reappropriation of the bed he lent to her (60) from the (significantly named) Dilepe Tribal Administration. He is said not to want to "do the dirty work [of recovering the bed] himself" (60). When Margaret shows up to ask for a period of grace, Moleka again betrays her by "not look[ing] up," "his face . . . like stone" (63). So, even though it is Maru who (through Ranko) thwarts any approach to Margaret by Moleka with the threat of death (78), Maru is to some extent justified in saying to Margaret that "Moleka did not want to approach you because he is such a tribalist" (122—cf. 94). Gover is the only (other) critic who seems to have noticed this strategy of testing used by Maru (Gover 114–115).

As far as Dikeledi is concerned, she barely stops herself from *saying* the protest which she does initially feel and think: "But you can't marry a Masarwa. Not in your position" (66).

177. One huge "complication" is illustrated in Maru's inner debate about Moleka (10).

178. His detestation is actually of the baseness of popularity—hence the paradox that Maru the "democratic liberator" also hates people (7, 68).

179. See the bottom section of p. 55; the middle of p. 57; p. 64 ("no other choice"); and the following: "It was different if his motivation was entirely selfish, self-centred, but the motivation came from the gods who spoke to him in his heart. They had said: Take that road. Then they had said: Take that companion. He believed his heart and the things in it. They were his only criteria for goodness. In the end, nothing was personal to him. In the end, the subjection of his whole life to his inner gods was an intellectual process. Very little feeling was involved. His methods were cold, calculating and ruthless" (73).

180. Its inclusivity, its *linking* (rather than separating) capacity is also indicated: "He dwelt everywhere. He'd mix the prosaic of everyday life with the sudden beauty of a shooting star" (34). This description links Maru's nature with the qualities of inclusive vision exhibited in Margaret's paintings.

181. Compare: "She had been mistaken . . . for another variant of the word 'Bushman'" [i.e., as "a Coloured"] (19), as well as Dikeledi's question, "Is your father a white man?" (24). Marilyn Miller-Bagley has written an excellent essay ("Miscegenation") on the "conflation" of the notions of being "coloured" and "Masarwa" in this text and in its relation to Head's life. Wicomb has commented astutely that Head's fiction is "haunted by the unacceptability of colouredness" ("Case" 9). (In South Africa the term "Coloured" is applied to people of supposedly mixed-race origins.)

182. Ironically, by doing so they give enough edge to Maru's detestation of them to make him decide to use his power to oust *them* from this society, instead. Earlier, Dikeledi deals a deathblow to Pete's headmasterly status by her protection of Margaret (44–48).

183. This status is not a matter of social ranking, of course, but might be termed "soul status" (compare "the standards of the soul"—126). It is most clearly expressed in the description of their first meeting, when Maru rejoices in the recognition that Margaret "had looked down at him, indifferently, from a great height where she was more than his equal" (64). His joy arises from the contrast between this inner nobility of Margaret's and the "grovell[ing]" attitude "almost everyone" else in his society shows towards him "because of his position" (64). Hence he elects Margaret as the person he wishes to marry and the one for whom he can abdicate from the chieftaincy (65).

184. See "a big hole in the child's mind" and what follows (15). Consider the essay by Miller-Bagley ("Miscegenation") on this point.

185. See "in her heart she had grown beyond any definition" (20).

186. See 126–127, as well as the way Maru earlier foresees this sort of consequence (59–60, 69).

187. Compare Head, *Alone,* 73.

188. This is of course very much like the way Head saw her own role as a (writing) artist—to be "the story-teller and dreamer, who . . . introduce[s] new dreams that [fill] the heart with wonder" (*Alone* 103)—a description that shows strong affinities between her and both Margaret and Maru. See her comment in the novel, that "any artistic observation of human suffering arouses infinite compassion" (14). Compare *Alone* 58–60.

189. "What did it really mean when another child . . . looking so angry, said, 'You are just a Bushman'?" (17) she asks, and decides that "there was only one thing left, to find out how Bushmen were going to stay alive on the earth" (18).

190. The immense power of racism by which societies are rigidly and hierarchically compartmentalized is analyzed by Head as being (A) primitive (see "the wild jiggling dance"—11, 17) and utterly un*thinking*, as is the decision to despise someone on the absurd ground that their appearance differs from your own; (B) evil (109—cf. "perpetrators," 10); and (C) "demented" (10). Head felt the novel communicated "urgent messages" (MacKenzie and Clayton 10).

191. In many of these necessary negotiations she is initially assisted, advised, and equipped by Margaret (Sr.) (see 16–20).

192. Compare the way Margaret exerts an "improving," enriching influence on those who come into real contact with her (Moleka has been discussed—compare Dikeledi, 105; and Maru, 107–108). Margaret is in her turn invigorated and assisted by them (99, 112, 114–115).

193. Although "allowance had to be made for all living beings . . . allowance for life ha[s] always been made [principally] for really vicious people . . . who spat at what they thought was inferior" (i.e., who do not themselves make decent "allowance" for others) (19).

194. Parallels with the marriages of Edward VIII of England to Wallace Simpson and of Sir Seretse Khama to Ruth Williams come to mind and may have been present in the author's memory. See Eilersen (117–118) for other possible historical parallels with some of the effects depicted in the novel.

195. Compare "the fury of centuries of oppression" (69) and Head's slightly earlier warning reference (in 1968) to "the underdog" as "a passionate person without any nice, fancy manners" (*Alone* 48; compare *Alone* 102: "Every oppressed man has this suppressed violence").

196. The tone of Head's sentence is prophetic, sounding a fierce warning (127).

197. Head, *Alone,* 68, and MacKenzie and Clayton, *Between,* 12.

198. For a contrasting opinion, see Ibrahim, e.g., the following: "Does [Head] wish to imply that race is secondary to creating a novel that only engages with race issues superficially? And does her subordination of the subject of race, in this novel, jeopardise the magical quality which she is at great pains to develop in her novel?" (*Bessie Head* 92).

199. The edition referred to throughout is that published by Heinemann in 1974.

200. It does evidently manifest itself in psychosocial and political dimensions, as Head demonstrates throughout, but she here features an apocalyptic, metaphysical perspective. In a 1976 letter about the novel she wrote: "Relatively little is known about evil: politically it cannot endure the light of day, so all those activities are secret. I felt that I could shed some light on the nature of evil" (quoted in Nichols 18).

201. That its nature is evil is made manifest in its dimensions of greed, lust, viciousness, persecution (of others), harshness, and ugliness. Consider Elizabeth's refer-

ence to "the roar of hell"—159; compare "the most appalling roar"—36; and "Dan's" "harsh, grating" but "unintelligible" shout of "Rrrrrrrrraaaaaaaaa" right into Elizabeth's skull—177: an act that vividly sums up the intrusiveness of evil by means of illustration. But "Sello," too, insofar as he is a power form, represents "terror"—as is signposted in his initial appearance to Elizabeth's mind, where we are told that "a sort of terror gripped her chest" (22). The life-threatening quality or effect of Sello's type of power is also indicated in his first questioning the length of her "stay" (22). Head wrote in a *Drum* article of 1982: "I associated evil in my mind with the acquisition of power" (see *Alone* 77).

202. Elizabeth states as a discovery, but also as an incontrovertible truth (in the conversation with Birgette): "The human soul is alone in the battle of life. . . . *I can be destroyed*" (86, emphasis added). Near the end of the novel she declares as (and despite its being) "the most horrific truth mankind had ever heard," that "no Lord ever would" "[appear] to help": a "victim simply stared in the face of evil, and died" (200). In Elizabeth's own experience, she finds that she "c[an]not retaliate" against Medusa (62), that she is "isolated in suffering" (118), that "God [is] no security for the soul" (65).

203. In referring to "Sello's" "own abyss," Elizabeth begins to sense "that the title God, in its absolute all-powerful form, is a disaster to its holder, the all-seeing eye is the greatest temptation. It turns a man into a wild debaucher, a maddened and wilful persecutor of his fellow men" (36–37). Significantly, "Sello" "said none of this" (37); "there was no explicit statement" (36)—Elizabeth has to work it out, unaided by him.

204. Head wrote to Lee Nichols that Elizabeth encounters "God roughly represented by 'Sello' and Satan roughly represented by 'Dan.' Both were destructive personalities to encounter and this encounter results in a nervous breakdown" (quoted in Nichols, 17). In the novel Head allows "Sello" to acknowledge that "[he] dominated the situation" (200) and Elizabeth says: "He *frightened* her deeply. He *conducted* a strange drama, *in a secret way*, and it had been so *terrible* that she had gone insane. He'd also, according to Dan, *included* her in his prophecies, which *endangered human life* because they *aroused jealousy*" (200, emphases added). All the italicized terms in the quotation indicate power characteristics. Compare p. 32: "He is controlling your life in the wrong way" as well as "Sello's" astoundingly cynical words on p. 41: "Ah I'm gaining control of the God show again." "Dan," "flaying his powerful penis in the air" (13), his sex organ described as "towering" and permanently "erected" (128), is of course a far more blatant power incarnation than "Sello" is, a point that confuses Elizabeth to some extent.

205. That goodness cannot be powerful.

206. The discovery by the former power figure "Sello," that "I am just anyone," is identified as "one of the most perfect statements" (11). Head also associates this proclamation with a dedication to "the brotherhood of man" (206).

207. Compare the caution Head expressed in a 1971 letter to Vigne: "I am afraid of the new song [an allusion to the conclusion of *A Question of Power*] 'The Kingdom of Heaven Is Inside People.' That kingdom holds greater demands of the person than celibate monks [ever] knew" (*Gesture* 151).

208. At the end of the novel Elizabeth proclaims: "There is only one God and his name is Man. And Elizabeth is his prophet," which she presents as a sort of corrective to monotheistic theologies like the Christian or the Muslim creed (to which she alludes): "There is only one God and his name is Allah. And Mohammed is his prophet" (206).

209. Elizabeth experiences "the evils overwhelming her [as] beginning to sound like South Africa from which she had fled . . . but this time the faces were black and it

was not local people. It was large, looming soul personalities" (57). Head wrote to Vigne from Botswana in 1969: "Here I am Bessie Head, the Bushman dog" (*Gesture* 85–86). In a 1983 interview she said, "My persecutors were so real to me that what seemed to the persecutor relevant was that I could be defaulted by being a Coloured and I would be defaulted by being sexually inexperienced" (MacKenzie and Clayton 25).

210. The sequence in the passage describing the latter event is important: Elizabeth feels a "terrible weight [to be] exterminating her" while "her mind struggle[s] with the question: 'Why . . . ? What have I done?'" Then "she *struck* an abyss of utter darkness, where all appeals for mercy . . . were simply a mockery" and then she "*struck* the old woman a blow on the side of the head" (173, emphases added).

211. Note "she ran, she screamed, she ran" (174). The abusive, libelous poster that Elizabeth subsequently puts up on the post office wall (175) is another such "scream" that she perhaps subconsciously realizes will (as on the previous occasion) lead, not to punishment (cf. "recklessly inviting her death"—175), but to a form of rescue in the many manifestations of caring and fellow feeling toward her that follow.

212. The first letter in the Vigne collection (dated 27 October 1965) contains the remarks "they don't want me here"; and "It's pretty terrible I tell you for a woman to be alone in Africa" (Head, *Gesture,* 9, 11).

213. Some might feel that "xenophobic" is a more appropriate term than "racist," but the emphasis is so explicitly on an African essentialism that contemptuously stresses Elizabeth's *racial* "impurity," that "racist" (with the necessary explanation, perhaps) seems the fitting appellation.

214. "Sello" uses and is used by "Medusa," who hints that the (imminent) appearance of "Dan" is preplanned by them both: "We are bringing you the real magic, this time" (93), she says gloatingly to Elizabeth. Ultimately, of course, they are all emanations from Elizabeth's own mind, but then, the mind is the mirror of (social and historical) experience, rather than self-generating.

Another indication of the suggestion that forms of power all resemble one another occurs in the detail (near the end of the novel) that "Dan" "looked like one of those Afrikaner Boers in South Africa who had been caught contravening the Immorality Act with a black woman" (98). Although the "Boer" seems primarily racist and "Dan" primarily sexist, they strongly resemble each other, and both societies are presented as phallocentric.

215. Possibly sexism could be construed as a form of racism, in identifying (usually the female) gender as the marker of a distinct and inferior, subhuman "race." A figure in Head's fiction who clearly illustrates this attitude is Garesego in *The Collector of Treasures* (92, 96, 100, 102).

216. "Would you like to be my brother ['in other lives']?" she asks him, saying that she is "better than [he] at organising family affairs" (201).

217. The deep ambivalence of the "Sello" figure is Head's warning against the yearning for "good power" or a "protective power." As Evasdaughter puts it in her essay on the novel, "Power over others has no good form" (77).

218. For example, that a "Sello" who decides without consultation that Elizabeth "needed the insight" is the exact parallel of the "Dan" whom he accuses of wanting "to remould [Elizabeth] in his own image" (200). Head's satirical echoing of biblical terminology is notable. "Sello's" heaping of all blame on "Medusa" is another wicked echo that Head employs here.

219. This point is indicated in Head's depiction of power abuse at the core of society, not only in the obvious case of South Africa, but *also* in Botswana. "Sello's" exhibitions of human history—the crater of excrement (53) and the continuous "roar"

behind the curtain (36)—also indicate the prevalence of power abuse and cruelty throughout history and in all cultures.

220. Her names or terms for Elizabeth—"Blabbermouth" (40), "warrior" (103), "prophet" (206), and even "punchbag" (93)—hint at this.

221. Indicated in the reference to "the arrogance of the soul, its wild flaring power, its overwhelming lust for dominance and prestige" (135), which Elizabeth makes in conversation with Tom, where that power is acknowledged to be present both in victims and in those who victimize others.

222. See the reference to "a creative force, . . . a power outside themselves that could invade and destroy them" (98). Compare Foucault: "Power . . . *produces* reality . . . domains of objects and rituals of truth" (*Power* 194, emphasis added).

223. Compare Elizabeth's reference to the "feeling behind" the cruel obscenities being shown to her as "a deep, cringing shame" (117).

224. Not only is Elizabeth "both God and Satan at the same time" (161), since "Sello" and "Dan" inhere in her psyche, but *both* "Sello" *and* "Dan" are simultaneously divine and demonic (throughout the novel both kinds of attributes are ascribed to them both). And in the p. 161 passage, too, the idea is clearly felt to be shameful ("'You wouldn't want anyone else to know?' she asked. . . . 'Yes,' he said. 'Because it's such a terrible idea'"). The platitudinous form of the idea that Elizabeth expresses to Tom ("The dividing line between good and evil is very narrow"—161) gives little indication of how horrifying and wrenching the *experience* of it is. To Elizabeth, it means "going insane" (161).

225. Compare "a tumultuous roar of mental confusion" (160).

226. Head wrote to Vigne (also in 1971): "In the end I really am a human being but the process of becoming so has worn me out and turned my hair stark grey" (*Gesture* 153).

227. Head described it elsewhere as "a horrible world of torture and very dangerous" (*Gesture* 143).

228. Head consistently and openly stated the autobiographical basis of the novel—e.g., "(Elizabeth and I are one)" (MacKenzie and Clayton 25). Coundouriotis comments that Head "self-consciously . . . tries to break down the artificial disjunction between some originating experience and the subsequent narrative about the experience" (17).

229. The sanity and inclusivity of Head's vision are indicated in the fact that she can *both* testify to the spiritual value ("beauty and harmony . . . intangible, unpraised efforts to establish the brotherhood of man"—157–158) of "the local-industries project" (154) *and* note its relatively unsuccessful financial side (155–157).

230. In the letter to Vigne, "practical[ity]" is associated with "sanity" (*Gesture* 69). In a passage from her 1983 interview, Head insists three times over on three notions that she links and that she feels were the major achievements of the period of *A Question of Power*. These seem to refer both to points of understanding (or of accurate "prioritizing") and to actual, practical activities. She refers to "the *tentative work* I had done about *building a kind of base*." (It is the notion of "work and effort," that of "building a . . . base" and the qualification of tentativeness that come up three times over.) She speaks here of "the solid work you do at the bottom" and of "a commitment to planning for people . . . in a beautiful way," in contrast with ideological social engineering. She expresses a sense of "horror" at "these camps of Marxism and socialism and so on" and a fear of "wild projects," which she associates with "Marxist-Maoism" (MacKenzie and Clayton 26, emphases added). In the novel, Elizabeth's interest is excited by the "*practical* genius of the Eugene man . . . so free and unconcerned" (61, emphasis added).

231. Pearse shares my opinion on this point: "The chain of evil is not necessarily broken," he writes, since "the real causes of anxiety and tension are still quite intact" (91–92). In proof he cites Head's letter (on this point) to C. Heywood (quoted in Pearse 93, n. 212). Ibrahim reads this equivocal final impression left by the novel as the author's failure, referring to "simplistic lessons learned" (168) and "resolutions" that she considers "simplistic" (169), and says that "Head can only talk about that aspect of Elizabeth's recovery in Christian platitudes," finding that the author "falls short of the grand design" (*Bessie Head* 169). By contrast, Evasdaughter's essay title—"Bessie Head's *A Question of Power* Read as a Mariner's Guide to Paranoia"—reflects the more widespread reading of the conclusion as in some sense "optimistic," depicting an overcoming of evil.

232. Compare Head's comment (in a 1971 letter to Vigne): "People simply want to believe in an infinite goodness without examining the basic ingredients of the soul" (*Gesture* 143).

233. In the Marquard interview (1983) Head said that "the work out [in the novel] of God is at that centre where all the horror happens. Not a pretty man in the sky, you know, who loves mankind" (Marquard 53).

234. Compare a comment in a 1971 letter to Vigne (Head is commenting on the *Question of Power* period in her life): "I began to understand a little of both sides of love—a heaven of perfection and a hell of degradation. You can't balance the two side by side, one eliminates the other and then dominates" (*Gesture* 150). Elizabeth's "relationship" with "Dan" is evidently the major illustration of power-perverted "love."

235. Compare her lengthy comments on the novel (to Vigne) on pp. 158–162 of *Gesture*; the expression "the sort of logic of war" that she applies to her experiences during this period in a later letter; and her description (in yet a later letter) of "the material of the book" as "desperate," since she (Head the writer; in the novel Elizabeth the protagonist) was forced to "observe [Satan's] values" by "get[ting] quite close" to that "ghastly sight" (*Gesture* 165, 175).

236. Quoted in Nichols, 17, from a letter (about the novel) that Head wrote at the end of 1976.

237. A quality caught in Elizabeth's description of the "air [in the vegetable garden as] alive with the tinkle of gently-seeping water" (73).

238. The narrator, through Elizabeth as focalizer, concludes that "any kind of demon is more powerful than normal human decencies, because such things do not exist for him" (150). Since "the important power-maniac" is blind, because he is capable "only [of seeing] his own power . . . his self" (19), he (it) is incapable of noticing or cherishing people.

239. Tucker refers to "the repetitions of power and oppression that Head's book seeks to defeat" (176).

240. A comment in a letter that Head wrote to Vigne in 1971, shortly after her own release from the Lobatse asylum, is especially poignant: "I am lost in a sorrow too deep for words," she said (*Gesture* 144). Compare the portrayal of Elizabeth: "There was a deep wail of tears inside her, as yet unexpressed" (131).

241. How terrible and far-reaching the devastation wreaked by evil power use can be is registered by Head's description of black South Africans' lives under apartheid: "Timid, docile and broken by violent assertions, black people allowed themselves to be shouted off the pavements of towns they had helped to build" (*Tales* 119).

242. Compare "Medusa's" boast to Elizabeth: "Africa is troubled waters, you know. I'm a *powerful* swimmer in troubled waters. You'll only drown here" (44, emphasis added).

243. Both "Medusa" and "Dan" are also introduced by means of flamboyant displays of sexual power (44, 106)—here, too, the achieved effect (in both cases) is a humiliation of Elizabeth. Head wrote to Tom Carvlin (17 September 1969) that evil is a force with a "propelling and almost eternal motion. To meet, in the flesh, a transmitter of this force is no joke. He's very similar to God, with his all-seeing eye and very attractive to weaker people because the power motive is THE thing with him" (quoted in Eilersen 128).

244. *Between* the fixities of "Old Father Time" ("Sello's" name near the end—201) and his records of history—on the one hand—and the falsehoods or "crookery" of "Dan's" ambition and power greed—on the other—Elizabeth finds the freedom to *record* "her *own observation* and *speculations*" (201, emphases added). She openly and deliberately chooses a "one-sided view" (201)—her own, with no godlike pretense of impartiality.

245. Contrast Elizabeth's reference to the way the missionary principal devastates her with the sudden information concerning the circumstances of her birth: "The story was an imposition on her life" (16). Under other circumstances, this account can be seen as "a sad story" and even a "beautiful story" (17). Other references to "story" (27, 29, 40, 199) all indicate manipulation of Elizabeth's self-image and role. By contrast, Head herself said that her "books [almost] wrote themselves, propelled into existence by the need to create a reverence for human life in an environment and historical circumstances that seem to me like a howling inferno" (*Alone* 77).

246. See Tucker's excellent comments (170–181) on the novel's structure as a "dismantl[ing of] the dichotomies" of power (171).

247. In a commentary by letter on the novel, Head wrote (in 1976): "I propose there is a fault in making an obeisance to anything" (quoted in Nichols 18). In desiring either a God who will save them and punish their oppressors, or a powerful (usually male) protector or love partner who will make them "queen" and look after them (114, 106), victims will end up with a "Dan."

248. Compare "Sello's" creed, the thought that finally saves Elizabeth from "Dan": "Elizabeth, love isn't like that. Love is two people mutually feeding each other, not one living on the soul of the other like a ghoul!" (197; cf. 12).

249. Using all the traditional resources of the novelist (plot development, characterization, irony, verbal echoes, parallels and contrasts, symbolic imagery, sociopolitical commentary, philosophical musing, dialogue, lyricism, description of setting, and circumstances), Head shapes a highly unusual and unforgettable text—a work that is simultaneously a novel of ideas, bildungsroman, *künstlerroman*, philosophical treatise, *testimonio*, autobiography, scare story, village tale, roman à clef, and a love story of a very special kind. She herself described it as "a big leap forward for me, internally" (*Gesture* 152). An account that constantly oscillates between joy and despair, it has the arresting intensity and urgency of meaning that mark a text of enormous significance. See also Evasdaughter (81) and the essay by Boyce-Davies.

250. She resumes her motherhood of Shorty; reseals her friendship with Tom, her comradeship with Kenosi, her alliance with Eugene; and she even gains a reverential regard for Mrs. Jones, whose somewhat vapid Christianity had formerly so irritated her. Her spiritual "partnership" with "Sello" is also reestablished—on Elizabeth's terms this time. See also Tucker's essay on this issue, and Ibrahim's comments in *Bessie Head* (166, passim).

251. This is described as "a terrible hatred," but "subterraneously" manifested (83), as "savage vengeance" (98) and "violent pride" (136)—all forms of destructive energy. See comments by Gover (119).

252. Tom tells her, "tenderly," on her return to Motabeng: "Lucrezia Borgia, . . . Don't you love everyone . . . not only . . . people but vegetables too?" (188). Throughout the novel, Elizabeth's warmth and the poignancy of her feelings appeal to the reader.

253. In the sense, not of "obsessive love" (11—although it is "Sello" who uses the expression here, it clearly applies equally to the Elizabeth-"Dan" "relationship"), but of a personally and socially linking energy, binding one creatively into family and community as a cherished and cherishing member. Elizabeth is shown throughout the novel to have a deep, but unsentimental, regard for others, and her humanity helps her to understand and cope with even "racialists" like Camilla and the Swiss psychiatrist who treats her. Compare her expression "a reverence for human life" (*Alone* 77).

254. My coinage is evidently derived from the name of the South African racial compartmentalization system of apartheid, which branded Elizabeth/Head "Coloured." Its exclusionary effects are traced in two dreams that Head had in Botswana, of which she wrote to Vigne (*Gesture* 86–87)—dreams in which Head experienced herself (surrealistically and deeply disconcertingly) set apart first from a group of whites and next from a group of blacks. The dreams clearly reflect the anxiety (in a person of "mixed" racial origin, in the context of a society where "race" is essentialized) that a woman of her origins cannot belong in either white or black society. Compare Elizabeth's vision, imposed on her by "Medusa," of the dying, homosexual "Coloured" men (45–47).

255. In contemporary terminology, it causes PTSD (post-traumatic stress disorder).

256. Elizabeth feels this recognition of "ordinariness" to be deeply embedded in African (in contrast with, say, Indian or European or *South* African) society, despite her sense of what she calls "the *surface* reality of African society . . . [as] shut in and exclusive . . . [with] a strong theme of power-worship" (38, emphasis added; cf. 137). Hence "Sello" can link the sense of Africa as "a rising civilisation" with the need to make "the ordinary man . . . teacher" (63). Compare Elizabeth's comments that "Africa isn't rising. It's up already . . . but it's a power that belongs to all of mankind and in which all mankind can share" (135). She rejects, as a false idea, even a dystopia, the "Black Power" cry (132–135). Compare Head's comments in an 1986 interview with Jane Bryce (quoted in Ola 74), in which she describes the novel as "a gesture towards Africa."

257. The historical and mythical names chosen ("Caligula," for "Sello's" earlier power incarnation, and "Medusa") also indicate this.

258. Camilla the racist Dane, the headmaster at the school where Elizabeth at first teaches, and the "comrade racialist" psychiatrist (184) are really the only *human* embodiments of power shown in the novel.

259. Compare Elizabeth's words to Tom: "Because of what I see inside. . . . Because of what I'm *learning*" (133, emphasis added—cf. the comments on her "learning" on p. 20).

260. The way this thought plagues Elizabeth is indicated by its recurrence throughout the text (38, 47–48, 51, 63, 104, 127, 129, 147, 159, 181). That Head's own actual experiences are reflected here can be traced in many passages in the Vigne letters (*Gesture* 9, 13–15, 24, 37, 64, 66–68, 71, 85–86, 89, 90, 93, 108–109, 124). The plaguing, *maddening* effect of racial ostracism is reflected in the "brain-washing" image of an incessantly played "record" (148). Head calls it the "power of assertion" and "pre-planned, overpowering statements," capable of "br[eaking] whole races of people" (47—cf. *Tales* 119). Adetokunbo Pearse refers to "the schism latent in Elizabeth's mulatto psychology becom[ing] overt in her psychosis" (83).

261. Dan's "girls" are probably Head's illustration of the way in which some women negotiate male power—by sexual attractiveness and skills—and they signify her sense of herself as unable or ill equipped to employ this mechanism; however, the large number and the term "girls" may indicate her sense of that sort of role as degrading to women. "Dan" could be thought of as a demonized version of the man depicted in Head's autobiographical essay/short story, "For 'Napoleon Bonaparte', Jenny and Kate," or of Elizabeth's husband. See also Coundouriotis 20–21.

262. Vaubel has demonstrated the extent to which the ideas in Head's novel are comparable to "the work of revolutionary theorists such as Fanon and Cabral, addressing . . . mental oppression of the colonized, . . . solidarity [among] the oppressed . . . and the empowerment of mass unity" (86).

263. Commenting on the ideas in the novel, Head wrote to Nichols in 1976 that instead of the idea of a both perfect and punitive God, recognition of "a basic fallibility is what is needed, an uncertainty about one's own goodness" (Nichols 18).

264. The edition referred to throughout is the only one yet to have appeared, published in 1984 by Ad. Donker. Eilersen documents the author's research periods and confirms that "*A Bewitched Crossroad* had taken ten years to materialise" (160). It is the work by Head most neglected, to date, by critics—though Newell's is a sound essay and Clayton's commentary is excellent—wide-ranging as well as probing.

265. What Head says here is similar to a comment of Fanon's:

> The settler makes history and is conscious of making it. And because he constantly refers to the history of his mother country, he clearly indicates that he himself is the extension of that mother country. Thus the history which he writes is not the history of the country which he plunders but the history of his own nation in regard to all that she skims off, all that she violates and starves.
>
> The immobility to which the native is condemned can only be called in question if the native decides to put an end to the history of colonization—the history of pillage—and to bring into existence the history of the nation—the history of decolonisation. (*Wretched,* 40; cf. 168–170)

Compare Boahen:

> First, although there is no theme in African history on which more has been written than that of the rise and fall of colonization in Africa, most of these authors have looked at the subject primarily from an Euro-centric point of view. Their principal preoccupations, in spite of the recent noise that has been made about African resistance, have been the origins, structure, operation, and impact of colonialism. The crucial questions of how *Africans* perceived colonialism, what initiatives and responses they displayed in the face of this colonial challenge, and above all how they reacted after the forcible imposition of colonialism have not been systematically dealt with. (i)

In Head's novel, the Boers, Rhodes, and the "Matebele" are the major "landgrabb[ers]" (105)—at one point the latter are referred to by Sebina as "thieves who had stolen their land" (61).

266. It is the awareness of this kind of psychic deprivation that lies behind Head's reference (in a 1982 letter) to her finding "Black historical treasure" in Botswana, because here "the African experience is continuous and unbroken" (quoted in Beard 42).

267. Head wrote in 1979: "I think it is bound to be as bewildering, Southern Africa, as bewildering as its past" (*Gesture* 218). Contrast Khama III's achievement of a "harmonious blending" of the ancient African with the new (European), of the Chris-

tian with the customary, in his reformist program (55). Compare Fanon, *Wretched,* 200.

268. That she herself thought of it in this way is an impression created in a passage from a letter written during this period: "It's early Southern African history . . . I am trying to gather several threads together to create a feeling of continuity in my work. . . . So this final work I am on will have the effect of rounding off my Southern African experience. I think I will then let it fall asleep in my mind" (Bruner 41).

269. Amilcar Cabral wrote: "The national liberation of a people is the regaining of the *historical personality* of that people, it is their *return to history* through the destruction of the imperialist domination to which they have been subjected" (Cabral 130, emphases added). Compare Edward Said, *Culture and Imperialism,* 212. Said's "idea that resistance . . . is an alternative way of conceiving human history" (216) can be inverted to make the statement that *an alternative conception of history* is itself an act of political and cultural resistance.

270. "I think that many writers in reaction against the humiliation of the colonial era, would like to build up an image of Africa, other than the humble humility of the sparsely furnished hut," she wrote in 1982 (*Alone* 79—the next sentence of this quotation appears in the main text).

Head also recognized that the refusal to see evil in a black skin was itself a form of racism—as if (she wrote) "[a] black man is not a whole man, with whole horrific satanic passions" (quoted in Eilersen 222). Ibrahim notes that "Head's envisioned history forces us to give up the view of Africans as either villains or victims" (235).

Head's focus on Khama III *as a reformer* is akin to Paul Gilroy's "attempts [in his own words, referring to his book *The Black Atlantic*] to show [his] students that the experience of black people were part of the abstract modernity they found so puzzling and to [cultivate] . . . their sense of embeddedness [as people of African origin] in the modern world" (ix).

271. Head wrote to Vigne in 1972:

> Khama is an extremely interesting personality and everything, the tone and feel of the country, are overshadowed by him—the sort of complicated, fluid, flexible hero of my other books but I think more confined to a power structure. . . . I have worked out my philosophies, anti-power, anti-social and never bothered to examine what it means to have a fluid, unbending personality within a power structure, to use power for one's own ends and others. (*Gesture* 171)

In a later letter she refers to his "compassion in social reform, compassion towards refugees and his personal power in leadership," mentioning that "the invading whites . . . all duly noted that powerful dignity he carried around with him." She says, "There are some men who did little but live accurately and people love this" (*Gesture* 180). She does acknowledge his "austere" nature (Head had originally wanted to name this "historical novel" "Mother Winter"—the astonishing praise name that had been bestowed on Khama by his people (Eilersen 191).

272. Newell writes that Head's "'novelisation' of the master-text of history is carried out in order to reanimate, expand and clarify the experiences of African populations who lived on the other side of the colonial researchers' literacy line" (80). Head wrote in an earlier work:

> Europeans despised black people and yet wanted to embrace them in salvation at the same time. The missionaries had another distinction—they produced the first written records of African history, and one is forced to refer to them when doing any research

> into the past. This hurts, because their writings are a desecration of human life. They keep an eye on the audience back home who will be titillated by the sensational material. Khama was not blind to this, in spite of his preference for the London Missionary Society. (*Serowe* 27)

"All that was written of this period by white historians," she also wrote, "trod rough-shod over [African] history dismissing it as 'petty, tribal wars,' denying for a long time that black men were a dignified part of the human race. . . . His master . . . was creating 'real' history" (*Serowe* 67); "white historians . . . for their own ends, damned African people as savages" (95). Clayton calls *Crossroad* "a corrective historical study" ("Elsewhere" 60).

273. The same point is reiterated in a 1984 piece of Head's: The "grandeur" of Khama, she writes, was used "at a crucial moment . . . [to] ma[ke] known the people's preferences as regards their independence and the ownership of the land" (*Alone* 87).

274. In a 1973 letter Head wrote: "One thing that interests me about Khama is the question of natural genius or intelligence, *without book learning*" (*Gesture* 180). In the novel she notes that "he had only had an elementary education . . . just sufficient to allow him to read the Tswana . . . Bible" (143).

275. I take issue with the suggestion, especially fully and forcefully articulated by Nixon, that Head's fascination with Khama III was chiefly the poignant sign of a psychological need or compulsion—a point he suggests in such comments as "her imaginary romance with Khama served both as the prototype and consummation of her partiality for 'great men'" ("Border Country" 125); "Head saw Khama not just as a champion of land rights and of women, but as a self-made oddity, whose invented eclecticism safeguarded his culture by radically transforming it. . . . Khama became, indeed, the great romance of her life" (126); Nixon refers to "Head's fondness for generating men with whom to fall in love. Her mythically resonant male leads tend to serve simultaneously as fathers and lovers; they also stand, paradoxically, as the offspring of female creative desire and the catalysts of female power (127).

> This complex process [Nixon continues] is most insistently played out through the figure of Khama the Great, who becomes the great romantic interest of Head's life while deputising for an idealized version of her spectral father. Head projects Khama as a Messiah who promises a past of integration that can help compensate for the orphaned, first generation "coloured" woman's record of abandonment and ostracism. She envisions Khama as the Father of the Nation who helped humanise the position of women, enhancing the power and liberty of the Daughters of the Nation. Khama represents "tradition" at its most accommodating: he stood, for her, as a man unafraid of mixing traditions and absorbing outsiders—like so many of her fictional characters, he risked affronting his people by transgressing the bounds of custom, in his case by marrying a Christian woman and converting to Christianity. He then caused further offence by refusing to take further wives, that is, by forsaking his hereditary prerogative to polygamy. The fortunate woman to whom this grand, munificent, transgressive, and visionary man devoted himself was none other than Elizabeta or, as she was popularly known, Mma-Bessie. Need one add that this was, for Head, the name that bore her tentative sense of female continuity: it was the name she [too coincidentally] had inherited from her mother and which she in turn passed on to the presiding, autobiographical character in *A Question of Power.* (Nixon 127—further arguments follow for which I have no space)

Nixon failed to note Head's own frequent and jocularly self-deprecating references to "love affairs" with male characters in her works (see, e.g., Cullinan, "I Try," 67, and Head, *Gesture,* 177: "I looked at the old man this way and that way and fell violently in love with him. He is . . . the great Lincoln of Southern Africa"), hence Nixon is presenting solemnly as an analytical discovery what Head had herself teased and joked about, quite self-consciously. Moreover, his comments seem to me dangerously reductive and, in effect, condescending toward Head and the important political and sociocultural purposes of her work. To write about her work in this way (as quoted above) is to "re-reduce" the author who overcame so many handicaps, to those very handicaps themselves—as if they explain what and why she wrote.

276. Khama told Shippard: "I wish to avoid all contact with the Boer government except through the government of Her Majesty, the Queen" (123). He tells his people: "I prefer to have nothing to do with the Boers . . . I prefer the ways of the English government" (90). Compare his letter on p. 114.

277. That Head was perfectly aware of the multiple qualifying ironies and even outright contradictions relating to such (frequently misplaced or betrayed) trust is amply documented throughout the text—for example in the reference to "the mingling of good intentions and self-interest that animated British imperialism" (103) and in the dry addition to the quotation appearing in the main text (above) of the statements that "the British government accepted this as an innovation they had acquired as part of their empire building. When it suited their interests they were prepared to play the role of 'protector' as against the interests of the brutal, voracious, land-grabbing, cattle-grabbing Boers" (108). Elsewhere Head refers to the "culture" of imperial Britain as "a confusion of evil and good" (160).

278. Head frequently emphasizes her belief that the achievement of humane rule would be "not the effort of a single man but a collaboration of many great minds in order that integrity be established in the affairs of men" (*Alone* 99–100). Hence her focus, in her "historical novel," on the collaborative leadership notion she had earlier explored in *Maru.*

279. For example, "But I feel that I am speaking to Gentlemen of the Government of England; shall I be afraid that they will requite me with deception leading to ruin? Rather may I not hope that they will see both sides of the question; that they will regard the Protection and then regard also the country which I now say is theirs" (118). See also "let us work together" (119) in the concluding sentence of the document.

280. Khama would be quick to protest in dignified outrage when the British did attempt to assert a more perceptible legal intervention than distant "Protectorate" status (in 1891), complaining, "This is not fair or open-handed; it puts me in the wrong with my tribe" (176).

281. That this is a real danger at the time is a point Khama is undoubtedly aware of. Head amply illustrates the cunning methods by which Europeans exploit permission to farm in tribal areas by resorting to land speculation (e.g., 104, as well as the "Stellaland" and "Goshen" wrangles and battles that she so fully documents).

282. The "unselfish power use," the inclusivity of Khama's vision, is confirmed in the "require[ment] that all the royal brothers and headmen of the town be witness to the document" (119). Although Maruapula predictably protests that "he alone is ruler and he sweeps us all along with him," Sebina attempts to teach Maruapula that "our ideas of leadership must change to suit the times" (120)—he even notes, "I can see too that you are proud to be a part of this nation which has such an able ruler" (120).

283. Two of her "historical tales," "Son of the Soil" and "The Coming of the Christ-Child" (*Tales* 116–124 and 131–140), are especially moving and harrowing accounts of South African (apartheid) history. Throughout the pieces collected in *A Woman Alone,* there are references to black dispossession and denigration in South Africa, contrasted with the retention of land and of dignity in Botswana (*Alone* 27, 62–64, 66, 69–73, 82–91, 94, 101–103).

284. In a 1978 letter she commented starkly: "Once people lost the land, they lost everything" (quoted in Eilersen 265). Clayton writes that "Head's historical work on Botswana subtends at every point the shadow of the South African nightmare" (Clayton 56–57).

285. Head refers to "the destruction of the Ndebele nation by missionaries, by British imperialism and by Cecil John Rhodes" (151).

286. Deftly qualified by the portrayal of Maruapula, whose suspicion of all that is "progressive" and, simply, of all change, clearly recalls the same type of resistance among the Ndebele people (as portrayed by Head) (see especially the middle paragraph on p. 71).

287. Head refers to the "dead wall" they present "against foreign penetration and exploration" (148).

288. Reiterated in "to show the oneness of British government and Chartered Company interests" (175).

289. Well known is the awful, "festive cynicism" of Hilaire Belloc's rhyme: "Whatever happens, we have got / The Maxim gun, and they have not" (Perham 32).

290. See, e.g., pp. 30; 32, 34, 35, 36, 37, 39, 87, 88, 89, 90, 92, 93, 96, 97, 105, 108.

291. Head quoted some paragraphs of Plaatje's writing in the Introduction she wrote for a new edition of his famous work *Native Life in South Africa*. Both Plaatje's words (and his work) and Head's words (in *Crossroad* and in other writings, for example, her 1982 reference to "the miserable history of the Great Trek, the land-grabbing, cattle-grabbing wars"—*Alone* 78—cf. 80–82 and 88–93), already embody the revision of history Njabulo Ndebele (later) calls for: "Why is the 'Great Trek' not the Calamitous Invasion?" (Ndebele 142). To both Plaatje and Head, it is indeed—and explicitly—just that.

292. "Cecil John Rhodes, his political career in ruins, could still be seen on the battlefield, gleefully counting dead black corpses: 'You should kill all you can,' he advised the officers. 'It serves as a lesson to them when they talk things over at night.' . . . [Head concludes her portrait of him by reporting his appalling boast:] 'I have taken everything from them but the air'" (193). Head's portrait is not a distortion or an exaggeration—compare William Plomer's *Cecil John Rhodes*, for example, the expression of Rhodes's Plomer reports on p. 13: "I prefer land to niggers" (cf., e.g., 31, 79, 130–131). Head likewise reports Rhodes's anxiety that "expansion into the interior of Africa [should not be] identified with 'a sympathy for the natives'" (110).

293. Head does not need to point the sarcasm—the expression implies, of course, that a man like Rhodes is "more suitable" to the expansionist greed of the British Cape government and settlers.

294. Compare the "amalgamation . . . of both London and Cape colonial interests" achieved in the founding of Rhodes's "British South African Company" (159–160), which will create such havoc in south-central Africa. MacKenzie's alternative "South African Committee" (160) stands no chance against Rhodes's wealth and the glamour of his power.

295. Head's predecessor in such morally outraged analysis of Rhodes's expansionism in the region is Olive Schreiner's *Trooper Peter Halkett of Mashonaland.*

296. Power forms such as Mzilikazi's, Lobengula's, the Boers', and Rhodes's clearly lack (in Head's presentation) these qualities, whereas Mambo and Mwenge, Moshoeshoe and Khama exhibit them. MacKenzie (48), Sebina (62–63), and Mazebe (173) are also shown to be true leaders *because* they exhibit these characteristics. Compare Head, *Alone,* 50.

297. That he serves as a model is clearly established (e.g., 44, 45–46).

298. To be contrasted with the empire building of Shaka and Mzilikazi. Sekgoma is identified as a "nation-builder" as well (43), but Moshoeshoe is the clearer and more illustrious example—he "began to build up his Basotho nation from the fugitives of the Mfecane" (27) and "from Thaba Bosigo *spun out* the new shapes and changes that were vitally to affect . . . the changing balances of power, the slow encroachment of white settlers, and the manner in which this encroachment could be dealt with" (28, emphasis added to indicate the energy of growth).

299. Head traces the trials and tribulations of his route to the chieftainship (48–49, 52, 53, 54) and afterwards (e.g., 137–139). The tradition of "strong central government under a paramount chief . . . characteristic of the northern Tswana kingdoms," in contrast with the "weak . . . authority" of those in the south (103), is, of course, a further factor in Khama's favor—in combination with his astute political maneuvers (e.g., 98–100).

300. In contrast with the "fanatical converts to Christianity" who blindly and indiscriminately "denounc[e] 'heathen customs'" (130), and in contrast with the missionary Hepburn's "embarrassment" as he compulsively denounces the African form of worship and theology of which Sebina informs him (72–73), Khama "pressed all his reforms into a conservative, traditional mould. He disrupted the old order in subtle and gentle ways," Head writes, so that "Christianity ramified its way into a social structure that had been tightly governed by custom" (165). It is through Christianity that Khama achieves greater emancipation for Bamangwato women.

301. Among which the haunting fear of a Boer attack (as on their "relatives" and neighbors the Bakwena—see p. 47—and illustrated in Maruapula's remark: "The Boers . . . could seize our land and enslave us at any moment"—137) looms largest. Attack from the Ndebele sometimes occurs (49) and at other times is rumored to be impending (153). Then there is the very real danger of being "cast away" by (i.e., losing the protection of) the English (187–188) at a crucial time.

302. To him and the Bamangwato, but not to Lobengula (153)—although Lobengula's sneer in his letter ("If you give your country over . . . they talk about boundaries"—148) is misplaced. Lobengula underrates Khama's political astuteness.

303. A remarkable passage on pp. 56–57 uses balancing rhythms and verbal echoes to illustrate the *interplay* in the field of power relations at this time. It moves from the reference to MacKenzie's moral influence as "powerful" to a glance at the "image" of "the great reformer" and "great Christian" (Khama), to the colonizing Europeans' recognition that "power was on their side" and that the African indigenes "had no power," yet concluding with a recognition of the "resistance of image and prestige" Khama would be able to offer to that onslaught (with his own kind of moral power). Old Sebina notes later: "I am impressed that the foreigners regard the chief of the Bamangwato with such great respect" (121).

304. The expression "the new learning" is an insistent refrain in the central section of the text, occurring at least ten times in eight pages (128–135), coupled with references to "new purchases" (140), "new occupations" (141), and even (!) "new innovations" (141). Old Sebina's first-time "signature" of a document is lovingly described as a magical, empowering moment (119–121). Head's recording of the point that "the choice was still left to the people as to whether they would become Christian or . . . follow traditional custom" (56) is nevertheless important, as is the detail that the Bamangwato acquire literacy "in the local language" (49).

305. See the contrast between the "tight, shut-in angry face" (83) of Maruapula, and (alternatively) the sense of "all life and thought float[ing] with graceful ease on a

broad, flowing, peaceful river" (82), an image characterizing Sebina's and Mazebe's, as well as Khama's, perspectives. Compare Head's comments on the Botswana of her own time providing both "innovations" and "roots" (*Alone* 88). The "broad, deep unruffled river" is Head's image for an "accommodating" culture (*Alone* 69–70), one that allows "dreaming" (72). A recent study by a South African political scientist describes Botswana as "arguably the most successful democracy in continental Africa" (Du Toit 5—cf. 16, 143, 151, 158, 165–166). Head herself bestowed on Botswana the ultimate accolade in calling it "a free land" (*Alone* 101).

306. See Head, *Alone*, 66:

> How do we and our future generations resolve our destiny? How do we write about a world . . . that reflected only misery and hate? . . . Botswana . . . has a past history that is unequalled anywhere in Africa. It . . . was never conquered or dominated by foreign powers and so a bit of ancient Africa, in all its quiet and unassertive grandeur, has remained intact there.

It is this recognition that lies at the root of Head's focus on the history of Botswana and its retention of African dignity, which made it, in her eyes, "a hallowed land" (196) and an inspirational example.

4

Dambudzo Marechera

To make the individual uncomfortable, that is my task.[1]
Friedrich Nietzsche, "Notes"

So enduring is Marechera's reputation as the iconoclastic *enfant terrible* of African writing[2] that an anecdote about his high school years strikes a particularly poignant note. A younger contemporary of the author's recalls that at boarding school "he had a short poem at his locker by Langston Hughes, starting 'Rest at pale evening' or something similar" (quoted in Veit-Wild, *Source Book,* 71). The full poem (called "Dream Variations")[3] reads:

To fling my arms wide
In some place of the sun,
To whirl and to dance
Till the white day is done.
Then rest at cool evening
Beneath a tall tree
While night comes on gently,
  Dark like me—
That is my dream!

To fling my arms wide
In the face of the sun,
Dance! Whirl! Whirl!
Till the quick day is done.
Rest at pale evening . . .
A tall, slim tree . . .
Night coming tenderly
Black like me.

Marechera's iconization of these particular verses indicates his youthful experience of membership of the "Dark," "Black," races of the earth as an uncomfortable, "exposing," disempowering condition,[4] given the context of "the problem of the twentieth century . . . [with] the color-line."[5] In the light of the global power distributions of our time, the fate of being "born black in a white environment" (Marechera, *Insider,* 87) is the experience of all Africans, whether within the continent or in exile from it in the "Western world." With time, the naked yearning for an accepting world that the Langston Hughes poem expressed for Marechera would (in his own work) mature into the strategies of irony, acute power analysis, subtle mockery, and satirical or serious expressions of righteous anger at the both impinging and excluding force of "the white world" (*Insider* 73). More especially, Marechera's understanding of the working of power formations in the world expanded geographically, historically, and philosophically to the point where he as an African writer could recognize that colonialist racism was *one* glaringly externalized instance of the cruelly inhibiting effect of power—which could adopt far more insidious forms. Experientially, Marechera learned this by joining "England's own walking wounded," who "internationalised his outlook,"[6] while intellectually the American "Beat" writers and the Russian novelists he read in translation[7] made him see the African author's position as a replication of a maddeningly persistent global problem. Finding "local" forms of persecution in postcolonial Zimbabwe brought further sophistication and urgency to his writing. The international breadth of his travels and his reading became a resource he could deploy in his battle (as a writer) to open others' eyes to the way institutions and wielders of power attempt to homogenize people for the purpose of control. This is why Marechera writes:

> I am against everything
> Against war and those against
> War. Against whatever diminishes
> Th' individual's blind impulse.
> (*Cemetery,* 59)

In the course of time Marechera came to see *mind-sets* as the worst danger to that human individualism that he thought of as the very principle of freedom and that he so cherished (in himself and others). He would warn (even) children, in one of his last works,[8] against "the secret club of big human beings," "Society," with its horrific brainwashing, "domesticating" methods[9] (*Scrapiron* 240). In *The House of Hunger* it is referred to as the "regiment[ation of] human impulses" (122). Marechera drew these warnings against the cunning strategies of power from his own experience.

> In the long run [his biographer[10] writes], political persecution was less detrimental for Marechera than the implicit suppression of his personality and work. His cosmopolitan outlook and anarchistic views did not fit into the

> landscape of Zimbabwe just after Independence. . . . Hence his attitude and his writing were often labeled as bourgeois and elitist.[11]

He found himself being "laughed . . . out of [the] offices" of the new elite, his poems "sealed in a deafening silence" (*Mindblast* 52). Marechera understood that the label of self-indulgent, irrelevant, and "un-African" artist attached to him was a power ploy to discredit his exposure of the emperor's nakedness.[12] His strategy was to go on writing—documenting[13] the attempted silencing and persecution itself as his "testament" and aid to other strugglers for freedom. Far from being self-obsessed, he was (as he explained) choosing to *use* a "private voice even when . . . dealing with a public theme."[14]

Analyses of power in its overwhelming and ubiquitous, insistent *presence* are much more in evidence in Marechera's writing than are examples or discussions of strategies for change.[15] Marechera conveys a tragic awareness of the preponderance of deadening power forms in individual lives, as in society as a whole. There is a note of lamentation throughout his writing, commemorating the precious energies of human potential, almost invariably (shown) strangled by convention, conformity, or more overt impositions of power—and the types of cowing or cowardice that result from this. Unmistakably, however, Marechera's texts constitute "protest writing" of a special kind—"against" exclusions or constrictions wherever he perceived them, not only against the "white world."

Indeed, Marechera found himself increasingly up against an African defensive strategy (against Western dominance) that he saw "backfiring" and itself becoming a new type of oppression, the intellectual equivalent of the political pseudo-change of neocolonialism (an unsheltering, exploitative social context in which white rulers have merely been exchanged for black ones).[16] The term he applied to this phenomenon was "the African image" (*Insider* 80). He saw its effects as a blinding of the self-critical consciousness of Africans, falsifying and constricting[17] thought and life, rather than providing the roomy shelter for a gracious life—for Africans—that it had initially seemed to promise. Instead of change, he saw ignominious stasis: "We will drive through to the independent countries where . . . original thoughts veer and crash into ancient lamp-posts," building "new towns crowded with thousands of homeless unemployed whose dreams are rotting in the gutters" (74, 79–80).

It is *in his writing itself* that Marechera attempts to "enact" as much as to promote transformative, vital lifestyles. In contrast with writing merely conforming to or parroting a static "African image," he described as his own artistic and political ideal "the voluptuous black*ening* image that commits me totally to writing" (quoted in Veit-Wild, *Source Book,* 4—emphasis added). Far from evincing apathetic despair, his "descriptions" (his texts)[18] constantly engage with forms of power and the activities by means of which power attempts to consolidate and extend control of people's lives. Indeed, it is because of the intensity of his efforts to make people realize the dangers of betraying their precious individuality to domination in its many guises (in the psychic, personal, social, or political spheres) that Marechera strove to create "language without a core," which he described as "frenetic, verbose" (*Cemetery* 130). The extreme aphoristic density of his style and its poetic, often surreal, qualities are the signs of the enormous effort this author put into his lifelong battle against that most insidious of all power forms, "accepted 'reality.'" His is, indeed, an energy for change, "in a struggle to construct an alternative language by which to exist" (Muponde, *Emerging,* 261).[19] In *Black Sunlight* Marechera pushes this battle to the very limits of "comprehensible" language. Power lies in wait not only in the large social and political forces and institutions, but "It's inside you. . . . Everything that sucks you in . . . it slams like a door once you're in" (*Sunlight* 70). Yet he could communicate the sophisticated insight that "civilization," complacency, and hypocrisy follow in the wake of power's victories (and are used to window-dress its savagery) with succinct and simple vividness, in a children's story: having teamed up to kill Green Baboon in a time of drought, White Baboon and Black Baboon decide to "eat him in a civilised way." They listen to Beethoven as they do so: "It was beautiful. / It was romantic. / It was the end of Green Baboon" (*Scrapiron* 232).

The quotation draws attention to the resource of humor that Marechera so often employs to debunk the pomposities and, generally, the pretensions of power and of the mighty and the well-off insiders of society. For all the tragic undertone of most of his work, he is one of Africa's great comic writers. His irreverence, iconoclasm, and exuberance work with great persuasive force to unmask the impressive disguises by means of which people are persuaded to worship and serve all kinds of power manifestations. A "court jester" of this kind provokes the mighty into fury and defensiveness, exposing their insecurity, as the narrator in *Black Sunlight* experiences (1–13). Marechera's mockery is seldom crude satire, but more often an impish kind or urbanely sardonic. He leaves none of the heavy stones of power structures unturned—nor does he fail to examine, iconoclastically, even his own nature or aspirations.

In fact, Marechera's controversial "self-preoccupation," the supposedly autobiographical nature of almost all his texts, exemplifies another *strategy* in his encounter with all powers, institutions, and roles. He expresses this succinctly and philosophically in *The Black Insider* when he writes, "The connection between what is happening inside us and . . . outside us in the Africa without had been made" (81), and symbolically when he emphasizes that the notion of "a man who walks away from his shadow" is "an illusion" (*Insider* 75).[20] The "shadow" image exemplifies the fate (in the present context, still too often the "stigma") of being African, the personal history of poverty and deprivation, as well as the subconscious "baggage" resulting from that background.

In Marechera's analysis it is, ultimately, "th' individual's blind impulse" that opposes power's obliterative force. His constant recountings of his own experience are not the writings of a self-obsessed defeatist, but instead of one who seeks to exemplify, emblematically, that particular, central insight. He clearly recognized (as he said of Soyinka) "the distance between self-exploration and self-mythification" (quoted in Veit-Wild, *Source Book,* 369).[21] The personally and artistically flamboyant Marechera could thus, with perfect sincerity *and* with no genuflection toward Deconstruction theory, say that "the writer is no longer a person: he has to die in order to become a writer" (quoted in Veit-Wild, *Source Book,* 366). The person and the person's experiences serve the writer, who aids individuation in others by baiting and mocking and denouncing the frightening bastion of power. His biographer (Flora Veit-Wild) recognizes this when she writes: "Marechera never missed a chance to speak publicly about the various forms of censorship that he perceived in his country, and he linked his fight for absolute freedom of speech with the necessity of a writer to talk and write about urgent social issues. Thus his artistic commitment was also strongly political" (335).

Marechera's insistence on the hardly deniable authenticity of individual impulse and experience cleared a space for that which the mighty seek to crush. Associated with this is his constant concern with the "embodiment," the "bodiliness" of human life—whether in the ecstasy of sexual fulfillment or in the weary decrepitude of the ailing.[22] Marechera measures the impact of power on the body as much as he celebrates ecstatic release in physically expressed love.

Though he acquired English initially as a disempowerment, a "sever[ance] from [his] own voice"—which seemed reduced "to a still small voice coming from the huge distances of the mind" (*Hunger* 30)—Marechera used it eventually to articulate the silenced, other "voices" in the psyche, or in his society, that conventions and oppressions had attempted to smother. With his vivid metaphors he castigated the barricades of power, writing of his aim "to loot the truths for so long packaged in lies," of the "scrap-iron of a lost empire," of the "fly-ridden promises" of the neocolony (*Cemetery* 31, 4, 91). Speaking *out* is perhaps the ultimate liberatory gesture: Marechera insisted that "history / Inside our mind is the headache / For ink and pen" (54).

After Marechera's death two of his Zimbabwean fellow writers paid tribute to the integrity that characterized both his life and his work, and that bound these spheres together. Hove called him "you who refused all shackles," and Zimunya said that "Marechera lived as he wrote and wrote as he lived."[23] As Nietzsche writes in "The Dawn," it is "the deviants, who are so frequently the inventive and fruitful ones."[24] The painfully earned insights of Dambudzo Marechera into the conditions prevailing in a postcolonial continent need to be reclaimed in the face of the superficial reading of this author's work as "un-African," as if he were an apostate rather than a *committed* critic of his society and the wider world.

The House of Hunger

No one can eat a House of Stone

Strike a match. See? No heart of darkness
Only stone for hungry teeth to crack and chew
Dambudzo Marechera,
"There Is Nowhere to Go Mister"

So sardonic and sophisticated is the articulation of the "cruel sarcasm" (6, 45) ruling the lives of the colonized subject expressed in *The House of Hunger*—the novella "House of Hunger" and ten "related" prose pieces, which was Marechera's first publication—that it aroused immediate controversy. Despite the author's deliberately scandalous behavior at the London reception after the joint award of the *Guardian* Fiction Prize to this work, plainly signaling that he was not about to allow himself to be absorbed into the (in his eyes patronizing) British literary establishment, the predictable accusations that his writing is "un-African" were soon forthcoming. Juliet Okonkwo wrote that Marechera had "grafted a decadent avant-garde European attitude ['nihilism'] and style to experiences that emanate from Africa" and declared that the continent "cannot afford the luxury of such distorted and self-destructive 'sophistication' from her writers" (Okonkwo 91),[25] apparently unaware that Marechera's prescience of such criticism had been written into his text, where "the Nigerian's taunts" (*House* 145) are recorded:

> He had, he said, read my stories and found them quite indigestible. Why did I not write in my own language? he asked. Was I perhaps one of those Africans who despised their own roots? Shouldn't I be writing within our great tradition of oral literature rather than turning out pseudo-Kafka-Dostoevsky stories? (142–143)

From a perspective concerned with power issues, it is noticeable that Marechera had provoked a powerful hegemony—the "African Literature 'Establishment,'" one might label it—by his demythologizing, iconoclastic approach to writing and to Africa. Marechera's exposure of "Africa" as the writhing ghetto of the twentieth century was misread (in these knee-jerk accusations and dismissals) as disloyalty to his African origins instead of being seen for what it is: one of the most brilliant analyses yet written of African urban degradation, admirably scrupulous in its pinpointing of the external *and* internal sources of this condition. Indeed, such dismissive criticism failed to hear what Marechera himself referred to as "the still sad music"[26] that is "at the heart of [his] art" (quoted in Veit-Wild, *Source Book,* 4). Rejecting "[influence] by other writers" (though he frequently and readily elsewhere listed the wide range of authors he admired) as a key inspiration of his work, he wrote: "I have been influenced to a point of desperation by the dogged though brutalized humanity of *those among whom I grew up*. Their actual lives, the way they flinched yet did not flinch from the blows dealt out to us day by day in the ghettos. . . . I *was* the drunken brawls" (quoted in Veit-Wild, *Source Book,* 1–2, emphases added).

The discomfiture of some critics with the African cosmopolitanism or African modernism embodied in Marechera's work might be linked with a representative passage in Ngugi wa Thiong'o's influential essay collection, *Decolonising the Mind* (1986): "By acquiring the thought-processes and values of the foreign tongue, [the African] becomes alienated from the values of his mother-tongue or from the language of the masses" (72).

The very fact that Marechera *seems*[27] to be a textbook case of this condition should alert one to the dangers of reductive, "essentialist" aspects of Ngugi's position. In an irrevocably "Westernized" Africa, where even "the language of the masses" and the "mother-tongue[s]" are almost invariably contaminated by the "thought-processes and values of the foreign tongue," it may be a type of escapism, or a romantic primordialism, to imagine that "the masses" are misrepresented by authorial accounts of "alienat[ion]" in African settings. Witnessing to the permeation of the colonized society (Rhodesia) by consumerism and deflected violence, Marechera is not betraying his people, but delineating their oppression, betrayal, and self-betrayal.[28] He writes (with irony and agony) interrogations and analyses of power bullying people's lives in a society where the bullies, too, are victims of structures and power sources beyond their reach—or even their understanding. Not holding out any comforting hope of change, Marechera highlights a changed, skewed, hemmed-in, ghettoized Africa. Yet his piercing, seeing-*through*[29] glance penetrates social and psychic deceptions and disguises, and this exposing stance is itself an achieved change. In some minimal way it balances imposed change, refusing power the compliance it buys with embourgeoisement—the privileges of assimilation. O'Brien refers to Marechera's "search for some third way between[30] colonial anti-nationalism and nationalist anti-colonialism" (O'Brien 89). The writer's position contends with the impingements of *both* these power formations. It can change perceptions by showing people how "to stop thinking in an institutionalised way" (Veit-Wild, *Source Book,* 41), stripping power of its guises and disguises. It cannot actually free the victimized, but to describe victimization so piercingly is a position evidently distinct from the cowed, silenced, abjectness of the overpowered. In his radically *unintimi-*

dated writing, Marechera's is a new African voice, articulating subalternity with an insider's experience and an outsider's intellectual and imaginative authority.[31] Duels with language (see Veit-Wild, *Source Book,* 4) are also battles for change, like liberation wars.

The brilliant tactical maneuvers by means of which Marechera tackles racist complacency "embrace" the Ngugi position, but surpass that rather primly solemn articulation by means of a cutting wit and mockery. In the first section (100–115) of "The Writer's Grain," the apparently typical English don who is the sole narrator suddenly (shockingly at odds with his hitherto genteel persona) tells in ghastly detail how he battered a "strange cat . . . with white fur gilded here and there" (109) to death in his room, using classic English tomes as his tools of extermination. Then it is revealed (as cunningly placed, seeming "relief" to the reader) that he is not a European after all, but an African—who is "cracking up" because *he* is so tortured by the "civilised" (111) English language "slur[ring] blackness—and I was teaching the bloody language and the bloody literature and also actually writing my novels in it" (111), he says. To this he adds: "If this is cracking up, then Jesus! let the whole world erupt." By now the expression "bloody whites" reliteralizes the conventional adjective, smearing the metropolitans' "civilized innocence" with gore. The narrator twists the knife of verbal vengeance, completely turning the tables on racist complacency in his devastatingly offhand sentence: "And the things which bloody whites—among them Jews—are doing to my family, to my countrymen, to black people everywhere, have never been done to animals" (111).[32] Using his surrealist strategy, Marechera elsewhere identifies the cat as "Melinda the Bloody White" (112)—a deliberate link between the cat and the narrator's English lover (107).[33] Chickens—or cats—come home to roost.

In the third section ("Protista"—127–133) of "The Writer's Grain," the narrator refers to the landscape of his banishment (for unidentified "political crimes"—127) as "this eerie region" that "overpower[s his] own imagination" with "the cramping effect of an overwhelming oppression" (131).[34] This is a particularly poignant comment, because "Protista" has been identified by Lilford (*Emerging Perspectives* 283–297) as one of Marechera's most recognizably "traditional" stories in many of its imaginative elements. The inappropriateness of critics' lambasting Marechera for what he is himself lamenting (in this example, cultural loss being figured as the grief of spouse loss) is especially glaring when an example in which the author traces the invidious, all-embracing effects of an alien power reconfiguring[35] a local society is considered.

The cunning ironies of Marechera's writing are the evidence of his implacable, oppositional engagement with power structures, among which colonialism, mental colonization of Africans, and racism are especially pertinent targets. In "Are There People Living There?" (149–151), the author's satirical echo of the Fugard play title (see p. 37) mocks the notion of the "Modern African Family," an entirely unreal notion in which the hype—"in each story the family *must be seen* to *consume* the products and manufactures of *white civilisation*" (149, emphases added)—is all that matters and the "House of Hunger," the African reality, is completely obliterated.

Yet Marechera expected the forces of what Gaylard has labeled "Nationalist Criticism"[36] to misunderstand his commitment. The painful impact of *this* power form with its simplistic hegemonic demands on the writer's sensitive soul have been illustrated (in the quotations of the "Nigerian's" comments—142–143). An even more vivid illustration of the point occurs in the passage in which the narrator's comrade (21–22) and former lover Julia "erupt[s]" with the vicious[37] accusation, "You hate being black" (45). He feels "impotent anger" at the remark, which underlines how cultural ostracism robs him of the very force of his own being. His African identity is, after all, inscribed in his appearance.[38] As Marechera writes in another piece whose title indicates his reading of Fanon ("Black Skin What Mask"—93–99), his "skin sticks out a mile" (93) and is, in a European context, an indelible liability. In that piece the narrator does have a double who attempts neurotically, eventually suicidally, "to scrub the blackness out of his skin" (93). (He is contrasted with the much more robust, sardonic narrator.) Over and over in *The House of Hunger*, claims about African "identity" impinge with shattering force upon relationships—whether in Rhodesia or in Britain.

The complexity of Marechera's reading of such identity questions—"No, I don't hate being black. I'm just tired of saying it's beautiful. No, I don't hate myself. I'm just tired of people bruising their knuckles on my jaw" (45)—made him vulnerable to attacks that he experienced and recorded, at once questioning the validity of "patriotic" racial essentialism (an entrapment "from within") and of contemptuous Eurocentric racism (an encapsulation from outside). An example of the second kind, relayed through a "brainwashed" black colonial subject, is Harry's father preaching to the narrator and his fellow schoolboys about "the ape in you . . . the heart of darkness" (35). So powerful is the assault of such racism on the psyche[39] (even though the old priest is later ignominiously routed—36) that the narrator "fall[s]" into a "dark pit" in which the feeling of being "boxed in" (37) is the overwhelming sensation.[40] Mocking, violent, and disturbing images of "ZIMBABWE" ("a star cut out of toilet paper") (39) swirl around him, emphasizing the extent to which the colonized condition is a surreal state of being.[41]

Marechera builds a description of the required stance of the African writer into his main narrative ("House of Hunger"). It is the response to colonial power imposition described in Philip's poems, which are "express[ive] . . . of discontent, disillusionment and outrage" (58). Since the entire description of these poems at first sight appears to be applicable to the very text (Marechera's) in which it features, a "double take" effect is achieved. This passage sounds like Juliet Okonkwo critiquing Marechera's text for "nihilism."[42] "There's white shit in our history . . ." (59), Philip says. Since his position seems so "politically correct" for an African writer, Marechera's subtle critique[43] of Philip's attitude is worth noting. Within his own text, so overwhelmingly preoccupied with the disrupted, fragmented ghetto experience, the author-narrator holds out for intimations of wholeness as the contribution the artist can bring to his shattered society. Although "only rarely do we see the imminence of wholes," "that is the beginning of art," he tells Philip (60). Such tentativeness is hardly a power, or a counterpower in the lives of degraded people, yet it may begin to inspire a change, a making "whole again" (39). Possibly[44] "those stitches, those poems" (39, 40), the narrator's type of text, "run[ning] like the great dyke across the country" (40), are seen as a precarious sewing up or stitching together of the deep gashes inflicted on the colonized society by the alien(ating) power.

It is in the concluding section of "House of Hunger," however (79–82), that Marechera most deftly maneuvers a space and stakes a claim for the validity, appropriateness, and need of writings such as his own to feature within the "iron net" (74) of the twentieth century. He does so by linking his own, supposedly "un-African," avant-garde writing with the ancient powers of African orature (oral literature): the old man's stories, "that were oblique, rambling, and fragmentary" (79)—exactly like the writer's![45] Since we have been told several times "earlier" in the narrative (2, 9, 45, 68) that "the old man died beneath the wheels of the twentieth century" (45), the section on pages 79–82 may be read either as a vivid, enduring, and inspiring memory in the narrator's mind or as an image of African resurrection and endurance. In fact, the latter seems more likely, given the old man's impish handling[46] of the traitor and police spy, Harry.

The psychic and physical vulnerability of the narrator is the principal mechanism by means of which Marechera links him with the other downtrodden, abused members of this society, a method that the author uses to focus on the "cruel sarcasm" (6, 45) of contemporary urban African existence. In "House of Hunger" he depicts the "U.D.I." period,[47] Rhodesia's own special form of colonialism,[48] when formal colonialism is embattled and fiercer, perhaps, because its days are numbered. ("I think Trouble is knocking impatiently on our door," the old man warns the narrator when he hands him Harry's spy notes—82.) An accommodating, compassionate vision is in evidence in *The House of Hunger*, alongside the more frequently noticed sardonic mockery.[49] Marechera draws attention to the white casualties of the Rhodesian impasse (like Richter) as well as to the far more numerous black ones, among whom the solitary figure of Edmund ("Sole survivor" among "twenty-two dead guerrillas laid out for display"—61, 60) is heroically prominent. Richter had been a conscript in Smith's forces, afterwards telling "harrowing accounts of atrocities he had either witnessed or taken part in, in the operational area" (69). Edmund, the butt of the school's "Africanist" bully, Stephen, becomes the true patriotic hero of their age set. Yet the two young men (black and white) are linked and doomed victims of the "House of Hunger": Edmund with a "dead-looking" face when captured; Richter "wander[ing] . . . in a drugged and drunken stupor . . . as though studying the abyss into which he must [and does] fall" (69).

Social degradation, rather than military defeat or overt political oppression, is, however, the recognizably most prevalent form of oppression in the community Marechera depicts.[50] Insidious, because seemingly detached from its initial source (the occupation of the society by an alien power and culture), oppression ramifies into the most private and intimate aspects of colonized subjects' lives.[51] The most awful and vivid example of such deflected oppression is the beating to which Immaculate is subjected by the narrator's brother Peter.[52] Raging with resentment against his own subjugation ("he hungered for the fight"—2), Peter has no way of identifying or getting at the source or perpetrators of his humiliation beyond his angry yet vague accusations against "the bloody whites" (2); his sense of impotence consequently merely intensifies, because he is "spoiling for a fight which was just not there" (2). In a context where it is "still believed that if one did not beat up one's wife it meant that one did not love her" (49–50), even marital sex is an "assault" (50), and wife beating a surrogate for political heroism. The entire community collaborates in this tissue of posturings[53] as it mirrors the people's own impotence and their ways of disguising the knowledge of degradation from themselves. The effect is that (unknowingly) the victim community collaborates in and even exacerbates its own debasement. "I'll beat it out of you yet" (4), Peter threatens Immaculate, indicating that he is unendurably shown up for a bullying, powerless coward by her enduring courage,[54] dignity, and unbroken spirit. Even the narrator, who loves Immaculate in his own baffled way, is disturbed and challenged (even agonized), rather than inspired, by her refusal to compromise her integrity or to stop "dream[ing]" (12, 17).

Immaculate's name and the "inner light" (28) that she radiates signify that it is she, rather than the narrator, who is closer to the "authentic black heroes[55] who [haunt his] dreams in a far-off [i.e., unreal] golden age of Black Arcadia" (24). Immaculate outshines "the grim squalor of our history" (21) as well as the corruption of her father (34–36) and her brother, Harry (10–21, 82, 88–92). The fact that it is she who bears the brunt of the ugly, "gluttonous merriment" (8) of Peter and the inadequate and compromised love (12) of the narrator is one of the saddest aspects of the situation Marechera depicts—its "cruel sarcasm," as he terms it (6, 45). Immaculate is subtly linked with the other victim-hero of the story, Edmund. It is with her that the narrator "walked *up* the ancient stone tracks that led *up* to the old *fortifications* which our warlike ancestors had used" (12, emphases added).[56] Like Edmund, when he courageously and resignedly goes out to defend his honor in the hopelessly unequal fight against the school bully, Stephen, she too uses the expression, "What else is there?" (12, 65).[57] Immaculate presumably means by this phrase an acceptance of actual local realities rather than futile dreams of some lost "Black Arcadia" (24). Like her "delicate skin," her vulnerability, gentleness, and idealism are shown somehow "stretch[ing] effortlessly over the pain" and the "grim squalor" of their township existence (12). In the narrator's view, however, "the rock and grit of the earth denied this" (12).

His despair is not shown up as any merely evasive, cowardly, or cheaply superficial attitude, though. The terrible double bind in which he is caught is the mirror image of the colonized subject's impasse: told of the need to "aspire" and yet punished for doing so. The family autocracy works in the same way: the narrator's mother "throw[s] her children into the lion's den of things white" (78), yet when the narrator rushes home joyously with an (English) anecdote for his mother, she punishes him with "stinging slap[s]" for "dar[ing]" to speak in English to her (13). The scene is an appalling one, indicative of the crushing of the child's spirit and the twisting of his hopes by a parent who feels herself to have been humiliated by the culture into which she is pushing her son.[58] What J.-P. Sartre termed the "nervous condition" of the "native"[59] is the natural result of such conflicting demands—of a sustained clash of cultures that leaves the narrator "awfully mixed up" to the unsympathetic eye, although it is the lucidity of his understanding of the layers of power hypocrisy that produced his condition that is so striking. The falseness of Peter's supposedly hearty invitation to the narrator, "This is home, man" (27), is immediately shown up by the power demonstration that Peter engages in when he forces the narrator to stare at him having sex with Immaculate—an ugly "top dog" ritual (28) fairly typical of the use of sex as surrogate power (compare Marechera's comments in Veit-Wild, *Source Book,* 13).

The rambling, circling, and intertwining memories of which "House of Hunger" is constructed (like the loose, yet linked, construction of *The House of Hunger* collection as a whole) are neither an arbitrary formlessness nor the result of a young writer's inability to control his material. Marechera himself said of the construction of *The House of Hunger* that he "was trying to experiment with the form which gave the largest range to [his] own experiences, but at the same time not to be so highly personal as to be opaque or meaningless to the reader" (quoted in Veit-Wild, *Source Book,* 26).

The power of Marechera's innate, highly verbal, and deeply metaphorical genius; the broad sweep of his learning; and the probing nature of his political, social, and psychological understanding are all in evidence in this remarkable first work.[60] The design of the work is not idiosyncratic, but perfectly appropriate to its two major points: first, its demonstration of the relatedness among the many varieties of colonial subjugation that it exhibits (even the bullies and profiteers like Peter, Harry, Stephen, and Harry's father, the "bullying" priest—see p. 34—being its victims), and second, its enactment of the entrapping nature of the condition. (Although "House of Hunger" opens with the classic rite of passage—leaving home—the narrator never gets away either physically or psychologically, as his past experiences resurface compulsively in his memory.) A cameo passage that exhibits the author's skill is the narrator's strange, dreamlike, semiconscious vision after one of his collapses (37–39). Its references to being "boxed in," "wound[ed]," to "falling" into a "dark pit," to "stitches," to "papering over the cracks," to a man with a "price-tag," to "scream[ing] quietly," to "CIVILISATION," "ART," "footsteps," "a mirror," "blackheads," a "struggle," "black heroes," "ZIMBABWE," "a toilet," a "story," and to "grim dirt," a "whitewashed wall," "flies," and a "spider" have multiple, weblike connections to the themes and images of the work as a whole. In its very fragmentedness something of "the imminence of wholes," which the narrator elsewhere refers to as "the beginning of art" (60), can be glimpsed.

"But the old man was my friend" (79) begins the concluding section of "House of Hunger," balancing its anguished and sordid fragments with a wholesome spirit breathed through the old man's "broken body" and his "fragmentary" stories. These stories bear an "oblique" but vital relation to the material and psychological realities depicted in the rest of the work. However dreamlike the stories may seem, they have (like their teller) "something of the earth" (79). The old man tells what is recognizably Marechera's own story (metafiction-style) to the narrator-persona—the tale of one "cast out," plagued by "[a]n unknown hunger" (79), laughed out of court when he "tried to enter" a "great city," deciding at last on a return to the deepest origins—"at the head of the stream[61] where all of man's questions begin" (80). He warns the narrator in one deft anecdote of both the independent, dangerous power and the limitations of the "circle" of art (81) and (in what might be a comment on Philip's style of "protest writing") suggests that an "angry youth" with an "angry mind" (81) may make not even a dent on the earth (82), and vanish unnoticed. Yet he also warns wisely against "tak[ing] these things too seriously" (82).

Marechera's approach (as his style indicates) is not solemn, despite the grave subjects of "soul-hunger" (1) and "gut-rot" (7) and their causes in the maldistribution and misuse of power. His remarkable mixture of anguish, mockery, surrealism, and sordid hyperrealism, qualified by an underlying compassion, brought an unforgettable work into being, reminding us that some human beings "have got that within [them] which does not kill when all the world out there is killing" (140)—a comment slipped into the midst of the charming and teasing piece, "The Christmas Reunion" (138–141)—a small, thought-provoking feast within *The House of Hunger*.

The Black Insider

in an uncertain country
Dambudzo Marechera,
The House of Hunger

The two lectures ("The African Writer's Experience of European Literature" and "Soyinka, Dostoevsky: The Writer on Trial for His Time"),[62] which Marechera delivered in Harare on 15 and 19 October 1986, provide numerous comments that appear to resonate from his earlier (at that stage still unpublished), most overtly intellectual work, the novel *The Black Insider*.[63] The fact that the (much earlier) novel covers a similar (enormous, both geographical and historical) range of references to other writers, from Petronius[64] to Gogol[65] and Soyinka,[66] indicates Marechera's concern, in *The Black Insider*, to place his own work in a broad literary and philosophical exploratory tradition. The novel can be read, therefore, as a claim to power of a specific kind: intellectual status. It makes such a bid not only for itself, or for Marechera, but for a number of other African authors to whom Marechera refers (among other literary greats), such as Armah, Okigbo, and Okara (82).

In its own uniquely Marecheran and "menippean"[67] way, *The Black Insider* is a work in the tradition of Plato's *Symposium*: a novel of debate. Because the discussions in the novel use the references and vocabulary of the entire "ideal cosmos" of literature,[68] criticism of the work as elitist (implying "un-African") helped to block publication during Marechera's lifetime (V-W, *S.B.*, 203; and Introduction, *Insider*, 7–12). What should be understood, though, is that the philosophical texture of ideas in this novel and its implicit plea for the intellectuals of Africa to be granted greater recognition[69]—both inside the continent and beyond its borders—address an African issue of great urgency.[70] In a piece published in 1980 in Britain, Marechera discussed the writing produced in his country and its contextual influences and issues:

> The country's educational system has for so long been fuelled by the political need (of the whites) to create a black population deranged to passivity by self-disgust and an acquiescent acceptance of western cultural and racial superiority. The result has been that much of Zimbabwean literature is a direct response to the obsessive and all-pervading theories about race, about racial conflict and the historical determinants of these. There is therefore a visceral unwillingness to define the individual by reference to that individual's self. (Quoted in V-W, *S.B.*, 232)

Marechera refers to the Rhodesian state's promotion of writing in the indigenous languages "depicting blacks in the appropriate image of clown and savage"[71] as well as to the way, "over the past fifteen years, war and injuries of the soul, exile and the emasculating effects of the black Zimbabwean diaspora, have taken their toll" (quoted in V-W, *S.B.,* 233).

Clearly a work like *The Black Insider* is a strategic response to these workings of overtly racist power structures as well as to racism of the more insidious, internationally hegemonic kind. Marechera associates his own type of writing with that of African writers like Soyinka and Okigbo, whom he calls "gadflies on their nation's leaping flanks" (quoted in V-W, *S.B.,* 370).

Central to Marechera's vision of literature as a vital, liberating force "exploding"[72] settled mind-sets and the political and social structures that such "complacen[t]" apathy endorses is his claim that "the irrational is the only true condition of man"—a "truth," he believed, that could inflict "burns on the body of both the individual and the State," appropriately and deliberately an "[affront]" (quoted in V-W, *S.B.,* 370). Marechera recognized that contemporary African writers find themselves—like the nineteenth- and twentieth-century Russian authors[73]—"in countries in a violent search for identity" (quoted in V-W, *S.B.,* 373), between the pressures of racist denigration from outside, on the one hand, and nationalist demands that they uphold a fine image of their own society, on the other.[74]

More overtly than in the novel *(Insider)*, Marechera in his (later) public address emphasizes the political centrality of writers and intellectuals as fighters for freedom against oppression: "The entire history of Russian terrorism can be summed up in the struggle of a handful of intellectuals to abolish tyranny, against a background of a silent populace. In independent Africa it is the university students who are in the forefront of the fight for the maintenance of liberty" (quoted in V-W, *S.B.,* 373).[75]

Speaking at a time (1986) when he could not have foreseen that *The Black Insider* would eventually be published, he uses in his speech images that clearly recall the novel, referring to Ngugi and Soyinka as "the new underground writers, sniping away from their nuclear bombshelter of high education and astonishing imagination" and to Dostoevsky and Gogol "connect[ing] with the [contemporary writer's] psychodrama of the intellectual trapped in a superficially rational world" (quoted in V-W, *S.B.,* 372, 374), quite like the novel's characters marooned in the "old Faculty of Arts" (23) as a refuge from the war raging around it.

The title of the novel itself can be considered a sarcastic oxymoron, a reminder of the excluded (outsider's) status of the African in "the white world" (73) of the twentieth century;[76] a pointer to the way those Africans who have apparently managed (usually by means of "Western" education) to get a foot in the door of the "white" establishment tend to be considered traitors or outsiders to their own society; or possibly an allusion to the Fanonian[77] condition of a "black" person assuming the trappings of the "white" world in a condition of cultural schizophrenia. The title of Marechera's work can, hence, itself be seen as a tool of power analysis. By choosing this title for his text,[78] the author brings to attention the power field of naming,[79] of "identifying" (either conferring or choosing an identity), and of definition of people.

Recognizing (on the one hand) that "identity is an act of faith, impossible to verify" (quoted in V-W, *S.B.,* 370), Marechera understands clearly (on the other hand) how fraught questions of identity are—especially in countries (like those in Africa) where "identities" are in dispute. His analysis of how (and why) identity questions become political issues, even sites of violence, is incisive: "Inevitably, the margin between literature and politics is breached" where a state and a people are "seek[ing] an [elusive] identity" (quoted in V-W, *S.B.,* 369).[80] The violent linguistic scorn with which Marechera in a poem from his London period lashes out against the "European" cartoon strip image of an Africa of "swamps savages Boukassas Amins Congos" (quoted in V-W, *S.B.,* 260) is to be understood in terms of this context of *contested* identities.[81]

Comments by Chantal Mouffe (in a 1993 essay) corroborate Marechera's understanding of the issues. She writes:

> There are no "natural" and "original" identities, since every identity is the result of a constituting process . . . the result of a multitude of interactions . . . [a] process [which] is always one of "overdetermination" . . . [, stemming from] the multiplicity of discourses and the power structure that affects it. . . . Instead of seeing the different forms of identity as allegiances to a place or as a property, we ought to realise that they are the stake of a power struggle. (Mouffe 110)

Using the image of a powerful identity as an "outfit," Marechera writes, "A naked man cannot have any statues but himself," whereas "clothed and belted he wields a power which is sickening to behold" (52). Contrastingly, "colonialism [was] that great principle which put anyone who was not white in the wrong" (79). Even in the supposedly postcolonial period when the African countries have regained independence, "Schweik" tells the narrator, "there are millions out there who also have designs [i.e., who confer identity]. Reducing you to a mere abstraction on a hate poster. Or just a shadow lurking among their fears" (79).[82]

"Schweik" describes colonialism sarcastically as "that great principle which put anyone who was not white in the wrong," a comment that probes the destabilizing, delegitimizing effect of this power formation on the sense of identity of anyone "not white." The logic of it is brutally simple: "equate whiteness with good and, of course, blackness becomes always tainted" (79).

Recalling a personal writing career, "Schweik" relates how he began by writing of a "romanticised Africa which could only exist in [the mind of] a pride-starved adolescent"—"Mother Africa" (80).[83] Colonial power *undermines* the individual identity[84] of the indigene. It assaults the psyche. Later years brought the recognition that this attempt to construct an alternative, admirable African identity was undertaken by most African writers ("all our best minds . . . had experienced the same anguish"—80), but also "that the African image we ourselves were constructing in our novels and poems was as limited and as false as in the white novelists' and poets' descriptions" (80).[85]

Moreover, colonial power can itself become an entrapment device employed by the neocolonial power ("a new kind of fascism based on the 'traditional' African image has arisen"—82).[86] The actual, dangerous, social and political consequences of this romanticized (African) image flown like a flag are that it masks and protects African power abuse.[87] In "Schweik"'s commentary, Marechera analyzes the way both the actual powerlessness of Africa in the international context and the lack of real nationhood are disguised by the trappings and posturings of merely military might: "We have rapidly armed ourselves to the teeth with the outward trappings of national advancement, as though by surrounding ourselves with these outward signs of social and national coherence we can will into our innermost craving the same edifices of peace and order" (85).[88]

Marechera also explores the effect on personal relationships of the large identity issues affecting all Africans in the twentieth century. It is when he is on his way "back to Africa" that the narrator, having broken up with his white companion Barbara, realizes that she had had a tender notion of "the African image she had seen" in him and had adjusted her original perspective from "the other side of the Common Market" (99). An exaggerated "identity" anxiety can become a handicap destructive to relationships: "Ignorance is to be filled with oneself" (100). Helen's artistic vision, "as though we were all changelings . . . [because] something indefinable was taken out of us long ago" (102) could be read as a description of an eviscerated, "identity-less" condition: the sense of a loss so crucial that it intensifies the narrator's "fear . . . of a world whose changes would never include a change for the better" (102).

By contrast, his relationship with his former wife, Tsitsi, at first sight seems ideal, since (he says) she "made me feel rooted in the middle of a universe" that was her body (107). "She was the insider" (108), the narrator says. Yet Tsitsi's career in "show business" ("far off in Beverly Hills"—112)[89] leads to barren isolation, their marriage ending in a failure: "It was a mistake to have married the African Dream" (112), as though in and through Tsitsi he could be faithful to his friend, her brother Owen, and to Africa. Crossing the "racial identity" barrier with Helen (113) is eventually his only real prospect of fulfillment. Initially, however, his racial otherness had presented a barrier[90] to her naïve racism—he stops her in the nick of time from stabbing him with a knife, an assault triggered by a spasm of racialism in her: "You frightened me. . . . I was suddenly appalled at myself. I've never done that with a black man before" (29),[91] she tells him afterwards.

Notions of fixed identities (like racial labels) are instruments of power and control, Marechera recognizes, but they are willingly absorbed, internalized, and sentimentalized by people. "Cicero" tells the narrator: "Talk of self-realisation and 'identity' and their attendant pathos and banality are the poorest of summings-up" (46). Earlier, the narrator had noted that "the only certain thing about these world descriptions is the damage they do, the devastation they bring to [people's] minds" (36). Notions of "'culture,' 'tradition,' 'history,' or 'civilisation'" (33) are characterized (by the narrator) as "endoparasites which actually live permanently in our minds" (33). *Words* govern,[92] or threaten,[93] people's lives, as if they have become detached from those who utter them: "Words are the waters which power the hydroelectricity of nations" (35), the narrator observes. It is because writers recognize the always arbitrary and instrumental nature of the descriptions we term "identities" and use *their* descriptions to expose this constructed nature that they are considered the enemies of the state. They point fingers "in spite of the emperor's new clothes" (82).[94] Marechera vividly describes the sort of mental colonization that has become known as "essentialism": "The idea of personality moulded by the cultural artefacts outside us and the sense of *identity with* a specific *time and place*, as though the human being is as rooted in his own kind of soil as any weed, is what creates for us the emperor's new clothes" (81, emphases added).

By means of such *de*scriptions, power *pro*scribes human dynamism and excludes and outlaws the "infinite" that "inexpressibly" (32) surrounds us.[95] Suggestions of the possibilities of change threaten the seats of power—hence, controlled from centers of power, "reading is an industry . . . breathing down the writer's neck" and telling the author that "he must write in a certain way and not in another way" (90), "Cicero" tells the company.

Marechera was convinced, however, that "beneath reality, there is always fantasy" and that "the writer's task is to reveal it, to open it out, to feel it, to experience it" (quoted in V-W, *S.B.*, 366).[96] What is in the novel referred to as "the wonder-garment of institutions, traditions, precedents, laws" are the "clothes" of "emperor[s]" (53) which writers need to expose as see-through garments. Fantasy, mockery, and mischief are the tools employed in *The Black Insider* to fight the "tyranny of straightforward things" and to escape "thoughts that think in straight lines . . . [taught by] . . . the missionaries and teachers" (37).[97] Because of such inflexible "straightforward[ness]," Africa has ended up ruled by what "Schweik" mockingly terms "Bible people" (97)—not implying that they are so pious, but so tyrannically and viciously self-righteous.[98] "This penny-certificate elite" as he snidely calls them, "has been ruling Africa since so-called independence was granted" (84), he says. The cynical maneuverings displayed in the brief play-within-the-novel (38–43) vividly illustrate how Marechera (adapting Shakespeare's *Julius Caesar* to the Smith-Muzorewa collaborative regime in Rhodesia-Zimbabwe) thought writers could blow the whistle on power collusions by heightening perception of the surrealism of the political sphere of "nation-making" (37).

Much misunderstanding of the writing of Marechera has been caused by excessive focus on the supposedly self-centered, autobiographical nature of his work. A quotation enlightening his purpose is the following (said of the Russian writer Pushkin): "He brought history nearer to himself and his readers by giving it biographical interest" (quoted in V-W, *S.B.*, 374).[99] In *The Black Insider*, given the period in Marechera's life when it was written, a major focus is on the experience of exile[100]—of being an African in an utterly un-African environment. He referred to "the terrible anxieties of exile"[101] in one interview (after his return) and explained this more fully in another (given in 1986):

> My main experience of Oxford University was loneliness and a certain questioning of why I found myself in a strange environment. . . . I asked myself exactly what had happened to my generation and what underlies those events which can erupt time and time again in any generation. Some of my friends had gone off to join the freedom fighters, some, like myself, found ourselves in countries where all we wanted to do was . . . survive mentally . . . hospitalise ourselves . . . our generation had more or less been raped and . . . like any rape case we would never really recover from the psychological consequences. (Quoted in V-W, *S.B.*, 152)

In a poem from this time ("Without"), Marechera refers to the condition of exile as a "soulless waitingroom" (*Cemetery of Mind* 28).[102]

Exile is never, in his presentation, a merely "personal" experience, however. Marechera acutely understood the power configurations that left the African in "Western" countries in "a world always without."[103] An especially poignant effect is achieved by the long passage (61–69) in which *The Black Insider*'s narrator relates the harrowing London encounter with his old friend and comrade Nyasha (69), which ends with Nyasha's throwing a glass of beer in his face (68–69). The corrosive effect (on personalities and relationships) of the exiled condition is vividly, terribly conveyed, not only in the portrayal of Nyasha, but deepened and made more complex by the way the anecdote is preceded and "interrupted" by some of the narrator's other and earlier experiences in London and Wales, producing a dense tapestry of impressions of the state of exile (61–69). The recollection is triggered by the narrator's metaphor of "the tearing cloth of exile," a very personal experience, but it is summed up in the bewildered, despairing, *angry* question with which Nyasha insistently confronts him: "What's happened to us? What's happening to blacks here in London?" (62). This makes clear how much broader than the merely self-preoccupied writer's Marechera's interest was, and how profound his empathy with others.

The condition of Africans in a European setting is succinctly characterized as "a new kind of decadence" masking "the inner unspoken discontent inside" (63)[104] and as manifesting its schizophrenic nature in an uncomfortable "obsequious assertiveness" (65). Marechera portrays it as a constant uncertainty. A phenomenon that poet W.H. Auden referred to as exiles' establishing "a malicious village" in the foreign capital[105] is described by Marechera as the "form[ing of] a black laager (defensive encampment) against the hordes of the white natives" and the "whiteman's sneer" (65)—an image effectively capturing the way the tables are often *not* turned on the European invasion of Africa, but merely ineptly imitated, when Africans come to Europe: the location of power remaining where it was. When "Schweik" defends himself from a late-night mugger's attack in Britain, it is assumed that he was the perpetrator—suddenly he feels himself alone "on an island that contained millions of whites . . . against [him]" (78).

Marechera greatly enlarges the reader's understanding of exile through his novel—it comes to be seen as the state of having been "born black in a white environment" (87), which is the twentieth century itself. "Naturalization" is seemingly unachievable. The author's probing analysis lays bare the roots of the "paralysing malaise" (30) infecting African intellectuals like himself. Not only are they never truly lodged in "Western" society, but they have become irrevocably distanced from their own people. "Cicero" says of the effects of his own education: "After a time I just couldn't understand my people and they couldn't understand me" (88).[106] Marechera carefully distinguishes between those educated Africans who snobbishly cultivate "their own elite separateness" (51)—the "presumption of superior intelligence . . . more likely to hurt . . . more likely to dehumanise" (52)—and those (like the characters in *The Black Insider*) whose intellectual endowments might serve their society, but who find themselves unvalued and rejected.[107]

It is with African intellectuals of the latter category that Marechera concerns himself in this novel. He does so, not in hopes of winning personal acceptance, but in order to point out that the continent *needs* the skeptical, questioning, imaginative minds of such people as "Schweik," "Cicero," and the narrator. That he has little hope of such acceptance is portrayed not only in the novel's major image of the Faculty of Arts (a version of the ancient ivory tower metaphor for the university—now an isolation enforced by the external conditions of mindless war with no discernible purpose or loyalties)—but also by its ending. The safety or refuge offered by the institution is merely provisional, ironically earned by becoming infected by the "plague" (25) of education, "exiles from the war out there" (25). That is why this shelter is characterized by means of the sinister image of the "dark wing" (25) under which the novel's personages are huddled. Africa itself is a "continent of refugees . . . of wounds" (79),[108] the narrator says. Exile is a continental condition for Africans—as well as being a metaphysical state.

Marechera's brilliant punning connects the various "states" he describes—hence, the narrator informs the reader that "the faculty is the last desperate ditch of a state of *my mind* bred in the tension of war" (31, emphasis added). The ancient, reassuring expression "there's no place like home" has its meaning inverted in the narrator's melancholy realization that "there *was* no place like home" (106, emphasis added).[109] With icy sarcasm he refers to the "careless abandon of *assimillados* who have not forgotten their place" (106), implying both that Africans co-opted into the Western system remain obsequious (65)—they have to show that they "know their place," in the snobbish phrase—*and* that they are forever haunted[110] by their sense of their own, very different origins—African, and probably indigent. The narrator says of himself and his friend Owen that they both "enjoyed the common and sordid freedom of being born in the slums and hacking [their] way out of them by the skin of scholarships," bringing them a "gritty insecurity" (104).

That theirs is a tragic condition is brought out in the tone of lamentation[111] discernibly underlying the narrator's generally tough-minded stance when he states, "The sense of having lost our nation was indivisible from the feeling of the nation having lost us" (105). It is not a "disloyalty"[112] that has brought about this condition of "lostness," but the international power shift; they live in "a world that had rapidly ceased to be [theirs, or their people's] and had become a whiteman's playground for investment, good living, and casual tormenting of Caliban" (105). That is the one force of exclusion. The other is described in one of the novel's most scathing passages: "The way forward increasingly meant the progress of inhumanity rather than the extension of the very freedoms which had given it life. Certainly, the machine of the nation-state gave the citizen a prefabricated identity and consciousness made up of the rouge and lipstick of the struggle and the revolution."[113]

If there is no room for principle or thought, the intellectual's choice becomes the decision whether to "stay . . . solidly in [his or her] own mind or in the real Africa of give and take" (75—cf. 74).

Although Marechera is well known for having said of himself, "I have been an outsider in my own biography, in my country's history, in the world's terrifying possibilities" (quoted in V-W, *S.B.*, 364), he gives one of the most evocative lines in the novel to his most eloquent alter ego, "Schweik": "Only the land that's framed by the empty blue sky is enclosed like a brain in my skull" (73)—a poignant claim to placement. Although the narrator laments that "dislodged" Africans like himself "[can] only give, and give unreservedly, in novels like this" (107—recurring from 64), the expression (still) registers a devotion, a commitment.

The novel also has an understated love theme. Although the narrator's love for Helen, herself a tragically damaged person (28, 50, 98, 101–102), ends tragically when she is killed, he experiences a profound sense of redemption through his commitment to her (98, 101–103), which makes even her death something worth fighting for, however suicidally (given the odds—113–115). This may be the only kind of change for which there is a touch of hope in the novel, to help "teach us the simple preciousness of all life" (106) and bringing the recognition that "we have to seek unborn routes . . . yet to come" (79).

Two short pieces from an interview (1986) may be used to introduce (in conclusion) a few very brief comments on the other pieces Veit-Wild published with *The Black Insider*: the first, Marechera's statement that "some of us from Africa had become part of an oppressive class"; and the second, his comment that he "was living with England's own walking wounded" (quoted in V-W, *S.B.*, respectively 27, 28).[114]

Power issues are evident in all five of these pieces: "Smash, Grab, Run" (117) treats all Britain as a prison; "Oxford, Black Oxford" (118–121) pursues the theme of alienation; "The Sound of Snapping Wires" (122–124) depicts the narrator's ejection by fellow Africans and his joining "England's . . . walking wounded"; "I Am the Rape" (125) imagines cross-racial sex as a form of international political "vengeance"; and "Night on My Harmonica" (126–127) depicts the sordidness and despair that exile can cause.

Black Sunlight

Charles Marechera is giving great trouble—he's nocturnal
Iris Hayter[115]

Kwame Nkrumah, president of Ghana, urged Africans first to seek the political kingdom if they wished to achieve other freedoms. Marechera's third novel, *Black Sunlight*,[116] is in some sense a major postcolonial text because it looks far past that (sort of) injunction, which at the time seemed so appropriate, but which later developments on the continent revealed as shortsighted. The novel urges a search for a freedom deeper and more difficult than the political, and it enlarges the subject beyond any national or even continental base.[117] The authority that Marechera's narrator evokes is not that of a political leader, but the ideas of a young urban guerrilla, Nicola,[118] tracing the thought that

> the more we "progress" the more we think as that progress demands and the less we think and feel as the life within us demands. All the forces of social and national man have been levelled against that tiny spark within us and seek to snuff it out with types of religion, education, legislation, codes and in the last resort, jails and lunatic asylums. The mass of men live underneath the hand of these forces. But a few of them still persevere, still implacably and at great cost to their own cherished lives, still go out there wielding the only banner, this tiny spark that will detonate all creation, and they wield it in the only manner which society cannot fail to understand. Some would say fear cleanses—Nicola does. Instil fear into society's heart and she will bare

> her fangs to protect her cubs. That kind of fear is not enough. It does not defrost the chilled spark within her. Inject her here and there with this and that strange and vivid idea and at the same time make memorable lifestyles out of the ruthless destruction and she will find her own cubs come running to us. The thaw will have begun. All those Ice Ages of the heart, they will have begun to thaw. The next thing she knows—it is the flood. But of course she is herself a cunning wench. She knows when to give rein to her children, when to let them hold out their hand to the flame, for they will come back crying and there will be even more snow and ice than ever before in the space within the human heart. I tried to say something of this at the meetings but why bother? It merely throws a damper on plans that sound world-wide. In the end they will get us one way or another. I know that. To evangelise the red-hot magma that bubbles within man is not my purpose in writing. Indeed I have no purpose. I merely see things in a certain way. (66)[119]

That in all this it is our very life (individually) that is at stake, as well as our capacity to care for one another as human beings, is illustrated in the following two sentences: "But where we are and what we do with each other have been subjected to that sum of allowable knowledge and know-how which diminishes the very life in us. Our material means, or lack of them, our belief in this or that ideology, our needs, our wants, they take up more room in us than do humane considerations" (68).

The quoted passage from Marechera's novel (66) is evidently centrally concerned with the idea of life as a perpetual, interlocking struggle between the socially ubiquitous forms of power and the individual's "red-hot" (66) potential energy of change—her or his true, vital core. What is done by and occurs around people is seen, not in political or national terms, but as a "struggle" between "our dreaming and our waking life": "Yet we retain for years on end [the narrator adds] the illusion of a linear and easily deciphered life" (67). Indeed, all of *Black Sunlight* is Marechera's major blow against what had in *The Black Insider* been labeled "the tyranny of straightforward things" (*Insider* 37).[120] One might say that *Black Sunlight* is a great cry against colonizations of the mind, in whatever guise or setting these occur, across time and space. The breadth of this attack on all oppressions is the purpose that generates the novel's blending of the modes of grotesque satire, realist narrative, intellectual speculation, and a type of free (modernist) verse in prose.[121] As Flora Veit-Wild wrote in an early essay on Marechera: "The 'power' of his words, always highlighted by critics, can be taken quite literally: with the power of the word and of the imagination, he seeks to counter the manifestation of power (i.e. violence) which he meets in all its forms in his own life, and which he abhors and fears more than anything else" (V-W, "Bullets," 114).

That long quoted passage (66) is, in fact, the answer given to the novel's main narrator, a photojournalist, by his double, the novelist (whose voice is subtly endowed with special authority by the surprising discovery of him typing away[122] at the very heart of the revolutionary center Devil's End), to the question: "What do you feel about violence?" (64).

The deeply troubling—indeed, crucial—nature of the issue is manifested in the novel not only in its numerous depictions of violent events and its constant exposure of the *violating* effects of institutions like the family, the school (14–21), and the state (e.g., 97–98), even language itself (87),[123] but in the way this particular question recurs. It is first (and rather startlingly) asked of the (main) narrator by the revolutionary Susan (43)—a question the narrator evades by claiming to have no feelings about violence, being "merely its photographic chronicler" (43). But Susan disallows his evasiveness by pointing out society's "institutionalised violence" (44)—the haunting thought of which will trigger the flood of memories and ideas that pour from the narrator in the last part of the text. Violence, constrictions, and regimentations are so ubiquitous and multifarious in the vision of this work because they are the experience of power impinging upon the very self. The extent to which this occurs is the source of the despair[124] that colors so much of the text. Near the end of the novel the narrator declares: "The things human beings construct have no connection with whatever it is a human being is: machines, mazes of streets, classified ads, water-closets, constitutions" (116). And yet, in art, this very "not-being-there . . . when it is *powerful* enough . . . *inspires us* with the deep and opposite thereness of everything that is human" (116), the italicized terms indicating something of a (temporary) triumph of transforming and liberating force,[125] adequate to the profound value that Marechera in this novel places on human selfhood.

The injunction from the long quoted passage, to "make memorable lifestyles out of the ruthless destruction" (66), is an expression indicating the link that Marechera in his text makes between political anarchism and the type of writing that *Black Sunlight* exemplifies. The common purpose shared by the political and literary activists is destabilization of all the dull and settled mind-sets hemming people in, which they allow to extinguish their own unique vitality. That such "destabilising" activity is risky, on both the literary and the political front, is a realization built into the text—toward the end of the novel when the revolutionary group seems safe, the narrator expresses the ominous feeling that "the Nazi ironclad [is] churn[ing] closer" (113), whereas the verbal attack by a student audience on Nick's poetry for its supposed "unintelligibility" and "modernistic European manner" (110) precisely forestalls the reasons given why the novel itself was (at first) deemed "undesirable" by the Zimbabwean censors. Marechera understood (and in the novel demonstrates) that "if you start translating your thoughts and your dreams into actual action, that's when society moves against you in terms of the police, the army or the secret service [or the censorship system, as Marechera wrote elsewhere]" (quoted in V-W, *S.B.*, 31).[126]

Throughout the text Marechera's images for the chilling effects of power are those of ice (66) and rain (15), and (contrastingly) for individuality his metaphors range from "black sunlight" (37) to "igneous fires" (51). There is, however, a complexity and an intellectual sophistication built into Marechera's depiction of the different methods of battling against "all those Ice Ages of the heart" (66). Satirical mockery, profound idealism, and serious, down-to-earth warning are all blended in this multifaceted text. In his own comments on what his novel depicts and intends, Marechera stressed its critical irony ("Intellectual anarchism is full of contradictions. . . . [If] it achieves any goal . . . then it is no longer anarchism"); its political realism;[127] and its "rigorous re-evaluation, especially of Western intellectual thought" (quoted in V-W, *S.B.*, 31). It is this complexity and breadth of reach that are reflected in the varying styles and highly unusual form of the work.

The most succinct expression of the crucial existential question permeating the novel in its entirety can be given in Marechera's own words:

> At what point can the individual realise that his brain is dead because it has been fed with irrelevant facts, fed with things which have nothing to do with the individual who carries that brain? And when one realizes that, what does one do? Does one resort to violence to destroy those institutions which have promoted such slow brain death in citizens? (V-W, *S.B.*, 40)[128]

It is clear from the novel that the vague "autobiography" of the narrator (beginning with his reference to his parents, "There was this woman . . ." and "There was this man . . . " [14] and proceeding more or less chronologically[129] until the encounter with the narrator's doppelgänger in the middle of the text) stresses the enforced experiences of family upbringing, school education, and a militarized, dominated society full of guns and "corpses" (21) as forms of assault on the individual sensibility.[130] As a schoolboy the narrator sees the prison guard's "dark glasses gleam[ing] like the sinister emblems of a powerful world" (21) and even at this early age he wonders: "How did one escape? In a rain of bullets? Or seeing red everywhere" until incarcerated in a lunatic asylum (21)?

Susan's is the most straightforward response to the issue. "I deal out death" (51), she declares. She describes her role as that of "an opposite and more direct force which can hammer this created tiger [society, the nation, any of the 'grand designs'] into bits and pieces of flying sparks" (50). Hers is therefore the conviction of justifiable counterviolence.[131] The narrator is aligned with her as her "chronicler" (51), through their sexual union (45–51) and through his admiration of her. She is, on the whole, extremely attractively presented, as warmly human, impetuous, almost shockingly honest—and very, very strong,[132] in every sense of the adjective. Although the narrator remains linked with and faithful to her in a profound friendship[133] and even becomes Susan's "assistant" in her violent revolutionary activities, he is never himself shown perpetrating any violent acts (nor will he leave his blind wife

Marie for her, even though Susan makes him think about this for the first time—47).

Something of the "irony" Marechera himself mentioned vis-à-vis anarchism (V-W, *S.B.*, 31) therefore accrues not only to Susan herself, but also to the violent activities of political anarchism depicted in the novel. (The entire "movement" is, of course, defeated by the end of the period depicted in the novel.[134]) The scene in which Susan assassinates a cabinet minister and the narrator photographs (technologically or mentally) how the woman's "headless body faltered at the third step" and how "the explosion blew the roof of the head into the sky," is also a scene where he registers some horror and outrage and (it seems) feels a protest[135] against "revolutionary violence": "Lethal blades of fire tore through the intellectual metal. . . . A film of blood between thoughts and the world out there—blotted something out" (84). A critically dissociative stance is also evident in the reference to Susan's "maniacal intelligence" (102).[136] When Susan's stare probes (he says "excavates") into the narrator in his drugged and hallucinating condition, the despairing and accusing question "What has not been done in the name of some straitjacket?" (88) includes her and her reign at Devil's End. This is pointed out by the narrator's alter ego, the novelist, when he warns of the danger of "be[ing] taken over by the collective delusion *either here or out there*" (62, emphasis added). He also describes Devil's End ("*here*") as "sordid and squalid [as well as s]adistic" (62).[137]

The author-protagonist refers somewhat sarcastically to Susan's motives as stemming from an inability to endure the existence of what is both "comprehensible" and yet unrelated to "her designs" (62)—which sounds like a classic case of megalomania. Yet he registers (is it with a mixture of horror and respect?) the idea that "they are really going out there to destroy, to kill" (63). For his own part, the narrator's alter ego abjures "private absolutes" and acknowledges that "the design is always bigger than its separate components"—yet the point that this is not a merely passive, acquiescent stand is indicated both in the humble admission that "I may be wrong again" *and* in the determination coloring the quiet statement "you can only persevere" (62).[138] His cryptic warning against "trying to bridge the gap between intelligence and terror" is probably a recognition of the way a commitment to acts of public violence can engulf the perpetrators—"a whirlpool that sucks you in, and not only involves you but tears inside out the shreds of what humane considerations you started out with" (62).[139]

I would thus argue that Susan's comment to the narrator (concerning his commitment to physical violence), "Your heart really isn't in it" (49), applies more generally to Marechera's depiction of the option of the revolutionary counterviolence practiced by the political anarchists in the novel. Yet he portrays Susan as an unmistakably "glamorous" figure,[140] and the type of physical counterviolence that she practices in her perpetual war against enslaving "grand designs" (50) remains the only political role with which he aligns himself. Nor does the novelist-narrator allow the serious *significance* of the activities of the "terror group" to be reduced to those activities[141] themselves: "Susan's ideas" remain the truly important matter (69). Her belief in the elemental "spark that sets creation on fire" (65) is the commitment that deeply links them.

It is notable nevertheless that Susan's bombing of two cathedrals (93–94) is not so effective a "demolition job" on the perceived inadequacies of Christianity (as a socially and psychologically salvific force) as the passage in an early chapter describing the narrator's visit to a church, which ends with the literal falling of the idol/ideal of the crucified Christ. The earlier account is compelling because the narrator enters the shrine in the *hope* of an alternative to an engulfing sense of "soullessness" (29), only to find in it human "narcissism" and sentimental delusion—what he calls "the impossible arcadia of a humane and visible world" (30). He finds Christianity a spent force.[142]

There is a wryness in the author's depiction of the photojournalist-narrator, however. It is a wryness that shifts from the hilariously comic perspective in the opening scenes of the novel to the deep melancholia of the closing section. Though it may be true (as Chris says) that "knowing two sides doesn't mean one has not a side" (56), the preference for destabilizing, liberatory activity by means of explosive *writing* rather than actual bombings[143] does not exclude recognition of its probable ineffectiveness—laying its practice open to accusations of evasiveness. In the opening scene the narrator calls himself "only a fucking court jester . . . not a dissident like Sakharov" (9) (not that this saves him from persecution in various undignified and grotesquely unpleasant forms!). Slightly later, somewhat gloomily, he notes that he has no public role other than to "perform as chronicler, subversive jester and teller of tales" (13). Despite the self deprecating tone, the perennial significance and need (in all societies) of exactly those functions, which only a principled writer can perform, might be noted.[144]

Throughout the novel ideas are constantly (mutually) readjusted and balanced, resisting any complacent resting place or finally approved choice. The "rigorous" questioning process that the author himself mentioned (quoted in V-W, *S.B.*, 31) leaves no position unchallenged and no role wholly approved. The narrator is told (by Chris): "There is a vacillation in you" (56). His alter ego pronounces oracularly:

> You seek a transformation that can never come to one of your nature, a twisting and turning nature. You think of making a breakthrough imaginatively and concretely but it's not the other side that you want but only the process towards it. That perhaps was your misunderstanding of Susan. She is less and yet more than you supposed. (63)

Clearly this is self-criticism by the author as well as the expression of agonizing doubts about the contrast between the political activist's oppositional role to power and the way in which the author challenges its institutions. The most anguished expression of doubt occurs near the end of the novel, in parenthesis: "(Steve Biko died while I was blind drunk in London. Soweto burned while I was sunk in deep thought about an editor's rejection slip)" (114). But whatever evasions she or he may practice, the violent assaults of power will not leave the writer alone: the acknowledgement "like everything else that hides behind a poetic attitude, I had to come out bloody and dirty" (14) sardonically registers this point.

To the question what sort of energetic, liberating force can effectively oppose the power forms of human society, the novel offers no naïvely hopeful answer. Besides the imagery of an icy mass (66), of the "GREAT CUNT" (59), of a controlling machine (100), and an "Armoured Insect" (115) for whatever dominates our lives, the novelist uses the image of a predator. Observing the scene of a "riot" being brutally quelled, the narrator notes that the "whole thing writhed like a jackal biting through its own trapped leg" (32). This is "society . . . the lioness" (69),[145] which uses its "fangs" (66) to protect its interests and to keep its "cubs" faithful. It reappears in "the bloodred leopard" in Nick's painting, "*War*" (109), and obliquely in the narrator's defeated sense that "the bestial fact" of overpowering institutions like the state "would always be there" (103). Even "the common speech, the aimless chatter" of conventional "members of society" conceals "the muted snarl sharpening its teeth" (58) of this same vicious beast.

To the question whether his most striking image of power, that of the "GREAT CUNT" (59, et passim) is indicative of an ambivalence toward women, Marechera replied that this was his attitude, not to "women alone, [but to] mankind[, since] the engulfing power is also the state" (V-W, *S.B.*, 219).[146] The image of the politician "with his microphone raping all his citizens" (V-W, *S.B.*, 219) is, indeed, distinctly male (97–98). Marechera's images of powerful *people* in this novel do tend to be those of female characters,[147] however—especially the authoritarian aunt who raises the narrator, the anthropologist Blanche, and the revolutionary Susan.[148] The aunt's seems to be a gloomy and disciplinarian presence with vaguely sinister overtones (her "lips were thin like threats"—15), oppressive toward the boy's open and imaginative nature (15–22). Blanche's "casual treachery" (92), inspired partly by her impatience with the narrator's "nightmare of neuroses" (113), seems to be his most abiding memory. When he imagines himself dying,[149] it is while "watch[ing] the gashes in [his] wrists leak . . . with meaning to flood . . . [his memory of his] embittered days with Blanche," who is given the overpowering identity of an "Amazon" (117). A yearning for her, a "grief underneath" (117) about his loss of her, resurfaces whenever his conscious guard is down (e.g., 78, 99, 112, 114). Since Blanche so clearly represents the "white" world of "Western" learning[150] ("ferret[ing] out the few bits and pieces of authentic people [and] reducing them to meticulous combinations of the English alphabet"—4), she is associated with that structure of dominance in both its colonial and neocolonial forms, however personally benign she may be.[151] Besides her "glittering" skin (6), she represents anthropological "distance" (110, 111), technological modernity, and consumerism (coffee and cigarettes, her watch, and cartons of Durex—10–11).

Especially marked in the narrator's association with Blanche is the way in which her shift of loyalties to a new lover (75–76) exacerbates in him intense feelings of anxiety and alienation, racially marked. He is reduced psychically to "a terrified ghostly shape, cringing into the trees" (81).[152] It seems as if his emotional dependence on her translates into a sense of cultural-racial intimidation, so that he imagines himself being ingested by her ("pushed down into her gut ready to be excreted"—81)[153]—another image of being *overpowered.*

The complicated disempowering effect of the narrator's European education can be brought up here. British (racial) condescension is alluded to when the narrator sarcastically refers to the effect of "an Oxford degree": "Making the monkey monkier. Erasing the solidity out of him to make him no more than a black insider" (77).[154] He is simultaneously kept at arm's length in the European context *and* (ostensibly and ostentatiously) severed from his Africanness by his education: "Language. Knotted tightly around my eyes like a bandage made of headaches. Language. Shards of a broken glued-together mirror. In it knotting my tie. English images came out of the barn with a thousand Zulus at my heels. . . . Big heavy words thumping onto my coffin" (73–74).[155]

When he speaks of "the assassin's knife plunging and twisting into his heart where the desert hurt" (77), the painful and life-threatening assault on the psyche comes both from "the English"[156] and from "the brothers" (78), his fellow Africans.[157] It is against this background that the narrator's disempowering sense of dislocation (Who are his "true people"?—4) must be understood. His reference to being "sometimes all the time . . . [i]n the wrong skin" or "this black skin" (4) is not a racial disavowal but a protest against the way this racial marker can be used by Europeans *and* Africans to encapsulate, essentialize, and deny the individuality of the (African) artist. It is another of the novel's images of entrapment.[158]

In contrast with these maddening superficialities, the novelist-narrator declares: "But there's nothing in looks. It's the inner things which matter" (60). This is where the central significance of the blind Marie, the narrator's gentle and sensitive wife, comes in. Marie grows from the "silent and scourged girl" (82), who "[does] not talk much" (18), to one who speaks from "the igneous heart of genius" (106) and who "ha[s] always known all about it" (103).[159] There is something in the suggestion[160] that it is her very powerlessness, her maimed condition, that binds the narrator to her. Her effect on him is far deeper (and more tender) than the exhilaration, the energized force that he experiences after his sexual union with Susan (51). In a more spiritual and inward way—in comparison with Susan—Marie too contains "the inspiring spark to set reality's façade on fire" (113). On their wedding night, the images of "her own black sunlight," a "song," "drumm[ing]," "the dark furnace roar[ing]," "stunned innermost reserves," "the blast of the song," "vibran[cy]," of the two of them "[riding] the crest," and especially the narrator's statement that he "shall not know such another till the waves recoil" (37) serve to indicate the beauty, value, and vitality of Marie and of his relationship with her. Even in Susan's company he recalls how he felt as though Marie "had begun to radiate with unseen insights" (47).[161] This visionary quality and the inspiring effect it has on the narrator come from her profound sensitivity, reflected in the fact that (like him) she is an artist.

Yet the point that all the children they conceive are stillborn is the tragic sign of an inadequacy in the relationship. It links with the fact that the narrator cannot find complete fulfillment with her and cannot wholly commit himself to her. "Then—[he] would be free" (36): it would be the liberation saving him from the weight of meaninglessness that the world's power forms push down on him. There are suggestions in the text that in contrast with the "glittering glory of [the] European tradition" represented by Blanche (6), to which the narrator is in a sense addicted, Marie represents suffering Africa[162] with its unnoticed "anguish" (113), its "diseases that have no esteem" (36). Hers is the "inner torment that trembled softly" (20), the condition the narrator shares with her.[163] The agony both of the continent and its most sensitive people is reflected in the nightmarish scene where the reporter-narrator, observing the campus riot, sees Marie in the midst of the flailing mass, "her mouth open, though I could not hear the scream" (32).[164] And yet in her is also the "black dream, arched her body taut like a full-drawn bow… loos[ing] the force that attracts the earth . . . [capable of] catapulting [the narrator] into the eerie depths" (113).[165]

The writing in the last half of *Black Sunlight* achieves a symphonic density, the predominant mood being one of tragic gloom and grandeur, shot through with glimpses of delight. The main issue is the question[166] whether a true transformation can occur in society.[167] Marechera's novelist-narrator adopts an almost evangelistic stance, exhorting "the few of us who . . . still have a sense of our elemental beginnings"[168] to try to "show the rest a glimpse of their own natural destiny" (69). The style is intensely lyrical, the narrator using the image of a new kind of being hatching out of the shells that at present enclose us (67).[169]

Sadly, the journalist-narrator is overcome by the "fear . . . of a world whose changes would never include a change for the better" (107).[170] The dulling banality of his life seems to have overwhelmed him.[171] When "the chasm of rock and ice smashe[s] upwards" (88) in the explosion that demolishes Devil's End, this represents simultaneously the crushing of his spirit. "The bestial fact would always be there" (103),[172] but for the "estranged hearts . . . there could be no ending": they *will* persevere, it seems.[173] Although the novel "fades out" on a glimpse of the "naked and vulnerable" humanity of the narrator (117), we are also reminded (just before this) of the eternal self-renewing vitality of the universe, its "spiralling nebulae . . . [and] galaxies, exploding wildly *outward*" (108, emphasis added)—expanding and transforming in creative liberty.

Mindblast

Write the poem, the song, the anthem, from what within you
Fused goals with guns & created citizens instead of slaves.

Do not scream quietly.

Dambudzo Marechera, "In Jail the Only Telephone Is the Washbasin Hole: Blow and We'll Hear!"[174]

The image of an explosive device in the title *Mindblast,* Marechera's third publication,[175] suggests the author's combative, disruptive intention[176] through participation in an ongoing battle for citizens' rights and needs, a battle that in African countries has almost invariably succeeded the disappointing "victories" of national "independence" won in liberation wars. In a continental context where the vast majority of the population remain the wretched of the earth, the pitfalls of national consciousness[177] became swiftly apparent—though among writers in his region, Marechera was one of the daring few to proclaim this loudly and immediately,[178] both in his writing and from other public platforms, at some risk to himself. He phrased his stance as follows in a 1985 interview:[179] "Now I am more preoccupied by individual liberty than by national liberation, the defence of those who cannot defend themselves. Now that we are independent I write, for example, about prostitutes. . . . [And yet he found that] . . . the writer becomes a problem. To criticise this or that is [considered] unpatriotic" (quoted in Caute, "Black and White," 101).

Close to the end of the Diary section of *Mindblast*, the concluding part of the whole text, the diarist reports himself

> thinking: I have just met the matter of this book, her and him [two Hararean down-and-outs, a grizzled bum and a woman who has resorted to prostitution]. The haus des hungers of Harare. Her, him, me. The rotting minced meat underneath the tablecloth of political slogans. And I thought of all the hundreds of unemployed youths—boys and girls. (153)

It is characteristic of the social inclusivity of Marechera's empathetic vision that it ranges from the young unemployed (mainly black) to the formerly employed (the white woman) and the petty criminal (the white bum). He aligns himself[180] with them, and he—as "outsider"-artist—writes on their behalf. More remarkable still is Marechera's acknowledgment and recognition *in himself* of the voluptuous opportunity and *desire to exploit* that weakness represents to the politically and sexually powerful (152–153). Power is represented as the desire to "pounce" and to conquer. Of the would-be, prematurely aged, prostitute the diarist says, "I felt her humanity but—and is it macho—despised her . . . white European female vulnerability. Feeling shit even as I felt this" (152). Deftly and vividly, the author links the personal and the political, gender and political power politics, in everyday, immediately accessible language—ranging from Caesar and his Roman conquests to "South Africa fucking Maseru. Or the Israelis sodomising the Palestinians. . . . Or the Nazis screwing . . . Europe" to "the gun-culture that is now a permanent feature of my country" (i.e., "postcolonial" Zimbabwe) (153).[181]

Marechera's adoption in most of *Mindblast*—a collage of three short plays, prose narratives, poetry, and the concluding Diary section—of a noticeably colloquial, mainly nonintellectual English must register his attempt to "get through to" the majority of his compatriots, to address their concerns and express their opinions. This is evident also in the name chosen for the major persona, since "Buddy" (as a nickname) indicates someone who is a reliable friend, in the same boat as oneself. This contrasts with, say, "*Comrade*" Norman Drake (22, emphasis added), whose "title"—for a white Zimbabwean—registers (ironically) his highly privileged and powerful position—a position partly earned by participation on the right side during the independence struggle, but since contaminated by ruthless ambition and shameless wheeling and dealing with the new black elite, equally happily corrupt. The set of three related playlets in which this scenario is established—"The Coup," "The Gap," and "Blitzkrieg"— in their titles and material introduce a *sardonic* perspective on power matters. The plays convey the view of those who are outside the opulence and power manipulations of the majority of the persons depicted on stage, on the absurd, mean, and grasping goings-on of the latter. By enabling his audience to laugh at the newly powerful and the nouveau riche and their hasty new alliances, Marechera uses comedy not only to expose the (suspected) dirty secrets of the "stylish"[182] rich and strong who now run the show, but also (simultaneously) to elevate the powerless and poor to judge their overlords and ladies (who are demeaned by his mockery).

Marechera's talent for sarcastic wit and the range of amusement he elicits—from low-life bawdry to quite esoteric, intellectual in-jokes—make him one of the continent's great comic writers. Comedy functions almost invariably irreverently in his writing and is used in the unmasking of power to expose the ordinary, mundane humanity hidden under the solemn posturings and the grandiose displays of power (per se) and its other form, wealth. An instance from *Mindblast* is the following short interchange, set against the background of that great social common denominator (which is the only stage prop), a noisy lavatory:

> MRS NZUZU: Am I not urgent business to you Norman?
> DRAKE: Of course you are. But this I have to do is even more pressing. A call of nature.
> MRS NZUZU: You are so poetic.
> DRAKE: I am not, Mrs Nzuzu, I mean Lydia. I just want to piss.
> MRS NZUZU: You do have a quaint turn of phrase. Yes all of us in the SADCC want peace. Zimbabwe more than most. (29)

How hilariously this excerpt from "The Toilet" mocks the sex-and-power manipulations of the "old" (colonial) and the "new" establishments—in the claims that are being staked, in the former and the presently fashionable catchphrases used, in both the misunderstandings and the mutual understandings of the predatory class, and even (of course) in the differences between "British" and "African" English, which is no bar to the deals eventually struck between them!

The embourgeoisement of Zimbabwean society went (typically) along with "hypocrisy towards sex and its close ally, power" (quoted in V-W, *S.B.*, 336).[183] The scene from "The Toilet" opens with the would-be suave, but forcible, seduction of The-Drake-on-the-make by the real holder of the reins of power, Mrs. Nzuzu. Staging the intertwinements of sexual and political connections so clearly for his audience, Marechera was of course treading on toes all around, not endearing himself to the new stakeholders. His role is the ancient one of the sociopolitical satirist, whereas Zimbabwe's rulers naturally desired praise-singing to be directed their way. Marechera soon began to see in Zimbabwe "a country very paranoid about sex and politics" (*Mindblast* 138). There are (thus) natural links between the perceptions of this society reflected in the titles of proposed plays listed in the Diary section, such as "the less than humanising activities of the Social Services," "bombastic hope followed by . . . the sudden mental/political blackout," and the depiction of "a society in the venereal grip of sexual/power paranoia" (128). Marechera's mockery relentlessly homes in on the sex-and-power games for which those at the top always—indignantly—demand privacy.

Although Mrs. Nzuzu is the most powerfully predatory figure in "The Toilet," outmaneuvering even Drake the master manipulator, Marechera clearly perceives that power manifestations are more usually male. As already noted, he confesses to (what he suspects is) the "macho" tendency to prey on a woman's vulnerability even in himself—a tendency that can assume de Sade–like perversity, mirroring political atrocity (152–153). Yet he also notes that, more commonly, women "[cope] quite casually with . . . male barbarity" (131). It seems to be with a mixture of cherishing tenderness, envy, and sadness that he registers his perception of femininity as powerlessness: "this deep notion in me that the essence of femaleness is an inbuilt vulnerability" (157). An especially vivid instance of this passes before the diarist's eyes as he sits typing in the park:

> The woman walking always three paces behind her husband, like a haiku. . . . A baby strapped onto her back. Another strapped against her belly. Yet another trailing behind. And on her head the huge crate of worldly possessions and the three paces behind her man, who is leisurely hurrying carrying nothing but the patriarchal power granted him by both custom and tradition. Thinking on the seventh wife . . . (144–145)

Although Marechera (as noted above) acknowledges his complicity in male power tendencies, a passage like the foregoing is especially poignant, perhaps, because the gaze *exposing* the impassive male exploitativeness is (here) that of a man.

Marechera throughout *Mindblast* intertwines supposedly personal experiences with public issues by exploring their power dimensions.[184] The mechanism by which he achieves this is his construction of the writer as *witness*, whose representivity (as in "political representative" as well as in the one who depicts or "represents") the writing establishes.[185] The most electrifying example of this technique occurs in "The Toilet," when the unknown, somewhat drunkenly belligerent character Alfie (a black man) suddenly reveals the Marecheran dimensions of his experience:

> The skull is a prison wherein weird thoughts pass the day in solitary confinement. . . . It was in prison that I started to write. . . . [Having become aware of] the blank wall that confronts the have-nots, . . . suddenly prison was no longer a prison but a school in which I was discovering that there are many shades of black but the only true one is that of the have-nots. (37)

Set in the midst of Drake's opulent party, these words ring with bitterness and conviction in the midst of the smooth complacencies of the newly constituted elite.

The long poem "Throne of Bayonets" (75–95)—rightly placed at the heart of *Mindblast*—is Marechera's most direct[186] accusation (in this text) of the new form of African power: no longer a throne of skulls,[187] but one established by and on the military hardware with which the continent is awash. The title image also emphasizes how brutally inaccessible the center of power is to the ordinary and the vulnerable members of society: it is an image of power bristling with violence. In the tradition of the prophet-poet[188] exhorting and exposing the ugliness of the city[189] (the concentration and manifestation of social power), Marechera directs his "X-ray" vision at Harare, "expos[ing] the corruption in the marrow of our bones" (quoted in V-W, *S.B.*, 372).[190] "I look at Harare, my hair stands on end" (75), the dramatic speaker frighteningly informs the reader. And fear—because of the fearful state of this society—is everywhere in evidence in the Harare of "Throne of Bayonets." This is summed up in the speaker's discovery of "terror the totem of truth" (75).

"Throne of Bayonets" is an important poem because it eschews the relatively easy role of mere denunciation of the powerful to examine and expose the many complicities[191] from which power derives its armor-plated[192] safety. Especially interesting and admirable is the way in which the artist, too, is taken to task and rigorously interrogated (by the dramatic speaker) concerning the adequacy of his fulfillment of his responsibility in the situation in which he finds himself.[193] Many of the accusations to which Marechera was subjected—of being effete, self-indulgent, irrelevant—are absorbed into the poem, which seriously, even agonizingly, asks the artist what he can achieve, what his role might be, in this difficult sociopolitical context.

Most of the allusions in the poem to "emblematic" social critics function as exhortations to the artist to risk ridicule, denunciation, and even death in order to be true to his role, which is to serve the lowly by exposing the injustices that prop up power. Antigone, Hamlet, Gogol, and (especially) Christ[194] are examples of such daring denouncers who "smell out the rot in public places" (92). The risk incurred is of being "hurled," "writer after writer," by the "seething" force of the social conformity demanded even—or especially—of artists (83). The ancient but (here) personally felt point that truth telling is a dangerous occupation in a society in the grip of power-mongers explains the early, cryptic reference to "terror the totem of truth" (75). Yet no cozy hideout is available:[195] "The friendly eye of thought" is assaulted by the "blows and kicks" of the offended and challenged (brutal) supporters of the social power base. Moreover, and more insistently, the artist's conscience challenges him[196] to speak out. His "song" is the expression of the repressed voices and "wrecked hopes" of the lowly, which are simultaneously the only (delicate) hope of new life[197] for this society. But this faint hope of the "battered" and badly accommodated members of society is also somehow unstillable, unsilenced, deep "within"—faintly, it "hums all the wrong" that it dares not speak out about (75).[198] To society's "wealthy shit," this sound is an "ominous song" (76).

"Throne of Bayonets" contains vivid—and biting—thumbnail sketches of both the supremely powerful and privileged members of society and of power's co-optees—the "comfortable" members of society. Among the latter group, the speaker's eye focuses on the "owning" attitude of the merely complacent (in female incarnation): "I watch them leisurely passing by / With their shopping bags, handbags, husbands / Their bland faces certain / Of the night and bedroom to come" (76). These, the socially sheltered, are contrasted with the group so often alluded to in the poem, the politically betrayed ex-combatants,[199] reduced to the condition of "Memories slumped on green park benches, / Veterans of black fire, these violets / Of terrifying beauty" (95). After "liberation," all the old injustices remain in place: "Fatrich, thinpoor—Power's / Gravy over the same rotting / Carcass" (76).[200] The colonial position of privileged comfort insensitive[201] to social suffering is now occupied by the new elite, "sit[ting] on the verandah of Destiny / Sipping Vermouth . . . / And the view a permanent drought of Probabilities" (82).[202] Especially repulsive is the image of corrupt, "Ring-studded black fingers / Around the pink gin of change" (87).

The revolutionary slogans (89, 91–93)—which so mockingly echo the betrayed ideals that brought the new elite into power—are interspersed (with cutting effectiveness) with Marechera's portrayals of the "happiness for the few" (95) that has been achieved, such slogans as the now-hollow rallying cry, "The people, / The people, / Always come first" (87). With lies like this and with its decadent comforts, power barricades itself against the weak. Marechera's images for this insensitivity range from the naturalistic ("shuttered houses / . . . the car speeding past"—76) to the surreal ("Bullet-proof brains"—84—and a "breastplate . . . table napkin"—93). All the images of threatened, gentle life and growth (in the poem) are shown excluded from the bastion of power. These images range from the "tiny blue eggs / In abandoned nest"·(75) to the "burning sparrow" (81) and the "flying fish" (80). Most significant is the recurrent metaphor of violets (80, 84, 85, 95)—helpless as these flowers are, there is some type of persistence in their growth.[203]

Marechera's indictment of postcolonial Zimbabwe is a powerful one. It is the more effective for avoiding the inevitable trap of the social satirist: self-righteousness. The poet, too, knows himself "time-warped" in the "maze" (87) of the postcolonial city,[204] a lost soul searching (80), weakly vacillating from "radical compassion" to "cynical resignation" (82); understanding the desire for glamour and comfort (84–85) from his position of homeless loneliness (76, 97, 82, 83, 88). The "knocks" of conscience (79, 82), "the fires of awakening" (80), and his sense of a duty to "the muted unborn" (84)[205] drive the speaker to ask: "Who and how the Artist in letters of blood / [can] Describe the terrible truth?" (94). It is exactly because this question eschews both political and aesthetic complacency that it validates the poem as a whole.

Among the other items in the poetry section (75–117), the poem that stands out for its both moving and fierce depiction of the power distributions in the postcolony is "Oracle of the Povo" (106–107),[206] which conveys the now "soured vision" (107) of the formerly hopeful. There is no shred of liberation in the lives of "lean harried squatters" harassed by "armed overlords / Touching to torch makeshift shelters / [of] / The most vulnerable and hungry of citizens"—oppression backed and legalized by "magistrate and village court," where "Drought Relief graintrucks" mysteriously vanish[207] without alleviating the plight of the starving (107). With bitterness the speaker in "The Coin of Moonshine" observes "our neon progress / Exhorting the homeless to bank with Beverley / Exhorting the thirsty to have a Coke and a smile" (112)—the obscene contrasts of a split "society" that has brought change only for "African mutants in transition" (97).[208] But he warns the wealthy and powerful (known in Zimbabwe by the term Marechera employs, the "shefs") to "Listen!"—for there *are* "voices / Rising in turmoil from the future ground floor" threatening to "lynch those . . . / Lining their pockets with coins from the povo's hymn" (117).[209]

Because all the prose sections of *Mindblast* tell and retell the story of the individualist / artist beset by the authoritarian and brainwashed[210] society in which he finds himself, it is clear where the perception of Marechera as a self-obsessed artist derives from—it is nevertheless necessary to recognize the extent to which this writer perceives in the artist's difficult, unappreciated role an index of how unfree his whole society is. The poems mentioned above indicate the extent to which he gives voice on behalf of those outside the doors of power. Being as homeless as the lowly and as contemptible—in the eyes of the fortunate—as they are, *his* worm's-eye perspective on the social hierarchy mirrors (and serves) that of the powerless. This point is expressed in the speaker's reference to "[his] heart's little hut / Of mud thatch and pole" (115).[211] It is also conveyed when "Buddy" writes, "That 'himself' no longer existed in him. What existed were the poems he wrote" (52).[212] Marechera's *Mindblast* makes the point that concern for "individual liberty" is no mere selfishness, typical of an aberrant artist's decadence, but is itself the expression of concern for all "those who cannot defend themselves"[213]—like the prostitutes and the legless war veterans on the streets of Harare, or the starving poor in the countryside.

Exhibiting and exposing what is said and done to "Grimknife Jr," to "Buddy," and to the diarist of the "Journal" section of *Mindblast* (199–159) is to lay bare the repressive dimensions of a not really new African state. But because he is a tramp with a typewriter, Marechera can register the slings and arrows inflicted by outrageous power with exceptional force, vividness, and variety.[214] Much of *Mindblast* is deeply sad rather than militant, typical protest writing. Yet it became a rallying point for many (especially young) Zimbabweans.[215] His very outrageousness, "the way I would talk and joke about things which people here are unable to talk and joke about" (152),[216] had a liberatory effect. The artist himself experienced the arduousness, "the donkey work of keeping sane among people obsessed not with ideas but with mammon" (63). Clinging to the artist's "dream" that "the individual can only find his society by searching to the utmost in himself" was "liveable," but "discouraging" (60)[217]—and harshly discouraged by the administrators of society, who considered such an attitude dangerously subversive.

Marechera never romanticizes or misrepresents the difficulty of the oppositional role of those facing the phalanxes of power and the bastions of luxury. To be "in fields where compromise is unthinkable" (59) is constantly to disturb and question the sources of the comfort of the fortunate members of society—but it involves being, oneself, *un*comfortable.[218] The "searing loneliness" (129) of this role is the aspect Marechera most often mentions in *Mindblast* (79, 83, 86, 88–89, 120, 129),[219] and it is the final impression we have of the diarist as the text ends (158–159)—the lonely figure sitting typing among "beggars and tourists, the povo and the shefs" (87).

The form of power especially in evidence in this text is wealth—conspicuous consumption, which Marechera terms "crudely materialistic" (120), a concern with "nothing but money" (137). "There are no / People, but dollars—or the want of dollars" (76),[220] he writes in a poem. The vandalism of unemployed youths he finds entirely unsurprising: "Their lives are a blank; the only model Zimbabwe offers them is that of a crude and corrupt capitalism: cars, videos, a suburban house, a telephone, a mistress, a name in society" (154).[221]

From this sort of power base, the Marecheran figure's devotion to his art appears either silly or seriously insane. As he is usually "penniless, homeless and friendless" (51), his position represents in their eyes a mere (or contemptible) powerlessness. But the artist's preference for "the inner spirit" (120)[222] "turn[s] in / Ward / To follow / That Within / Which teacher / And priest / Taught / Divine" (79). It is only in this devotion to "what's inside you" (61), when one feels intensely, that anyone can "giv[e] all [their] soul to the black electricity of [their] inner nerves" (121). It is Marechera's only hope of electrifying and life-giving change being achieved in the stultifying and material-minded wasteland of modern Harare: "How to split the atom of the story and in the mindblast survive the . . . psychological holocaust. All this dead skin I have to scrape off with literary fingernails. And seed the clouds for the rain to come. Tears that have not yet been shed for ninety years" (144).[223]

To the songwriter Grace, Buddy assigns the testimony that "attacks of triviality and futility . . . had to be fought . . . by songs, poems, novels, sculptures. It was the hardest kind of life the individual could choose" (68). Here, then, art uncompromised by materialist ambition is seen as the true life force of society, and the artist's role (however thankless) of giving a sense of meaning to life is defined as a heroic one.

Especially hypocritical and especially discouraging to the artist, then, are the statements of those in (government) "offices" (representing their power position) who tell him, "We want poems that will uplift the people . . . you write capitalist poems. . . . We want simplicity and directness, something the workers and the peasants can understand" (52).[224] Buddy's question, "Why does every revolution result in the alienation of its artists?"[225] is answered by Grimknife Sr's counterquestions: "Is it the slogans have become stale? . . . Or is it more change results in no change?" (58). Marechera exposes the especial absurdity of rulers' desire for tamely parroting citizens most satirically in the "Prologue—Grimknife Jr and Rix the Giant Cat" section of the text (45–50).

But the ridiculous, mindless foolishness of the Reorientation Officer Rix (45)—who attempts unsuccessfully to subject Grimknife Jr to political brainwashing—does not obliterate the truly fatal nature of the danger he represents to the nonconformist: without the required brain death (called a "transformation"), Grimknife Jr "will be hanged by the neck" until dead (49). That the youngster manages instead by an immense effort to "[transform] himself," by means of "laughter," becoming "brighter" and "shimmering" with incandescent vitality (50), gives this particular story an upbeat ending. Although it is probably not meant to signify the simple or final defeat of his adversary "Officer Rix" (50), transformative energy is *embodied* here. The equivalent to Rix's "voice with the eye of authority" (in the story-within-the-story) is that of an "army officer" who tells Buddy: "We do not have to read the trash you write. We do not even have to interrogate you. We just know you're not one of us" (54).[226]

The sinister note in those words reflects not only the demoralizing effect (on the writer) of the discouragement[227] of his art, but actual risk and threat from the upholders of power and its central prop—ideology expressed in slogans. The demand is for "positive / Affirmation"; "schools need books / Not critical looks" (92). The classification of Buddy's position as "nihilistic individualism" occurs, inevitably, because "he had always had a problem with slogans" (62).[228] Marechera indicates that censorship of the artist's work can go as far as imprisonment[229] of the writer—so infuriating is open dissidence to authoritarian power. More destructive, though, is the psychological cost. Marechera illustrates this horrifyingly clearly in the scene where Buddy, contemptuously dismissed for his supposedly irrelevant,[230] inappropriate,[231] "capitalist" poetry, starts "coughing horribly, raucously; he coughed blood. It trickled down his chin and onto his dirty heat-thinned-out shirt. He looked at the blood with wonder. He swabbed it with the back of his hand and began to rub the blood into the ground. The so precious soil. The land he had returned to" (52).

However "accidental" Marechera's actual return to Zimbabwe had in fact been, the gesture of commitment—of the author giving his lifeblood[232]—in the above passage is not dismissiable. As Marechera said in one of his own comments on *Mindblast*, "The book consists of many voices . . . the only way to have access to the hearts and minds of all those people out there is to first of all know my own humanity, my own failings of emotion" (quoted in V-W, *S.B.,* 311). Because of his complex, critical loyalty to the society from which he had originated and to which he returned, Marechera had the creative energy to produce, in *Mindblast*, the sort of work that would both contribute to bringing about, and itself exemplify, what he saw as "the future of modern African literature. Complex, unstable, comic, satirical, fantastic, poetic, insane, . . . and sort of mindboggling *in its pursuit of truth*" (emphasis added).[233]

Scrapiron Blues

the struggle's aftermath
Dambudzo Marechera, *Scrapiron Blues*

Living and writing within Zimbabwe (as he did from his return there in 1982 until his death at thirty-five in 1987), the allegedly "international," "unpatriotic," "un-African" Marechera produced the material collected in *Scrapiron Blues*,[234] which evinced a remarkable degree of local commitment, more obviously so than is the case in most of his previous writing. In fact the author around this time expressed his ambition to write a work that "would reflect in all its national contradictions and national achievements . . . what it is to be Zimbabwean today," exhibiting "a panoramic fictional landscape which would have the reader actually feel the soil here, feel the grime and rhythm of our cities": a work "that would do something for our nation as Dostoevsky's and Tolstoy's novels did for 19th century Russia." Yet in Marechera's hands, writing that would express "the pace and tempo of a whole nation"[235] would never be either a conventional novel in form or the expression of a merely fulsome patriotism. In the fragmented nature of its composition and in its recourse to dislocating and disconcerting techniques (such as surrealism, absurdism, sudden shifts, imaginatively taxing images and allusions, close-ups of violence and blood) Marechera's "menippean" writing remains true to its author's vision.[236]

Most clearly discernible as the distinctive tone of this text is Marechera's (to many readers, probably unexpected) concern with Zimbabwe's rapidly disappearing past: the uncomfortable reminders of the terrible frictions and actual atrocities of the liberation war period are the chief power base that the author employs in this text to launch its challenges to the postwar, independent Zimbabwean realities and structures. Even though Marechera was himself away in Britain while many of the events he describes were occurring, he fulfills the authorial "gadfly"[237] role in pieces for which he could find no publisher (see V-W, *S.B.*, 337–352; and the *New African* interview—64), resuscitating a past that many preferred buried and forgotten. Emblematic in this respect are the appeals to the author (reported within the text itself and elsewhere) by ex-combatants and others with "uncomfortable" stories to tell of the recent past[238] that he help them to broadcast their knowledge. Although he shows himself unable (and for principled reasons unwilling) to tell others' stories directly, the text as a whole eventually takes up that responsibility[239] in its combination of fiction with autobiographical testimony, urgently *addressing* society's power sources of the immediate past and present: it holds them to account by its "recounting" approach to Zimbabwean realities. On the one hand, Marechera remains true to the earliest impulse of his writing, "the silent but desperate voices *inside you*" (*The House of Hunger* 136—emphasis added), but on the other hand, there is at this stage of Marechera's writing career a clearer and more recognizable indication that these "voices" are not merely self-confined, since they articulate the agonies of the multitude[240] in the cruel grip of power contentions to which they are mere fodder. *Scrapiron Blues* attempts, in the words of the poem appearing on the last two pages of the text, "to cry, what no scream ever whispered"; to be "the small scream underneath the boot of the Sky" (250, 249).

In the 1987 interview[241] published as *An Articulate Anger*, Marechera said: "I dredge up all the mess from which my generation more or less survived, and I ask myself, what has happened to my generation? . . . this kind of diaspora that had happened to this generation. Exactly what does it mean to *the inner development of a people*?" (12, emphasis added).

This suggests something of that excavatory, "archeological"[242] approach that characterizes Marechera's writings of this period. Although, Cassandra-like, the author found himself writing in circumstances on the whole highly discouraging to his work,[243] the somewhat more muted tone of much of the writing can be read as an attempt to gain access to a Zimbabwean readership, rather than any diminution in the urgency of his concern (which remains the discernible driving force). It is nevertheless necessary to consider Marechera's disempowered and isolated position in independent Zimbabwe as the condition making him especially aware of, and therefore the more determined to express, the "voices" of the socially marginalized. Shortly before his death he reiterated (in an interview) his concern with the "helplessness of the victims of society [as something he] was always very much aware of" (Petersen, *Articulate,* 30). The categories of such victims on which the *Scrapiron Blues* pieces focus are those of unusually sensitive or vulnerable persons (especially among children), down-and-outs, ex-combatants, the despairing, even the occasional swaggering and brutal racist commander (about to be bombed into oblivion).

What Marechera wanted to do with and in his writing was exactly what was frowned upon by the powers that be: to "explore the subconscious of our new society" (quoted in V-W, *S.B.,* 39). Power structures and strictures require and insist upon bland *surfaces*, yet the weight of this demand could not quash Marechera's perpetually rebellious, oppositional creative spirit, although it succeeded at the time in suppressing his writing.[244] Ironically, the vitality, the very power to disturb, of his writing remains alive in his posthumously published pieces. The collection of pieces that opens *Scrapiron Blues* is an illustration of this author's ability to contrast, tellingly, the social surface and the discomforting "underground" of that collectivity. The manuscript that Marechera submitted (unsuccessfully) for publication[245] in 1983 opened appropriately with the sketch called "Tony and the Rasta" (212–216 in *Scrapiron*). As a children's story it shocks all conventional expectations raised both by the choice of genre and the simple candor of the style (of the "Tony is small," "Tony likes him" variety—213, 215), which Marechera effectively employs to expose (here) the *absence* of *all* the privileges and pleasures that feature in the typically middle-class world of such stories.[246] The realities of the social power hierarchy are exactly what (it is usually believed) children should be sheltered from; Marechera tells a story with a protagonist overwhelmingly conscious of social inequalities and injustices. Even the figure closest to a "fairy godfather" (the "Rasta," his teacher) gets beaten up (215).

In his vitality and fierceness[247] ("Tony hates people who hate Rastas. . . . He really hates them"—216), his open-eyed social awareness[248] ("Tony knows everything that goes on in Shantytown. . . . The stealing, fighting, fucking, the incest and rape"—216), his questioning attitude,[249] and (above and despite all this) his sensitivity,[250] little Tony is a Marecheran figure of sociopolitical protest.[251] He is an augury of hope, signifying at least the possibility of change in his society. Most of the details delineating Tony's Hararean township remind one clearly of the author's descriptions of Vengere township (Rusape) and Tangena (a shantytown) in which Marechera grew up and that he, even as a boy, detested and resented as furiously as Tony does his birthplace (see V-W, *S.B.,* 1–19. Marechera understood the power imbalance between the "cruel externality" of his circumstances and his own "physical and mental insecurity" (quoted in V-W, *S.B.,* 2, 3), because of a "violence which surrounds you from birth" (quoted in Petersen, *Articulate,* 27). But some changes, some "advance" is registered within the story itself, because the "Rasta" teacher (representing maturity in his understanding tolerance toward Tony's aunt, his responsible and care-giving attitude toward Tony, and his cautioning against hatred—215, 216) is also to be associated with the dreadlocked author,[252] now in a (socially) parental role (having emerged *from* the township squalor). Nevertheless Marechera deftly maintains the integrity of each perspective:[253] "[The Rasta teacher] was cursing the bureaucrats 'up there.' Tony looked up but could not see any bureaucrats, all he saw were badly dressed clouds, a thin, starved moon, and a few hungry stars that were quietly screaming for food" (215). Writing of such wryness and poignancy exhibits its own sort of power, intensifying the will to social betterment and transformation.

The collection of "Pub Stories" gathered under the title "Tony Fights Tonight" (1–29) are among the most interesting of Marechera's writings. Despite the apparent triviality and "irrelevance" of the lives they depict, they do engage with social and political realities in unobtrusive but carefully contrived ways. Marechera's unusual blending or, rather, paralleling—in these two types of stories—of the "pub chat" world of the unemployed[254] (the one type) with his dreamed-up couple, Tony and Jane's sphere (the other type), exemplifies the stories' origin in that "moment" (in the author)[255] when "low-life naturalism meets its *doppelgänger*, the existentialist" (quoted in V-W, *S.B.,* 367). In his easy association with and actual recording of the profane anecdotes of Fred, the author partakes of that "low life," but his writer's imagination needs and therefore creates the very different "existentialist" dimension that he embodies in

Tony and Jane.[256] Indeed, so intense is that need that he imagines Tony disputing and Jane becoming sexually intimate with him, their author (16–17). Yet, he shows, "tragedy peers over *everyone's* shoulder" (quoted in V-W, *S.B.*, 367, emphasis added): the pub haunters' lives are in fact more dreary[257] than those of the haunted characters Tony and Jane (who eventually seem to gain both prosperity and peace of mind: a meaningful place in the new society—26). The author in these stories can be thought of as engaged in a power struggle of the imagination in which the two sides (both clamoring for his recognition) are "this too much, this cruel externality" and (contrastingly) what is seen through, or with, "the inner eye of dream" (quoted in V-W, *S.B.*, 2, 43).

It is mainly through Tony and Jane that Marechera attempts to access "the subconscious of [the] new society" (quoted in V-W, *S.B.*, 39). That "subconscious" is, in most of the *Scrapiron* pieces, the past of the Zimbabwean "Struggle" against "internal colonization." It appears lightly in the "Fred" pieces;[258] but is much more painfully, vividly, and centrally present in Tony's "hard work trying to wash invisible blood from perfectly clean walls," which remain stubbornly (perhaps ineradicably) "covered with the gore of misunderstanding" (6–7). Tony "had been part of the thing called the Struggle" (14). Although Tony fiercely resists the traditional exorcism invoking "the spirits and ancestors" (14), it is evident that in the figure of this almost unlikely ex-combatant[259] Marechera is depicting the condition that has been labeled "post-traumatic stress disorder." Tony's compulsive washing represents not only physical cleansing but that of "conscience," as the author-narrator himself points out to his character (16). "It is a superhuman task" (10), it is noted. Marechera (in Tony's behavior) creates a vivid, even eerie, image of the "terrible" danger of an unexamined past: "It lurked in wait. . . . It lay in ambush" (14).

The role of a writer in such a situation is "to drag it all into full consciousness" (8). That his is an effortful, resistant role (opposing the forgetfulness that is decreed by power and its administrators)[260] is indicated by the author-narrator declaring that he "will not let go [his] story of Tony and Jane . . . [who] are [even, now] the only evidence that [he is] still alive" (9)—that is, *imaginatively aware*. He is the one capable of producing (and not merely exploiting) "a social and historical document" (24) in the unexpected shape of his strange, surreal tales. As Jane says, "Dreams are the only reality" (6) because they tell the truths unwelcome in the mundane world of privilege and might. Tony's "quest," his "dream," is to "exorcise out of his short plump body the rippling incredible Power" (10) that looms over him.

Far from representing life in a cocoon of privilege,[261] Jane's refuge in a world of her own dreams, the "only reality" she can stomach (6), is the survival mechanism of an excessively sensitive person. Hers is not a sphere of selfish isolation—she is tenderly aware of the "vulnerable unsuspecting dreams" (15) of the pupils she teaches and of the powerless position of those on the fringes of Hararean society:

> Those overalled dreams bowed down by pick and shovel. Those snotty-nosed urchin dreams that were reluctantly creeping out of the alleyways to face another day of cold and hunger. Those pot-bellied dreams already casting their pessimistic but appraising eye on those passing by who would want a quick one against some crumbling wall. Or were they the wrinkled white dreams that sulked past you as though you were personally responsible for the downfall of their racial and political supremacy? (13)

Through her, Marechera addresses the difficult, mediating role an author has to play in a traumatized (postcolonial) society. She is "heard" by the author-narrator screaming her protest at the idea of his possibly usurping someone else's story of his "Struggle" experiences (23). "She hunger[s] for the time when the spill of blood and the crump of bombs would have been wiped off the face of the countryside and the streets" (14–15). Although Marechera in *Scrapiron Blues* pays tribute to Chimurenga (the liberation war) by reviving the awkward[262] memories of this time, he also criticizes war psychosis and the enforced, uniform loyalties demanded by the "liberation forces" (itself a power form) as the unnatural, psychically distorting attempt (in Jane's words) of "everyone tr[ying] to live everyone else's dream" (14). This, she says, is "death" (14). Its aftermath comes in the shape of exploitative "relatives and friends. Sulky, yet sharp-eyed," putting social and even "religious" pressure on her and on Tony in their attempts at bullying the couple into conformity, for gain (14). Her awareness of power realities is expressed in her own terminology: "The future is controlled by people who inflict *their* dreams on other people" (15, emphasis added).

The unsatisfactory sociopolitical shape that such "dreams" may end up taking is vividly encapsulated in the opening paragraph of the text:

> A hard day. Nerves shrieking. The head tight and taut with the fact of heat, crime, lust, power, boredom and food. The ambulance still wailed in the distance. The Air Force had just brutally peeled the enamel from my teeth. The House Guards were riding by, back to barracks. And there was the Army Ceremonial Band—a controlled din of brass and trumpet, and the uncanny rhythm of stomping feet. Under the eyes of cynical, cheerless, drunken, curious, fascinated eyes. In navy-blue suit and necklace of oxtail bones, I watched it all pass by. I had looked out of the pub windows. I had come out to watch. I was standing cold and hard by the pavement. So this was the Opening of Parliament. (2)[263]

Authorial disenchantment with the overt, bragging display of the new form of power is cunningly communicated in the details that show its jarring impact on the author-narrator: "peeled the enamel from my teeth," "a controlled din," "the uncanny rhythm of stomping feet," his own "cold and hard" stance. In combining "Tony and the Rasta" (213–216) with the "Pub Stories" (1–29) (as he originally did), Marechera shows the other side of the coin of this smoothly efficient power (in his own words): "the harsh facts of poverty and the struggle's aftermath."[264]

The author-narrator's perception of his society is akin to Jane's, but it is Tony with whom he is (subtly) especially closely associated, not only as a fellow writer, but because both of them are psychically "plagued" personalities, a point figured in the imaginary "red ants" both believe to be eating at their minds.[265] It seems to be an image representing in both cases the nagging of "conscience" (16)—it stirs the author into writing, as it drives Tony to wash the walls of his flat. The implicit claim of association with a "Struggle" veteran (by the author-figure) is an interesting one, though, especially as it recurs in several forms in the *Scrapiron* collection. In the rather melodramatic story (significantly) titled "The Skin of Loneliness" (112–122), the author-figure ends up "cleared" (120) by "one of our finest commanders" (119) and is partnered by a desirable but psychologically damaged ex-combatant, Grace, who uses her "demob money" to buy the protagonist a bookshop—since he is "the one with the education" (118). Although violently irritated[266] initially by their interventions into his privacy (power impositions he resents), the protagonist by the end seems to anticipate a hopeful future with Grace (122). The whole of the story seems fueled by a wish-fulfillment drive, a yearning[267] of the author's for the sort of full and honorable (re)acceptance into Zimbabwean society he was never to have. He also creates, in the unmistakably both vulnerable[268] and powerful Grace, the sort of ideal partner with whom he could overcome his tendency "always to associate sex with the expression of[, especially, patriarchal] power and all its disgusting uses" (119). When he feels "out of place, as it were, superfluous to our history," it is Grace who, by "interlac[ing]" her fingers with his own (120), "reabsorbs" him into the heroic elite of the local community. Although there is great pathos in the discernible probable originating impulses[269] that produced the story, it is (partly because of its uncharacteristically overt patriotism) one of Marechera's least successful texts.

A suggestive remark from Gaylard's "Nationalist Criticism" essay, that "Marechera operated as some sort of urban *n'anga* or *sangoma*, seeing to the psychological and spiritual health of the people" (102), actually links up with the author's own wry reference to "those n'angas who think I'm competing for customers" (*Mindblast* 147) and with his recognition that to "describe and live in [one's] descriptions" is "in African lore, akin to witchcraft" (*Mindblast* 123). In *The Black Insider* Marechera had noted the blasted nature of Zimbabwean society: "We are a devastated garden in a time of drought" (37). In their essay, Levin and Taitz say of Marechera's writing project:

> The reconstruction of his individual identities entails a reconstruction of that community of which Marechera forms part. He fuses the role of artist and historian as individual recollections become part of or point to collective

> memory. In so doing, he disidentifies with constructed categories, which accounts for the reception of his work as challenging notions of community and wholeness of identity. . . . The materials of the past are shaped by memory and imagination to serve the needs of present consciousness. (*Emerging Perspectives* 168)

These comments emphasize the presence of a power (of a nonexploitative and unauthoritarian kind) akin to that of a healer or a social visionary in Marechera's writing: an energy for social change.

Such a function is evident in the strong theatrical piece called "The Alley," which moves from its Beckett-like opening ("hell is an Alley like this"—37) toward an agonizing and eerie confrontation with the violent, racially dichotomized Zimbabwean past. The initial harmony[270] between the former partners (professionally, and later in crime), the black Rhodes and the white Robin, soon fissures when the past that is hidden behind the "wall" of repression (37)[271] starts resurfacing.

Marechera in his writings consistently parallels political or racial power abuse with pedophilia and incest, especially a father's sexual exploitation of his daughter.[272] The connection is a symbolic one, yet also a sociological reality. Marechera is expressing the sexuality of power. In his role as a Rhodesian army officer, Robin tells his victim (Cecilia Rhodes): "We'll screw the ancestors out of you . . . and your God will be the Big White Cock!" (41). Such words are terrifying because they not only function powerfully on a symbolic level, but also effectively mimic the hate speech by means of which violent oppressors whip themselves into action. Examining such awfulness is necessary despite Rhodes's sardonic recognition that "nobody talks about the war. It's indecent to remind ourselves of all that. Bayoneting children, ramming primed grenades into vaginas, bombing cattle, and herdboys, shooting schoolboys in so-called cross-fire, murdering missionaries and blaming it on the boys. . . . Genocide . . . massacres . . ." (43).

Allowing the past to remain a dirty secret helps power to hide its evil uses so that it can more easily erupt in the future, compromising others and making alliances in the present.[273] As Rhodes, the play's voice of conscience, says, the "hundreds of skulls and ribs *dug up* from those mass graves" (emphasis added) are unlikely to "talk about reconciliation" (45).[274] The unassuaged pain has become "the song that will forever blow like an unsettled spirit from the Zambezi . . . so that . . . we can retell their story, which is not our story" (46). This becomes the "howling wind . . . gathering momentum" (46): an image simultaneously threatening and promising a cleansing storm—a hint of possible future change.

Many of the shorter pieces in *Scrapiron Blues*, however, express or depict an utter absence of hope for change or for a future of meaningful social participation. They range from the obscure surrealist piece "Killwatch"

(96–106)[275] to the brief sketch "First Street Tumult" (108–111) to "Black Damascus Road" (123–124: the account of a Struggle veteran's wedding-day suicide), and from the dreary white upper-class world of "Evening Star over 28 Highland Avenue" (125–126) to the piece titled "Fragments" (127–130), with its alienated protagonist.[276] All are similar in their bleakness—in the sense of exclusion from meaning or the dearth of hope. In a variety of class, sexual, and racial guises, they are the "bad dreams" of Harare that Jane[277] found so disturbing: its unfortunate realities.

The aforementioned pieces are all somewhat slight; however, Marechera produced some of his most unforgettable writing in three pieces from the collection of interlinked writings entitled "The Concentration Camp" (157–209).[278] They are the three sketches[279] depicting the life of the inmates of the "keeps," correctly identified as "concentration camps" by Marechera, in which native Zimbabweans were incarcerated under brutal conditions during the liberation war period. Especially well achieved is the perspective of the boy Tonderai, the chief protagonist. The "feel" of the writing reflects its (for Marechera, unusual) origin in "interviews" with those who had been prisoners in or guards at the camps—yet so concerned was he not to usurp others' stories that he declared his determination *not* to produce writing with a would-be documentary quality, by (instead) "using a kind of expressionist technique and here and there certain surrealist techniques and here and there straight narrative" in order "to bring out the psyche . . . of that particular period" (*Scrapiron* xiv).[280] It is in these three pieces that Marechera employs, on the one hand, the adult resource of hatred (as Tonderai's father does, under the extremity of torture) in order to withstand the humiliation and pain inflicted on his people by the overwhelming power of militarized racism (whether perpetrated by whites or by black Zimbabwean co-optees):

> Mr Murehwa was reliving those moments which, little by little, had gathered into his heart a congregation of pure hatred. It is one thing to hate only with the mind; when the body physically hates, that is something else. If the mind cannot overcome pain, the body's intense and passionate hatred can do so, after all. Memory, physical memory, was coming to his aid. (199)

Mr. Murehwa *uses* the bodily memory of previous torture[281] to defend himself against physical anguish and psychic stress under interrogation. He develops a revitalizing energy by the very effort "to remember every detail of this gross and evil time" (200). Marechera, by writing of this, verbally reenacts the terrible, but invigorating, resistance achieved by the torture victim.

The other resource against brutality to which Marechera draws our attention is the children's inviolate innocence.[282] On the one hand, a boy like Tonderai is shown "learning little by little from the horrifying stories whispered around the concentration camp" (160), from seeing his "beaten" and "weakening" father (159), and from such a "panoramic scene of horror" as that in which he and the other herdboys are wantonly strafed from a Rhodesian army helicopter, leaving four of his companions mere "mangled bundles." At such times it is as if he sees "the whole world through a thin screen of blood" (161).[283] But the little girl Rudo's tenderness toward Tonderai "splashe[s]," like reviving water, a "strange sweetness into [his] heart . . . there was something in these children which made them *resist* being changed overnight into little cynical adults" (163, emphasis added). When the horrors of the camp life seem to intensify *because* the inmates sense that it will soon end, "it was the children who held out" (194).

Marechera admirably resists the temptation to turn children into "little cynical adults" and shows himself (in these two sections and in other of the *Scrapiron Blues* pieces) capable of respecting the integrity of a childhood vision[284] without sentimentally and dishonestly editing out the horrors that do impinge on the lives of the unfortunate. In depicting a boy like Tonderai's purity, he allows a glimpse of the hope of change, balanced with a poignant awareness of the vulnerability of innocence to the world's massive powers.[285]

The strange and moving poem that opens Part 7, "Tonderai's Father Reflects" (195–203), takes up the theme of modes of survival under the assaults of destructive power. It seems to be wrung from Mr. Murehwa, subjected to yet another bout of torture (which he expects not to survive, it seems, hence the elegiac tone of the poem, as a sort of last will and statement). Fascinatingly and fittingly, the speaker's perspective takes up that of the artist-in-words, Marechera, whose own health was declining at this stage:

> Well it's done
> Across this stuttering tongue of sea
> My ship, The Wordhorde, sails
> My burial ship, wrought from tough hardwood word
> Sails . . .
>
> (195)[286]

Remembering the torture (and probably death) he inflicted for political reasons on the woman who was perhaps his wife, Hannes (from the surrealist playlet also called "The Camp," 168–176) "gradually falls into a paroxysm of grief," eventually "burst[ing] himself inside out in a strangely silent scream" (176). The grotesquely vicious Rhodesian army officer nicknamed "Win-Some-Lose-Some" shows only a vestige of humanity and conscience when he recalls the "mere boy" (Tonderai?), an emblem of self-sacrificing courage, whose "brains" he "blew . . . out" (202). Compared with these two representatives of the brutal power with which native Zimbabweans were faced during the Chimurenga, the serenity in the face of death exemplified in the verse quotation (above) causes a reconsideration of shallow notions of defeat and victory. Such a reevaluation, albeit subtle and full of complex correctives, was the contribution Marechera could (by means of this "final text") make to the psychic healing of his society. A monument and a haunting Zimbabwean anthem have been wrought from (or in) *Scrapiron Blues*.

Notes

1. The epigraph, seemingly so "Marecheran," in fact comes from a period about a hundred years earlier than the African writer's and was written by the German philosopher Friedrich Nietzsche—himself one of the intellectual world's great destabilizers ("Notes" [1875]: VII, 216, in Kaufmann). Compare Marechera's commitment to "cur[ing] by [means of] literary shock treatment," what he called "slow brain death in citizens" (quoted in Veit-Wild, *Source Book,* 41).

2. Veit-Wild writes that he "embodies . . . the . . . image of the writer-tramp . . . the Steppenwolf who survives on the fringe of society . . . his every public appearance . . . an opportunity for him to attack and ridicule the Establishment" (Veit-Wild, "Words as Bullets," 113), while T.O. McLoughlin writes that "his serious concerns with the metaphysics of creativity and with language itself as a violent instrument take his fiction beyond the accepted bounds of 'African' literature" (McLoughlin, "Black Writing," 111).

3. Taken, here, from *The Norton Anthology of African-American Literature,* 1256–1257. Reprinted by permission.

4. Hence, most of his titles signpost "blackness" (however ironically): *The Black Insider, Black Sunlight,* the unpublished works "Portrait of a Black Artist in London" and "The Depth of Diamonds," the lost manuscripts "The Black Heretic" and "A Bowl for Shadows," even the township reference in the title *The House of Hunger* (see Veit-Wild, *Source Book,* 343, 345, 199 for references to the unpublished titles).

5. As W.E.B. Du Bois saw it in his famous work, *The Souls of Black Folk* (10).

6. Quoted in Veit-Wild, *Source Book,* 28, 29.

7. Marechera read widely in "world literature," and his deep erudition is evident in all his writings. Among the "Beat Generation writers," he mentions Ginsberg, Kerouac, Snyder, and Leary (Veit-Wild, *Source Book,* 26) (and elsewhere Burroughs), whereas among the Russian writers he lists Gogol, Turgenev, Pushkin, Goncharov, Lermontov, Dostoevsky, Tolstoy, Mayakovsky, Yesenin, Tsvetaeva, and Pasternak (*Source Book* 366).

8. Unfinished and unpublished in his lifetime, it is called "Fuzzy Goo's Guide to the Earth," posthumously published in *Scrapiron* 239–247).

9. For example, "the big ones will make you stand in line in the streets and wave stupid little flags and sing horrible national songs, and be kissed by the thick drunken lips of the biggest of the big human beings" (*Scrapiron* 241). The "Reorientation Officer Rix" tells Buddy that "honest citizens only think what they are told" (*Mindblast* 45, 47). The "African Schweik" tells how he gets "beaten up . . . for not behaving like people [want] him to" (*Insider* 74).

10. Veit-Wild, *Source Book,* 337.

11. Interestingly (though indeed quite accidentally) this phrase calls to mind the Langston Hughes poem, confirming that Marechera never found the context of loving acceptance he had apparently dreamed of attaining.

12. Alluding to Andersen's tale of the exposure of foolish pomp and compliant hypocrisy (and greed), "The Emperor's New Clothes"—which Marechera used extensively in *The Black Insider*.

13. *Because* he did so despite the discouragement of nonpublication, his readers (of his posthumous works) can recognize the validity of his sociopolitical analyses as well as the vital creativity of his writing.

14. A point made in a 1984 interview with Veit-Wild, printed at the end of *Cemetery of Mind,* a collection of his poetry (211). Compare his reference elsewhere to a "dream" to which he clings, although it is "dangerous": that "the individual can only find his society by searching to the utmost in himself" (*Mindblast* 60—only male pronouns in the original).

15. An especially melancholic statement comes from the narrator of *The Black Insider*: he refers to "the fear inside [him] of a world whose changes would never include a change for the better" (*Insider* 102). In *The House of Hunger* the young narrator speaks of his generation's sense of the future itself as an engulfing power: "We knew that before us lay another vast emptiness whose appetite for things living was at best wolfish" (*Hunger* 3).

16. "We raise the African image to fly in the face of the wind and cannot see the actually living blacks having their heads smashed open with hammers in Kampala" (*Insider* 84)

17. He refers to it as "limited and false" in *The Black Insider* (80).

18. "I am what I am not because I am an African or whatever but because it is the basic nature of *a maker of descriptions, a writer*" (*Mindblast* 123, emphasis added).

19. Muponde refers to Marechera's "unusual capacity for dissent" (254).

20. Part of thc meaning here is that Marechera knew he could not and did not ever attempt to deny his "Africanness"—an unjust and extremely hurtful accusation so often made against him that he built it (as well as exposures of its falseness) into most of his texts—as will be seen inter alia in the discussion of his prose works.

21. (As Ngugi, he implies, did not always manage to do.) The two South African writers, Serote and Gordimer, both report their "discovery" of the falseness of Marechera's reputation for being a merely "self-obsessed person" or writer (both quoted in Veit-Wild, *Source Book,* 330, 331).

22. "And O the delight of pure sexual pleasure," Marechera writes in a small introductory section to his "Amelia Sonnets," "when thought and calculation are banished out of sight. A melodrama of the voluptuous" (*Cemetery* 167). He longed for "an overwhelming irreducible glimpse of the body's fiery core," but found himself at last dying, "condemned . . . to this slow, long lingering disease," "tired of the blood / And the coughing" (164, 163, 207).

23. The postmortem tributes are quoted in Veit-Wild and Schade, *Marechera,* 12, 16. Both Zimuyna and Hove had, in fact, made highly critical comments on Marechera's writing in earlier years (quoted in Veit-Wild, *Source Book:* Zimuyna 98, 126, 128; Hove 349–351).

24. Quoted in Kaufmann, *The Portable Nietzsche,* 81. Nietzsche's characterization of Socrates' thought and social role, "the gay kind of seriousness and that wisdom full of pranks" (quoted in Kaufmann 69), is also reminiscent of Marechera.

25. Other examples of such criticism are the following: "His literary analogies owe very little to the African tradition, and rob his work of a Zimbabwean authenticity" (Mzamane 212); "Marechera's story seems to resonate amongst the attitudes and idioms of the European literati. . . . *The House of Hunger* is racked with the *inward* tortures of an *individual* and *rampantly esoteric* sensibility" (Wylie, "*Thieves,*" 60, emphases added); "The vision is preponderantly private and indulgent. The social and moral undertaking is cynically dismissed at the expense of the aesthetic motive. The artist curries favours and succumbs to the European temptation in a most slatternly exhibition. . . . Masochistic artistic engagement overwhelms the social and moral intent.

Pleading for admission to the neurotic twentieth century is the worst way to go about revitalising a culture depleted by the self-same Europe" (Zimunya 126, 128).

In a late (1986) interview, Marechera said: "*The House of Hunger* was very difficult to write because . . . [after my] having been expelled once again from Oxford . . . the exiled Zimbabwean community started moving away from me and even beating me up, simply saying, 'Dambudzo . . . you are giving Zimbabweans a bad image'" (quoted in Veit-Wild, *Source Book,* 25).

26. From the remarkable piece "Dambudzo Marechera interviews himself" (Veit-Wild, *Source Book,* 1–5). The expression "the still sad music" derives from Wordsworth's famous poem "Composed . . . Above Tintern Abbey" (line 91) and indicates a compassionate awareness of human suffering. Fraser used Marechera's expression in referring to Marechera's "ear for the still small voice of national calamity to which others were deaf" (*Emerging Perspectives* 188).

27. I use "seems" because of the implicit irony in Marechera's candid, *unapologetic* answer to the question, "Did you ever think of writing in Shona?" which he puts to himself in the self-interview. His reply reads:

> It never occurred to me. Shona was part of the ghetto daemon I was trying to escape. Shona had been placed within the context of a degraded, mind-wrenching experience from which apparently the only escape was into the English language and education. The English language was automatically connected with the plush and seeming splendour of the white side of town. As far as expressing the creative turmoil within my head was concerned, I took to the English language as a duck takes to water. I was therefore a keen accomplice and student in my own mental colonization. At the same time of course there was the unease, the shock of being suddenly struck by stuttering. (Quoted in Veit-Wild, *Source Book,* 3–4)

He did, in fact, write one section of a play in Shona (see *Scrapiron* 61–72). The section from "House of Hunger" on the "interminable argument" between the narrator's Shona and his English "side" (30) and the double bind of parental demands—that he acquire an English education but not bring it home (13–14)—are particularly pertinent here. Ironically, Marechera's writing *has* of course attracted a considerable popular following both in Zimbabwe and elsewhere in Africa as coming from a writer on the side of the "povo" (the poor and "voiceless").

28. More perceptive Marechera critics have noted that "he was rigorous in examining *all the varieties* of oppression" (Gaylard, "Nationalist Criticism," 98, emphasis added), recognizing that "an African nationalist reading of Marechera is inadequate . . . a post-colonial reading would be more helpful, as he was writing most directly about post-colonial and neo-colonial issues. Marechera clearly understood that . . . imperialism had to be combated 'at home' or [that] nationalist rhetoric could exclude and obscure . . . neo-colonialism" (91). Taitz writes that he "uses indeterminacy" (*Emerging Perspectives,* 41); and Foster observes, "Marechera demonstrates the tyranny implicit in all expressions of cultural centrality" (Foster 60–61).

29. I adapt Marechera's reference to "things which exist out there . . . which [he says he] can *see through* the inner eye of dream" (quoted in Veit-Wild, *Source Book,* 43, emphasis added) to indicate both the penetrating quality of his sociopolitical understanding and his predilection for surrealism.

30. One is reminded of Fanon's famous reference to "this zone of occult instability where the people dwell" (*Wretched* 183). In his own way, Marechera's writing is more "Fanonian" than his critics have recognized—"the truths of a nation are in the first place its realities" and "you must bring about and render possible the meeting of

your people and other men" (*Wretched* 181, 237) are two key comments by Fanon that Marechera's writing exemplifies.

31. Compare Trinh T. Minh-ha's articulation of the advantages (contra Ngugi, one might say) of such a "straddling" position: "The moment the insider steps out from the inside she's no longer a mere insider. She necessarily looks in from the outside while also looking out from the inside. Not quite the same, not quite the other, she stands in that undetermined threshold where she constantly drifts in and out" (Minh-ha, "Not You," 418). Foster writes that Marechera "reclaim[s] his . . . people's . . . experiences from the margins" (Foster 59).

32. Byron, in *Don Juan,* Canto 10, 81 (line 8), refers to the British with similar shocking effect as the people "who butcher'd half the earth, and bullied t'other" (Byron 788).

33. This helps to decipher the emphasis on the whiteness of the cat's fur and on the indications of privilege ("fur gilded here and there"—109), which provoke the narrator's (probably envious, or vengeful) fury. Compare a later poem ("I Am the Rape"—*Cemetery* 30) in which the speaker refers to the experience of making love (as a black man, to a white woman) as a type of racial revenge: "Your white body writhing underneath / All the centuries of my wayward fear." In Marechera's comments on the "Amelia Sonnets," he articulates similar feelings (*Cemetery of Mind* 215). Compare Tayeb Salih's famous novel *Season of Migration to the North* (translated from Arabic).

34. In terms of the collection's "hunger" trope, the "oppression" and "overpower[ing]" of the imagination mentioned are linked in the same passage with details of starvation: "the great shortage of water and the shortage of food" (131). Compare Mphahlele, *Down Second Avenue*: "Hungering sharpened the edge of our longings" (221). Taitz in his *Emerging Perspectives* chapter quotes Fanon, *Wretched,* 30: "The native town is a hungry town."

35. See the reference in this story to "[Mr.] *Robert's* side of the river, *where it was fenced and there was a notice about trespassers*" (129, emphases added). Is "[Mr.] Robert" perhaps "Barbara's father" (130), the villain of the piece?

36. See note 25.

37. "Her sharp little teeth gleamed" (45).

38. Like the Jewish yellow star, it is a racial identification that carries its own penalty—as the scars on his face testify:

> "Take a close look at me," I said, "And then see if you can repeat what you've just said."
>
> She took a long detailed look at my incredible face.
>
> And she burst out laughing. (45)

39. Compare the humiliated, grievously assaulted Edmund (attacked verbally and physically by his "Africanist" fellow student Stephen) ending up pathetically, excruciatingly "jabbering" "I'm a monkey, I'm a baboon" (66). This attack from the African "patriot" Stephen is shown having the same devastating effect as that of the sell-out's (Harry's father's) words on the narrator. Both *these* attacks are comparable to the incident in which the narrator and Philip spit on an old white man for addressing them as "Kaffirs" (56), which seems the cause of the police assault which follows (57)—and can also be compared to the racist attack on the narrator and Patricia by a white mob (72–73).

40. Compare the reference to Patricia as "one of those disturbingly concise and adult youths whom our country either breaks or confines in prisons and lunatic asylums" (71), and the narrator's comment, "It was the House of Hunger that first made

me discontented" (77). In "The Slow Sound of His Feet" (134–137), a vicious occupying force of "white soldiers" (135) extinguishes the very voice of the narrator.

41. Compare the complex, nightmarish crisis of identity (emotional, sexual, racial) exemplified in "Burning in the Rain" (83–87).

42. Okonkwo 91—a scathing review of *The House of Hunger* earlier referred to. Here, the narrator likens the experience of reading Philip's poems to that of falling into a pit-latrine (58).

43. The description of Philip's posture ("he placed an ankle over a knee and began to light a cheap cigar"—60) recalls the narrator's dream vision of a "sell-out" African (37–38), a hint confirmed when Philip's office ("This was what mother had always wanted me to become"—63) is seen to contain "a stupid Boer magazine on African current affairs" (63)—perhaps a sign of the source of his income.

44. The unlikely, unprepossessing resistance war hero, Edmund, is said to have a "stitched-together warthog face" (66). Yet near the end of "House of Hunger" the image of an iron net is used for mental oppression (73–75), a net that also consists of "stitches," which (the narrator says) "have nipped me maddeningly" (73—cf. 75).

45. Isabel Hofmeyr's comments on Marechera's old man (as) signifying a twentieth-century "resuscitation" of orature are especially interesting (Hofmeyr 88, 92).

46. There is a very satisfying poetic justice in the way the old man *uses* Harry's desire for "white chicken" to get him beaten up at "the white soldiers' whore-house" (82)—a passage full of ironic echoes from the earlier one where Harry (appallingly) dismisses the women of his own nation ("Nigger girls are just meat"—13).

47. That is, when Ian Smith's white government of Rhodesia issued the Unilateral Declaration of Independence from Britain (without the latter's consent). The other stories that seem to be set in Rhodesia (apparently all the other pieces were written before "House of Hunger"—Veit-Wild, *Source Book,* 25) are "Burning in the Rain," "The Transformation of Harry," and "The Slow Sound of his Feet"—and "Thought-tracks in the Snow" has interspersed memories of a "Rhodesian" (i.e., preindependence) past.

48. Marxist scholars coined the expression "colonialism of a special type" to distinguish the system of settler oppression in South Africa during the apartheid period from other forms of colonialism.

49. Gurnah (116) refers to Marechera's "savage and sarcastic humour," though he notes "a yearning for lost wholeness" (110). Fraser recognizes the role of the author as enabling the "projection . . . of distressed states of mind," which have been prohibited self-expression (*Emerging Perspectives* 188).

50. Yearning for "black heroes" (12), the narrator is instead haunted by "three men in *threadbare* clothes and [a] woman [in a] *faded* shawl" (28, emphases added).

51. The South African poet and novelist Mongane Serote's *To Every Birth Its Blood* is another brilliant and moving depiction of the psychic invasiveness of racial oppression.

52. Marechera's compassionately analytical understanding of (rather than sensationalist or sadistic interest in) this type of social malformation, and of the way it stems from inadmissible or inaccessible (alien) power sources, is confirmed in comments from a 1986 interview:

> Poverty can drive one into obscure sexual passions: if economically you cannot assert yourself, you try to assert yourself as a human being sexually. . . . Poor people . . . [not] having any kind of power . . . turn on each other. . . . And because at that time black men were used to being the slaves of the whites, . . . the only slaves they had were their women. That's why women were the ultimate victims of racism in this

country. . . . I have depicted that. . . . Because it affected me very much. (Quoted in Veit-Wild, *Source Book,* 13)

53. Compare: "It was all a show for me" (4); Peter's removing the covering blanket (28); and the unnamed wife's public sexual humiliation (50). "And because he hungered for the *fight* everyone saw it in his eyes and liked him for it" (2), the narrator says of Peter. This role of Peter's is a parallel to Stephen's boasting that "Africa always rises up to every new challenge" (65) before viciously beating up the puny, "undernourished" Edmund (60, 65–66), whom he had insulted (64)—whereas it is Edmund who turns out to be the truly heroic patriot (60–61).

54. In a fine phrase, the narrator refers to the visible "*pulses* of her raw courage" in her eyes (4, emphasis added).

55. Compare the same detail in Philip's poems (58). The narrator mentions that "the best lessons we had in hardihood were not from the example of the males" (50) and he twice refers to "the woman who led the 1896/7 uprising" who was executed by firing squad (68, 50), linking her with contemporary women who "make do" by means of prostitution. See also the essay by Huma Ibrahim on gender roles in the colonized society Marechera depicts (Ibrahim, "Violated").

56. The preposition ("up") indicates Immaculate's inspirational effect on the narrator ("She made me want to dream"—12), and "fortifications" indicates a form of power through resistance and through linking with the indigenous culture.

57. Of course, Harry uses the expression as well (12, top)—in his case, to justify his cultural betrayal in his pursuit of (what he conceives of as) "civilis[ation]" (11)—the truly abject nature of his inspiration measured in his celebration of the "snot" that is his proof that "[his] white chick" "gave" him her cold (15)—that is, infected him!

58. It is no cynical betrayal, but a validly analytical comment of the narrator's, to refer to his "family life" as "decaying," a condition of "stench" (7). In a parallel with Peter's abuse of Immaculate, the narrator's father, too, fails completely to recognize his clever little son's anguish as a consequence of the "English" incident, hitting him with a blow that breaks his front teeth as further "punishment" (14). Significantly, both parents are eating in this scene, whereas the boy is reduced to the despicable, hungry role of "a cockroach in a delicatessen" (14).

Marechera's editor reports, "Asked later about the problems and worries of his childhood, Marechera replied in one word: 'Home.' As his only pleasure he remembered: 'School'" (Veit-Wild, *Source Book,* 53).

59. In his Introduction to, and on the evidence of, Fanon's *The Wretched of the Earth* (17). The sardonic reference in Part 1 (100–115) of "The Writer's Grain" to parents who "starved themselves to give [you] education" yet in the process "sell you mind and soul to the bloody whites" (112) is a parallel passage. A surrealist version of the same idea occurs in "Protista" (127–133), in the "nightmare" of the "white manfish" who insists that the narrator come to him (130)—Mr. Warthog's "counter-education" in Part 2 of "The Writer's Grain" (116–125) being itself a nightmare, despite the elements of the parody and mockery of conventional education in this tale. See also the comments of the editor on Marechera's education in its sociopolitical context (Veit-Wild, *Source Book,* 61).

Marechera's compatriot Tsitsi Dangarembga has written another famous account of the psychically baffling paradoxes of the colonial education experience in her novel *Nervous Conditions.*

60. It is noteworthy that his work itself encompasses the "downtrodden hero" Edmund's writing (with its two themes, first "the painstaking exploration of the effects of

poverty and destitution on the 'psyche' and [second] the higher themes . . . concerned with something of what Gogol tried to do for the Russian character"—61).

61. The expression has both a Shona cultural reference (see the Lilford essay) and a biblical echo. It was Marechera's initial title for the "House of Hunger" (Veit-Wild, *Source Book,* 177–178).

62. (Because of the increased frequency of the reference, the abbreviation "V-W, *S.B.*" is from this point used for "Veit-Wild, *Source Book.*") V-W, *S.B.,* 361–375.

63. *The Black Insider* was written in 1978 when Marechera, having been expelled from Oxford University for his "disorderly" behavior, was living a squatter's existence in London; it was one of the manuscripts he wrote (there were two others, now lost) in response to his publisher Heinemann's request for a novel to follow the shorter pieces collected in *The House of Hunger* (Introduction, *The Black Insider,* 7). This novel was "found" in 1984 and eventually (posthumously) published only in 1990 by Baobab Books (the edition referred to in this section).

64. Quoted in V-W, *S.B.,* 363; *Insider* 83.

65. Quoted in V-W, *S.B.,* 374; *Insider* 83.

66. Quoted in V-W, *S.B.,* 363–375; *Insider* 32.

67. Marechera adopted this term (a reference to the ancient author Menippus of Gedara) as the appropriate name for his preferred style of writing: "Everything in the world is so serious you [have] to take it with a light touch, a sleight of hand. But this [is] always underlined by an eternally imminent terrible vision" (from the unpublished manuscript "The Depth of Diamonds" by Marechera, quoted in Gaylard, "Menippean Marechera," 185). In this style of writing, according to Marechera, "fantasy and symbolism are combined with low-life naturalism" (quoted in V-W, *S.B.,* 363). He thought it a way of writing appropriate to the "incredible conflicts of the twentieth century," the renewed evidence of "animal aggression" in humanity, the "monstrous midway" in which modern societies seem to be caught (which he called "the mid-point of the scream"). Because of these common factors and the literary responses they elicit, Marechera concluded that "it is no longer necessary to speak of the African novel or the European novel: there is only the menippean novel" (quoted in V-W, *S.B.,* 363, 362, 364).

68. As Marechera termed it (quoted in V-W, *S.B.,* 362, where he also calls it a "unique universe"). To the question whether he considered himself a specifically African writer, Marechera replied that he did not. "For me, a writer is a writer," he said, expressing the anxiety that "nationalistic" pigeonholing of authors might lead to a type of "fascism" (quoted in V-W, *S.B.,* 39—from a 1986 interview; see also *Insider* 82). Compare his reference to Ngugi and Soyinka's "X-ray poems and articles expos[ing] the corruption in the marrow of our bones" (quoted in V-W, *S.B.,* 372).

69. As Marechera recognized, "Military regimes, corrupt civilian regimes, murders, civil war, apparitions like Bokassa and Idi Amin, the struggles for liberation in Southern Africa, the horrors of famine, etc." (quoted in V-W, *S.B.,* 375) dominate the impressions of Africa held all over the world.

70. Readers have tended to overlook the numerous clear indications that the novel is set in Africa and that most members of the cast of characters are black (only Helen, Liz, and her son, among those gathered in the Faculty of Arts, are white). Such misreading perhaps reflects unconscious racism—a failure to recognize the intellectuals and professionals depicted in debate in the novel as African people, and to "allow" a Faculty of Arts an African location.

Of course, Marechera does not stress the Zimbabwean location, and the novel is to an extent set in an imagined future (interestingly, imagining his own "return"—see p. 23—in the main protagonist, who so strongly resembles the author). On the way (in this case, the African) setting is taken for granted, Marechera's reference to Gibbon's observation that the Koran nowhere makes mention of camels should be noted (quoted in V-W, *S.B.*, 371).

71. Marechera described in this article "a *delirium tremens* of experiment with the available genres, a reassessment of the traditional oral resources and, as it were, an unendurable but resolute self-consciousness" as the admirable and appropriate response by Zimbabwean authors to the way in which those occupying the structures of power would have preferred blacks to write (quoted in V-W, *S.B.*, 234).

72. Elsewhere (in an interview, earlier in 1986) Marechera spoke of the dangers of imaginative and intellectual ossification, referring to such a condition (which props up institutions—to him all, virtually by definition, oppressive power structures) as "slow brain death in citizens" needing to have their unthinking reliance on "traditions and morals" exploded or "short-circuit[ed]" by means of his own sort of "literary shock treatment" (if power is to be dislodged from its imposition on our lives) (quoted in V-W, *S.B.*, 40–41). Volk writes, "Fundamental change, Marechera insisted, was possible only by freeing the imagination" (*Emerging Perspectives* 301).

73. Compare "the writer . . . is in Africa, in the same situation the Russian writer was under the Czar" (quoted in V-W, *S.B.*, 373—and see 374). See also *The Black Insider* (83).

74. See as a political parallel (in the novel) the decision taken at an "Africa Centre" meeting not to broadcast the betrayal of African freedom fighters by African heads of neighboring states (*Insider* 66), which Marechera presents in a deadpan way, with implicit sarcasm. Volk says, "The insider knows the intricacies of mental and physical oppression" (*Emerging Perspectives* 307).

75. Making the academic Liz the provider of weapons in *The Black Insider* (86), and ending his novel with the bookish narrator "cradl[ing]" a gun, ready to shoot as many as possible of the invading, significantly "face-blackened" hordes (115), Marechera is probably (almost cartoon-fashion) responding to the common accusation that intellectuals are useless in situations requiring military action against overwhelming power.

76. See Marechera's essay "Why There Will Be Race Riots" (quoted in V-W, *S.B.*, 230–232) and *The Black Insider* 57, 77–78.

77. I am thinking especially, of course, of Fanon's *Black Skin, White Masks*. Marechera frequently refers to Fanon's work (e.g., on p. 363 of the lecture quoted in V-W, *S.B.*).

78. Marechera draws attention to the expression by (A) making it the only "name" for the narrator/protagonist that the reader is ever told; (B) having the outspoken, significantly "named" "African Schweik" (whose own "name" gives his voice authority and who is especially closely linked in ideas and opinions with the narrator) actually apostrophizing the narrator with the expression "Oh, black insider!" (74) at a central point in the novel; and (C) showing the narrator noticing and asking for an explanation of the expression—an explanation that is withheld, so that the whole of the text must be searched for an answer/definition.

79. See *Insider* 49: "Others like myself chose other facets of English hegemony and were christened Charles [as was Marechera], William, Patrick or Derek, etc. The English language has certainly taken over more than the geography of the African image." Compare also: "I still speak English and sound quite foreign to myself" (*Insider* 24).

80. Compare again a quote cited earlier: "countries in a *violent* search for identity" (quoted in V-W, *S.B.*, 373—emphasis added).

81. Understood in the poem as a context that can turn the tables on "white" power by presenting *it* (e.g.) as the violent, rapist, child-abusing father. The long poem from

which the quotation is taken was found with the manuscript of *The Black Insider* and seems to have alternative titles, either "Portrait of a Black Artist in London" or (more provocatively) "I Ain't Got My Balls (On the Chip on My Shoulder)"—see V-W, *S.B.*, 250–268 for the full poem.

In *The Black Insider* the narrator refers to himself as having grown up "in the very midst of the cultural cerebral rape of my people" (51). He also speaks of colonialism effecting "brain transplants" (52) on the indigenes of colonized countries.

82. At the time Marechera wrote *The Black Insider*, the racist right-wing movements in Britain (e.g., the National Front) were on the rise (see V-W, *S.B.*, 230–232, 239, 250–268, as well as *Insider* 57 and 77–78). Compare: "The notion that you're as black as you're painted does seem to derange some of our best black minds. . . . The clenched fist is more often a self-therapeutic device than a potential blow against Enoch Powell's jaw" (quoted in V-W, *S.B.*, 231). (Powell was a right-wing British politician.)

83. These comments can be directly related to Marechera's personal history—for example, the "recurring dream" he described (in his final school year) of Zimbabwe as a violated woman ("I love her very much alright, but it's hard for me to take") (quoted in V-W, *S.B.*, 90). It is to be noted that even at this youthful age Marechera does not have an unproblematic sense of "the African image," but instead the notion of a *soiled* motherland. See also his use of a similar image in several early poems (*Cemetery of Mind* 6, 14–15, 29).

84. In the context of colonial humiliation, Marechera recognizes that the sense of personal "identity" becomes so precarious and evanescent that the writer feels the persistent need not merely to revalidate the self, but even constantly to reconstitute selfhood ("I *needed* to *stamp* myself with the evidence of my own existence"—80, emphases added).

85. Comments like these illustrate what Veit-Wild has referred to as Marechera's "relentless iconoclasm." She describes his as a "sceptical, post-colonial stand." As she observes, "politically, he was a heretic" (V-W, *S.B.*, 240).

86. An illustration from Zimbabwe postdating Marechera's comments would be the condemnation of homosexuality as un-African by President Mugabe.

87. "Schweik" observes: "We raise the African image to fly in the face of the wind and cannot see the actually living blacks having their heads smashed open with hammers in Kampala. . . . For a people seeking freedom we are much practised in intolerance among ourselves" (84).

88. The character "Cicero" voices the opinion that this "militarisation of identity" is an even wider, international, twentieth-century problem, an inevitable consequence of the domination of science: "We have been inexorably put on a path of more menacing discoveries" (88), he says. Might, technologically embodied, becomes a loose cannon beyond apparent human control, threatening us all. The unidentified invading hordes shown at the end of the novel may personify this notion.

89. She wants to be "a sort of noble savage version of Brigitte Bardot," "the number one black actress to come out of Africa" (108). Yet the narrator "cannot remember her face's features" (111). He does "nevertheless" attribute to her "a powerful and human awareness of—as she said—'the importance of being one's self'" (112), in contrast with the narrator's (her husband's) and her brother's fruitless "philosophical" speculations (113).

90. In the narrator's initial, sardonic "colour coding" of Helen, he refers to her "E.M. Forster pinko-grey throat" (26), a mocking parody of racism that (naturally) revives after *her* racist assault on him, when he notices that the knife has fallen from her "pink palm" (28).

91. Helen's "guardian," the middle-aged academic Liz, tells the narrator, "I've never met any black writers," although she has been teaching at the Zimbabwean "Faculty of Arts" for a long time (48). (She is British—92.) Nevertheless she confidently (in a wonderfully satiric description) pigeonholes African writers as invariably belonging to one of the following "categories": "angry and polemic"; "grim and nocturnal"; "realistic and quavering"; or "indifferent and European" (49). Here Marechera simultaneously "gets at" European intellectual arrogance and ignorance, his fellow African writers, and even himself, teasing everyone simultaneously and extremely wittily.

92. A point exemplified in "your thoughts think of themselves in the words you have been taught to read and write" (35).

93. "The word 'primitive' is applied to all those who take their alphabet neat from rivers, sewers, and natural scenery" (i.e., Africans et al.) (34). Compare this comment from an interview: "It was so easy to make us kids feel that we were shit, that we were the product of an inferior race" (quoted in V-W, *S.B.,* 10).

94. Armah, Okigbo, and Okara are here mentioned by Marechera, as well as Ngugi's imprisonment in postcolonial Kenya (82).

95. "We are provisional, yet contain seeds of limitlessness." Note the extension of the idea of control from the political (external) sphere to the psychic: "The inquisitor in the mind controls the sources of the imagination" (quoted in V-W, *S.B.,* 365).

96. In a 1986 interview (i.e., after having been back in Zimbabwe for some years), Marechera complained of the way, in the context of his own society (as he put it then), "literature was now seen merely as another instrument of official policy and [it was frowned upon if the writer dared to] explore the subconscious of our new society" (quoted in V-W, *S.B.,* 39).

97. These analytical comments on the colonial education process as mental entrapment can be linked with Marechera's somewhat sarcastic expression "Graeco-Roman thinking" (63).

98. See the "Jezebel" passage (94–97) as well as the portrayal of "the Bishop" (Muzorewa) in the play-within-the-novel (38–43).

99. Compare Marechera's saying (of the writer): "His whole life is lived in the expectation of what is going to be written. The writer is a vampire, drinking blood—his own blood" (quoted in V-W, *S.B.,* 366). Pattison ("Inside . . . *Insider*" 228) writes: "The author is at the centre of the text. And yet *The Black Insider* is not autobiographical."

100. Having been expelled from the University of Rhodesia for political activities, Marechera was given (with the help of some of his lecturers) a scholarship to Oxford University. Yet as Buuck writes, "Marechera [was] ostracised by academic institutions both at home and abroad" (Buuck 129).

101. *New African* 200 (1984): 65.

102. See the reference to the narrator's "waiting room" in *The Black Insider* (100).

103. From the same poem ("Without," in *Cemetery of Mind,* 28). The title probably alludes both to a condition of *lack* (being without particular necessities) and to an excluded state (being without rather than within).

104. I would suggest that the adverb "inside" recalls the ironic title of the novel.

105. In Auden's poem "The Capital" (*Collected Shorter Poems* 122–123).

106. Marechera's editor, Flora Veit-Wild, writes:

> To attend a secondary school was a rare privilege for a black child during Marechera's time. The lucky few who managed to get a place found themselves under immense emotional strain, as the system was highly selective and competitive. This was height-

> ened by the great expectations of their families. The pupils also underwent the usual process of acculturation through colonial and Christian education which alienated them from their traditional background. (V-W, *S.B.*, 61)

Pupils discovered themselves to have been "mentally colonised by the same system their compatriots were fighting," a "conflict" exacerbated by their despairing sense of "their limited future" (V-W, *S.B.*, 61). The uncomfortable moral and political ambivalences reflected here are extended in a small sequence from an interview (1986) in which Marechera first mentions that he "was always reading, already at primary school. Just to escape, from hunger, actual physical hunger"; although at university he "wanted to become part of the national struggle," it was also there that he felt that "it was irrelevant for [him] to continue to be part of the house of hunger because the house of hunger has no voice in any decision-making process" (quoted in V-W, *S.B.*, 19–20). He did not, of course, ever manage to become an *assimillado*, and in his tramp's existence during the last part of his life returned to the "house of hunger." In *The Black Insider*, the narrator's comrades' "amnesia" about him when he is expelled from Oxford and the humiliating public search to which a black policeman subjects him in London illustrate this point (58–59).

107. See the reviewer's comments on the narrator's short stories—quoted on 109.

108. This theme is first broached in the opening pages of the novel, when the narrator states: "The people in the house are all refugees in one way or another, exiles from the war out there. . . . The place stinks of psychological wounds, which gives it a human fragrance" (25).

109. "There is no sense of home any more, no feeling of being at one with any specific portion of the earth" (79).

110. The psychological *dislocation* of this condition is portrayed by Marechera when he writes, "The mind reeled between the mirage of a snug mud-hut in the middle of nowhere and the noise of a gong in a draughty city apartment" (106). Compare the telling contrast, in the two opening paragraphs of "Oxford, Black Oxford" (*Insider* 118), between the "dull gold inwardness, narrowness" of Oxford and the "reek and ruin of heat and mud-huts" in the land of the narrator's origin.

In a 1986 interview Marechera said about his own acquisition of education that "it also meant ignoring the poverty of others" (quoted in V-W, *S.B.*, 17). During his period in England he felt that "some of us from Africa had become part of an oppressive class" (quoted in V-W, *S.B.*, 27). An especially poignant instance of the psychological "haunting" here referred to occurs when the narrator, drunk at a party to celebrate his first publication, walks around asking his guests whether they have seen his father (who is long dead) (30).

111. He refers to Owen's "bitter and inconsolable experience of losing his nation" (104). Compare: "We are no good to both sides" (85).

112. Despite accusations like Nyasha's (68) and the reviewer's (109), the narrator evidently bears the burden of Africanness wherever he goes, whereas Owen indeed "remained [when the narrator left for England] and fought [albeit not in the liberation war, it seems, but] for the survival of his sanity" (104).

113. It could be contended that Marechera tends to write usually in the spirit of Fanon's warnings and castigations concerning the postcolonial condition in the chapter of *The Wretched of the Earth* called "The Pitfalls of National Consciousness" (119–165). He is perhaps generally more harsh and mocking in his criticism and less exhortatory (because less hopeful?) than Fanon. (See Pattison, "Inside . . . *Insider*," 223–224.) See the first paragraph of "Schweik's" rambling statement on p. 72, with its terrifying prediction.

114. He is alluding here to his living in a series of "squats" in England (mostly in London) after he was expelled from Oxford.

115. These words are from the 1975 diary of Iris Hayter (quoted in V-W, *S.B.*, 163), wife of the Warden of New College, Oxford, from which Marechera was expelled in 1976. The quotation is used as epigraph because it serves to indicate the larger anti-*establishment* stance (in its widest sense) of which this novel is Marechera's most eloquent expression.

116. It was actually his second substantial work to be published. *Black Sunlight* was initially banned from distribution in newly independent Zimbabwe on the grounds of the alleged obscenity and obscurity of the work—a ban subsequently set aside on appeal (see V-W, *S.B.*, 290–299). The edition referred to here is that published by Heinemann in 1980 (first publication).

117. Though Marechera deliberately gave no racial identification to a number of the novel's characters, the narrator's (black) racial markers and Blanche's whiteness are vividly identified, and the setting of most of the text in Zimbabwe is lightly indicated (e.g., in the "acacias" and "flame lilies" mentioned on pp. 45–46). Marechera's comments on these matters are quoted on pp. 29 and 220 of Veit-Wild's *Source Book*—for example, "nobody ever knew that it was about post-independent Zimbabwe, that it was my projection into the future of my country" (V-W, *S.B.*, 220).

118. The "gelignite" she carries (100) identifies her as practicing urban terrorism along with Susan and other members of the (mostly female) anarchist group. Her major preoccupation is with what she considers the tyranny of the intellect.

119. For an earlier (comic) version of the list of oppressive forces and institutions in the quotation, see "The History of the Runner" (8–9). Other passages making similar points are Susan's reference to "all these grand designs," "societies . . . [l]ike nations" (50) needing in her eyes to be shattered to atoms, and "Christian's" reference to the guillotine, electric chair, and noose being "the implements of a human tradition" (58). Just before the quoted passage the novelist-narrator refers to Susan's seeing "the development of social and national and international man [as] one long denial of that in [people which she] sees as our natural destiny" (65). As Mark Stein has noted, the passage quoted has a "distinctly Foucaultian ring" (*Emerging Perspectives* 65). Marechera, however, goes further than Foucault in both his delineation and his abhorrence of power.

120. It is said to be "more oppressive" and "degrading" than either (even) "apartheid . . . and Jew-baiting" (*Insider* 37), among other things.

121. I prefer this description to the label "stream of consciousness."

122. This is the sign (it is also articulated in this passage) that *he* (i.e., the "double," who is then interviewed) is the *author* of the narrative we have been reading up to this point in the novel. The encounter occurs at the center of the novel.

123. Here the hallucinating narrator recalls "the armed lorries of language" (87). A comparable image is that of language "knotted tightly around my eyes like a bandage made of headaches" (73).

124. "Discovering how infinitely a human condition despair was" (107) is a description that occurs in the passage in which the narrator describes the "almost domestic" scene of the regathered revolutionaries. Compare "the grief underneath" (117) mentioned in the penultimate sentence of the novel. Chennells writes that "the novel seems to confront the pessimism which is inherent in its multiple meanings" (*Emerging Perspectives* 54), while Mark Stein notes that the "humour" employed in the exposure of "the overpowering influence of the state . . . cannot hide the anguish that seems the bottom-line of the text" (*Emerging Perspectives* 60).

125. This links with and reiterates the exhortation in the first-quoted, central, and "centered" passage (66), that "strange and vivid ideas" and "memorable lifestyles" need to be used to break the icy stranglehold of power in society.

126. He refers to the writer's Cassandra-like fate of being "cursed by censorship, by persecution" for having the "talent to . . . analyse people's destinies" (quoted in V-W, *S.B.,* 42). He was (nevertheless) devastated by the initial ban on *Black Sunlight,* referring to the intense "crisis of expectation [built up by] people in exile," so that the news came like a "bombshell" (quoted in V-W, *S.B.,* 290).

127. A realism that cuts both ways—simultaneously warning that there are people who, although they may be acting in terms of "some banal [presumably anarchist] slogan can, when actually act[ing this] out, [cause] destruction and death" because of the intensity of their convictions, *and* that the political consequences for such anarchists are likely to be viciously punitive (quoted in V-W, *S.B.,* 31).

128. Marechera added that this question "forms the basis of anarchism in *Black Sunlight* and also in *Mindblast*" (V-W, *S.B.,* 40), although I will take it slightly further than this to explicate the dilemma implicit in the question.

129. Besides this faint narrative line, the text of course also contains in "scrambled" form, in all its other sections, whether straightforward realist description, fantasy, hallucination, or free-flowing meditation, an account and assessment of a life—the life of a British-educated African intellectual who has returned to his own country. Chennells ("Unstable Identities") writes that "a formal narrative . . . lies like a body entombed within the text. That narrative is a political autobiography" (*Emerging Perspectives* 45).

130. Compare "the hounded thoughts that begin at home. . . . The way to Hell paved by good intonations [Marechera's 'Oxford accent' was notorious and famous]. . . . The chasm of rock and ice" (88).

131. She is a great deal more efficient—and effective—than the "hungry horde . . . attacking any sign of authority," predictably overpowered and quelled by "soldiers" (27).

132. Sordid Joe, who medically treats her wounded shoulder after the campus riot, describes her amusingly as being "as virile in the soul as an ox" (35)! She takes charge of most situations in which she finds herself and even seems to be the eventual sole breadwinner (through prostitution) of the group in a scene that is placed early in the novel (5–6), but that probably precedes the narrator's stint with the chief (the passage that teasingly begins the novel *and* ends what there is of a chronological "narrative"). On the dislocations in the narrative "line," see Chennells 48–50 and Crehan 269–275 (*Emerging Perspectives*).

133. Having judged her as one who (like Katherine) has "come through" (104), the narrator near the end pays tribute to her successful "transformation," which he seems to read as a slight softening (compared to her earlier "[b]urning . . . anger"—101), to a "glittering" and a leading role in an "almost domestic" scene (107).

134. "Stamped out ruthlessly," etc. (13).

135. He seems to sense similar protest from the gentle Marie and the principled pacifist Blanche (84, bottom of page—compare p. 78, where Blanche rebukes the narrator for shooting a shark that was about to attack her). As literary parallels one may think of Soyinka's *Season of Anomy,* in which the protagonist also to some extent *dis*sociates himself from the techniques of his *as*sociate, the political assassin nicknamed The Dentist, or of Hamlet's reluctance to fulfill the duty of vengeful execution of his father's brother and murderer, Claudius.

136. The expression ironically aligns her momentarily with "that brutal unrecognisable intellect that was the machine running all destiny" (100). Blanche, too, *uses*

her intellect to hurt and get rid of the narrator in Oxford: "As soon as it became clear we were not going to 'hit if off.' . . . She had begun to talk as though she needed to observe herself clinically from afar whenever I was in her vicinity" (110).

137. The clues to totalitarian tendencies are represented by certain details (mainly articulated by Chris) concerning the revolutionary organization at Devil's End—the regimentation implied in required answers, permitted substances (no tobacco, only vodka!), and thought control (the intercom "Sally's" voice) (52–59).

138. Compare Marechera's own statement that despite being "cursed by censorship, by opposition," the writer, "precisely because" of his "talent" to analyze people's lives effectively and probingly, "must continually activate it, in spite of any opposition from any quarter. If I am a committed writer," he said, "that's what I am committed to"—adding, "A vision like that transcends any political programme" (quoted in V-W, *S.B.*, 42).

139. Compare p. 68 (quoted earlier): "Our material means . . . our wants . . . take up more room in us than do humane considerations."

140. The feminist cartoon cameo in which Susan outbullies and, in fact, virtually demolishes the male owner of a "borrowed motorbike" (101–102) is a case in point.

141. Described as mere "superficial ripplings" (69).

142. In typical Marecheran fashion, however, there is a "balancing" of this dissociation from Christianity in the narrator's instinctive choice of the *name* "Christian" (which he also applies to his alter ego, the novelist) for himself, in "Devil's End" (53).

143. Marechera said in a 1986 interview that he tried in his writing to "short-circuit, like in electricity, people's traditions and morals. Because only then can they start having original thoughts of their own," and that he "would like people to stop thinking in an institutionalised way" in order that they might "see those impossibilities within themselves, emotionally and intellectually—that's why most of what I have written is always seen as being disruptive or destructive. For me, that slow brain death . . . can only be cured by this kind of literary shock treatment," he added (quoted in V-W, *S.B.*, 40–41). Clearly the ideas expressed here are closely related to the issues raised in *Black Sunlight*. In another relevant quotation from this interview he said: "A pen is not a gun. A gun will actually kill somebody but a pen can stimulate thought and in this sense the pen should be given unlimited freedom" (quoted in V-W, *S.B.*, 42).

144. Compare an essay by Nuruddin Farah, "The Creative Writer and the Politician," for example, the observation that in contrast with a politician, "a writer lives in a capsule of ideas; and the world is his constituency, and he owes no allegiance to a power-base of clansmen and clanswomen, but to a constituency of ideals" ("Creative Writer" 29).

145. Compare Susan's image of "this created tiger" (50) for societies, states, even habits. The eerie and "startling roar of a leopard" (7) outside the chief's camp, a reminder of "some long ago beastiality" (7), arouses a sense of "feral threats" (8), which the chief's magic cannot assuage, and leads (with deliberate incongruity) to the expression of a sense of meaninglessness in modernist verse (8), supposedly by the tribesmen. This confirms the persistence through time of fear and hopelessness as the control mechanisms used by power.

146. In the novel the question is answered when Frank's brother explains: "It's inside you. It's everything you are. . . . Everything that sucks you in . . . basically we are it. We are the great cunt. . . . In fact, it's the DNA in us, that great cunt." To this the novelist-narrator adds: "Disease, war, persecution, rapine, these are our ancestors, you know" (70, 71). Everyone, in other words, is contaminated by power.

147. Huma Ibrahim sees Marechera's female characters as (especially in *Black Sunlight*) figures of revolutionary hope in contrast with those who are male, whom she sees as complicit in oppression, if not actual perpetrators of violence ("Violated"). Clearly, my own reading does not discern so clear-cut a "gender divide"—in *Black Sunlight* or his other works—although I find Ibrahim's a suggestive reading.

148. The point was made earlier that Susan's forcefulness *is* touched with some ambivalence, and the association between her and "the GREAT CUNT" highlights her more frightening qualities. She is nevertheless mainly presented as a liberating force, more so in personal relationships (interestingly) than in her political activities. She has a (re)vitalising, sometimes comforting, and literally *energizing* effect on her associates, especially on the narrator (see the exhilarated descriptions on p. 51—"exulted . . . new . . . arrived . . . glittering . . . new," and on p. 46—"quickening," as well as p. 108—"small lightning," relating to their sexual encounters). Hers is an incandescent presence throughout—she *is* perhaps "the revolutionary spirit," like Blake's Orc. Her "amazing energy" (39) never flags.

149. Is it suicidally, overcome by despair at the way "words" and "meaning" represent an alien power that will always, eventually, overcome the individual sensibility? A trace of racial anxiety is also in evidence here because this psychic condition is associated with his rejection by Blanche, her "green and frozen" (European) eyes and a "blind sky bleached white" (117). Blanche's name stresses her racial whiteness and her surname (Goodfather) associates her with European paternalism.

150. Compare the narrator's description of her, swimming nude in Africa "in the tanned and glittering glory of her European tradition" (6).

151. She is clearly given the role of a "comrade" when the narrator says, "Blanche would carry on here what needed to be done and more professionally [probably, than himself], too" (13).

152. This is the "Conradian" vision of Africa exhibited in *Heart of Darkness*, which Marechera mocks so wholesomely and heartily in the opening section of the novel (where, significantly, the narrator is unproblematically reunited with Blanche) (1–13).

153. The image is of course reminiscent of the "Jonah complex" passage (73)—the narrator's being "swallowed" into the digestive tract ("down her gullet into the large folds of the stomach"—81) or "swallowed alive by the great cunt" (73) is terrifying—whatever the power system that exploits one, it is implied, the reduction or loss of selfhood is similar.

154. This ancient racist insult about monkeys directed at Africans features in many of Marechera's writings. In *Black Sunlight* he seems to combine it with the African image of the "desert" (75–77 and elsewhere) representing the way he is rejected or "othered" in England.

155. The image of the Zulus at his heels recalls the childhood experience recounted in *House of Hunger*, of the youthful narrator's hallucinations in which he is pursued/haunted by a small group of poor Africans (28–34)—as here, probably imaging a sense of guilt at his "abandoning" his own people by accepting a privileged (Western) education.

156. This source of threatening power is indicated in: "But this last book—it would break the hinges off all the doors they had locked in his teeth" (77).

157. Who taunt him, saying, "Can't you talk in our own language any more?" (78); and "You may be a writer but you're still as coal black as I am" (76).

158. The image explains why the narrator thinks of "escape" (14) and (sardonically) of "The history of the Runner" (8–9). But (as the narrator realizes, quoting Horace): "The exile takes himself with him" (87, 116).

159. The knowledge here referred to probably includes awareness of the revolutionary group's existence and activities, the political condition of the country, and the narrator's sexual relationship with Susan.

160. It is Susan who says with characteristic, harsh bluntness: "Your wife is blind and you probably fuck her the better for it" (44). This echoes the narrator's own earlier expression of an (occasional) fear "that her blindness was the only thing I loved about her" (36). He refers to the "fragile shell of blindness" (36) in which she is enclosed.

161. Compare his vision of Marie's very body, her nipples: "charged with insight. Radiating a total and unflinching clarity" (98), as well as an earlier recognition of a "strange *quickness* in her face" (22, emphasis added). Even when they are children, the narrator recognizes that she, too, is a visionary, when he hears her "singing of a world which was not there but of which [he] had the wildest intimations" (20).

162. Marechera in an interview reviewing his ghetto childhood identifies a blind, homeless couple that made an indelible impression on him as the "source" of Marie's blindness in *Black Sunlight* (V-W, *S.B.,* 2). On returning from Oxford, the narrator discovers in Marie "a desert I had never thought to find in another" (82). I have earlier suggested that the desert image indicates both the narrator's alienation (in Europe) and his African origin. See also the combination of associations linking Marie with Africa on p. 113: "anguish . . . admitting neither her youth nor her blindness. But only the enticing mouth of the African Dream" (113).

163. Marechera himself speaks of readers' tendency not to hear "the still sad music at the heart of [his] art" (V-W, *S.B.*, 4).

164. Edvard Munch's famous painting *The Scream* is called to mind. The description has a similar emblematic force.

165. The description of the bow recalls Marie and the narrator's wedding-night union (37). Compare also Marechera's own reference to "the voluptuous *blackening* image" (V-W, *S.B.,* 4—emphasis added) inspiring his writing.

166. Saying this, one must add that just as the narrator knows that "there [are] no answers" (101), Marechera realized that his fiction offered no "solutions" (V-W, *S.B.,* 40, 221). As Jane Bryce says finely, "A voice emerges [speaking] of the extremes of anguish and ecstasy with equal measures of emotional honesty, intellectual authority and technical virtuosity" (*Emerging Perspectives* 222).

167. The novelist-narrator distinguishes between "transformation" of social conditions (which he sees as desirable, but inadequate) and true, far-reaching transformation. The first kind, he says, does "not [transform] the nature of available reality at all" (69). "How *change* might then be conceivable is one of the key questions pursued in *Black Sunlight,*" writes Mark Stein (*Emerging Perspectives* 59).

168. He uses the beautiful image of "the gleamings that . . . [make] us furnaces of an eternal present" (62–63).

169. The novelist-narrator says: "To sit still and then hatch out in the natural time—that would be something. But I suffer from claustrophobia, impatience. A hungering after exactly what is outside my shell which I am breaking out into" (67).

170. Compare: "And crowded out any thought of ideas ever truly changing in the world [because] . . . the ghastly shape was a living thing. In an instant it could bare its teeth, its soldiers, its police, its informers, its paymasters" (83). The stasis in which the narrator finds himself is "akin to a marriage of fear and freedom" (114), each keeping the other at bay.

171. He refers to his occupation as "chronicling shit. And now, warped and twisted into some stringent desire that carried cameras, fucked Marie, wrote, watched Susan blow things, et al. A series of indefinable electric shocks smacking my brain with a less and less insistent impact" (100).

172. The expression links the idea of oppressive social convention with the image of a predatory creature (as before).

173. Daniela Volk writes: "For Marechera the 'true people' are those aspiring to free themselves but the aspiration is only the beginning" (*Emerging Perspectives* 301).

174. Marechera elsewhere refers to Erin Pizzey's "book . . . about wife-beating, *Scream Quietly or the Neighbours Will Hear*," adding, "I think I am in a similar position: people threaten to beat me up [or do so—as in the notorious incident when a colonel in the Zimbabwean army attacked him in a men's toilet], but ask me at the same time to 'scream quietly, Dambudzo, or the international community will hear, our enemies will hear'. Now, whenever I'm in trouble, I scream out loud" (quoted in V-W, *S.B.*, 43–44). One might add here Marechera's statement that he "was arrested the very day [he] published *Mindblast*" (quoted in V-W, *S.B.*, 35) (he was arrested and detained by the Central Intelligence Organisation, or CIO, for six days). "Once the revolution has achieved its objectives," he said, "it usually discards those very writers and artists who inspired that revolution" (quoted in V-W, *S.B.*, 38—cf. *Mindblast* 58).

175. *Mindblast or The Definitive Buddy* (its full title) was published in Zimbabwe, after some delays and difficulties (with earlier and prospective publishers), in 1984. This is the publication referred to in this commentary.

176. Once again recalling a key passage in the 1986 (Lansu) interview with Marechera, in which he said that the question whether one should resort to violence to destroy the "institutions which have promoted . . . slow brain death in citizens . . . form[ed] the basis of anarchism in *Black Sunlight* and also in *Mindblast*." He explained that the type of violence he himself employed was to "try to write in such a way [as to] short-circuit, like in electricity, [conventions], traditions and morals . . . [so that people] start having original thoughts of their own. . . . [For, he said] that slow brain death . . . can only be cured by this kind of literary shock treatment" (quoted in Lansu 40–41).

177. Here the expressions allude obviously to the title of Fanon's most famous work in its English translation (*The Wretched of the Earth*) and to the title of its third chapter ("The Pitfalls of National Consciousness," 119–165), which concludes with the admonition that if "nationalism . . . is not . . . deepened . . . into a consciousness of social and political needs, in other words into humanism, it leads up a blind alley. . . . [It should aim] first to give back their dignity to all citizens, fill their minds and feast their eyes with human things, and create a prospect that is human, because conscious and sovereign men dwell therein" (Fanon, *Wretched,* 165). It was because he saw so little of this Fanonian vision being realized in newly independent Zimbabwe that Marechera resorted to his *Mindblast.*

178. After meeting Marechera for the first time in 1983, M.W. Serote (South African poet and novelist) stated how struck he was by the "intensity" and the "insight into issues" (easily overlooked by others "at moments of euphoria") that Marechera's writing displayed, finding this consistent with his role as persistent "rebel" who "identified strongly with the dispossessed." N. Gordimer (South African Nobel prize–winner in literature) also noticed that despite his seeming a "self-obsessed person," Marechera "was the one who took up a burning social issue . . . and turned all this anger and concern away from himself to others" (both statements quoted in V-W, *S.B.*, 330–331). "Marechera confronted the burning political issues of the early 1980s," writes Veit-Wild (V-W, *S.B.*, 326—see also 328 and 335–337).

179. With the Parisian daily *Liberation.*

180. Having registered the degree of guilt he had felt in "escap[ing] from hunger, actual physical hunger" (V-W, *S.B.*, 19) as well as from the spiritually constricting effects of poverty (which meant "ignoring the poverty of the others . . . selfish[ly]"—

V-W, *S.B.,* 17), "because the house of hunger has no voice in any decision-making process" (V-W, *S.B.,* 20), Marechera's almost inadvertent (see V-W, *S.B.,* 32) return to what was now Zimbabwe can be "read" as to some extent a realignment with the occupants of the house of hunger and an attempt to give them a "voice" (V-W, *S.B.,* 20) in another sphere—his writing. His down-and-out lifestyle made the same point "practically" (cf. his "full circle" comment, *S.B.* 43). His perspective was "informed" "because I know the poverty here. I know the house of hunger here, in the ghettos, in the rural areas. . . . For the working classes and the peasants, it's still the same. . . . [The ex-combatants, he said, are mostly] now unemployed and live in the streets. This is what I wrote about in *Mindblast.* It's actually based on Harare" (V-W, *S.B.,* 35). So popular did his work prove, especially with younger Zimbabweans (who felt it expressed their own disillusionment and anger), that reference to the "Mindblast generation" became common (V-W, *S.B.,* 310 and especially 390–392, a young Zimbabwean's testimony).

181. The point being that a supposedly demilitarized society is still permeated with military weaponry and that citizens are beleaguered by the threat of violence from trigger-happy, dissatisfied ex-combatants—a situation familiar to numerous African countries and often the roots of follow-up wars and rebellions. Compare Cyprian Ekwensi's novel *Survive the Peace.*

182. Note the playwright's insertion of the following encomium, spoken by "the Minister" (Nzuzu) to his host, the social (and political) climber Norman Drake: "Now, it is a magnificent party. Informal yet formal. Dignified yet casual. VIPees and a few representatives of the povo [i.e., the poor masses]. Marvellous, Mr Drake" (33), the effect of which is biting (coming as it does from the recipient—in this very scene—of three fat bribes from the host: two envelopes of cash and a Rolls-Royce. No wonder Nzuzu is purring!).

183. Toward the end of the book, the diarist observes: "Here there is all this nationalism, this glorification of the state, this 'respect' for education, this bowed attitude towards the notion of society. We are in the nineteenth century and know and like it" (157)—as it were, detecting a Victorian attitude (in this respect as well) in his society.

184. When Olga reveals that she is keeping her options open as far as her choice of a male partner is concerned, for instance, the diarist's mind links and parallels this with the political corruption that (in his words) has "already" turned Zimbabwe into "a Kenya" (147–148).

185. The diarist writes that it is his writing that enables him to maintain the belief "that humans are human" despite "all the horrors and the crushing waste [of] the earth" (151). A later Zimbabwean writer, Yvonne Vera, maintains in her work a similar balance between a splendid vitality of language and the depiction of horror and squalor.

186. Admittedly its employment of the resources of poetic language—in metaphor and tone modulation—is less "populist," less accessible than the colloquial prose of most sections of the text, so (in another sense) the author hits harder because he has the "protection" of poetic indirectness.

187. As in the satirically exaggerated picture of the Chief in the opening scenes of *Black Sunlight*—although that portrait is balanced by a quick "correction" to the portrayal when the narrator (there) notes that the "unpredictable tyrant" had "in his heyday" been "a mighty wrestler, a Casanova, a fair and just man" (etc.) (6).

188. The *risky* role of the prophet who exposes power is shown to be in the poet's mind when he calls to mind the beheading (in the biblical account of John the Baptist (84).

189. Blake's "London" and Eliot's "The Waste Land" seem to have been two of Marechera's inspirational sources, which he effortlessly adapts and "Africanizes" in this poem. Dirk Klopper's piece (*Emerging Perspectives* 121–135) is a substantial analysis of the poem.

190. Such "X-ray" vision is apparent in the poem—for example, in the speaker discerning greedy and materialistic "goldthought" and "goldvein" underneath people's apparently human skins (77).

191. He notes apathy ("Black lassitude"—87), conformity and bedazzlement by vulgar pleasures in "placid faces" (83), "wide bellies" (84), "platform boots and imitation Levis" (85), and "striptease[s] for the Minister / And the clerk" (83).

192. An image employed in the poem, touched on again later in this discussion.

193. "With the dying the hungry milling / Round, / Is it enough to write lines like / These: / . . . Between bough and branch / Birdsong and sky"? (78), the speaker asks himself.

194. References to "the bitter cup / That will not pass" (82) and to sipping "vinegar" (83) and European-language biblical quotes (85) link the speaker with Christ; the Hamlet parallel is invoked on p. 85, whereas Antigone and Gogol are brought in on pp. 92 and 93, respectively.

195. The poem opens on a question that expresses a yearning for security: "Where to sit / And slam the door / Against fear of tomorrow?" (75).

196. The image used for this is that of "brute black rain / Pummel[ing] my brainpaths" and of "thought," despite being "muddled" by the assault of power's brutes, "shak[ing] the dust / To all humanity" (75). Compare also: "Only escape to sit down and write" (77).

197. Marechera uses the image (simultaneously lovely and gloomy) of "tiny blue eggs / In abandoned nest" (75).

198. Elsewhere in "Throne of Bayonets" the poet writes: "The poem hastens slowly. / Like the slow shimmering sights of Winter-dawn [another hopeful anticipation of social change] / The poem screams quietly" (reverting to the image of torture and abuse of the powerless, the *expression* of anguish is at least unapathetic and noncomplicitous: a form of protest) (80).

199. Evidently, from the Zimbabwean war of liberation. They are portrayed as ghosts haunting the social conscience: "Time's mutilated beggars" or "Gaunt skeletons" (75) or "Phantoms at Second Street bus stop" (82).

200. The carcass "Stinks the neighbourhood / But [surreptitiously] feeds the Cats at night" (76): a brilliant image of corruption and its beneficiaries; however, the poet's searing vision nightmarishly, "in the region / Of heartgloom," discovers even himself "gleefully at banquet" (79).

201. The complacent isolation bred by power is elsewhere depicted as the ability to wander through Harare's streets: "Deaf to the prostitute's pitiful shrieks / Blind to malnutrition's glazed look" (92), ignoring "homeless poverty illiterate despair" (93).

202. Elsewhere in the poem the speaker notes, "The Cityman cometh to no pain / When rural grounds receive no rain" (88).

203. In Klopper's chapter on the poem, this image is well analyzed (*Emerging Perspectives* 127).

204. He is uncertain of (ever) achieving "coherent poetry in the gibberish rhythm / Of available 'reality,'" perhaps capable only of "Stuttering, trembling, ejaculating / At the edge of the ruthless dream" (86).

205. When others drown their woes in drink, the poet "will think on Hurt / How its tattered skirt endures" (90).

206. As indicated above, "povo" is a term commonly used in Zimbabwe and in the formerly Portuguese dominated areas of Africa (from which the term derives), signifying the poor masses. Here, of course, they are represented, emblematically, by a single woman. Flora Veit-Wild has commented illuminatingly and in detail on this poem in her chapter in *Emerging Perspectives*, on pp. 96–97. Nhamo Mhiripiri's chapter on Marechera's poetry in the same collection (151–160) is also worth noting.

207. Another type of corruption is castigated in Marechera's tribute to those who died at "Soweto, June 16 & Sharpeville," called "The Undying Testament" (110–112), which sneeringly reports the failure to show "African solidarity" (with apartheid's victims), which is evident in the "tired half-hearted revolutionary yawn" of privileged Zimbabwean university students.

208. From the poem about the decolonization negotiations that brought about first the Smith-Muzorewa regime and eventually independent Zimbabwe, "The Lancaster House Dressing Table" (97). Marechera does in some poems celebrate (e.g., "Eve ate, Adam delved, Nehanda / Oiled her AK47"—98) or warn others about African militancy (e.g., 108–109, 115–116).

209. The quoted lines occur in the poem "Sunday Service" (117), where the speaker's "special" hearing detects this militant undertone in the apparently placid, otherworldly sounds of the hymns sung in church.

210. Using a technique that might be described as satirical surrealism, the diarist refers to "the heads of these men and women all cabbages, waiting always to be boiled by the mothers of politicians in power" (145). He also experiences his sense of human "uniqueness . . . dispelled" by the "shrieked insult[s]" provoked from various social sectors by his own off-beat appearance and behavior (147). The "glorification of the state" (157) in newly independent Zimbabwe, which so appalled Marechera, has been earlier referred to.

211. From the poem "The Light of Landscapes in Strings" (115).

212. Compare: "The writer is no longer a person: he has to die in order to become a writer" (V-W, *S.B.*, 366).

213. These are quotations from a newspaper interview that appear in Caute's essay "Marechera in Black and White" (101).

214. McLoughlin writes that Marechera's poetry "affirms . . . the necessity of poetry as the medium through which the helplessness of silence finds a voice" (*Emerging Perspectives* 138).

215. See V-W, *S.B.*, 310, 328, and (especially) 390–392.

216. Compare the Reorientation Officer's accusation against Grimknife Jr: "You do not think the way everyone else thinks" (46), and Buddy's being subjected to the "demand" of the conformity that is termed "patriotism, loyalty and responsibility," which has the effect of "stifling" him (54).

217. Such discouragement is spelled out in the diarist's reference to "the anger, the angst, the overwhelming desire to just give up" (142), in his expressing his feeling of being "tired of living like this" (147), and in his recording of Olga's observation, "It's fucking you up . . . your living like this" (148).

218. "Bohemianism is not a lifestyle for the serious writer," the diarist writes: "It is dictated by harsh poverty which is imposed by the fact that fulltime writing brings in little or no return in the early stages of one's career" (138). He also writes that "when the revolution is over and the changes have turned sour . . . the artists [are] unable to join the ruling class and rejected by the Povo as effete" (143). In V-W, *S.B.*, 41–42, Marechera uses the analogy of the unappreciated prophetess Cassandra for the writer.

219. "Buddy" is introduced as an isolated figure: "The neatly pressed safari suits of the shefs bludgeoned his senses, gouged his eye. But the povo too were no better.

Their wretched ragged respectability made his thoughts ache" (51). "How to face alone / This Christian festive dawn?" he asks in a poem (88). Compare Marechera's saying (in the Lansu interview, 1986), "The isolation is driving me crazy" (Lansu 36).

220. Compare: "Finger-fat delusions wash themselves / in the dish of dollars" (84) and (from another poem) "The fast expensive imported cars / Leave in their wake mangled workers / Deranged peasants and crazed radical intellectuals" (112).

221. On p. 125 a similar catalog is listed (cf. also p. 64 for its portrayal of the bourgeois milieu).

222. The songwriter Grace, another artist figure, has feelings and notions "which she hid[es] 'inside'" (66), of which tears are the outward manifestation. (Compare Marechera's definition of poetry as "the art of making invisibility visible"—quoted in V-W, *S.B.,* 352.)

223. The recurrence here of the title image of the (whole) text signals the centrality of this passage. Marechera repeatedly mentions the ninety-year time span, which represents the period of white domination in the former Rhodesia.

224. These comments exactly reflect reasons given to Marechera why much of his material was deemed "unpublishable"—for example, 338, 349, 350–351 (quoted in V-W, *S.B.*).

225. Compare V-W, *S.B.,* 38, Marechera's comment on revolutions betraying (their) artists.

226. The literary agency Marechera attempted to set up in Harare proved hugely popular but was forced to close after four and one-half days, probably by state security officers (*Mindblast* 133–135; cf. V-W, *S.B.,* 327–328).

227. Grimknife Sr remarks: "There is so little encouragement for what we do" (58), while Grace registers "the futility, the feeling of shame when it was said that the Third World did not want Art, it wanted food" (etc.) (67).

228. The type of slogan (one might label it fake Marxism) with which Marechera had to contend is exemplified in *Mindblast* especially in the second half of "Throne of Bayonets" (87–93). He also brings in two of Pete Seeger's songs (156–159)—in Olga's voice—to castigate mindless conformity.

229. As Marechera himself experienced (299).

230. See *Mindblast*, 67, 92; and V-W, *S.B.,* 34, 39, 43–44, and 312.

231. Comments by editors and readers indicating the difficulties Marechera experienced in seeking publication of his work during this period are quoted on pp. 338–339, 346–347, 349, and 350–351 of the *Source Book*. Only Olga, in *Mindblast*, is shown as a discerning and appreciative reader of the writer's work (141).

232. Blood spilt by and injuries to the writer feature prominently throughout (52, 57, 59, 60, 62, 72, 84, 141). The most appalling scene is at the end of the second "Buddy" section where the devastating "fall" of the poet, in blood, vomit, and self-doubt, occurs. It is Marechera's most vivid portrayal of the degradation of the committed artist in an authoritarian society, in contrast with "the full luxuries of conforming" (63).

233. In ironic confirmation of Marechera's *Mindblast* depiction of suppression of ideas and censorship of writing, the quotation occurs in "The Depth of Diamonds," a work of Marechera's that has not yet been published. The quotation is cited in Gaylard, *Emerging Perspectives*, 78.

234. The edition used is the original publication; compiled, edited, and with an Introduction by Flora Veit-Wild, copyright to the Dambudzo Marechera Trust, and published posthumously in 1994.

235. All these quotations from p. 65 of the interview printed in *New African* 200 (May 1984). It is clear that they contrast somewhat startlingly with the *generally* accu-

rate perception of Marechera's position represented by a description given by Marechera's biographer, champion, and editor, Flora Veit-Wild: "Marechera refuses to identify himself with any particular race, culture, or nation; he is an extreme individualist, an anarchistic thinker" ("Words as Bullets" 113). In *Mindblast* (published in 1984) Marechera described himself (with some bitterness in the irony) as "homeless yet home" (136), although he also writes, "After all I must find and define my place in this new Zimbabwe" (137).

236. *Scrapiron Blues* was not assembled by the author, but it was posthumously put together by his editor Flora Veit-Wild. Yet it recognizably functions by means of a technique of "assemblage" or collage parallel to that which Marechera himself usually employed to express the multiplicity, the "many voices" (quoted in V-W, *S.B.,* 311), of his fragmented society (see his catalog of some of those "many voices" quoted in V-W, *S.B.,* 1).

237. An image originally applied to the philosopher Socrates in Ancient Greece due to his persistently questioning attitude toward official morality and state rules and structures (for which he was eventually punished by enforced "suicide"), Marechera uses the same term to apply to African writers like Soyinka and Ngugi (see V-W, *S.B.,* 370 and 372), who in his eyes were maintaining the same duty of "disturbance" of official complacencies and who were therefore hounded and imprisoned (as he was himself, intermittently, in independent Zimbabwe—see V-W, *S.B.,* 290, 307–311, 326, 328–336).

238. "Even the fighters, the ex-combatants, are not allowed to write about their direct experiences as guerrillas. They have to get permission. . . . Most of those who want to write about their experiences will not glorify anything. . . . [When Marechera opened a literary agency that had to shut down within days due to intimidation from what he strongly suspected were state security officials], hundreds and hundreds were queuing outside [his] office door. The majority of them were ex-combatants. . . . [He adds:] anyone who has direct experience of the struggle is finding it hard to write about it; it's not permitted" (quoted in V-W, *S.B.,* 45—cf. the last paragraph on p. 328 and the first on p. 336). Compare also *Mindblast* 133–135 and *Scrapiron* 23–24, 43, 45–46.

239. As did, more recently, Shimmer Chinodya, who despite being a noncombatant (like Marechera) produces in (the second part of his novel) *Harvest of Thorns* a compelling account of the experiences of and the moral quandaries besetting participation (as a freedom fighter) in Zimbabwe's war of liberation.

240. Compare the wide range of people (occupations, roles, classes, genders, races) mentioned by Marechera in his "self-interview" (quoted in V-W, *S.B.,* 1) as being the most direct influence on his work: a diversity replicated in *Scrapiron Blues.* Of the section in it called "The Concentration Camp," Marechera said that he had never before attempted writing of this kind, "for which [he had] to interview people"—former inmates of the so-called protected villages as well as those who had been (black) guards at the camps, serving under a white officer (quoted in Introduction, *Scrapiron* xiv).

241. Conducted and published in booklet form by Kirsten Holst Petersen.

242. In the Foucaultian sense of the term.

243. His difficulties with publishers have been mentioned; he also found Zimbabwean society generally narrow-minded and constrictive (see *Scrapiron* 26, 28), exhibiting authoritarian tendencies, and demanding the kind of conformity and uncritical support that he considered it his life's work to challenge and oppose (see V-W, *S.B.,* 32–46, 290–291, 312, 319–320, 326–28, 333–352). He found that he had come back "armed with a profession [considered] irrelevant to development," that "every [Zimbabwean] writer is aware of the national programme which unofficially does not allow

certain things," that like Cassandra "with all this enormous talent to actually analyse . . . people's destinies . . . [he would be] cursed by censorship, by persecution . . . [even though] a pen is not a gun" (quoted in V-W, *S.B.,* 34, 39, 42). Even his unconventional dress and lifestyle raised eyebrows and were considered provocative, yet proof of his "irrelevance" (*Mindblast* 120). Even fellow writers, he reports, "think I deserve what I get because I criticise too much" (quoted in V-W, *S.B.,* 45–46).

244. Marechera himself refers to the "heavy political atmosphere" (quoted in V-W, *S.B.,* 39). He is in a 1984 interview (already) described as being "virtually silenced as a writer" and mentions that, despite having "written at least five works" since his return, he could not get most of them published and hence had no reliable source of income (*New African* 200—64).

245. Titled "Killwatch or Tony Fights Tonight," it contained (according to the *Scrapiron* editor—xi–xii), the pieces now printed as "Pub Stories" (2–29), the play "Killwatch" (96–106), and the "unfinished" story, "Tony and the Rasta" (213–216).

246. The chapter on Marechera's children's stories in *Emerging Perspectives* (253–263) by Robert Muponde ("Reconstructing Childhood: Social Banditry in Marechera's Children's Stories") is highly illuminating.

247. "He shouts the biggest screams in the streets. / He fights the dirtiest battles in the playground" (213).

248. He knows and notices that his aunt "starves him"; senses that she exploits him by making him "do all the jobs around the house," which "is not really / a house"; that the township is shockingly underresourced (213); that his aunt is having an affair; and that "men and women dressed in / rags get drunk . . . and fight and curse / and kick the children" (214—the power/oppression pyramid in operation!); that township people are hounded by a black government just as blacks are by the white South African government (214); that at school "classes are crowded" with "few" teachers, who "are always drunk and ogling the schoolgirls" (215).

249. Although he knows "there are no answers," Tony nevertheless asks, "Why do the men have no jobs? Why do all these people live in these horrible houses?" and (when his aunt beats him up) "Why is she always angry?" (214). He does so because "Tony feels a great deal; he thinks too much" (216).

250. "Tony dreams strange dreams" (213); he feels that the "questions" (previous note) "seem too big"; he senses that "everyone in Shantytown is frightened," the whole settlement seeming to have "dragged itself out of . . . sewerage" (214). "Tony loves [Shantytown, but] with great bitterness"; "He hates not being loved"—he knows that most "shanty people . . . are afraid of peace because they have never known it" (216).

251. See also the poem "The Zimbabwe Children's Liberation Festival" (Marechera, *Cemetery of Mind,* 140–142) in which especially the child called "Fatboy" is the voice of social critique.

252. Like him, too, in being often "with a fractured jaw and broken ribs[, having been] beaten up" (215).

253. Here I disagree with Muponde's implied suggestion that the adult Marechera "usurps" the child's voice/vision (*Emerging Perspectives* 256–257).

254. Consisting mainly of the narrator and Fred, with the latter's "girlfriend" Jill as a peripheral presence.

255. Described as the mere instant in which one can become "the raw person": "a person without titles, without a label" (quoted in V-W, *S.B.,* 367). This is, it seems, simultaneously a moment of social disempowerment and of artistic empowerment or liberation, such as Marechera experienced in his marginalized position—expelled from Oxford, homeless in Britain, now homeless in Harare.

256. About Fred's tales and autobiographical anecdotes the narrator (identified as an author) says:

> I try not to listen. . . . Because I am trying to pounce on my own story too. I am trying to grasp the kind of story that will take in the swimming-pool skin of Harare skies, the slightly mocking darkness that underlines sunset's briefly glowing coals, before the black hand of anxiety clenches its darkness round the city. In the mind the roof rattles. The plaster comes down. And millions of tiny red ants slowly but inexorably creep through the egg-cracks into the sleeper's dream. (5)

Clearly, writing of this type expresses an existentialist perspective on Zimbabwean "realities."

257. "There is this shallowness to everything. This elaborate hollowness" (26). Emerging after a year of imprisonment for debt, the author-narrator feels "the horror and hollowness of [his] coming out into yet another prison" (28), Hararean society. He cannot "retrieve" Tony and Jane.

258. "Is it so surprising," the author-narrator wonders, "that everyone is so obsessed with the past?" (22), just before he recounts how he was asked (and refused) to write up an ex-combatant's "experiences in the Struggle" (23). While scratching "dead skin," the sign of his ill health, from the back of his hand, the author-narrator says: "I hate dead skin. There's an Ian Smith in it" (alluding to the "UDI" regime in Rhodesia and its aftermath when Smith continued to govern, along with Bishop Muzorewa—the period during which black Zimbabweans fought bitterly and bloodily for political independence). Fred, too, remembers "the time South Africa bombed our pipeline" (3). Even in independent Zimbabwe, the author-narrator cannot stop "worrying about South Africa bombing us" (9).

259. He is described as "a short plump guy who wears wire spectacles with very thick lenses" (5).

260. Who are associated with death: the imminent threat of which "old-age pensioners" resist by compulsive newspaper-reading—*their* reading paralleling this author's writing activities (8–9).

261. Despite the middle-class comforts of life in the flat with Tony—eggs and coffee breakfasts (9) and wine and cheese suppers behind velvet curtains (7).

262. In contrast with official, glorifying "histories" that falsify the terrible realities of that period: "Massacres . . . atrocities. . . . The dying sons and slogans. . . . Vivid hatreds. Minds exchanging nightmares of blood and mutilation" (14). Compare one of Marechera's earliest poems, which takes a similarly disenchanted view of "heroic" battle ("Liberty," in *Cemetery,* 3).

263. Compare lines from the poem "Parliament": "Always the guards / At the horned gates / To the people's forum, / There are guns / At each end / Of democratic expressions" (*Cemetery of Mind* 106).

264. Marechera wrote elsewhere: "It is difficult for a novelist to justify his exclusive devotion to his typewriter when all round him are the harsh facts of grim poverty and the struggle's aftermath" (Veit-Wild and Schade, *Marechera,* 25). In the *Scrapiron Blues* pieces he resolved the dilemma by writing about exactly these subjects.

265. On p. 5 the author-narrator feels that "millions of tiny red ants . . . inexorably creep . . . into the sleeper's dream"; on p. 6 we are told that Tony "coughs a lot, trying to get rid of the tiny red ants he thinks have made their nest in his fragile chest." See also pp. 8 and 24 for recurrences of this image.

266. He decides, later, that "we were all for Zimbabwe, all in it together. My resentment was ridiculous—unless I was against Zimbabwe" (121)—beginning to

sound (himself) almost like the state security personnel who had plagued Marechera's life in the newly independent country! Afterwards, conciliatingly, he tells Grace that "Zimbabwe takes some getting used to. Like you" (121)—directly and emblematically associating her with the country. For her part, she urges him not to "stop writing"; adding that "The Struggle never stopped" (121). Grace *also*, it seems, represents Harare, "the city as demon lover" (122), further (over)loading the symbol(ism).

267. The title, especially, confirms this reading.

268. References to physical violation and damage (121) as well as to her psychically traumatized state (116–117) do record yet again (in this collection) the ugly and terrifying aspects of the liberation war, especially the women veterans' histories, so seldom reported (or allowed to be recorded).

269. I suggest that the attempt to escape the "searing loneliness" Marechera suffered from in Harare (*Mindblast* 129, etc.) was such an originating impulse.

270. "But we are all brothers now. Comrades Down and Out alias Black and White" (34), Rhodes says sardonically.

271. In *Scrapiron Blues* Marechera frequently uses the image of a wall, or walls, to indicate the suppression of ugly, evil, or "uncomfortable" memories: 5–7, 9, 10, 12, 16–17, 28–29, 37–47. The floor and trapdoor in the piece (also with two male characters) called "The Camp" (174–176) fulfill the same function.

272. It is a main theme in the playlet "The Breakdown Scrapiron Blues" (48–60). Compare also "Apartheid is only real / To faggot Afrikaners / Who fuck their daughters" (178), and pp. 39 and 41–43 of "The Alley."

273. Another (but related) point is made in the poem "The Zimbabwe Children's Liberation Festival" (*Cemetery of Mind* 140–142): "Fatboy says reconciliation only works when justice is seen to be done. / Otherwise all whites are lumped with the killers" (141). The relevance of this comment to the functioning of the South African Truth and Reconciliation Commission is unmistakable.

274. Contrast the gently satirical piece "The Servant's Ball" (in a Shona version by Marechera and an English translation by others—61–84), which does end with an image of racial "reconciliation" (84)—whereas the proof of such reconciliation (a loving and passionate interracial marriage) is precisely what triggers vicious, even murderous, racial persecution in the supposedly new society, Zimbabwe, *from both black and white* ("Alien to the People" 85–95)—deep *irony* shown to be attendant upon the overt racial power shift (as Marechera "reports" it in the three different depictions of "reconciliation").

275. There is one vague hint that the elder of the two watchers in "Killwatch" is thought of as a liberation war veteran (now dead, of course): First Watchman tells his younger partner: "We fought hard to create all this, you see. I watched death and dying for years ravaging all this. It was a time of brutal sickness. You did not have to think but *knew, simply knew*, terror. It was a terrible time. [Pause] That is why I do my duty to sustain the structure of all life" (99). The suicide in "Black Damascus Road," correspondingly, seems to personify the war-ravaged psyche—"the mind of a man who has seen too much too soon" (123).

276. Because a number of auto/biographical details in this piece link the protagonist with the narrator, his alienation probably expresses Marechera's own sense of marginalization at this time.

277. The character in the "Tony Fights Tonight—Pub Stories" sequence.

278. According to the editor (Introduction, *Scrapiron,* xiii) these were written in 1986, the year before Marechera's death.

279. Titled, respectively (and in "chronological" order), Part One: "The Camp" (158–163—not to be confused with the two-character surrealist playlet also—confus-

ingly—called "The Camp," 168–176), Part Six: "The Camp" (192–202), and Part Seven: "Tonderai's Father Reflects" (195–203).

280. Identified by Marechera as the period from 1978 to the end of 1979, according to him the "most dangerous time" for the camps' inmates, because by then "Ian Smith's soldiers knew that they were losing the war" (quoted in the Introduction, *Scrapiron,* xiv, above—as are the quotes appearing above in my main text).

281. Being made to consume (by himself) all of his family's food (accused of having wanted to "feed the terrs," or terrorists), being kicked and having his right hand broken merely and maliciously (it seems) because he is right-handed. He adds to this the terrible memory of the day Tonderai was critically injured (by the Rhodesian army) (199–202).

282. Compare Ben Okri's moving and terrible short story "Laughter Under the Bridge" in *Incidents.*

283. In a brilliantly written paragraph, Marechera depicts the enormous *weight* of oppressive power all but overwhelming the boy's consciousness (this is just after the helicopter attack on the herdboys):

> The boy tottered to his feet. His eyes were coming into focus, but it was as if he was seeing the whole world through a thin screen of fresh blood. He still clutched his present for Rudo. He looked up into the sergeant's face. All the darkening twilight of the universe was streaming into the sky from a point at the back of the sergeant's head. Getting darker and darker, minute by minute, month after month, year after year. Century after century. (161)

284. As he does so appealingly in the novella of family life in the township to which Veit-Wild appended the title "When Rainwords Spit Fire" (131–156). However, as in the short narrative "The Intellectual's Revolt" (179–192), a strong impression of the vulnerability and mortality of the innocent is also conveyed. Compare the last three narrative pieces in *Scrapiron Blues* (not discussed here): "The Magic Cat," "Baboons of the Rainbow," and "Fuzzy Goo's Guide to the Earth" (217–247), as well as the excellent discussion of Marechera's writing for children in Muponde's essay (*Emerging Perspectives* 253–263). Muponde says inter alia that in these works Marechera is "proposing a grammar of . . . [dissident] dreams and perception" (261).

285. Exemplified (for instance) in the looming presence of the brutal sergeant "tower[ing] over" Tonderai as he slowly regains consciousness after the bomb attack (161).

286. Marechera's "stuttering tongue" was well known (see, e.g., V-W, *S.B.,* 46–48). In this particular poem one can catch a vague echo of a well-known poem ("The Ship of Death") by D.H. Lawrence, whose work Marechera had read avidly and (especially as a youngster) admired. The emphasis on words in the poem certainly calls the poet and story writer Marechera to mind, as do the later lines "(Darkness visible!) memory's very light / Baptizes the Towerman's exilebroken / Return" (195).

5

Brief Conclusions

Be attentive, for here, now, you are arriving
Hamidou Kane, *Ambiguous Adventure*

In the foregoing chapters I have primarily attempted to establish the practically relevant and intellectually profound qualities of the three selected writers' presentations, simultaneously *assessments,* of the African circumstances of which they write, as well as the value of the method of analysis employed here to access, and to convey, the kinds of concepts that their works embody. The texts have been discussed as exemplifications of the authors' concern with the difficulty as well as the dire need, in the kinds of societies that they describe, of (re)establishing or maintaining and liberating local, communal forms of life within the contemporary context of globalized modernity—a context within which African regions have remained by and large the neglected backyards of late twentieth-century prosperity.[1]

These preoccupations of the three chosen writers become evident when their concern with issues of change and power, embodied in their many and various presentations in the texts they write, is carefully pinpointed and analyzed. The present study contends that the methodology of a more literary-oriented style of analysis (meaning, here, readings as attentive to the verbal texture of the authors' prose as to their sociopolitical and psychological delineations of specific African contexts and conditions, as manifested in details and patterns of the works selected) yields for the reader recognitions in the texts of both actual social, political, and psychic conditions, *and* deeply thoughtful analyses of the circumstances portrayed—insights that theory-filtered readings are less successful at accessing, because the literary texts are not, as they are here, the primary focus of attention. Prioritizing the literary texts makes possible the discovery of the extent to which these texts simultaneously embody and assess types of African social structures. The conclusion argued here is, then, also a plea for a recentering of African realities, if the ills of the continent are to be more successfully addressed than heretofore, and for a role of greater authority in such a process being accorded to such witnesses and analysts of African conditions as the authors whose texts the present study examines. If a label is worth choosing, the readings that have been offered might be called "sociometaphorical," since the texts discussed are treated as "interactive" with actual societies and circumstances—in the senses both of emanating from societies like those that they depict and of commenting analytically on these societies, yielding insights that are, then, usefully applicable or transferable also to other social situations with significant similarities to those that have been represented in the literary texts.

In the struggle to change the politically fraught conditions of many African states to more viable social circumstances, in the need to cope with the constant threats and difficulties presented by the besetting global and local forms of power, writers like the three who feature in this study, and others like them, represent an inestimable spiritual[2] as well as intellectual resource—no less so in their role as social critics than as pointers to hopeful possibilities or truths neglected and overlooked. The balanced and ironic sense of history in Achebe, the powerful wellspring of hope in Head's writing, and the anguished despair of Marechera are all vividly African in their origin and in the supple, lucid English by means of which they communicate their impressions. In their different ways, these three writers encounter power and change textually and "vicariously," writing the "*stories*" that can help to "*create people.*"[3]

In a world much aware of international power relations, Shakespeare's play *The Tempest* is now frequently read as an early and deeply ambiguous study of territorial expansionism or colonization by critics examining the Elizabethan playwright's portrayal of the manner of the occupation of the island that is its setting. Toward the end of this play the European nobleman who is the central character, significantly named Prospero, is shown victorious, at last, over his enemies—a group that includes his rebellious, but now penitent, servant-slave Caliban, who is the son of an African mother.[4] Speaking to his newly gained ally, the King of Naples, Prospero disdainfully explains the supposed "strange[ness]" of Caliban by saying, "He is as disproportion'd in his manners / As in his shape" (5.1.289–291). In their dismissiveness these words recall what Marechera writes in *The Black Insider* (65): "There is no answer to the whiteman's sneer."

The telling contrast shown in *The Tempest* between Prospero's "story" of Caliban with Prospero's "story" of himself (5.1.304) calls to mind the Manichaean dichotomy of Eurocentric worldviews and histories. The way in which such a perspective combines denigration of non-Europeans with a paradoxical type of psychic dependency on the world's darker people[5] has often been pointed out. V.Y. Mudimbe formulates the point as follows:

> From Herodotus onward, the West's self-representations have always included images of people situated outside of its cultural and imaginary fron-

> tiers. The paradox is that if, indeed, these outsiders were understood as localised and far away, geographically, they were nonetheless imagined and rejected as the intimate and other side of the European-thinking subject. (Mudimbe, *Idea,* xi)[6]

In *The Tempest,* Prospero redirects his "guest's" attention from Caliban toward "The story of [his—that is, Prospero's] life"—a reference emphasized by Alonso's repetition of the expression (5.1.304, 312). It is *his* "story" that Prospero has been staging for the audience up to this final point in the play: a story that has swelled far beyond the bounds of his (and its) origins. If the bogeyman image (like Prospero's description of Caliban) of Africans and other colonized people as "cannibals" is read along the lines of the symbolic logic employed here, that type of image might be interpreted as an unconscious projection of the "swallowing" of land and of people (and the claiming of "history") by the European invaders. The ironies and mysteries with which Prospero's "story," with its blatant self-staging and its many gaps, is surrounded stem from Shakespeare's vision, not from Prospero's mind, with its concentration on power. Any *single* story is automatically questionable. Said writes (in words highly appropriate to the terms of the present study): "In human history there is always something beyond the reach of dominating systems, no matter how deeply they saturate society, and this is obviously what makes change possible, limits power in Foucault's sense, and hobbles the theory of that power" (*World* 246–247). "Ignorance is to be filled with oneself," remarks a Marechera character (*Insider* 100).

When Duke Prospero—in a line shortly before the sections of *The Tempest* discussed—says of Caliban: "this thing of darkness I / Acknowledge mine" (5.1.275–276), what is missing from his grudging "acknowledge[ment]" is exactly the "reciprocal" *recognition* that Fanon[7] sees as an end to be struggled for, if "the creation of a human world" is to occur (*Black Skin* 155).[8] Like acknowledgment, recognition requires knowledge—but more: an admission (unlike Prospero's), in humility and with fellow feeling, of one's *equal* kinship with another. Most especially, it requires the ability to *see* (to notice) and to *hear* (to be attentive to) what others feel and proclaim themselves to be. As long as Africans are identified as "thing[s] of darkness" by non-Africans, no such recognition can occur—and no fully human world can be constituted. Marechera, Head, and Achebe are three of the writers from this continent who can assist in the founding of a responsible complementarity as we begin to address the aftermath of colonialist power impingements as well as the effects of African social failures.

Unlike Caliban, who resentfully proclaims his "profit" from the arrival of Prospero as the knowledge of how to "curse" the conqueror in "[his] language" (1.2.365–366), these authors *address* both their African compatriots and their former conquerors, exhibiting their own and their people's human dignity in the shapeliness of the works that they (as artists) produce. It is time to end the confrontational standoff between the Afrocentric and the Eurocentric claims to "civilization" and to strive for a balanced inclusivity. "For" (in the words of Bessie Head) "largeness of heart is what we need for a civilisation and big, big eyes, wide enough to drink in all the knowledge of the heavens and earth" (*Alone* 50).

Notes

1. Pieterse refers to "a global 'South Africanisation,' that is, zones of prosperity and high employment next to sprawling Bantustans of poverty, . . . dispersed across the globe" (375).

2. In the sense of (A) being inspirational, suggestive, encouraging; (B) being concerned with the profoundest human needs—for example, for justice, for acceptance, and for a recognition of one's identity and worth.

3. I am again echoing (here) what Achebe calls "the universal creative rondo": "*stories create people create stories*" (*Hopes* 162).

4. Sycorax (in Prospero's description) the "blue-ey'd hag" (1.2.269) is said to have been banished to the island from Algiers (1.2.265). Caliban's name is commonly interpreted as an anagram of "can(n)ibal." An article by Rob Nixon that appeared in 1987, "Caribbean and African Appropriations of *The Tempest,*" usefully summarizes something of the variety of ways in which the Shakespearean text has been employed by authors like Mannoni, Lamming, and Césaire to address problems of colonization and decolonization (557–578).

5. Not to be confused with the dependency on their labor and "raw materials": Prospero says of Caliban: "We cannot miss him: he does make our fire, / Fetch in our wood, and serves in offices / That profit us" (1.2.312–315)—a comment provoked by a complaint against Caliban's ugliness and surliness.

In an essay entitled "Power in the Global Arena," Noam Chomsky cites an American politician who (exactly like Prospero) refers to "*our* raw materials" when the "materials" indicated are found in Third World areas (quoted in Chomsky, "Global," 7, emphasis added).

6. In *Culture and Imperialism* Said speaks of "the authority of the [European] observer . . . confining the non-European to a secondary racial, cultural, ontological status. Yet this secondariness is, paradoxically, essential to the primariness of the European" (70). See also Ashcroft et al.:

> In one very significant way the "discovery" of Africa was the dominant paradigm for the self-discovery of the twentieth-century European world in all its self-contradiction, self-doubt, and self-destruction, for the European journey out of the light of Reason into the Heart of Darkness. As such, the more extreme forms of the self-critical and anarchic models of twentieth-century culture which modernism ushered in can be seen to depend on the existence of a post-colonial Other which provides its condition of formation. (*The Empire Writes Back* 160)

7. In the passage used as epigraph to Chapter 1 of this study.

8. The full quotation reads: "Do battle for the creation of a human world—that is, a world of reciprocal recognitions" (Fanon, *Black Skin,* 155).

Bibliography

Abdel-Messih, M.-T. "Identity Text History: The Concept of Inter/Nationalization in African Fiction." *Research in African Literatures* 26.4 (1995): 163–171.

Abrahams, C., ed. *The Tragic Life: Bessie Head and Literature in Southern Africa.* Trenton, N.J.: Africa World Press, 1990.

Abrahams, P. *Wild Conquest.* London: Faber and Faber, 1951.

Achebe, C. "Chinua Achebe Speaks on the Role of the African Writer." *New African* 242 (1987): 47–48.

———. "An Interview with Chinua Achebe." By A. Appiah, J. Ryle, and D.A.N. Jones. *Times Literary Supplement.* 26 Feb. 1982. 209.

———. "Interview with Chinua Achebe." By O.O. Enekwe. *Okike* 30 (1990): 129–133.

———. "Mapping Out Identity." *The Classic* 3.1 (1984): 24–25.

———. "The Role of the Writer in a New Nation." *Nigeria Magazine* 81 (June 1964): 158.

———. "The Uses of African Literature." *Okike* 15 (1979): 8–17.

———. *African Short Stories.* Ed. C. Achebe and C.L. Innes. London: Heinemann, 1985.

———. *Anthills of the Savannah.* London: Heinemann, 1987.

———. *Arrow of God.* London: Heinemann, 1974.

———. *Beware, Soul Brother: Poems.* London: Heinemann, 1972.

———. *Girls at War and Other Stories.* London: Heinemann, 1972.

———. *Hopes and Impediments: Selected Essays.* New York: Doubleday, 1989.

———. *A Man of the People.* London: Heinemann, 1988.

———. *Morning Yet on Creation Day: Essays.* London: Heinemann Educational, 1975.

———. *No Longer at Ease.* London: Heinemann, 1987.

———. *Things Fall Apart.* London: Heinemann, 1986.

———. *The Trouble with Nigeria.* London: Heinemann, 1983.

Adam, I., and H. Tiffin, eds. *Past the Last Post: Theorizing Post-Colonialism and Postmodernism.* New York: Harvester Wheatsheaf, 1991.

Adedeji, A. "Africa's Strategic Agenda." In *Africa Within the World: Beyond Dispossession and Dependence.* Ed. A. Adedeji. London: Zed Books, 1993. 207–222.

Adedeji, A., ed. *Africa Within the World: Beyond Dispossession and Independence.* London: Zed Books, 1993.

Adeeko, A. "Contests of Text and Context in Chinua Achebe's *Arrow of God.*" *Ariel: A Review of International English Literature* 23.2 (1992): 7–22.

Ahmad, A. "Jameson's Rhetoric of Otherness and the 'National Allegory.'" In *The Post-Colonial Studies Reader*. Ed. B. Ashcroft, G. Griffiths, H. Tiffin. New York: Routledge, 1995. 77–82.

———. *In Theory: Classes, Nations, Literatures*. London: Verso, 1992.

Amadi, E. *The Concubine*. London: Heinemann, 1966.

Amadiume, I. *Reinventing Africa: Matriarchy, Religion and Culture*. London: Zed Books, 1997.

Amuta, C. *The Theory of African Literature: Implications for Practical Criticism.* London: Zed Books, 1989.

Anderson, B. *Imagined Communities: Reflections on the Origins and Spread of Nationalism*. London: Verso, 1983.

Appadurai, A. "Globalization and the Research Imagination." International Symposium on Globalisation and Social Sciences in Africa. The Graduate School for the Humanities and Social Sciences, University of the Witwatersrand, Johannesburg. 14 Sept. 1998.

Appiah, K.A. "Cosmopolitan Patriots." *Critical Inquiry* 23 (1997): 617–639.

———. "Is the Post- in Postmodernism the Post- in Postcolonial?" *Critical Inquiry* 17 (1991): 336–357.

———. "New Literatures, New Theory?" In *Canonisation and Teaching of African Literatures*. Ed. Raoul Granqvist (*Matatu* No 7). Amsterdam: Editions Rodopi B.V., 1990. 57–89.

———. "Reconstructing Racial Identities." *Research in African Literatures* 27.3 (1996): 68–71.

———. *In My Father's House/What Does It Mean to Be an African Today?* London: Methuen, 1992.

Armah, A.K. *The Beautyful Ones Are Not Yet Born*. London: Heinemann, 1969.

———. *The Healers*. London: Heinemann, 1979.

Arnove, A. "Pierre Bourdieu, the Sociology of Intellectuals, and the Language of African Literature." *Novel/A Forum on Fiction* 26.3 (1990): 278–296.

Ashcroft, B., G. Griffiths, and H. Tiffin. *The Empire Writes Back: Theory and Practice in Post-Colonial Literatures*. London: Routledge, 1989.

Ashcroft, B., G. Griffiths, and H. Tiffin, eds. *The Postcolonial Studies Reader*. London/New York: Routledge, 1991.

Auden, W.H. *Collected Shorter Poems 1930–1944*. London: Faber and Faber, 1966.

Bahri, D. "Once More with Feeling: What Is Postcolonialism?" *Ariel: A Review of International English Literature* 26.1 (1995): 51–82.

Bakhtin, M.M. *The Dialogic Imagination: Four Essays*. Ed. M. Holquist; trans. C. Emerson and M. Holquist. Austin: University of Texas Press, 1981.

Balakrishan, G. "The National Imagination." *New Left Review* 211 (1995): 56–69.

Balibar, E. "Racism and Nationalism." In *Race, Nation, Class: Ambiguous Identities*. By E. Balibar and I. Wallerstein. London/New York: Verso, 1991. 36–67.

Balibar, E., and I. Wallerstein. *Race, Nation, Class: Ambiguous Identities*. London: Verso, 1991.

Barber, K. "African Language, Literature and Postcolonial Criticism." *Research in African Literatures* 26.4 (1995): 3–29.

Bayart, J.-F. *The State in Africa: The Politics of the Belly*. Harlow: Longman, 1993.

Bazin, N.T. "Weight of Custom, Signs of Change: Feminism in the Literature of African Women." *World Literature Written in English* 25.2 (1988): 183–197.

Beard, L.S. "Bessie Head, Cape Gooseberry, and the Question of Power." *ALA Bulletin* 12.2 (1986): 41–44.

Beier, U., ed. *Introduction to African Literature: An Anthology of Critical Writing.* London: Longman, 1979.

———. *The Origin of Life and Death: African Creation Myths.* London: Heinemann, 1966.

Benjamin, W. *Illuminations.* Trans. H. Zohn. London: Fontana Press, 1973.

Bernal, M. *Black Athena: The Afroasiatic Roots of Classical Civilization.* London: Vintage, 1991.

Beti, M. *The Poor Christ of Bomba.* London: Heinemann, 1971.

———. *Remember Ruben.* London: Heinemann, 1980.

Bhabha, H.K. "Freedom's Basis in the Indeterminate." *October* 61 (1992): 46–57.

———. "Postcolonial Authority and Postmodern Guilt." In *Cultural Studies.* Ed. L. Grossberg, G. Nelson, and P. Treichler. New York/London: Routledge, 1992. 56–68.

———. "Sly Civility." *October* 34 (1985): 71–80.

———. *The Location of Culture.* London/New York: Routledge, 1994.

Birch, K.S. "The Birch Family: An Introduction to the White Antecedents of the Late Bessie Amelia Head." *English in Africa* 22.1 (1995): 1–18.

Blaut, J.M. *The National Question: Decolonising the Theory of Nationalism.* London: Zed Books, 1987.

Bloom, H. *The Western Canon—The Books and School of the Ages.* London: Macmillan, 1995.

Boahen, A.A. *African Perspectives on Colonialism.* Baltimore, Md.: Johns Hopkins University Press, 1989.

Boehmer, E. "Of Goddesses and Stories: Gender and New Politics in Achebe's *Anthills of the Savannah.*" *Kunapipi* 12.2 (1990): 102–112.

———. "Postcolonial Diasporas." *Pretexts: Studies in Writing and Culture* 7.1 (1998): 141–143.

———. "Transfiguring Colonial Body into Postcolonial Narrative." *Novel: A Forum on Fiction* 26 (1993): 268–277.

———. *Colonial and Postcolonial Literature.* Oxford: Oxford University Press, 1995.

Bollard, J. *Language and the Quest for Political and Social Identity in the African Novel.* Accra: Woeli Publishing Services, 1996.

Booker, M.K. "African Literature and the World System: Dystopian Fiction, Collective Experience, and the Postcolonial Condition." *Research in African Literatures* 26.4 (1995): 58–75.

Boyce-Davis, C. "Private Selves and Public Spaces: Autobiography and the African Woman Writer." *College Language Association Journal* 24.3 (1991): 267–289.

Brown, H.R. "Igbo Words for the Non-Igbo: Achebe's Artistry in *Arrow of God.*" *Research in African Literatures* 12.1 (1981): 69–85.

Brown, L.W. *Women Writers in Black Africa.* Westport, Conn.: Greenwood Press, 1981.

Bruner, C.H. "Bessie Head: Shock and Loss." *ALA Bulletin* 12.2 (1986): 39–41.

Bryce, J. "Inside/Out: Body and Sexuality in Marechera's Fiction." In *Emerging Perspectives on Dambudzo Marechera.* Ed. F. Veit-Wild and A. Chennells. Trenton, N.J.: Africa World Press, 1999. 221–234.

———. "Writing as Power in the Narratives of African Women." *Kunapipi* 16.4 (1994): 618–625.

Bryce-Okunlola, J. "Motherhood as a Metaphor for Creativity in Three African Women's Novels: Flora Nwapa, Rebecca Njau and Bessie Head." In *Motherlands—Black Women's Writing from Africa, the Caribbean and South Asia*. Ed. S. Nasta. London: The Women's Press, 1991. 200–218.

Burns, T.T., and W. Buckley, eds. *Power and Control: Social Structures and Their Transformation*. Beverly Hills: Sage Publications, 1976.

Buuck, D. "African Doppelgänger: Hybridity and Identity in the World of Dambudzo Marechera." *Research in African Literatures* 28.2 (1997): 118–131.

Byron, G. *Byron: Poetical Works*. Ed. F. Page. London: Oxford University Press, 1970.

Cabral, A. *Return to the Source: Selected Speeches of Amilcar Cabral*. Ed. Africa Information Service. New York: Monthly Review, 1973.

Campbell, E. "Bessie Head's Model for Agricultural Reform." *Journal of African Studies* 12.2 (1985): 82–85.

Campbell, J.M. "Beyond Duality: A Buddhist Reading of Bessie Head's *A Question of Power*." *Journal of Commonwealth Literature* 29.1 (1993): 64–81.

Carroll, D. *Chinua Achebe*. London: Macmillan Commonwealth Writers Series, 1980.

———. *Chinua Achebe: Novelist, Poet, Critic*. London: Macmillan, 1990.

Cary, J. *Mister Johnson*. Harmondsworth: Penguin, 1962.

Cary, N.R. "Religious Discourse in the Writing of Bessie Head: A Bakhtinian Reading." *World Literature Written in English* 34.2 (1995): 38–50.

Caute, D. "Marechera and the Colonel—A Zimbabwean writer and the Claims of the State." In *The Espionage of the Saints: Two Essays on Silence and the State*. London: Hamish Hamilton, 1986. 1–96.

———. "Marechera in Black and White." In *Cultural Struggle and Development in Southern Africa*. Ed. P. Kaarsholm. London: Currey, 1991. 95–111.

Césaire, A. *Discourse on Colonialism*. Trans. J. Pinkham. New York: Monthly Review Press, 1972.

Chabal, P. "The African Crisis: Context and Interpretation." In *Postcolonial Identities in Africa*. Ed. R. Werbner and T. Ranger. London: Zed Books, 1996. 29–54.

———. *Political Domination in Africa: Reflections on the Limits of Power*. Cambridge: Cambridge University Press, 1986.

Chambers, I., and L. Curti, eds. *The Postcolonial Question: Common Skies, Divided Horizons*. London: Routledge, 1996.

Chennells, A. "Unstable Identities, Unstable Narratives in *Black Sunlight*." In *Emerging Perspectives on Dambudzo Marechera*. Ed. F. Veit-Wild and A. Chennells. Trenton, N.J.: Africa World Press, 1999. 43–55.

Chetin, S. "Myth, Exile and the Female Condition: Bessie Head's *The Collector of Treasures*." *Journal of Commonwealth Literature* 24.1 (1989): 114–137.

Chinery-Hesse, M. "Divergence and Convergence in the New World Order." In *Africa Within the World: Beyond Dispossession and Independence*. Ed. A. Adedeji. London: Zed Books, 1993. 97–117.

Chinodya, S. *Harvest of Thorns*. London: Heinemann, 1989.

Chinweizu. "An Interview with Chinua Achebe." *Okike* 20 (1981): 19–32.

Chinweizu, O. Jemie, and I. Madubuike. *Toward the Decolonization of African Literature*. Washington: Howard University Press, 1980.

Chomsky, N. "Market Democracy in a Neoliberal Order: Doctrines and Reality." *Pretexts: Studies in Writing and Culture* 7.1 (1998): 9–33.

———. "Power in the Global Arena." *New Left Review* 230 (1998): 3–27.

Clapham, C. "Governmentality and Economic Policy in Sub-Saharan Africa." *Third World Quarterly* 17.4 (1996): 603–624.

Clayton, C. "'A World Elsewhere': Bessie Head as Historian." *English in Africa* 15 (1988): 55–69.
Clayton, C., ed. *Women and Writing in South Africa: A Critical Anthology*. Johannesburg: Heinemann, 1989.
Cobham, R. "Introduction: Special Issue on Women Writers." *Research in African Literatures* 19.2 (1988): 137–142.
Coetzee, P., and C. MacKenzie. "Bessie Head: Rediscovered Early Poems." *English in Africa* 23.1 (1996): 29–46.
Cole, H.M., and C.C. Aniakor. *Igbo Arts: Community and Cosmos*. Los Angeles: University of California Press, 1984.
Collins, R.O., ed. *Problems in the History of Modern Africa*. Princeton: Markus Wiener Publications, 1997.
Colmer, R. "Quis Custodies Custodiet? The Development of Moral Values in *A Man of the People*." *Kunapipi* 12.2 (1990): 89–101.
Conrad, J. *Nostromo*. London: Dent, 1963.
———. *Youth, Heart of Darkness, The End of the Tether*. London: Dent, 1946.
Cook, D. *African Literature: A Critical View*. London: Longman, 1977.
Coombes, A.G. "The Distance Between Two Points: Global Culture and the Liberal Dilemma." In *Travellers' Tales: Narratives of Home and Displacement*. Ed. G. Robertson et al. London/New York: Routledge, 1994. 177–186.
Cooper, B. *To Lay These Secrets Open: Evaluating African Writing*. Cape Town: David Philip, 1992.
Cooper, B., and A. Steyn, eds. *Transgressing Boundaries: New Directions in the Study of Culture in Africa*. Cape Town: University of Cape Town Press, 1996.
Corner, R. "The Start of Weeping Is Always Hard: The Ironic Structure of *No Longer at Ease*." *Literary Half-Yearly* 21.1 (1980): 121–135.
Coronil, F. "Can Postcoloniality Be Decolonized? Imperial Banality and Postcolonial Power." *Public Culture* 5.1 (1992): 89–107.
Coundouriotis, E. "Authority and Invention in the Fiction of Bessie Head." *Research in African Literatures* 27.2 (1996): 16–32.
Crehan, S. "Down and Out in London and Harare: Marechera's Subversion of 'African Literature.'" In *Emerging Perspectives on Dambudzo Marechera*. Ed. F. Veit-Wild and A. Chennells. Trenton, N.J.: Africa World Press, 1998. 285–302.
———. "Ironies of Balance in Achebe's *Girls at War*." *English Studies in Africa* 40.1 (1997): 15–30.
Cullinan, P. "I Try. In Bits. (Letters from Bessie Head 1963–1982)." *New Contrast* 21.4 (December 1992): 66–71.
———. "On the Edge of Everything." *Southern African Review of Books* 4.1 (1996): 4–5.
Currey, J., A. Hill, and K. Sambrook (in conversation with) K.H. Petersen. "Working with Chinua Achebe: The African Writers Series." *Kunapipi* 12.2 (1990): 149–159.
Dangarembga, T. *Nervous Conditions*. London: The Women's Press, 1988.
Darian-Smith, K., L. Gunner, and S. Nuttall, eds. *Text, Theory, Space: Land, Literature and History in South Africa and Australia*. London/New York: Routledge, 1996.
Dathorne, O.R. *African Literature in the Twentieth Century*. London: Heinemann, 1975.
Davidson, B. "For a Politics of Restitution." In *Africa Within the World: Beyond Dispossession and Dependence*. Ed. A. Adedeji. London: Zed Books, 1993. 17–27.
———. *Africa: History of a Continent*. London: Weidenfeld and Nicolson, 1966.

———. *Africa in Modern History: The Search for a New Society*. London: Lane, 1978.
———. *The African Past: Chronicles from Antiquity to Modern Times*. London: Longman, 1964.
———. *The Black Man's Burden: Africa and the Curse of the Nation-State*. London: Currey, 1992.
———. *Can Africa Survive? Arguments Against Growth Without Development*. London: Heinemann, 1975.
———. *Discovering Africa's Past*. London: Longman, 1978.
———. *Modern Africa: A Social and Political History.* London: Longman, 1989.
———. *The Search for Africa: A History in the Making*. London: Currey, 1994.
Daymond, M. Introduction to *The Cardinals—with Meditations and Short Stories* by Bessie Head. Cape Town: David Philip, 1993. vii–xviii.
Desmond, C. *The Discarded People*. Harmondsworth: Penguin African Library, 1971.
Dickens, C. *Little Dorrit*. Harmondsworth: Penguin, 1967.
Diop, C.A. *The African Origin of Civilization—Myth or Reality*. New York: Lawrence Hill, 1974.
———. *The Cultural Unity of Black Africa: The Domains of Matriarchy and of Patriarchy in Classical Antiquity*. London: Karnak House, 1989.
Dirlik, A. "The Postcolonial Aura: Third World Criticism in the Age of Global Capitalism." *Critical Inquiry* 20.4 (1994): 328–356.
Doherty, C. "Dambudzo Marechera: *Cemetery of Mind*." (Review). *New Coin* 29.2 (1994): 58–62.
Driver, D. "Gestures of Expatriation and Belonging." (Review of *The Cardinals*). *Southern African Review of Books* 5.5 (September/October 1993): 16–18.
Du Bois, W.E.B. *The Souls of Black Folk*. New York: Bantam Books, 1989.
Duerden, D., and C. Pieterse, eds. *African Writers Talking: A Collection of Interviews*. London: Heinemann, 1972.
During, S. "Postmodernism or Post-Colonialism Today." *Textual Practice* 1.1 (1987): 32–47.
———. *Foucault and Literature: Towards a Genealogy of Writing*. London: Routledge, 1992.
During, S., ed. *The Cultural Studies Reader*. London: Routledge, 1993.
Du Toit, P. *State-Building and Democracy in Southern Africa: A Comparative Study of Botswana, South Africa and Zimbabwe*. Pretoria: HSRC Publishers, 1995.
Eagleton, T., F. Jameson, and E. Said, eds. *Nationalism, Colonialism and Literature*. Minneapolis: University of Minnesota Press, 1990.
Egudu, R.N. "Achebe and the Igbo Narrative Tradition." *Research in African Literatures* 12.1 (1981): 43–54.
Ehling, H.G., ed. *Critical Approaches to Anthills of the Savannah*. Amsterdam: Rodopi, 1991.
Eilersen, G.S. *Bessie Head/Thunder Behind Her Ears: Her Life and Writing*. Cape Town: David Philip, 1995.
Ekeh, P. "Colonialism and the Two Publics in Africa." *Comparative Studies in Society and History* 17 (1975): 91–112.
Ekwensi, C. *Survive the Peace*. London: Heinemann, 1976.
Elder, A.E. "Bessie Head: New Considerations, Continuing Questions." *Callaloo* 16.1 (1993): 277–284.
Eldredge, E.E. *A South African Kingdom: The Pursuit of Security in Nineteenth-Century Lesotho*. Cambridge: Cambridge University Press, 1993.
Eliot, T.S. *Collected Poems 1909–1962*. London: Faber and Faber, 1963.

Emecheta, B. *The Joys of Motherhood*. London: Heinemann, 1980.
Emenyonu, E.N. "Chinua Achebe's *Things Fall Apart*: A Classic Study in Colonial Diplomatic Tactlessness." In *Chinua Achebe: A Celebration*. Ed. K.H. Petersen and A. Rutherford. Oxford: Heinemann, 1991. 83–88.
———. *The Rise of the Igbo Novel*. Oxford: Oxford University Press, 1978.
Emmerij, L. "Co-Responsibility Versus Double Standards." In *Africa Within the World: Beyond Dispossession and Dependence*. Ed. A. Adedeji. London: Zed Books, 1993. 97–117.
Enekwe, O.O. "Interview with Chinua Achebe." *Okike* 30 (1990): 129–133.
Englebert, P. "The Contemporary African State: Neither African nor State." Feature Review. *Third World Quarterly* 18.4 (1997): 767–775.
Evasdaughter, E.N. "Bessie Head's *A Question of Power* Read as a Mariner's Guide to Paranoia." *Research in African Literatures* 20.1 (1989): 72–83.
Eze, E.C., ed. *Postcolonial African Philosophy—A Critical Reader*. London: Blackwell, 1997.
Ezenwa-Ohaeto. "Patriots and Parasites: The Metaphor of Power in Achebe's *Anthills of the Savannah*." In *Critical Approaches to Anthills of the Savannah*. Ed. H.G. Ehling. Amsterdam: Rodopi, 1991. 23–24.
———. *Chinua Achebe: A Biography*. Oxford: James Currey, 1997.
Fabian, J. "Popular Culture in Africa: Findings and Conjectures." *Africa* 48.8 (1978): 315–334.
———. *Power and Performance: Ethnographic Explorations Through Proverbial Wisdom and Theater in Shaba, Zaïre*. London: University of Wisconsin Press, 1990.
Fanon, F. *Black Skin, White Masks*. Trans. L. Markmann. St. Albans, Hertfordshire: Paladin, 1970.
———. *A Dying Colonialism*. New York: Grove Press, 1965.
———. *Towards the African Revolution*. Harmondsworth: Pelican, 1970.
———. *The Wretched of the Earth*. Trans. C. Farrington. Harmondsworth: Penguin, 1967.
Farah, N. "The Creative Writer and the Politician." *The Classic* 3.1 (1984): 27–30.
———. *Close, Sesame*. London: Allison & Busby, 1983.
———. *Maps*. New York: Pantheon, 1986.
———. *Sardines*. London: Heinemann, 1982.
———. *Sweet and Sour Milk*. London: Heinemann, 1980.
Fido, E.S. "Motherlands: Self and Separation in the Work of Buchi Emecheta, Bessie Head and Jean Rhys." In *Motherlands*. Ed. S. Nasta. London: The Women's Press, 1991. 330–349.
Fieldhouse, D.K. *The Colonial Empires/A Comparative Survey from the Eighteenth Century*. London: Methuen, 1982.
Foster, K. "Soul-Food for the Starving: Dambudzo Marechera's *House of Hunger*." *Journal of Commonwealth Literature* 27.1 (1992): 58–70.
Foucault, M. *Discipline and Punish: The Birth of the Prison*. Trans. A. Sheridan. New York: Pantheon, 1977.
———. *Power/Knowledge: Selected Interviews and Other Writings 1972–1977*. Ed. C. Gordon. Trans. C. Gordon et al. Brighton: Harvester, 1980.
Fourny, J.-F., and M.-P. Ha. "Multiculturalism. Introduction: The History of an Idea." *Research in African Literatures* 28.4 (1997): 1–7.
Fraser, R. "The Slow Sound of His Tongue: Speech Impediments and Political Impediments in Marechera's Work." In *Emerging Perspectives on Dambudzo Marechera*.

Ed. F. Veit-Wild and A. Chennells. Trenton, N.J.: Africa World Press, 1999. 177–192.
Frost, R. *Complete Poems of Robert Frost*. London: Jonathan Cape, 1966.
Gagiano, A.H. "A.C. Jordan's *Tales from Southern Africa*." *Alternation* 4.2 (1997): 68–80.
———. "'Barbarism' and 'Civilization' in Shakespeare's *Titus Andronicus* and Marechera's *Black Sunlight*." *The Literary Griot* 10.1 (1998): 13–27.
———. "Bessie Head's Questioning of Power." Paper given at the conference "Women, the Arts and South Africa" held at the University of Natal (Pietermaritzburg). (Conference Proceedings 1) (1995): 67–75.
———. "Blixen, Ngugi: Recounting Kenya." In *Ngugi wa Thiong'o: Texts and Contexts*. Ed. C. Cantalupo. Trenton, N.J.: Africa World Press, 1995. 95–110.
———. "Encountering African Novels in English." In *Cultural Synergy in South Africa: Weaving Strands of Africa and Europe*. Ed. M.E. Steyn and K.B. Motshabi. Randburg: Knowledge Resources, 1996. 131–145.
———. "Finding Foundations for Change in Bessie Head's *The Cardinals*." *The Journal of Commonwealth Literature* 31.2 (1996): 83–96.
———. "'I Do Not Know Her, But Someone Ought to Know Her': Chenjerai Hove's *Bones*." *World Literature Written in English* 32.2 and 33.1 (1992–1993): 33–43.
———. "Mongane Serote's *To Every Birth Its Blood*: Painting the True Colours of Apartheid." In *An Introduction to the African Prose Narrative*. Ed. L. Losambe. Pretoria: Kagiso Tertiary, 1996. 122–130.
———. "Patterns of Leadership in Bessie Head's *Maru* and *A Bewitched Crossroad: An African Saga*." Paper given at the Bessie Head Conference at the National University of Singapore, 1996.
———. "Serote's Novel and Visser's Criticism." *The English Academy Review* 6 (1989): 84–91.
———. "The Symbolic Dimension of Achebe's *No Longer at Ease*." Paper given at the African Literature Association at the University of Texas in Austin, 1998. ALA Annual 1998 (forthcoming as "Multiculturalism and Hybridity in African Literatures").
———. "'The Tree Goes On': Reconsidering Alex La Guma's *Time of the Butcherbird*." *English in Africa* 24.1 (1997): 23–30.
Gakwandi, S.A. *The Novel and Contemporary Experience in Africa*. London: Heinemann, 1977.
Gardner, S. "Bessie Head: Production Under Drought Conditions." In *Women and Writing in South Africa: A Critical Anthology*. Ed. C. Clayton. Johannesburg: Heinemann, 1989. 225–235.
Gardner, S., and P.E. Scott, eds. *Bessie Head/A Bibliography*. Grahamstown, South Africa: The National English Literary Museum, 1986.
Gates, H.L., Jr. "Critical Fanonism." *Critical Inquiry* 17.3 (1991): 457–470.
———. *Figures in Black: Words, Signs and the "Racial" Self*. New York: Oxford University Press, 1989.
———. *The Signifying Monkey: A Theory of Afro-American Literary Criticism*. Oxford: Oxford University Press, 1988.
Gates, H.L., Jr., ed. *Black Literature and Literary Theory*. London: Methuen, 1984.
Gaylard, G. "Dambudzo Marechera and Nationalist Criticism." *English in Africa* 20.2 (1993): 89–105.
———. "Marechera's Politic Body: The Menippeanism of a 'Lost Generation' in Africa?" In *Emerging Perspectives on Dambudzo Marechera*. Ed. F. Veit-Wild and A. Chennells. Trenton, N.J.: Africa World Press, 1999. 75–91.

———. "Menippean Marechera: Africa's New Antirealism." *inter action* 111 (1995): 181–192.

Gellner, E. *Plough, Sword and Book: The Structure of Human History*. Chicago: University of Chicago Press, 1988.

———. *Reason and Culture: The Historic Role of Rationality and Rationalism*. Oxford: Blackwell, 1992.

Gikandi, S. "Chinua Achebe and the Poetics of Location: The Uses of Space in *Things Fall Apart* and *No Longer at Ease*." In *Essays on African Writing 1: A Re-evaluation.* Ed. A. Gurnah. Oxford: Heinemann, 1993. 1–12.

———. "Introduction: Africa, Diaspora, and the Discourse of Modernity." *Research in African Literatures* 27.4 (1996): 1–6.

———. *Reading Chinua Achebe: Language and Ideology in Fiction*. London: Currey, 1991.

———. *Reading the African Novel*. London: Currey, 1987.

Gilroy, P. *The Black Atlantic: Modernity and Double Consciousness*. Cambridge, Mass.: Harvard University Press, 1993.

Gordimer, N. "To Hold the Yam and the Knife: *Anthills of the Savannah*." In *Writing and Being* (The Charles Eliot Norton Lectures 1994). Cambridge, Mass.: Harvard University Press, 1995. 70–93.

Gover, D. "The Fairy Tale and the Nightmare." In *The Tragic Life: Bessie Head and Literature in Southern Africa*. Ed. C. Abrahams. Trenton, N.J.: Africa World Press, 1990. 113–121.

Griffiths, G. "Chinua Achebe: When Did You Last See Your Father?" *World Literature Written in English* 27.1 (1987): 18–27.

———. "Imitation, Abrogation and Appropriation: The Production of the Post-Colonial Text." *Kunapipi* IX (1987): 13–20.

———. "Language and Action in the Novels of Chinua Achebe." *African Literature Today* 5 (1971): 88–105.

Gugelberger, G.M., ed. *Marxism and African Literature*. London: Currey, 1985.

Gurnah, A., ed. *Essays on African Writing (1): A Re-evaluation*. Oxford: Heinemann, 1993.

Gurr, A., ed. *The Yearbook of English Studies*, Vol. 27 (1997). Special Number: "The Politics of Postcolonial Criticism." London: W.S. Maney and Son Ltd. for "The Modern Humanities Research Association," 1997.

Ha, M.-P. "Relations of Cultures." (Review). *Research in African Literatures* 28.4 (1997): 154–164.

Hall, S. "Cultural Identity and Cinematic Representation." *Framework* 36 (1989): 69–70.

———. "Introduction: Who Needs 'Identity'?" In *Questions of Cultural Identity*. Ed. S. Hall and P. du Gay. London: Sage Publications, 1996. 1–17.

———. "Random Thoughts Provoked by the Conference Identities, Democracy, Culture and Communication in South Africa." *Critical Arts* 11.1–2 (1997): 1–16.

Harlow, B. *Resistance Literature*. New York and London: Methuen, 1987.

Harris, W. *The Womb of Space/The Cross-Cultural Imagination*. London: Greenwood Press, 1983.

Harrow, K.W. "Bessie Head's *The Collector of Treasures*." *Callaloo* 16.1 (1993): 169–179.

———. "Flying Without Perching—Metaphor, Proverb, and Gendered Discourse." In *Thresholds of Change in African Literature—The Emergence of a Tradition*. Portsmouth, N.H.: Heinemann, 1994. 109–137.

———. *Thresholds of Change in African Literature: The Emergence of a Tradition.* London: Currey, 1994.
Harvey, P. "Black and White from Rhodesia: Memories of Dambudzo." In *Emerging Perspectives on Dambudzo Marechera.* Ed. F. Veit-Wild and A. Chennells. Trenton, N.J.: Africa World Press, 1998. 255–266.
Hayer, S. Interview with Bessie Head. *CRNLE Reviews Journal* 2 (1991): 1–7.
Head, B. "For 'Napoleon Bonaparte,' Jenny and Kate." *Southern African Review of Books* 3.6 (1990): 12–15.
———. "Reply." *Index on Censorship* 4.2 (1975): 23.
———. *A Bewitched Crossroad: An African Saga.* Johannesburg: Ad. Donker, 1984.
———. *The Cardinals—with Meditations and Short Stories.* Ed. M.J. Daymond. Cape Town: David Philip, 1993.
———. *The Collector of Treasures and Other Botswana Village Tales.* London: Heinemann, 1977.
———. *A Gesture of Belonging: Letters from Bessie Head, 1965–1979.* Ed. R. Vigne. London: Heinemann, 1991.
———. *Maru.* London: Heinemann, 1972.
———. *A Question of Power.* London: Heinemann, 1974.
———. *Serowe: Village of the Rain Wind.* London: Heinemann, 1981.
———. *Tales of Tenderness and Power.* Ed. G.S. Eilersen. Johannesburg: Ad. Donker, 1989.
———. *When Rain Clouds Gather.* London: Heinemann, 1987.
———. *A Woman Alone: Autobiographical Writings.* Ed. C. MacKenzie. Oxford: Heinemann, 1990.
Hofmeyr. I. "Not the Magic Talisman: Rethinking Oral Literature in South Africa." *World Literature Today* 70.1 (1996): 88–92.
hooks, bell. "Feminism: A Transformational Politic." In *Multicultural Experiences, Multicultural Theories.* Ed. Mary F. Rogers. New York: McGraw-Hill, 1996. 415–421.
Hove, C. "Zimbabwe: One State, One Faith, One Lord." *Index on Censorship* 20.6 (1991): 32.
———. *Bones.* Cape Town: David Philip, 1988.
Ibrahim, H. "The Violated Universe: Neo-Colonial Sexual and Political Consciousness in Dambudzo Marechera." *Research in African Literatures* 27.1 (1990): 79–90.
———. *Bessie Head: Subversive Identities in Exile.* Charlottesville: University of Virginia Press, 1996.
Innes, C.L. "Reversal and Return in Fiction by Bessie Head and Ama Ata Aidoo." In *"Return" in Post-Colonial Writing: A Cultural Labyrinth.* Amsterdam: Rodopi, 1994. 69–75.
———. *Chinua Achebe.* Cambridge: Cambridge University Press, 1990.
Innes, C.L., and B. Lindfors, eds. *Critical Perspectives on Chinua Achebe.* London: Heinemann, 1979.
Irele, A. "The African Imagination." *Research in African Literatures* 21.1 (1990): 47–67.
———. "The Criticism of Modern African Literature." In *Perspectives on African Literature.* Ed. C. Heywood. London: Heinemann, 1971. 9–24.
———. *The African Experience in Literature and Ideology.* London: Heinemann, 1981.
Jameson, F. "Third-World Literature in the Era of Late Capitalism." *Social Text* 15 (1986): 65–88.

———. *The Political Unconscious: Narrative as a Socially Symbolic Act*. London: Methuen, 1981.
JanMohamed, A.R. *Manichean Aesthetics: The Politics of Literature in Colonial Africa*. Amherst: University of Massachusetts Press, 1988.
Jeyifo, B. "For Chinua Achebe: The Resilience and the Predicament of Obierika." In *Chinua Achebe: A Celebration*. Ed. K.H. Petersen and A. Rutherford. Oxford: Heinemann, 1991. 51–70.
———. "The Nature of Things: Arrested Decolonization and Critical Theory." *Research in African Literatures* 21.1 (1990): 33–46.
Jeyifo, B., ed. *Contemporary Nigerian Literature: A Retrospective and Prospective Exploration*. Lagos: Nigeria Magazine, 1985.
Johnson, J. "Structures of Meaning in the Novels of Bessie Head." *Kunapipi* 8.1 (1986): 56–69.
Jones, E.O., E. Palmer, and M. Jones, eds. *Women in African Literature Today* (*A.L.T.* 15). London: Currey, 1987.
Joseph, M.S. "A Pre-Modernist Reading of 'The Drum': Chinua Achebe and the Theme of the Eternal Return." *Ariel: A Review of International English Literature* 28.1 (1997): 149–166.
Julien, E. *African Novels and the Question of Orality*. Bloomington: Indiana University Press, 1992.
Jumbam, K. *The White Man of God*. London: Heinemann, 1980.
Kanaganayakam, C. "Art and Orthodoxy in Chinua Achebe's *Anthills of the Savannah*." *Ariel: A Review of International English Literature* 23.2 (1993): 35–51.
Kane, C.H. *Ambiguous Adventure*. Trans. K. Woods. London: Heinemann, 1972.
Kanneh, K. "What Is African Literature?: Ethnography and Criticism." In *Writing and Africa*. Ed. M.-H. Msiska and P. Hyland. New York: Addison Wesley Longman, 1997. 69–86.
———. *African Identities: Race, Nation and Culture in Ethnography, Pan-Africanism and Black Literatures*. London: Routledge, 1998.
Katrak, K.H. "Decolonizing Culture: Toward a Theory for Postcolonial Women's Texts." *Modern Fiction Studies* 35.1 (1985): 157–179.
———. "From Pauline to Dikeledi: The Philosophical and Political Vision of Bessie Head's Protagonists." *Ba Shiru* 12.2 (1985): 26–35.
Kaufman, W., ed. *The Portable Nietzsche*. New York: Viking, 1954.
Kedourie, E., ed. *Nationalism in Asia and Africa*. London: Weidenfeld and Nicolson, 1970.
Kendall, K.L. *Basali! Stories by and About Women in Lesotho*. Pietermaritzburg: University of Natal Press, 1995.
Kibera, V. "Adopted Motherlands: The Novels of Marjorie Macgoye and Bessie Head." In *Motherlands*. Ed. S. Nasta. London: The Women's Press, 1991. 310–327.
Killam, D.G. "A Personal Note." *Kunapipi* 12.2 (1990): 160–162.
———. *The Novels of Chinua Achebe*. London: Heinemann, 1969.
Killam, D.G., ed. *African Writers on African Writing*. London: Heinemann, 1973.
———. *The Writing of East and Central Africa*. London: Heinemann, 1984.
King, B. "The Revised *Arrow of God*." *Echos du Commonwealth* 5 (1979): 93–102.
King, B., and K. Ogungbesan. *A Celebration of Black and African Writing*. Zaria, Nigeria: Ahmadu Bello Press, 1975.
Klopper, D. "The Edge of the Ruthless Dream." *Southern African Review of Books* 5.2 (1993): 15–16.
———. "Freeing White and Black." *Die Suid-Afrikaan* 46 (1993): 46–47.

———. "The Outsider Within: Marginality as Symptom in Marechera's 'Throne of Bayonets.'" In *Emerging Perspectives on Dambudzo Marechera*. Ed. F. Veit-Wild and A. Chennells. Trenton, N.J.: Africa World Press, 1999. 121–135.

Kossick, S.G. "Bessie Head: *The Cardinals*" (Review). *Unisa English Studies* 32.1 (1994): 36–37.

Kristeva, J. *Nations Without Nationalism*. Trans. L.S. Roudiez. New York: Columbia University Press, 1993.

Kubayanda, J. "Unfinished Business: Dictatorial Literature of Post-Independence Latin America and Africa." *Research in African Literatures* 28.4 (1997): 38–53.

Kunene, D.P. "Language, Literature and the Struggle for Liberation in South Africa." *African Literature Today* 18 (1991): 37–50.

La Guma, A. *Time of the Butcherbird*. London: Heinemann, 1979.

Lamming, G. *The Pleasures of Exile*. London: Alison and Busby, 1984.

Landau, P.S. *The Realm of the Word: Language, Gender, and Christianity in a Southern African Kingdom*. London: James Currey, 1995.

Lansu, A. "Interview with Dambudzo Marechera." *Dambudzo Marechera: A Source Book on His Life and Work*. London: Hans Zell, 1992.

Lazarus, N. "Disavowing Decolonization: Fanon, Nationalism, and the Problematic of Representation in Current Theories of Colonial Discourse." *Research in African Literatures* 24.4 (1993): 69–98.

Lemarchand, R. *Burundi: Ethnocide as Discourse and Practice*. Cambridge: Cambridge University Press, 1994.

Levin, M., and L. Taitz. "Fictional Autobiographies or Autobiographical Fictions?" In *Emerging Perspectives on Dambudzo Marechera*. Ed. F. Veit-Wild and A. Chennells. Trenton, N.J.: Africa World Press, 1999. 163–175.

Lewis, D. "*The Cardinals* and Bessie Head's Allegories of Self." *World Literature Today* 70.1 (1996): 73–77.

Lewis, G. "Interview with Chinua Achebe." In *Conversations with Chinua Achebe*. Ed. B. Lindfors. Jackson: University Press of Mississippi, 1997. 185–191.

Lewis, M.E.B. "Beyond Content in the Analysis of Folklore in Literature: Chinua Achebe's *Arrow of God*." *Research in African Literatures* 7 (1976): 44–52.

Leys, C. "Confronting the African Tragedy." *New Left Review* 204 (1994): 33–47.

Lilford, G. "Traces of Tradition: The Probability of the Marecheran Manfish." In *Emerging Perspectives on Dambudzo Marechera*. Ed. F. Veit-Wild and A. Chennells. Trenton, N.J.: Africa World Press, 1999. 283–297.

Lindfors, B., ed. *Approaches to Teaching Achebe's* Things Fall Apart. New York: The Modern Language Association of America, 1991.

———. *Conversations with Chinua Achebe*. Jackson: University Press of Mississippi, 1997.

———. *Folklore in Nigerian Literature*. New York: Africana Publication Co., 1973.

———. *Research Priorities in African Literatures*. Oxford: Hans Zell Publishers, 1992.

Lindfors, B., et al., eds. *Palaver: Interviews with Five African Writers in Texas: Chinua Achebe, John Pepper Clark, Dennis Brutus, Ezekiel Mphahlele and Kofi Awoonor*. Austin: African and African-American Research Institute, University of Texas at Austin, 1972.

Lo Liyong, T. "Interview with Raditlhalo." *New Coin* 33.1 (1990): 46–59.

Loomba, A. *Colonialism/Postcolonialism*. London/New York: Routledge, 1998.

Losambe, L., ed. *An Introduction to the African Prose Narrative*. Pretoria: Kagiso Tertiary, 1996.

MacKenzie, C. "Allegiance and Alienation in the Novels of Bessie Head." In *Essays on African Writing 1: A Re-Evaluation.* Ed. A. Gurnah. Oxford: Heinemann, 1993. 111–125.

———. *Bessie Head: An Introduction.* Grahamstown, South Africa: National English Literary Museum, 1989.

MacKenzie, C., and C. Clayton, eds. Bessie Head interviewed by Michelle Adler et al. *Between the Lines: Interviews with Bessie Head, Sheila Roberts, Ellen Kuzwayo and Miriam Tlali.* Grahamstown, South Africa: NELM (1989): 5–29.

MacKenzie, C.G. "The Metamorphosis of Piety in *Things Fall Apart.*" *Research in African Literatures* 27.2 (1996): 128–138.

Maes-Jelinék, H. "Another Future for Post-Colonial Studies? Wilson Harris' Post-Colonial Philosophy of the 'Savage Mind.'" *Wasafiri* 24 (1996): 3–8.

Mahood, M.M. *The Colonial Encounter.* London: Rex Collings, 1977.

Maithufi, S. "Bessie Head's *When Rain Clouds Gather*: A Novel of Monopolies, Exclusion and Institutionalism." *Vista Occasional Papers* 4.1 (1996): 46–51.

Maja-Pearce, A. *A Mask Dancing: Nigerian Novelists of the Eighties.* London: Hans Zell Publishers, 1992.

Mamdani, M. *Citizen and Subject: Contemporary Africa and the Legacy of Late Colonialism.* Princeton, N.J.: Princeton University Press, 1996.

Mannoni, O. *Prospero and Caliban: The Psychology of Colonization.* New York: Praeger, 1964.

Maqagi, S. "Taboo: A Positive Transgression? A Study of Bessie Head's *The Cardinals.*" Paper given at the AUETSA Conference, July 1995, Pietermaritzburg.

Marechera, D. "Dambudzo Marechera: Zimbabwe's Prodigal Son." (Interview). *New African* 200 (1984): 64–65.

———. "Jumping on the Bandwagon of Oppression: A Book Review." In *Emerging Perspectives on Dambudzo Marechera.* Ed. F. Veit-Wild and A. Chennells. Trenton, N.J.: Africa World Press, 1998. 269–270.

———. *The Black Insider.* Harare: Baobab Books, 1990.

———. *Black Sunlight.* London: Heinemann, 1980.

———. *Cemetery of Mind.* Poems: Comp. and ed. F. Veit-Wild. Harare: Baobab Books, 1992.

———. *The House of Hunger.* London: Heinemann, 1978.

———. *Mindblast or the Definitive Buddy.* Harare: The College Press, 1984.

———. *Scrapiron Blues.* Comp. and ed. F. Veit-Wild. Harare: Baobab Books, 1994.

Marquard, J. "Bessie Head: Exile and Community in Southern Africa" (Interview). *London Magazine* 18.9/10 (1978/1979): 48–61.

Martin, R. *The Sociology of Power.* London: Routledge and Kegan Paul, 1977.

Matsikidze, I.P. "Toward a Redemptive Political Philosophy: Bessie Head's *Maru.*" *World Literature Written in English* 30.2 (1990): 105–109.

Maughan-Brown, D. "*Anthills of the Savannah* and the Ideology of Leadership." *Kunapipi* 12.2 (1990): 139–148.

Mazrui, A. "Language and the Quest for Liberation in Africa." *Third World Quarterly* 14.2 (1993): 351–363.

———. *The African Condition: A Political Diagnosis.* London: Heinemann, 1980.

Mbembe, A. "The Banality of Power and the Aesthetics of Vulgarity in the Postcolony." *Public Culture* 4.2 (1992): 1–30.

———. "Prosaics of Servitude and Authoritarian Civilities." *Public Culture* 5.1 (1992): 123–145.

———. "Provisional Notes on the Postcolony." *Africa* 62.1 (1991): 3–37.

McClintock, A. "The Angel of Progress: Pitfalls of the Term 'Post-Colonialism.'" In *Colonial Discourse and Post-Colonial Theory: A Reader.* Ed. P. Williams and L. Chrisman. Hemel Hempstead, Hertfordshire: Harvester Wheatsheaf, 1994. 291–304.

———. *Imperial Leather: Race, Gender and Sexuality in the Colonial Context.* London: Routledge, 1995.

McClintock, A., A. Mufti, and E. Shohat, eds. *Dangerous Liaisons: Gender, Nation and Postcolonial Perspectives.* Minneapolis: University of Minnesota Press, 1997.

McLoughlin, T.O. "Black Writing in English from Zimbabwe." In *The Writing of East and Central Africa.* Ed. D.G. Killam. London: Heinemann, 1984. 100–119.

———. "Resistance and Affirmation: Marechera's 'My Arms Vanished Mountains.'" In *Emerging Perspectives on Dambudzo Marechera.* Ed. F. Veit-Wild and A. Chennells. Trenton, N.J.: Africa World Press, 1999. 137–150.

Memmi, A. *The Colonizer and the Colonized.* New York: Orion Press, 1965.

Menager-Everson, V.S. "*Maru* by Bessie Head. The Dilepe Quartet from Drought to Beer." *Commonwealth: Essays and Studies* 14.2 (1992): 44–48.

Metrovich, R., ed. *Nigeria: The Biafra War.* Pretoria: The African Institute, 1969.

Mhiripiri, N. "Danger! Stay Away from Meaningless Poems!" In *Emerging Perspectives on Dambudzo Marechera.* Ed. F. Veit-Wild and A. Chennells. Trenton, N.J.: Africa World Press, 1999. 151–160.

Michel, M. "Positioning the Subject: Locating Postcolonial Studies." *Ariel: A Review of International English Literature* 26.1 (1995): 83–99.

Mignolo, W.D. "Afterword: Human Understanding and (Latin) American Interests—The Politics and Sensibilities of Geocultural Locations." *Poetics Today* 16.1 (1995): 171–214.

Mihailovich-Dickman, V., ed. *"Return" in Post-Colonial Writing.* Amsterdam: Rodopi, 1994.

Miller-Bagley, M. "Miscegenation, Marginalisation and the Messianic in Bessie Head's *Maru.*" *World Literature Written in English* 34.2 (1995): 51–69.

Minh-ha, T.T. "Not You/Like You: Postcolonial Women and the Interlocking Questions of Identity and Difference." In *Dangerous Liaisons: Gender, Nation and Postcolonial Perspectives.* Ed. A. McClintock, A. Mufti, and E. Shohat. Minneapolis: University of Minnesota Press, 1996. 415–419.

———. *Woman, Native, Other/Writing Postcoloniality and Feminism.* Bloomington: Indiana University Press, 1989.

Mongia, P., ed. *Contemporary Postcolonial Theory: A Reader.* London: Arnold, 1996.

Moore, G. *Twelve African Writers.* London: Hutchinson University Library for Africa, 1980.

Moore-Gilbert, B. *Post-Colonial Theory: Contexts, Practices, Politics.* Verso: London/New York, 1997.

Morell, K.L., ed. *In Person: Achebe, Awoonor, and Soyinka at the University of Washington.* Seattle: African Studies Programme, Institute for Comparative and Foreign Area Studies, University of Washington, 1975.

Morna, C.L. "Chinua Achebe Speaks on the Role of the African Writer." *New African* 242 (1987): 47–48.

Morrison, T. *Playing in the Dark: Whiteness and the Literary Imagination.* Cambridge, Mass.: Harvard University Press, 1992.

Mouffe, C. "For a Politics of Nomadic Identity." In *Travellers' Tales: Narratives of Home and Displacement.* Ed. G. Robertson et al. London/New York: Routledge, 1994. 105–113.

Mphahlele, E. *Down Second Avenue.* London: Faber and Faber, 1959.

Msiska, M.-H., and P. Hyland, eds. *Writing and Africa*. New York: Addison Wesley Longman, 1997.
Mudimbe, V.Y. *The Idea of Africa*. Bloomington: Indiana University Press, 1994.
———. *The Invention of Africa: Gnosis, Philosophy and the Order of Knowledge*. Bloomington: Indiana University Press, 1988.
Muponde, R. "Reconstructing Childhood: Social Banditry in Dambudzo Marechera's Children's Stories." In *Emerging Perspectives on Dambudzo Marechera*. Ed. F. Veit-Wild and A. Chennells. Trenton, N.J.: Africa World Press, 1999. 253–263.
Mwangi, M. *Carcase for Hounds*. London: Heinemann, 1974.
———. *Striving for the Wind*. London: Heinemann, 1988.
Mzamane, M.V. "New Writing from Zimbabwe: Dambudzo Marechera's *The House of Hunger*." *African Literature Today* 13 (1983): 201–225.
Ndebele, N.S. *Rediscovery of the Ordinary: Essays on South African Literature and Culture*. Johannesburg: COSAW, 1991.
Newell, S. "Conflict and Transformation in Bessie Head's *A Question of Power, Serowe: Village of the Rain Wind* and *A Bewitched Crossroad*." *Journal of Commonwealth Literature* 30.2 (1995): 65–83.
Ngara, E. "Achebe as Artist: The Place and Significance of *Anthills of the Savannah*." *Kunapipi* 12.2 (1990): 113–129.
———. *Art and Ideology in the African Novel: A Study of the Influence of Marxism on African Writing*. London: Heinemann, 1985.
———. *Stylistic Criticism and the African Novel: A Study of the Language, Art and Content of African Fiction*. London: Heinemann, 1982.
Ngcobo, L.G. "Bessie Head: A Thematic Approach." In *Perspectives on South African English Literature*. Ed. M. Chapman, C. Gardiner, and E. Mphahlele. Johannesburg: Ad. Donker, 1992. 342–351.
Ngugi wa Thiong'o. *Decolonising the Mind: The Politics of Language in African Literature*. London: Currey, 1986.
———. *Devil on the Cross*. London: Heinemann, 1982.
———. *Homecoming: Essays on African and Caribbean Literature, Culture and Politics*. London: Heinemann, 1972.
———. *Moving the Centre: The Struggle for Cultural Freedoms*. London: Currey, 1993.
———. *Petals of Blood*. London: Heinemann, 1977.
———. *The River Between*. London: Heinemann, 1965.
———. *Weep Not, Child*. London: Heinemann Educational, 1964.
———. *Writers in Politics: Essays*. London: Heinemann, 1981.
Nichols, L. "In Memoriam: Bessie Head." *ALA Bulletin* 12.3 (1986): 16–18.
Nicholls, B. "Post-Colonial Politics in Homi Bhabha's *The Location of Culture*." *Southern Review* 30.1 (1997): 4–25.
Niven, A. "Chinua Achebe and the Possibility of Modern Tragedy." *Kunapipi* 12.2 (1990): 41–50.
Nixon, R. "Border Country: Bessie Head's Frontline States." In *Homelands, Harlem and Hollywood: South African Culture and the World Beyond*. New York/London: Routledge, 1994. 101–130.
———. "Caribbean and African Appropriations of *The Tempest*." *Critical Inquiry* 13 (1987): 557–578.
———. "Refugees and Homecomings: Bessie Head and the End of Exile." In *Travellers' Tales: Narratives of Home and Displacement*. Ed. G. Robertson et al. London/New York: Routledge, 1994. 114–128.

———. "Rural Transnationalism/Bessie Head's Southern Spaces." In *Text, Theory, Space—Land, Literature and History in South Africa and Australia*. Ed. K. Darian-Smith, L. Gunner, and S. Nuttall. London/New York: Routledge, 1996. 243–253.

Nkosi, L. "Sex and the Law in South Africa." In *The Transplanted Heart*. Benin: Ethiopia, 1975. 22–30.

———. *Home and Exile and Other Selections*. London: Longman, 1965.

———. *Mating Birds*. Johannesburg: Ravan Press, 1987.

———. *Tasks and Masks: Themes and Styles of African Literature*. London: Longman, 1981.

Nnaemeka, O. "From Orality to Writing: African Women Writers and the Re(Inscription) of Womanhood." *Research in African Literatures* 25.4 (1994): 137–157.

Nnaemeka, O., ed. *The Politics of (M)Othering—Womanhood, Identity, and Resistance in African Literature*. London: Routledge, 1997.

The Norton Anthology of African-American Poetry. Ed. H.L. Gates Jr. and N.Y. McKay. New York: Norton, 1997.

Nwabara, S.N. *Iboland: A Century of Contact with Britain, 1860–1960*. London: Hodder and Stoughton, 1977.

Nwachukwu-Agbada, J.O.J. "A Conversation with Chinua Achebe." *Commonwealth: Essays and Studies* 13.1 (1990): 117–124.

Nwoga, D.I. "The Igbo World of Achebe's *Arrow of God*." *Research in African Literatures* 12.1 (1981): 14–44.

Obiechina, E. *Culture, Tradition and Society in the West African Novel*. Cambridge: Cambridge University Press, 1975.

O'Brien, A. "Against the Democracy Police: The Contradictions of Nation-Language in Dambudzo Marechera's *House of Hunger*." *Current Writing* 6.2 (1994): 77–92.

Ogbaa, K. *Gods, Oracles and Divination: Folkways in Chinua Achebe's novels*. Trenton, N.J.: Africa World Press, 1992.

Ogede, O.S. "Achebe and Armah: A Unity of Shaping Vision." *Research in African Literatures* 27.2 (1996): 112–127.

Ogu, M. "Bessie Head and the Pragmatic Spirit in *Maru* and *The Collector of Treasures*." Paper delivered at the AUETSA Conference hosted by the University of Natal, Pietermaritzburg, July 1995.

Ogundele, W.M. "*Natio*, Nation and Postcoloniality: The Example of Ngugi." In *Ngugi wa Thiong'o: Texts and Contexts*. Ed. C. Cantalupo. Trenton, N.J.: Africa World Press, 1995. 111–131.

Ogungbesan, K. "The Cape Gooseberry Also Grows in Botswana." *Présence Africaine* 109–112 (1979): 92–106.

Okara, G. *The Voice*. London: Heinemann, 1970.

Okigbo, P. "The Future Haunted by the Past." *Africa Within the World: Beyond Dispossession and Dependence*. Ed. A. Adedeji. London: Zed Books, 1993. 28–38.

Okonkwo, J. "The House of Hunger." (Review). *Okike* 18 (1981): 87–91.

Okpewho, I. *African Oral Literature: Backgrounds, Character, and Continuity*. Bloomington: Indiana University Press, 1992.

Okri, B. *Incidents at the Shrine*. London: Heinemann, 1986.

Ola, V.U. *The Life and Works of Bessie Head*. Lewiston, N.Y.: The Edwin Mellen Press, 1994.

Olaniyan, T. "Narrativizing Postcoloniality: Responsibilities." *Public Culture* 5.1 (1992): 47–55.

Olaogun, M. "Irony and Schizophrenia in Bessie Head's *Maru*." *Research in African Literatures* 25.4 (1994): 69–87.

Omotoso, K. *Achebe or Soyinka? A Study in Contrasts*. London: Hans Zell, 1996.

———. *Just Before Dawn*. Ibadan: Spectrum Books, 1988.

———. *Season of Migration to the South: Africa's Crises Reconsidered*. Cape Town: Tafelberg, 1994.

Ondaatje, M. *The English Patient*. London: Picador, 1992.

Ong, W. *Orality and Literacy: The Technologizing of the Word*. London: Methuen, 1982.

Owomoyela, O., ed. *A History of Twentieth-Century African Literature*. Lincoln: University of Nebraska Press, 1993.

Oyono, F. *Houseboy*. Trans. J. Reed. London: Heinemann, 1966.

Pakenham, T. *The Scramble for Africa 1876–1912*. New York: Random House, 1991.

Palmer, E. *The Growth of the African Novel: Studies in African Literature*. London: Heinemann, 1979.

———. *An Introduction to the African Novel: A Critical Study of Twelve Books by Chinua Achebe, James Ngugi, Camara Laye, Elechi Amadi, Ayi Kwei Armah, Mongo Beti, and Gabriel Okara*. London: Heinemann, 1972.

Parker, M., and R. Starkey, eds. *Postcolonial Literatures: Achebe, Ngugi, Desai, Walcott*. New York: St. Martin's Press, 1995.

Parry, B. "Problems in Current Theories of Colonial Discourse." *Oxford Literary Review* 9.1 and 2 (1987): 36–44.

———. "Signs of Our Times—Homi Bhabha's *The Location of Culture*." *Third Text* 28/29 (1994): 5–24.

Pattison, D. "Call No Man Happy: Inside *The Black Insider*, Marechera's Journey to Become a Writer?" *Journal of Southern African Studies* 20.2 (1994): 221–239.

———. "The Search for the Primordial I in the Novel's *Black Sunlight* and *The Black Insider*." In *Emerging Perspectives on Dambudzo Marechera*. Ed. F. Veit-Wild and A. Chennells. Trenton, N.J.: Africa World Press, 1999. 193–208.

Pearse, A. "Apartheid and Madness: Bessie Head's *A Question of Power*." *Kunapipi* 5.2 (1983): 81–92.

Perham, M. *The Colonial Reckoning*. London: Collins, 1961.

Perocchio, P. "A Black Insider: The Man Walking Away from His Shadow." In *Emerging Perspectives on Dambudzo Marechera*. Ed. F. Veit-Wild and A. Chennells. Trenton, N.J.: Africa World Press, 1999. 209–219.

Petersen, K.H. *An Articulate Anger/Dambudzo Marechera 1952–87*. Sydney: Dangaroo Press, 1988.

Petersen, K.H., and A. Rutherford, eds. *Chinua Achebe: A Celebration*. Oxford: Heinemann, 1991.

Phillips, A. *The Enigma of Colonialism: British Policy in West Africa*. London: Currey, 1989.

Phillips, M. "Engaging Dreams: Alternative Perspectives on Flora Nwapa, Buchi Emecheta, Ama Ata Aidoo, Bessie Head, and Tsitsi Dangarembga's Writing." *Research in African Literature* 25.4 (1994): 89–103.

Pieterse, J.N. *Empire and Emancipation: Power and Liberation on a World Scale*. London: Pluto Press, 1989.

Plaatje, S.T. *Native Life in South Africa, Before and Since the European War and the Boer Rebellion*. London: King, 1916.

Plato. *The Symposium*. Trans. W. Hamilton. Harmondsworth: Penguin, 1951.

Plomer, W. *Cecil Rhodes*. Cape Town: David Philip, 1984.

Quayson, A. "Realism, Criticism and the Disguises of Both: A Reading of Chinua Achebe's *Things Fall Apart* with an Evaluation of the Criticism Relating to It." *Research in African Literatures* 25.4 (1994): 117–136.

Radakrishnan, R. "Postcolonial and the Boundaries of Identity." *Callaloo* 16.4 (1993): 750–771.
Rajan, R.S. "The Third World Academic in Other Places; or, the Postcolonial Intellectual Revisited." *Critical Inquiry* 23 (1997): 596–616.
Ranger, T. "Postscript. Colonial and Postcolonial Identities." In *Postcolonial Identities in Africa.* Ed. R. Werbner and T. Ranger. London: Zed Books, 1996. 271–281.
Rasebotsa, N. "*Maru* and Bessie Head's Place in Botswana." *Current Writing* 5.1 (1993): 25–35.
———. "Wild Cannon." *Southern African Review of Books* 41 (1996): 3–4.
Ravenscroft, A. *Chinua Achebe*. London: Longman, 1969.
Richards, D. "Repossessing Time: Chinua Achebe's *Anthills of the Savannah.*" *Kunapipi* 12.2 (1990): 130–138.
Riemenschneider, D. "Short Fiction from Zimbabwe." *Research in African Literatures* 20.3 (1989): 401–411.
Rose, J. "On the 'Universality' of Madness: Bessie Head's *A Question of Power.*" *Critical Inquiry* 20 (1994): 401–418.
Rutherford, A., ed. *From Commonwealth to Postcolonial*. Sydney: Dangaroo Press, 1992.
Said, E. "Figures, Configurations, Transfigurations." *Race and Class* 32.1 (1990): 1–16.
———. "Identity, Authority and Freedom: The Potentate and the Traveller." *Pretexts/Studies in Writing and Culture* 3.1–2 (1991): 67–81.
———. "Reflections on Exile." In *Out There*. Ed. C. Ferguson et al. New York: New York Museum of Contemporary Art, 1990. 357–363.
———. *Culture and Imperialism*. London: Vintage, 1994.
———. *Orientalism*. New York: Routledge, 1978.
———. *The World, the Text and the Critic*. Cambridge, Mass.: Harvard University Press, 1983.
Salih, T. *Season of Migration to the North.* Trans. D. Johnson-Davies. London: Heinemann, 1969.
Samatar, A.I. "Leadership and Ethnicity in the Making of African State Models: Botswana Versus Somalia." *Third World Quarterly* 18.4 (1997): 687–707.
Samkange, S. *On Trial for My Country*. London: Heinemann, 1967.
———. *Origins of Rhodesia*. New York: F.A. Praeger, 1969.
Sarup, M. "Home and Identity." In *Travellers' Tales: Narratives of Home and Displacement*. Ed. G. Robertson et al. London/New York: Routledge, 1994. 93–104.
Sarvan, C.P. "Bessie Head: *A Question of Power* and Identity." [Women in] *African Literature Today* 15 (1987): 82–88.
———. "Bessie Head: Two Letters." *Wasafiri* 12 (1990): 11–15.
Scheub, H. "A Review of African Oral Traditions and Literature." *African Studies Review* 28.2–3 (1985): 1–72.
Schipper, M. "Knowledge Is Like an Ocean: Insiders, Outsiders, and the Academy." *Research in African Literatures* 28.4 (1997): 121–141.
Schirato, T. "Relocating Post-Colonialism: Bhabha's *The Location of Culture* and Contemporary Cultural Theory." *Southern Review* 28.3 (1995): 358–365.
Schreiner, O. *Trooper Peter Halkett of Mashonaland*. Johannesburg: Ad. Donker, 1974.
Schwab, A. *The Mirror and the Killer-Queen: Otherness in Literary Language*. Bloomington: Indiana University Press, 1996.
Sebina, A.M. "Makalaka." *African Studies* 6 (1947): 82–96.
Sembène, O. *God's Bits of Wood*. London: Heinemann, 1970.

———. *The Last of the Empire: A Senegalese Novel*. Trans. A. Adams. London: Heinemann, 1983.

———. *Xala*. London: Heinemann, 1976.

Serote, M.W. *To Every Birth Its Blood*. Johannesburg: Ravan, 1981.

Seshradi-Crooks, K. "At the Margins of Postcolonial Studies." *Ariel: A Review of International English Literature* 26.3 (1995): 47–71.

Shakespeare, W. *The Tempest*. Ed. F. Kermode. London: Methuen, 1964.

Sharma, G.N. "The Christian Dynamic in the Fictional World of Chinua Achebe." *Ariel: A Review of International English Literature* 24.2 (1993): 85–99.

Sharpe, J. "Figures of Colonial Resistance." *Modern Fiction Studies* 35.1 (1985): 137–155.

Shaw, D. "Transgressing Traditional Narrative Form." In *Emerging Perspectives on Dambudzo Marechera*. Ed. F. Veit-Wild and A. Chennells. Trenton, N.J.: Africa World Press, 1999. 3–21.

Shelton, A.J. "The Offended *Chi* in Chinua Achebe's Novels." *Transition* 13 (1964): 36–37.

———. "The 'Palm Oil' of Language: Proverbs in Chinua Achebe's Novels." *Modern Language Quarterly* 30 (1960): 87–93.

Shillington, K. *History of Africa*. Rev. ed. London: Macmillan Educational, 1995.

Simons, J. *Foucault and the Political*. London: Routledge, 1995.

Simonse, S. "African Literature Between Nostalgia and Utopia: African Novels Since 1953 in the Light of the Modes-of-Production Approach." *Research in African Literatures* 13 (1982): 451–487.

Sisulu, W. "Academic Freedom and Intellectual Empowerment." *Pretexts/Studies in Writing and Culture* 3.1–2 (1991): 62–66.

Slemon, S. "Monuments of Empire: Allegory/Counter-Discourse/Post-Colonial Writing." *Kunapipi* IX (1987): 12–21.

———. "Post-Colonial Allegory and the Transformation of History." *The Journal of Commonwealth Literature* 22.1 (1988): 158–159.

———. "The Scramble for Postcolonialism." In *De-Scribing Empire: Post-Colonialism and Textuality*. Ed. C. Tiffin and A. Lawson. London: Routledge, 1994. 15–32.

———. "Unsettling the Empire: Resistance Theory for the Second World." *World Literature Written in English* 30.2 (1990): 30–41.

Slemon, S., and H. Tiffin, eds. *After Europe: Critical Theory and Post-Colonial Writing*. Sydney: Dangaroo Press, 1989.

Smith, A. *East African Writing in English*. London: Macmillan, 1989.

Sörsen, G. "Development as a Hobbesian Dilemma." *Third World Quarterly* 17.4 (1996): 903–916.

Sougou, O. "Language, Foregrounding and Intertextuality in *Anthills of the Savannah*." In *Critical Approaches to Anthills of the Savannah*. Ed. H.D. Ehling. Amsterdam: Rodopi, 1991. 35–54.

Soyinka, W. *Collected Plays*. Oxford: Oxford University Press, 1986.

———. *Ibadan: The Penkelemes Years: A Memoir*. London: Methuen, 1994.

———. *Myth, Literature and the African World*. Cambridge: Cambridge University Press, 1976.

———. *The Open Sore of a Continent: A Personal Narrative of the Nigerian Crisis*. Oxford: Oxford University Press, 1996.

———. *Season of Anomy*. London: Arrow, 1988.

Spivak, G.C. "Can the Subaltern Speak?" In *Marxism and the Interpretation of Culture*. Ed. C. Nelson and L. Grossberg. London: Macmillan, 1988. 271–313.

———. "Neocolonialism and the Secret Agent of Knowledge." *Oxford Literary Review* 1 (1991): 220–251.

———. *In Other Worlds: Essays in Cultural Politics*. New York: Methuen, 1987.

———. *Outside in the Teaching Machine*. New York: Routledge, 1993.

———. *The Post-Colonial Critic: Interviews, Strategies, Dialogues*. New York: Routledge, 1990.

Starfield, J. "The Return of Bessie Head." *Journal of Southern African Studies* 23.4 (1997): 655–664.

Stein, M. "*Black Sunlight*: Exploding Dichotomies—A Language Terrorist at Work." In *Emerging Perspectives on Dambudzo Marechera*. Ed. F. Veit-Wild and A. Chennells. Trenton, N.J.: Africa World Press, 1999. 57–72.

Stevens, W. *The Collected Poems of Wallace Stevens*. New York: Vintage, 1990.

Stratton, F. *Contemporary African Literature and the Politics of Gender*. London: Routledge, 1994.

Style, C. "Dambudzo Marechera." *London Magazine* 27.9/10 (1987/1988): 106–110.

Taitz, L. "Knocking on the Door of the House of Hunger: Fracturing Narratives and Disordering Identity." In *Emerging Perspectives on Dambudzo Marechera*. Ed. F. Veit-Wild and A. Chennells. Trenton, N.J.: Africa World Press, 1999. 23–42.

Taitz, L., and M. Levin. "Fictional Autobiographies or Autobiographical Fictions?" In Emerging Perspectives on Dambudzo Marechera. Ed. F. Veit-Wild and A. Chennells. Trenton, N.J.: Africa World Press, 1999. 163–175.

Ten Kortenaar, N. "Beyond Authenticity and Creolization: Reading Achebe Writing Culture." *Publications of the Modern Languages Association* 110.1 (1995): 30–41.

———. "'Only Connect': *Anthills of the Savannah* and Achebe's Trouble with Nigeria." *Research in African Literatures* 24.3 (1993): 59–72.

Thompson, L. *Survival in Two Worlds: Moshoeshoe of Lesotho, 1786–1870*. Oxford: Clarendon Press, 1975.

Tiffin, H. "Post-Colonial Literatures and Counter-Discourse." *Kunapipi* 9.3 (1987): 17–34.

———. "Post-Colonialism, Post-Modernism, and the Rehabilitation of History." *The Journal of Commonwealth Literature* 23.1 (1988): 169–181.

Townsend, R. "Beyond Racism: Bessie Head's Vision of a New World." *Unisa English Studies* 32.1 (1994): 27–31.

———. "In Search of Self: Fictional Autobiography as a Means of Reconstituting the Subject in Charlotte Brontë, Jean Rhys and Bessie Head." Paper given at the AUETSA Conference, July 1995, Pietermaritzburg.

———. "Life Stories: Fiction and Autobiography in Bessie Head." In *An Introduction to the African Prose Narrative*. Ed. L. Losambe. Pretoria: Kagiso Tertiary, 1996. 141–154.

Tucker, M.E. "A 'Nice-Time Girl' Strikes Back: An Essay on Bessie Head's *A Question of Power*." *Research in African Literatures* 19.2 (1988): 170–181.

Turner, M.E. "Achebe, Hegel, and the New Colonialism." In *Chinua Achebe: A Celebration*. Ed. K.H. Petersen and A. Rutherford. Oxford: Heinemann, 1991. 31–40.

Tutuola, A. *The Palm-Wine Drinkard and His Dead Palm-Wine Tapster in the Deads' Town*. London: Faber and Faber, 1961.

Uchendu, V.C. *The Igbo of Southeast Nigeria*. New York: Holt, Rinehart and Winston, 1965.

Udumukwu, O. "Ideology and the Dialectics of Action: Achebe and Iyayi." *Research in African Literatures* 27.3 (1996): 34–49.

Vaubel, N. "The Battlefield of Politics and Selfhood in Bessie Head's *A Question of Power*." In *Nwanyibu: Womanbeing and African Literature*. Ed. P.A. Egejuru and K.H. Katrak. Trenton, N.J.: Africa World Press, 1997. 83–106.

Veit-Wild, F. "Carnival and Hybridity in Texts by Dambudzo Marechera and Lesego Rampolokeng." *Journal of Southern African Studies* 23.4 (1997): 553–564.

———. "Words as Bullets: The Writings of Dambudzo Marechera." *Zambezia* 14.2 (1987): 113–120.

———. *Teachers, Preachers, Non-Believers: A Social History of Zimbabwean Literature*. London: Hans Zell, 1992.

Veit-Wild, F., ed. *Dambudzo Marechera: A Source Book on His Life and Work*. Harare: University of Zimbabwe Publications, 1993.

Veit-Wild, F., and A. Chennells, eds. *Emerging Perspectives on Dambudzo Marechera*. Trenton, N.J.: Africa World Press, 1999.

Veit-Wild, F., and E. Schade, eds. *Dambudzo Marechera 1952–1987*. Harare: Boabab Books, 1988.

Vera, Y. *Why Don't You Carve Other Animals*. Harare, Baobab Books, 1994.

Visel, R. "'We Bear the World and We Make It': Bessie Head and Olive Schreiner." *Research in African Literatures* 21.3 (1990): 115–124.

Volk, D. "'In Search of My True People': Universal Humanism in Marechera's Writing." In *Emerging Perspectives on Dambudzo Marechera*. Ed. F. Veit-Wild and A. Chennells. Trenton, N.J.: Africa World Press, 1999. 299–312.

Walcott, D. *Conversations with Derek Walcott*. Ed. W. Baer. Jackson: University of Mississippi Press, 1996.

Wallerstein, I. "The Ideological Tensions of Capitalism: Universalism Versus Racism and Sexism." In *Race, Nation, Class—Ambiguous Identities*. E. Balibar and I. Wallerstein. London/New York: Verso, 1991. 29–36.

———. "Social Conflict in Post-Independence Black Africa: The Concepts of Race and Status-Group Reconsidered." In *Race, Nation, Class—Ambiguous Identities*. E. Balibar and I. Wallerstein. London/New York: Verso, 1991. 228–232.

Washington, P. "'Being Post-Colonial'/Culture, Policy and Government." *Southern Review* 28.3 (1995): 273–282.

Weber, M. *The Protestant Ethic and the Spirit of Capitalism*. Trans. T. Parsons. London: Unwin, 1930 (repr. 1965).

Weinstock, D., and C. Ramadan. "Symbolic Structure in *Things Fall Apart*." *Critique: Studies in Modern Fiction* 2.1 (1969): 33–41.

Werbner, R., and T. Ranger, eds. *Postcolonial Identities in Africa*. London: Zed Books, 1996.

Whiteley, W.H. *A Selection of African Prose*. Comp. W.H. Whiteley. Oxford: Clarendon, 1964.

Wicomb, Z. "Postcoloniality and Postmodernity: The Case of the Coloured in South Africa." In *AUETSA 1996 Conference Proceedings,* Vol. 1. Ed. H. Wittenberg and L. Nas. Bellville: University of the Western Cape Press, 1997. 5–16.

———. "To Hear the Variety of Discourses." *Current Writing* 2.1 (1990): 35–44.

Wilhelm, C. "Bessie Head: The Face of Africa." *English in Africa* 10.1 (1983): 1–13.

Wilkinson, J. *Talking with African Writers: Interviews with African Poets, Playwrights and Novelists*. London: Currey, 1990.

Williams, A. "Literature in the Time of Tyranny: African Writers and the Crisis of Governance." *Third World Quarterly* 17.2 (1996): 349–362.

Williams, P., and L. Chrisman, eds. *Colonial Discourse and Post-Colonial Theory: A Reader*. New York: Wheatsheaf, 1993.

Williams, R. "Critical Resources—the Politics of Literacy." (Interview). *Pretexts/Studies in Writing and Culture* 3.1–2 (1991): 136–143.

Winters, M. "An Objective Approach to Achebe's Style." *Research in African Literatures* 12.1 (1976): 53–58.

Wolf, E.R. *Europe and the People Without History*. Berkeley: University of California Press, 1982.

Wren, R.M. "Achebe's Revision of *Arrow of God*." *Research in African Literatures* 7 (1976): 94–103.

———. *Achebe's World: The Historical and Cultural Context of the Novels of Chinua Achebe*. Harlow, Essex: Longman, 1981.

Wright, D. "Things Standing Together: A Retrospect on *Things Fall Apart*." *Chinua Achebe: A Celebration*. Ed. K.H. Petersen and A. Rutherford. Oxford: Heinemann, 1991. 76–82.

Wright, E. *The Critical Evaluation of African Literature: Essays*. London: Heinemann, 1973.

Wylie, D. "Language Thieves: English-Language Strategies in Two Zimbabwean Novellas." *English in Africa* 19.2 (1991): 39–62.

———. "Taking Resentment for Wisdom: A Posthumous Conversation Between Marechera, N.H. Brettell and George Grosz." In *Emerging Perspectives on Dambudzo Marechera*. Ed. F. Veit-Wild and A. Chennells. Trenton, N.J.: Africa World Press, 1999. 315–331.

Xie, S. "Rethinking the Problem of Postcolonialism." *New Literary History* 28.1 (1997): 7–19.

Young, R.C. *Colonial Desire: Hybridity in Theory, Culture and Race*. London/New York: Routledge, 1995.

———. *Torn Halves: Political Conflict in Literary and Cultural Theory*. Manchester: Manchester University Press, 1996.

———. *White Mythologies: Writing History and the West*. London: Routledge, 1990.

Zabus, C. "The Logos-Eaters: The Igbo Ethno-Text." In *Chinua Achebe: A Celebration*. Ed. K.H. Petersen and A. Rutherford. Oxford: Heinemann, 1991. 19–30.

Zack, N., ed. *Race/Sex: Their Sameness, Difference, and Interplay*. New York: Routledge, 1997.

Zimunya, M. *Those Years of Drought and Hunger*. Gweru: Mambo Press, 1982.

Index

About the Book

Concentrating on issues of power and change, Annie Gagiano's close reading of literary texts by Chinua Achebe, Bessie Head, and Dambudzo Marechera teases out each author's view of how colonialism affected Africa, the contribution of Africans to their own malaise, and above all, the creative, pragmatic role of many Africans during the colonial and postcolonial periods.

Gagiano contends that Achebe, Head, and Marechera play an important role in the necessary reconceptualization by Africans of themselves and their place in the global system. Treating both the consummate verbal art of these writers and their social relevance, she reveals them to be penetrating analysts who convey lucid, convincing evaluations of the failures and prospects of contemporary African societies.

Annie H. Gagiano lectures in English at the University of Stellenbosch (South Africa).